EXPLORATIONS IN PSYCHOANALYTIC ETHNOGRAPHY

EXPLORATIONS IN PSYCHOANALYTIC ETHNOGRAPHY

Edited by

Jadran Mimica

Berghahn Books
NEW YORK • OXFORD
www.berghahnbooks.com

First published in 2007 by

Berghahn Books

www.berghahnbooks.com

© 2007 Berghahn Books

Library of Congress Cataloging-in-Publication Data

Explorations in psychoanalytic ethnography / edited by Jadran Mimica.
    p. cm.
      "Originally published as a special issue of Social analysis (volume 50,
issue 2, summer 2006)."
    Includes bibliographical references and index.
    ISBN 978-1-84545-402-9 (pbk. : alk. paper)
    1. Ethnopsychology. 2. Cognition and culture. I. Mimica, Jadran.
II. Social analysis (Adelaide, S. Aust.).

    GN502.E977 2007
    155.8—dc22

                                                    2007010293

British Library Cataloguing in Publication Data

A catalogue record for this book is available from the British Library.

Printed in the United States on acid-free paper

In memory of Geza Roheim, George Devereux,
Erik H. Erikson, and John Layard

CONTENTS

ACKNOWLEDGMENTS

I wish to express my gratitude to the late Kingsley Garbett, the editor of *Social Analysis*, for first suggesting that I organize a volume on the topic of psychoanalysis and ethnography. He will be missed by all of us who knew him and his work. I especially thank Bruce Kapferer for supporting this project from its inception to its final realization, and for his constructive appraisal of all the articles. Special thanks are due to my wife and companion, Ute Eickelkamp, for generously assisting me in my editorial work and translating from German the text of conversations incorporated in Florence Weiss and Milan Stanek's article. I also wholeheartedly thank all of the contributors, without whom this project would never have seen the light of day. My special thanks are due to Henry Abramovitch, Keith Hartman, and Leslie Devereaux for their comprehensive critical assessment of and comments on all the individual papers. Finally, I thank Shawn Kendrick for outstanding and painstaking copyediting work. For all mistakes and shortcomings that remain in this volume, I am solely responsible.

INTRODUCTION
Explorations in Psychoanalytic Ethnography

Jadran Mimica

This collection of essays is about psychoanalytic ethnography. Its concern is the psychic depths of human cultural life-worlds as explored through psychoanalytic practice and/or the psychoanalytically framed ethnographic project. The authors engage various aspects of the human condition within a wide range of conceptual frameworks that are representative of contemporary psychoanalytic understanding and practice. The anthropological contributions come from scholars whose ethnographic research is grounded in psychoanalysis and whose overall approach to human existence is articulated in terms of or gravitates toward psychoanalysis as a foundational framework for anthropological understanding. A strong version of this position (not shared by all contributors) maintains that anthropological interpretation of human existence is not sustainable without psychoanalysis. Critical here is the primary level of concrete ethnographic research whose horizons are delimited by the psychoanalytic perspectives on the unconscious matrix of the human psyche and, correlatively, on the unconscious depths and dynamics of the intersubjective (social) reality of any given cultural life-world.

Five of the contributors to this volume are primarily practicing psychoanalysts and psychotherapists (including one Jungian and one Lacanian analyst). One of them is also a scholar of comparative religion. Another four are both practicing psychoanalysts and ethnographers, and yet another is a political scientist and a psychoanalyst.[1] This amplified representation of psychoanalysis is important for the project of psychoanalytic ethnography since, in my view, without immersion into concrete psychoanalytic work concerning diverse human predicaments, no adequate comprehension of psychoanalysis, its field of evidence, interpretive constructions, and therapeutic action is possible. And likewise, without immersion into ethnographic research, which generates primary evidence and understanding of diverse cultural life-worlds, no adequate grasp of anthropological knowledge can be achieved. Given this view, I think that the articles in this volume will interest a psychoanalytic ethnographer as much as a practicing psychoanalyst. And, if only because of their ethnographic focus, they will also appeal to anthropologists with no interest in psychoanalysis. My invitation to the contributors was to write not about the problems of and the relations between anthropology and psychoanalysis[2] but about the realities of the human condition that they, as practitioners, deal with on a daily basis.

The individuals who undergo psychoanalysis exemplify in their motley predicaments and, more often than not, unfortunate suffering the fundamental dynamics of human existence—the life of embodied psychic being and its unconscious matrix. The realities encountered and metabolized by analysts in their daily practice belong to and are generated by the same mind-body matrix as the familiar and seemingly less problematic 'normal' realities of the socio-cultural life-world. But it is the former that reveal the inner conditions and the workings of the latter, and with it the full extent of the possibilities and limitations of human self-actualization fueled by the desire for both freedom and abysmal unfreedom.[3] This primal twinship of human desire is equipollent. The self-knowledge and unique wisdom borne out of psychoanalytic practice and thus produced evidence show this with abundant case material.

Psychoanalysis spans the entire twentieth century and has been internationalized for almost as long. The studies published in psychoanalytic journals alone (here I will disregard the general psychiatric and psychological journals) in English, French, German, Spanish, Italian, Swedish, Hebrew, and Japanese[4] offer a wealth of testimonials to the human soul as lived by contemporary humanity and made intelligible primarily within the ontological and epistemological frameworks of the Western intellectual tradition. Over the last hundred years, thousands of individuals have been in analysis, and the existing journals and other publications contain a vast amount of information on and insights into the at once intra- and intersubjective realities of the human psyche. Every mode of desire, phantasy, thoughts, feelings, and nightmarish possibilities that the imaginary matrix of human reality and existence can and does engender is given some sort of expression, a semblance of objectivity, and made intelligible in the context of psychoanalytic engagements with individuals and groups.[5]

Being familiar with this plenitude of the productions of the human unconscious and its correlative existential conditions, I am always struck by the myopia of so many would-be critical pronouncements about the field of psychoanalytic evidence, which commonly draw on Freud's paradigmatic case studies. These critics assume that on that basis one can argue about the psychoanalytic field as a historical and present-day dynamic totality and, still worse, about the scope and nature of psychoanalytic experience, the method of its inquiry, its claims about itself and its therapeutic effects and validity, and, most vitally, its object—the human psyche and mind. Such critiques are legion, and it would require a separate work to deal with them.[6] This is not my intention. It will suffice to point out that these 'postmodern/deconstructionist discourses' have to be comprehended in their appropriate psycho-cultural context, that is, the current Western 'megapolitan'[7] civilization and its temporal (epochal) cum geopolitical threshold that dictates the life of humanity as a whole—by and large, without reciprocity. By this I mean that the appetites and desires of inhabitants of, say,

New York, London, Paris, Moscow, and Shanghai determine, mutatis mutandis, in the chain of differential vectorial influences, the lives of the villagers in the sticks of, say, Papua New Guinea but not vice-versa.[8]

It is exactly with this geopolitical perspective in view that I see psychoanalysis, in combination with Husserlian and existential phenomenology,[9] as a critical framework that provides anthropology with the foundations for the practice of critical self-knowledge despite all the negative will and the desire not to know 'thyself'. When I am asked about psychoanalysis and anthropology, my response is to point out that without a commitment to the ongoing reading of professional (analytic) publications, one will not be able to secure sufficiently informative data pertaining to the basic empirical dimension of the human experience and modes of existence that make psychoanalytic understanding and practice possible. One's own life experiences and critical self-reflections are the necessary starting point, but there is more to each of us than we may be willing to submit to self-scrutiny. Except for the actual experience of analysis, to read case studies rather than numerous critical academic disquisitions on psychoanalysis is the best way to get some footing in the psychoanalytic field. The same applies to the anthropological field of evidence where ethnographic literature provides the 'stuff' of knowledge. It is the diversity of human cultural life-worlds and modes of humanness—which so many ethnographers have explored and interpreted—that constitute (and will remain) the foundational domain of critical anthropological knowledge of humanity and its self-reflection.

All of the contributors to this volume are imbued with and motivated by the realities of their long-term practice and experience of psychoanalysis and ethnographic research. Each article is an exploration in and, through its very specificity, of the field of psychoanalytic ethnography at large. The dialectics of the singular experience/practice in a given life-world context and the dynamic unfolding of the universal yet socio-culturally specific shapes of human psychic being are intrinsic to each article. This is also true of the wealth of theoretical psychoanalytic knowledge and perspectives that each contributor draws on in the pursuit of his or her project as a practicing analyst, therapist, and ethnographer.

The Essays

Given that each contributor was free to choose his or her topic, I could not have hoped for a more fitting article to head the collection than that of Sudhir Kakar. A Hindu and a Punjabi Khatri by birth, Kakar is a master psychoanalyst with profound knowledge of diverse cultural life-worlds in both the Western and Indian civilizational spheres. It is important to point out in this connection that his first major work was a psycho-historical study of Frederick Winslow Taylor (1856–1915), the 'Father of Scientific Management', whose work—to the extent that it incipiently gave a particular practico-ideological articulation of the "efficiency craze that gripped the United States in the decade before World War I, a craze which has been called a 'normal American madness'" (Kakar 1970: 1)—has since those days contributed to the global malaise of the 'post-industrial world' in a myriad of ways (see also Doray 1988). This work was done under the influence of Erik Erikson. In subsequent decades, Kakar (1981, 2001) produced a number of psychoanalytic studies of Indian civilization, which in their thematic diversity, acuity of insight, critical reflection, and attunement to the inner feelings of the cultural *Weltstimmung*, as well as in their literary quality, exemplify the finest achievements of psychoanalytic ethnography.[10]

Kakar's essay in this collection outlines the problematics of psychoanalytic practice as it refracts through the relationship between the analyst and the analysand. In this instance, set in a Western European context of professional psychoanalytic engagement, the two belong to and actualize qua and through themselves their respective yet different cultural universes. Drawing on his lifelong experience as a practicing psychoanalyst and set in relation to his still developing lifework, Kakar endeavors to answer the question, how should a Western psychoanalyst approach the issue of cultural difference in his or her practice? Regardless of this particular framing of the problematics and the answers given,[11] his responses pertain to the human situation as a whole and to the pursuit of the project of anthropological qua ethnographic knowledge. The psychoanalytic framework radicalizes and brings this project to its authentic existential dimension, namely, the psyche as the conditio sine qua non of all human reality. Reflecting on Kakar's exemplary work as a whole, this present account of the problematics of the psychoanalytic knowledge of culture underscores a prior condition of psychoanalytic and ethnographic undertaking: the necessity to experience and acknowledge another cultural life-world as absolutely real—in and for itself—on a par with the same demand that the psyche exacts on both the one who is its subject (and may suffer it as such) and the one who is prepared to analyze it and perhaps transform it into a more viable semblance of its total self and its life-world.

The contribution by Florence Weiss and Milan Stanek derives from their work with Fritz and Marco Morgenthaler among the Iatmul people of the East Sepik Province, Papua New Guinea, who were originally described by Gregory Bateson in his renowned 1936 monograph *Naven*. The Morgenthalers and Weiss's 1984 monograph, *Gespräche am sterbenden Fluss*,[12] also represents the style of a distinctive Swiss ethno-psychoanalytic research methodology developed by Paul Parin, Goldy Parin-Matthey, and Fritz Morgenthaler, whose principal research was done in West Africa, specifically among the Dogon of Mali and the Anyi of Ivory Coast. The monograph on the Anyi is their sole major work available in English, albeit in a somewhat shortened form of the original (Parin, Morgenthaler, and Parin-Matthey 1980). All three were medical doctors and practicing psychoanalysts.[13] To the extent that they chose to involve themselves passionately with ethnographic research, their work has parallels with that of L. Bryce Boyer (1979) among the Apaches, which is better known among anglophone anthropologists of psychoanalytic bend.

Weiss and Stanek's article focuses on the most basic aspects of human intersubjective relations, which in Freud's original clarification of the analytical framework of experience became formulated as transference and countertransference.[14] Its irreducible psychosomatic matrix is the mother-infant dyad, which, as the primary circuity of relatedness, positions and mediates the father; further, through the circuity of the infant-mother-father triad, it mediates the siblings and all other human relations. This primary familial circuity of selfhood enables one to become a socialized egoity and self-consciousness, possessed of 'toilet-trained' embodiment and language and a whole plethora of other tacit bodily habits and skills. This constitutive parental mediation, at once generative-providing and frustrating-negating, will exercise its presence and shape every person's desires, spontaneity, and choices of oneself in his or her relations with other persons throughout life. But for most people, this self-otherness, which inhabits and calibrates one's self-conscious egoity, remains unnoticed. Indeed, one often lives it as the most vital effluence of one's unreflected-upon embodied self.

As already indicated by Kakar in his article, this infra-dimension of human selves becomes particularly problematic in the context of the psychoanalytic situation and more so when there is a cultural difference between the persons involved. Yet at the same time, these dynamics are crucial to the development and outcomes of the psychoanalytic process as a whole. When Freud asked Jung "out of the blue, 'And what do you think about the transference?'" the latter replied, "with the deepest conviction that it was the alpha and omega of the analytic process, whereupon he [Freud] said, 'Then you have grasped the main thing'" (Jung 1969: 8). Regardless of the specificities of psychoanalytic technical formulations and the uses of the transference–counter-transference, together with incorporation, introjection, projection, and identification,[15] these dynamics unfold in various ways in all human relationships. They do so more intensely in the context of ethnographic fieldwork, where defensiveness, regressive anxieties, and the swings of archaic impotence and omnipotence are likely to bedevil the researcher more so than the individuals she or he is living and working with. In this regard, Devereux's (1967) classic but largely neglected systematic treatise on the psychoanalytic foundations of ethnographic research methodology remains as pertinent as ever.

Detailed in Weiss and Stanek's article are the vicissitudes, the anxieties, the highs and lows of Weiss's relationship and conversations with an Iatmul woman called Magendaua. As such, it is a meticulous ethno-psychoanalytic account of the fieldwork situation. The most common manifestations and shapes of desire in intersubjective relations are critically attended to and used constructively for the purpose of gaining knowledge and insight into the inseparable unity of the unconscious dynamics of specific individuals and their cultural life-world. In the mediation of Weiss and her Iatmul interlocutor, there emerges a unique horizon of experiential meanings of the famous *naven* and, like a hologramic condensation, the totality of the Iatmul's human-saurian cosmos.[16] Along the way, one also learns about the mode of critical-interpretive synthesis of understanding that is achieved not just through the self-interpretations of the single ethnographer (Weiss) but through the dialogue with her ethnographic co-worker (Stanek) and the psychoanalytic supervisor present in the field (Morgenthaler).[17]

My own contribution is extracted from a very long work in progress on the father-son relationship among the Yagwoia people of Papua New Guinea (see also Mimica 1991). In the Yagwoia mythopoeic cosmo-ontological imagery and formulations, the fatherhood of man is articulated as the implantation of his bone into the male and female progeny. It means that the Yagwoia sonship is an irreversible and unstoppable process of incorporation of the father's bone across the generations. This dynamic structural relation and its cultural imagery can be readily rendered through the conceptual prism of anthropological understanding as 'patri-filiation'. However, comprehended from within the mythopoeic cosmo-ontological matrix of the Yagwoia life-world, this structural relationship is a dynamic process of the totalizing life-death flow as specifically articulated through the succession of male progenitors and their male progeny. It is further co-articulated and completed through five stages of male initiations (literally, 'man-making'). Simultaneously, this procession of the ceaseless life-death flow through the bodily substance of human progeneration and the 'making of men by men', mediates and totalizes in each mortal human corpuscle (male and female) the substantial self-replication of the Yagwoia imperishable Cosmic Self. This auto-generative monadic totality is literally the concrete cosmos as synthesized and lived by the Yagwoia within the bounds of their life-world (Mimica 1981, 1988, 1991).

I will recast this formulation into a psychoanalytic frame. The Yagwoia fatherhood and sonship are structured as an original and irreducibly pre-Oedipal constellation of desire wherein the father is driven by the desire for self-perpetuation not just to 'implant' but, fundamentally, to abdicate his phallic power ('bone') to his sons. Here, the son is not only 'the father of the man' but also his living bodily ossuary (Mimica 1991). What may appear as an Oedipal (ternary) relational circuitry, constitutive of the social field and its morphology, is an original morphism driven by a primary, narcissistic automorphic dynamism. Following Neumann (1954), I characterize it as 'ouroboric' (Mimica 1991, 2003). That human desire is fueled by its immanent self-difference—namely, the dialectics of the life-and-death instinctual drives (libido-mortido)—is, for me, a universal aspect of human existence. As I document in this article, the facts of Yagwoia existence highlight this fundamental auto-polar instinctual dynamics with unparalleled acuity.[18]

The ouroboric dialectics of fatherhood and sonship has multiple actualizations whose concrete reality and significance can be adequately understood only through individual-biographical life situations and trajectories. Accordingly, the focus is on the lifelong trajectory of the relationship between a man and his father through which the individual specificities of the ouroboric incorporative dynamics of implantation and bone extraction are consummated in diverse modes. One of these results in a common psycho-cultural form of Yagwoia egoity and self-consciousness wherein, after his death, the father becomes his progeny's protective spirit, especially his son's. The article also shows the critical importance and reality of the culturally specific archetypal themes and imagery in the life of individuals; it makes evident that the imaginary matrix (Castoriadis 1987) of the cultural life-world has no actualization independently of the psyche of concrete persons.

Waud Kracke's psychoanalytic ethnographic work among the Parintin Indians of Brazil and his contributions to psychoanalytic anthropology are well known in anglophone anthropology.[19] In the contribution to this volume, he discusses Parintin shamanism, which appears to have waned, and the importance of dreaming, a subject that has figured prominently in his work (e.g., 1979, 1981, 1999, 2003a, 2003b). The present article deals with the dreams of two of his informants who were not shamans, though each in his own way had an interest in this practice. Of particular significance are the dreams of Pedro Neves Dire, one of Kracke's older informants. He could not become a shaman because his birth was not 'dreamed' by a shaman. Nevertheless, his dreams manifest his deep desire to become a shaman, and in one he performs a shamanistic celestial ascent. Kracke takes up Lincoln's ([1935] 1970) well-known view that "culture-pattern dreams" are too stereotyped to have personal meaning. Similarly to my presentation of the Yagwoia archetypal dreams, Kracke shows that although Dire's shamanic dream is, in Lincoln's terms, a culture-pattern dream, by the same token, it is no less deeply and personally meaningful for the dreamer. Yet again one is prodded to reflect on the transpersonal psychic depths of the human unconscious and, correlatively, of the rootedness of all cultural reality and objectivity in the psychic depths of its concrete members.

Like most of his previous publications, Rene Devisch's article is about the Yaka people of the southwestern Congo. But here Devisch applies a critical perspective to his life itinerary and development as specifically a Belgian anthropologist working in the country whose very name is eponymous of the brutalities and the dialectics of the last 100 years of Western geopolitics—from the classic late nineteenth-century European colonialism and the would-be revolutionary liberation crises of the 1960s to the current neo-liberal–post-colonial globalism in which the Congo is but a marginal African blot in the planetary geopolitical field. Whether as King Leopold II's 'private possession', the Belgian Congo, or the short-lived People's Republic of the Congo (of the 'second liberation'), declared by Christophe Gbeyne's rebels in Stanleyville in August 1964, or, again, as Mobutu's Zaire (named so in 1974) and, in the most recent reiteration, as the Democratic Republic of the Congo, this country was always marked by a surplus of violence. To be sure, it was and is not just an expression of some vile eruptions unique to a tropical 'heart of darkness'. Rather, this violence was and is the systemic expression of the Western civilizing project—its immanent imaginary and the dialectics of desire wherein abject greed, realpolitik, and mercenary opportunism go hand in hand with the pursuit of human freedom and emancipation.[20]

Throughout the 1960s, the Congo was indeed a major theater of Western capital and political interests, the praxis of violent life and death, and the ideological clashes out of which emerged the current, 'post-colonial' epoch.[21] No matter how absurd it may have appeared 30 years later, the would-be 'Congolese revolution', which didn't happen in the 1960s when Laurent Kabila was a 26-year-old rebel who collaborated with Che's *companeros* (Che Guevara 2000), did come about in 1996 when Kabila's rebels ended Mobutu's reign with the aid of Rwanda and Uganda.[22] But the white world has changed; it has turned post-modern, which is to say that it mainly approves of neo-liberal projects. And, as it were, the present-day Congo and other regions inhabited by, as I will call them, the 'post-wretched of the earth', are subject to the post-colonial styles of 'negotiation' and 'representation' regarding their place in the planetary casino.

Devisch's sojourn began in the Congo as it was created by the Belgians, Americans, Soviet Russians, United Nations, and white mercenaries and their employers—the black generals, presidents, prime ministers, and ministers of motley ideological persuasions and self-images. He went there moved by his love of philosophy and anthropology, and, I venture to say, his desire for human redemption. Psychoanalysis came later. Devisch's article reflects the richness of some 30 years of outstanding research, teaching, and reflection. But it is also a testimonial of an attempt to articulate an authentic ethical position of a psychoanalytic ethnographer faithful to his project of critical knowledge that is inextricably bound to the vagaries of the Yaka people and their more recent fate in the shanties of Kinshasa as *les citoyens de la République démocratique du Congo*. In its personal tenor, Devisch's article also intimates the inner workings and tensions of a mature experience of the reparative power of depressive guilt under the sway of Eros. And herein is its specifically psychoanalytic import, since it casts light on the dialectics of his personal self-synthesis of the relation between his native country, the former colonizer, and the formerly colonized country that he chose to make into his ethnographic alma mater.

This dialectics, which is constitutive of the human reality in so many colonized countries, has also been explored in the work of Craig San Roque, a Jungian analyst and therapist who spent over 12 years living and working in the Aboriginal life-worlds of Central Australia. He did so under the aegis of the Northern Territory Health Department, focusing specifically on the impact of alcohol, gasoline sniffing, and other forms of intoxication that have had malignant effects on the indigenous peoples of this continent inhabited by hunters and gatherers for some 60,000 years.[23] San Roque was profoundly affected by the experiential reality of the Central Australian 'Dreaming' traditions (*Tjukurrpa*). Accordingly, he has formulated a radical perspective on thinking activity that relates these traditions to the ideas of Klein, Bion, and Jung. He conceptualizes the thinking process as formed around culturally shared internal geo-psychic objects held and maintained in the *Tjukurrpa* stories and enacted in ceremony. Apart from being about the Dreaming, this essay is also an ethnography of a 'failure'.

The failure pertains to the reality of human suffering, its meanings, and the severe limitations of such forms of intervention as mental health services, their administration by the state bureaucracy, and the experiences of a Jungian psychotherapist who is compelled to see through the delusions of a managerial ideology that sets up and implements the parameters of acceptable reality. This is the dynamics of self-normalization whereby the civic society projects and enforces its desirable self-image, based on the profitable success of economic goals and means, through the distortions and disavowals of its habitual self-deceptions. While there are no therapeutic methods for curing a whole society of its immanent malignancy, human suffering and its alleviation are the fundamental domain of psychoanalytic practice and understanding, regardless of the scale of magnitude. It is in the context of psychotherapeutic engagement with and reflections upon concrete human predicaments (marked by numerous limitations and conditions that hamper humans in their life pursuits) that psychoanalysis fully affirms itself as a system of knowledge of and intervention into the human condition. Correspondingly, the radical reality of the psyche is revealed when a person is subjected to the painful realization that she or he cannot be and is not free to be free in respect of his or her own self. The individual is a troubled, even a tormented soul, and this causes problems not solely in relation with others but principally with oneself. Furthermore, no others, including one's own mother, can ameliorate that predicament. With the soul imperiled and wounded, one is stuck with oneself. The only way out is to deal with one's psyche.

The problematics of the indisputable fact that psychic malady and suffering are intrinsic to the human condition are further examined by Renata Volich Eisenbruch, a Lacanian psychoanalyst and therapist. Humans everywhere are subject to experiencing and living with various conditions involving painful afflictions and alterations of the soul, although the meanings of and reactions to these conditions vary between different life-worlds and across temporal (historical) trajectories. In her article, Volich Eisenbruch offers an insightful comparative perspective that deals with psychic malady within a contrastive framework of twentieth-century Western psychiatric and psychoanalytic outlooks on mental health. Of particular interest is the impetus she derives from Jaspers's ([1913] 1997) exemplary discussion of the differences between psychiatric-scientistic and phenomenological-interpretive approaches to psychopathology, which she applies to her exegesis of the Lacanian conceptions of the human unconscious, the dynamics of symptom formation and transformation, and the significance of mental malady for the understanding of the structure of the human subject.[24] Her concluding reflections make it clear enough that these are not exclusive to the self-world dialectics of an individual existence; instead, they pertain to humanity and political society at large.

The reality of human suffering, corruption, and malaise that plagues humans in the context of their own socio-political arrangements and relations, as well as the possibility of their cure, has been at the center of James Glass's psychoanalytical and philosophical-political explorations from his earliest (e.g., 1974, 1976) to his most recent publications (2004). An extraordinary political scientist, he conducted long-term psychoanalytic research in the 'halls' of the Sheppard and Enoch Pratt Hospital in Towson, Maryland, where Harry Stack Sullivan (1974) had carried out his acclaimed work with schizophrenics. Glass's trilogy (1985, 1989, 1993) provides ample demonstration of his view that "political theory should be an activity that focuses on the relationship between the self (particularly its unconscious structures) and political life" (1985: 247). In concord with such paradigmatic thinkers as Plato, Machiavelli (Glass 1976), Hobbes, Rousseau, and, of course, Marx and Freud, Glass espouses the same radical spirit of theoretical reflection on the possibilities of transformation of existing civil societies, namely, that "it is not possible to conceive of a political theory in terms of readjusting laws or institutions; change becomes meaningless unless it reaches to the structure of motivation and desire, to unconscious and psychical reality" (1985: 260).[25] And, I would add, conversely, the condition of self-production and the persistence of any society at any moment of its existence is the unconscious and the "radical imaginary" (Castoriadis 1987) of its constitutive members. Glass's article, following his more recent work on Nazi Germany (1997, 2004), most cogently illustrates this dynamics of human social life.[26]

In a slightly different metapsychological key, it can be said that Glass explores specifically the corruptive and destructive modes of the negative (Green 1999b, 2001) inherent in the dynamics of the unconscious. In its core, this negative knows no "no" (Freud [1915] 1984, [1925] 1984), for it pertains not to the human dimension of compassion, language, and judgment but to the vital order of self-generation. As such, its own self-negation is the auto-generative condition of its self-affirmation. Here, the process of life reigns supreme, which is to say, it subsumes death as its own vehicle of ceaseless self-generation. The question of its (im)perishability is as (in)decisive as the destiny of the creative process that has brought into existence and sustains the cosmos as we humans have—thus far—come to understand it.

The last two articles deal with the dynamics of religious experience. Through its choice of topic and evidence, each touches on the dialectics of the negative that lives in and as the human unconscious. Dan Merkur's article explores the sphere of religious experience in reference to Rudolf Otto's ([1923] 1958) classic contribution to the phenomenology of religion, namely, the notion of the numinous. To underscore the depth of Merkur's perspective, I would like to emphasize the breadth and diversity of his empirical and textual scholarship, which ranges from Eskimo shamanism and cosmology (Merkur 1991, 1992) to the traditions of Christian and Jewish gnosis (e.g., Merkur 1993). His psychoanalytic work, then, combines his experience as a practicing psychoanalyst with the phenomenologically tempered critical perspective of an explorer of diverse cultural practices and manifestations of human experience known in the West as 'religious' (Merkur 1998, 1999, 2001). From either vantage point, Merkur articulates an inside view of the phenomena he explores. Although intrinsically related to his previous book on mystical experience and unitive thinking (Merkur 1999), the present interpretation of the dynamics of the numinous through the figures of *mysterium tremendum* and *fascinans* (overwhelming and fascinating mystery) is a beautifully crafted whole, in terms of both psychoanalytic understanding and phenomenological fidelity to experience. For those not familiar with Merkur's growing work, this article provides an excellent introduction as well as a novel way of plumbing the depths of religious experience. In this regard, Merkur's work will be of interest especially to those psychotherapists and psychoanalysts who work primarily with patients entangled in religious object relations.[27]

The final contribution exemplifies a poetic mode of psychoanalytic reflection. It comes from a psychoanalyst whose theoretical perspective is informed by a Buddhist outlook on the human condition.[28] There is no better way of stating Shahid Najeeb's view of psychoanalysis than to cite a passage from an essay originally intended to be his contribution to this volume: "Psychoanalysis is a name for a complex multifaceted relationship between two people. It is true that the name defines the parameters of what we call psychoanalysis, yet psychoanalysis keeps spilling over those parameters and extending into the world-as-it-is. Equally, the world-as-it-is keeps spilling over the parameters that define psychoanalysis. The world as it-is lives fully within the parameters of psychoanalysis, and psychoanalysis is fully a part of the world-as-it-is. When we fail to understand this, we fail to understand the meaning of psychoanalysis; we fail to understand the truth" (Najeeb 2004: 16).

This sort of ontological view of the symmetry between psychoanalysis and "the world-as-it-is" is rare and radical. It is fair to say that even the most committed among psychoanalysts, those unreservedly dedicated to and desirous of knowledge about this great science,[29] would deliberate over this one. This position indicates the radical depths of the human psyche and, correspondingly, the realities brought about by a psychoanalytic engagement with human beings. But let me try to be more concrete about the "world-as-it-is" from a generalized Buddhist perspective. This configuration—"world-as-it-is"—is the totality of all unconditioned (absolute and eternal) entities (*nirvana*), including the Buddha, and the conditioned, relative, temporal beings (*samsara*). The two realms, the unconditioned and the conditioned (or in the more familiar Western formulation, the infinite and finite), co-arise and co-cease together. Hence, the 'ultimate' in Buddhism is neither conditioned nor unconditioned, neither relative nor absolute, neither temporal nor eternal, neither infinite nor finite. It is this neither^nor median that circumscribes the notion of emptiness (*sunyata*). The Buddhist notion of no-self can be quite appositely approached in terms of this neither^nor vantage point. Masao Abe (1997: 151) argues: "If one clearly understands that the Buddhist notion of no-self is essentially connected with its doctrine of dependent origination and sunyata or Emptiness, one may also naturally understand that the Buddhist notion of no-self does not signify the mere lack or absence of self, as an annihilationist may suggest, but rather constitutes a standpoint which is beyond both the eternalist view of self and the nihilistic view of no-self."

But in terms of the field of psychoanalytic experience and of its evidence, the concrete process of ascendance to this vantage point (this being the self-awakening whereby egoity experiences and, fundamentally, makes its project the realization of the truth of itself as the no-self) inevitably leads to disequilibration and the erosion of the narcissistic structuration of the personality. I am inclined to think that the most painful experience would be in the sphere of the archaic egoity and object relations, where omnipotence, grandiosity, and symbiotic ambivalence are predominant narcissistic modalities. To put it somewhat differently, the pursuit of the realization of one's no-self would in some ways lead through those vicissitudes involved in the mastery of the depressive position—and a great deal more. Abe (1997: 73) writes that the "question of selfhood has been formulated in a way peculiar to Zen: 'What is your original face before your parents were born?'"[30] How, in concrete terms, does it happen in analytical experience that one can come to 'see' one's 'face' beyond the mirror-ing face of the primal, maternal self-object? What can be said about death and loss as the inevitabilities of the life process on the basis of the experiences of self-erosion and psychotic self-dissolution (and other greater and lesser modes of ego death that occur) in the psychoanalytic process? How much pain may one experience (or how painless may it be) before coming to that inner self-certitude surmised, for instance, by Nishida (1958: v), who wrote: "The bottom of my soul has such depth. Neither joy nor the waves of sorrow can reach it." I am inclined to think that psychoanalysis, through its experiential domain and evidence, can immensely contribute to the task of clarification of the Buddhist outlook on the world and existence (and vice versa; see, for instance, Engler 1983). Here I am merely sketching out some implications of Najeeb's statement about the interdependence of psychoanalysis, the human self, and the "world-as-it-is," for it alone can be the appropriate backdrop for Najeeb's article. Its examination of psychoanalysis and religion completes the central theme of the issue—the dialectics of interpenetration of world and psyche in the dynamic constitution of human cultural life-worlds.

The Self and the World

I will place this fundamental human process into a perspective that amplifies its proper spatio-temporal depths. Anyone who does long-term ethnographic research and toils in the process on and through a non-Indo-European lan-guage is in the perfect position to witness the destruction of many human life-worlds and their original modes of existence. Take, for instance, the region of New Guinea where I work. Together with the Australian continent, modern humans have been in this region for some 60,000 years, an eon of human presence and self-world making extending over some 2,000 generations. The effective European presence in this region spans scarcely 8 generations, that is, a mere 240 years. However, it is this Western presence that has decisively and irreversibly transformed the entire region into a domain of self-perpetuation of the Western ecumene and its existential designs for itself and in its own terms. Accordingly, every local life-world has ended up bearing a certain resemblance to the Western 'cost-efficient' civic state, whose existence is dictated by the exigencies of the geopolitics, desires, self-idealizations, and hypocrisies of the dominant powers. Everywhere in this region (as elsewhere) the indigenous inhabitants are expected to become dutiful replicants of the Western ecumeni-cal megapolitans, a certain semblance of good citizens who conduct their civic life (including electioneering) in accordance with the legalities of cost-efficient life and death, in compliance with the legal codes and values of the civilized international *Gemeinschaft* and its techno-efficient organizational institutions. They are to pursue their competitive self-interests on the global market, thus transmuting their private vices into global virtues and prosperity.

These original life-worlds, which until eight generations ago had been living and dying for themselves and on their own terms, had created well over a quarter of the world languages (up to about 1,700 different languages). Many are, if in dwindling numbers, still spoken in this antipodean Oceanic region. They have co-articulated and sustained these life-worlds in terms of, and for the sake of, their own self-generation and self-world intelligibility, whereby the world truly was bespoken and thus sustained in its being from within the matrix of its originary human presence. This lingual cornucopia is presently disintegrating and with it so many human existential designs and noetic universes.[31] In order to get a sense of what is at stake, one would best think of these languages in the way Schilder (1950) thought about the human body image, which he, rightly in my view, saw as "the ultimate gestalt of all human experiences" (Bender, in Schilder 1976: viii). Indeed, the relation between language and body image, and between that of the self and the world, is intrinsic, and more so when language has no other mode of objectification but through living speech (i.e., it is not captured by writing). Understood in this matrix of living embodiment, languages are revealed as the veritable autopoietic structures whereby humans create and sustain the fundamental dimensions of their cultural life-worlds as the universes of self-world creation and intelligibility.

The fact is that nowhere else and never again in this astrophysical universe of ours, no matter how isotropic it is, was there, is there, or will there be anything similar to what those 2,000 generations of humans had created and perpetuated as and for themselves. Whatever and wherever it may be, it is something other than what has been here, at the outskirts of the Virgo super-cluster, in this outer quarter of the Milky Way wherein this solar system is, on this planet, and in this antipodean sector of the globe. It is something other than these particular forms of humanity, who speak Australian, Papuan, and Austronesian tongues that have progenerated and bespoken their desert, rain forest, and oceanic life-worlds.[32] This also holds true for all other regions of the globe occupied by 'first peoples'. At once the fully fledged domains of the biosphere, they were and to an extent still are the provenance of unrepeatable human existence, no less real when actualized in dreams than in wakeful activity. This is the perspective from which I look upon the irreplaceable value of the project of ethnographic fieldwork and writing. All ethnographies (no matter how deficient they may be) are invaluable for anyone who wants to learn about the diversity of human cultural life-worlds that have hitherto inhabited this planet.

The field of psychoanalytic evidence corresponds with this cosmically underscored concrete universality qua individuality of human self-actualization and diversification on this planet whereby the pre-human biosphere became transmuted into the *milieu humaine*, the realm of socio-cultural self-world making. In this delineation, the field of psychoanalytic ethnographic inquiry is that of the originary humanization and diversification of this planet. The depth and breadth of the human psyche and its expressions in and as so many human cultural life-worlds have made this planet what it is—the sole known home of terrestrial humanity.

Only within this vital dimension of diversity and particularities of the human condition can there be discerned the authentic horizons, figurations, movements, and transformations of its universal protagonist, the embodied human self. One way to characterize the fundamental project of psychoanalytic ethnography is to say that its aim is to discern and comprehend the concrete dialectics of this self amidst all the *maya*—all that is transitory and illusory—spun out of the originary 'twinkle in the maternal eye' that from infancy confers upon and beholds its primordial self-unity of being but also conceals its true unconscious matrix. Each explorer has to discover it for him- or herself alone and transform it into critical self-knowledge and knowledge of others.[33] Rather than describing the ego's total embodied unconscious ground (or field) as his or her other (or 'Other', or varying spheres of otherness), I characterize it as the egoic self, for this ground is self-centered through all its parts, and the ego derives its own centricity from the omni-self-centeredness of its ground, regardless of whether the ego knows and/or likes it or not. It is this total matrix that generates all of its parts, starting with the ego, which is always the individuating figure and dimension of its total ground and its parts. Categories such as the Lacanian Other or the Kohutian self pertain to the same ground of human egoic being.[34] Their metapsychological differences and incommensurability are not to be taken as final. For me, to paraphrase one of Lacan's (1993: 9) own quips, neither author "has an odour of sanctity." Open research has recourse to a phenomenologically grounded exploration of human psychic being, of the field of psychoanalytic evidence, and will endeavor to examine critically the conceptualizations by different theorists.

Such open-minded inquiries, especially when ethnographically grounded, allow for a more productive and informative exploration of the constitution of the embodied mind and its dynamic structural configurations. The ego's constitution with regard to others ('objects'), the concrete relations with others (mother, father, society, i.e., intersubjective relations), includes the otherness of the world at large, which as such is always cosmopathically[35] conterminous with the development of the body image. The latter too is mediated by and mediates concrete relations with these living others (Schilder 1950). The intimations of the ego's own internal otherness, such as the super-ego, or other presences (objects), some of which may have divine or demonic qualities to the point of insinuating themselves as the radically autonomous 'Other' (e.g., Freud's [via Groddeck] ID, "other thing" [*das Andere*], or Lacan's archi-signifier and the "Law" giver), all of these modes of constitutive otherness I see as the modes of the primal, constitutive Self (Jung 1971: 460–461), which is in-and-for-itself. The ego that has awakened to this truth of its facticity will thereafter endeavor to make this Self into his or her Self. She or he will endeavor to modulate this Self in accordance with the lucidity and maturity of the ego's knowledge of itself and its primal unconscious ground. Neither master nor slave, the Self will thereby become more self-aware of what it is to be a concrete human egoity, the Self's own presence on this side of infinity—the realm of human transience and mortal finitude known as social-cultural-temporal existence. This, as a first approximation, will be the meaning of Freud's "Where id was, there shall ego be." Neither a dupe of the other, the two will have become the one whose egoity has broken into its unconscious matrix, has ascended to and claimed it as the authentic knowledge of its own Self. Thereafter, and all along this road, neither the one nor the other will be the same figure and the ground that they originally were.

Notes

1. It is worthwhile pointing out the international diversity of the contributors. They are from India, Australia, Belgium, Brazil, Switzerland, Czech Republic, Canada, the US, and the former Yugoslavia.
2. For recent disquisitions on this topic, see Heald and Deluz (1994); Bidou, Galinier, and Juillerat (1999), especially the essays by Green (1999a) and Gillison (1999); and Molino (2004). See also Weiner (1999) and Schwartz, White, and Lutz (1992), especially the essays by Ewing (1992), Cohler (1992), Westen (1992), and Crapanzano (1992).
3. I emphasize human freedom precisely because in the present epoch of intensifying desire for and will to unfreedom, the dominant ideological value promoted in geopolitical-cum-academic fora is that of 'rights'. This is wholly consonant with the civic condition of those who endorse this value, for despite all the writings about 'human agency', they have inherited the freedoms fought and died for by past generations. It is through this historical violence that the Western pursuit of freedom became transmuted into civic 'rights' promulgated and sustained through the might of Western military technology. Fundamentally, the inner horizon of the Western ideology of 'rights' and 'law' is real-politik. This is why the present generations, especially those of academic 'postmodern' citizens, act as if they exist in a human world in which everything is 'negotiated' and implemented through democratic debate and legal ratification, willfully oblivious to the fact that it is not so even in their most immediate institutional domains, including 'partnership' (aka conjugal) arrangements and families. Reflecting on the 'postmodern' worldview and practices confirms on a daily basis Sartre's (1958: 557–775) determination of self-deception/bad-faith as the basic structure of human egoity and its intersubjective milieu. Accordingly, one can appreciate Meltzer's (1991: 49) surmise that virtually "all of psychopathology could be said to be the consequence of self-deception."
4. To the best of my knowledge, *Samiksa*, the journal of the Indian Psychoanalytic Society, is published in English.
5. The literature on group analysis and psychotherapy is enormous. I list here only a handful of references indicative of this fact: Foulkes (1990), Anzieu (1984), Hinshelwood (1987), Brown and Zinkin (1994), Schermer and Pines (1994), Kernberg (1998), Volkan (1997), Koenigsberg (1975, 1977), H. F. Stein (1985, 2001, 2004), and Hopper (2003).
6. A good example of this ideological critique of psychoanalysis that is emblematic of the 'postmodern/deconstructionist' style of current academic performative criticism, purportedly written in the name of non-Western cultural life-worlds, is Brickman (2003; see also the references therein). For a critical review of this work, see Eickelkamp (2006).
7. A modification of 'metropolitan' intended to emphasize not only the enormous size of present-day cities but also the irreversible trend whereby the majority of human populations will soon live in cities.
8. As I see it, rather than representing a critical perspective on the geopolitical situation, let alone promoting significant opposing actions, Western academia and its 'postmodern' sensibilities are symptomatic ideological manifestations of the current civic mentality and its will to conformist discontent. Under the guise and theatrics of moral correctness and the post-colonial aesthetic world-mood (*Weltstimmung*), the postmodern academic 'discourses of the humanities' normalize and reinforce the malignant global negativity of the latest epochal bout of neo-liberal expansion and geopolitical re-equilibration.
9. This combination is well exemplified in such early works as Schilder's (1928, 1942a, 1942b, 1950, 1951, 1953), Federn's (1953), and Sartre's (1958: 557–775) 'existential psychoanalysis' (see also Sartre 1963, 1981–1993). Sartre's critique of the unconscious in terms of his concept of "bad faith" (1958: 47–70) is well known. Husserl's view of the unconscious is outlined by his disciple Eugene Fink (in Husserl 1970: 386–387). For Merleau-Ponty's comments on phenomenology and psychoanalysis, see his "Preface to Hesnard's *L'Oeuvre de Freud*" (1969; see also Lacan 1982–1983), and Pontalis (1982–1983). Schilder's proclivity to treat the unconscious through his concept of the "sphere"

relates it in an original manner to Leibniz's and Kant's concepts of "apperception" and "transcendental subjectivity," and to the phenomenological distinction between the pre-reflective and reflective experience and consciousness. Ricoeur's (1970) discussion of the concept of the unconscious is still the best introduction to the phenomenological problematics of the unconscious. See also Boss (1963, 1990). For a more recent attempt to approach the psychoanalytic field in terms of phenomenology and self-psychology, see Atwood and Stolorow (1984) and Stolorow, Brandchaft, and Atwood (1987). For a phenomenological approach to Jungian analytical psychology, see Brooke (1991, 2000).

10. For a critical view of Kakar's work on Hindu childhood and psychoanalytic theorizing, see Kurtz (1992).

11. For a discussion of related issues, with the focus on the Asian and North American life-worlds, see Roland (1996). See also Kakar (1985, 1995).

12. *Gespräche am sterbenden Fluss* (Conversations by a Dying River) was published in German in 1984 and translated into French with a preface by Georges Balandier in 1987 as *Conversations au bord du fleuve mourant*. The latter is readily available, whereas the German edition has been out of print for a long time. There is no English translation, and the book is virtually unknown, as I found out, even among the Anglophone ethnographers and linguists specialized in the Sepik life-worlds. In this regard, the article presents the first and only sample in English from the contents of this valuable ethno-psychoanalytic ethnography.

13. As young and newly graduated medical doctors, Parin and Matthey served in 1944–1945 as volunteers in the Yugoslav Partisan Liberation Army of Marshal Tito (Boyer 1979: xv), a deed indicative of deep personal convictions, courage, and humanistic ideals.

14. See Freud ([1910] 1963, [1912] 1963, [1915] 1963), Klein ([1952] 1988), Heimann (1950, 1956), Giovacchini (1989), Searles (1979), Jung (1969), Samuels (1985a, 1985b), Schwartz-Salant (1991), and Lacan (1977b, 1985).

15. See Freud ([1917] 1984), Klein ([1940] 1988, [1946] 1988, [1955] 1988), Grinberg (1990), Grotstein (1981), and Meissner (1982).

16. For a discussion of the saliency of crocodilian identity of the human self among the Iatmul, see Mimica (2003).

17. A useful and critical comparison can be made between Parin, Parin-Matthey, and Morgenthaler's ethno-psychoanalytic monographs (including *Conversations by a Dying River*) and Herdt and Stoller's (1990) *Intimate Communications*, especially since the latter is presented as a paradigmatic example of 'clinical ethnography'. For a critical assessment of Herdt's work, including the psychoanalytic dimension of his and Stoller's clinical ethnography, see Mimica (2001).

18. I should state here, as a sort of theoretical prophylaxis, that my positive adherence to the conception of Eros and Thanatos, and with it to the very idea of such psychosomatic vital substratum as instinctual drives matrix, does not, in this context, compromise my relation to such frameworks as 'relational theories' (e.g., Fairbarn 1952; Mitchell 1988; Sullivan 1953), self-psychology (Kohut 1971, 1977, 1996), or Lacan's (1977a) language-centered refiguration of the unconscious. All three have creatively problematized Freud's original conceptualizations of the vital psycho-energic sphere of the psychic being. But in countless commentarial derivations and refractions of these developments one encounters opinionated views adverse to any notion of instinctual drives, that is, the psycho-organismic dynamics; they assume, erroneously I should stress, that Freud's meta-psychology presupposes a view of the human psyche that is void of the intersubjective (inter-human relational) matrix.

19. For Kracke's most recent reflections on the field of psychoanalytic anthropology, see Kracke and Villela (2004).

20. This violent praxis was also responsible for the death of a white secretary-general of the United Nations (Dag Hammarskjold)—until now a unique event in the history of that organization. It is not for nothing that in the 1960s Congo was the home not only of Belgium mining consortia and vestigial colonial bureaucracy but also of such individuals

as Joseph Kasavubu, Moises Tshombe, Joseph Mobutu, 'Mad Mike' Hoare, Siegfried 'Congo' Muller, Patrice Lumumba, Pierre Mulele, and, for a brief period, Che Guevara and his one hundred all-black Cuban internationalist revolutionaries dedicated to the globalization of the revolutionary project that purportedly would end Western imperialism (Che Guevara 2000). Kasavubu was the first president of the independent Congo until he was ousted in a coup by the commander-in-chief of the Congolese National Army, General Joseph Mobutu. Immediately after independence, Tshombe led the secession of Katanga, the wealthiest province in the Congo, and started a succession of crises that ended in 1967. Along the way, he became one of several Congolese prime ministers following the assassination of the Soviet-backed socialist prime minister, Lumumba. Mulele was originally a minister in Lumumba's government. In 1964, backed by the Chinese, he started the first rebellion against the Kasavubu-Tshombe government backed by the Belgians, the Americans, and the British. Hoare and Muller, together with the French ex-marine Bob Denard and the Belgian colonel Vanderwalle, were the leading white mercenaries employed by Tshombe and Mobutu. The core mercenary force that fought for Tshombe during the secession of Katanga in 1960 also included former French Foreign Legionnaires, who had already done most of the dirty work for France in Indo-China and Algeria. In November 1964, backed by the CIA, which, among others, had supplied anti-Castro Cuban pilots and Belgian paratroopers, Hoare's and Vanderwalle's mercenaries broke the rebel forces that held Stanleyville. In late April 1965, Che Guevara and his Cubans joined the rebels fighting in a mountainous region in the border area of Rwanda and Tanzania, near Lake Tanganyika. Their revolutionary project turned into a fiasco, and they left in dismay on 20 November of the same year. On 24 November, Mobutu deposed Kasavubu, who beforehand had deposed Tshombe from the position of prime minister.

21. General Mobutu's Congo, backed by the US, was effectively consolidated and ushered into stable existence in November 1967 following the last Congolese crisis of the so-called mercenary revolt led by a Belgian military man, Colonel Jean Schramme. The episode ended with the mercenaries' retreat to Rwanda, where they were disarmed and eventually repatriated to Europe.

22. No sooner than August 1998, an insurrection backed by Rwanda and Uganda turned against Kabila and ushered the Congo into its current period of violent life and death. Among the few white mercenaries involved in the Congolese affairs of the 1990s were ex-soldiers from the former Yugoslavia who had perfected their art of perdition on the Balkanian home soil but had made no fortune there. Accordingly, if belatedly, they went on to seek it in the Congo. It should be pointed out that their rates were considerably lesser, and with chronic arrears, than the daily fees of the development experts and consultants who make their own not-so-small fortunes in the present day Congo and other regions of the so-called post-colonial world.

23. See also San Roque (2001). For more information on Jungian perspectives on Aboriginal life-worlds and for a précis of San Roque's "Sugar Man" project, which was designed to provide a mythopoeic framework for alcohol-induced experience and behavior, see Petchkovsky, San Roque, and Beskow (2003).

24. The exegetical literature on Lacan is an academic industry, but detailed clinical studies of Lacanian orientation are rare. Apart from the early work of Mannoni (1972, 1973) and the essays compiled by Schneiderman (1980), Lefort's (1994) and Leclaire's (1998) works are exceptional examples. Two other recent works that illustrate well the clinical dimension of the Lacanian framework are Tendlarz (2003) and Apollon, Bergeron, and Cantin (2002), while Verhaeghe (2004) offers a Lacanian "manual for clinical psychodiagnostics."

25. Without diminishing the value and originality of Glass's work, it is not out of place to link his work to the tradition represented by Fromm (1941, 1955), Gabel (1975), Kovel (1981, 1988), or Lerner (1986).

26. Glass's essay draws mainly on examples from Germany under Nazism, and the documentary literature on and critical studies of the period are massive. However, I cannot think of a more appropriate piece of psychoanalytic ethnography to supplement this article than

Beradt's (1968) *Third Reich of Dreams*. Sartre's (1960) remarkable short story, "The Childhood of a Leader," set against the backdrop of the French fascist leagues, may also be read profitably in relation to Glass's essay.

27. I am thinking of such practitioners and authors as Oden (1967) and Spero (1992), but of course many others could be listed.

28. For three comprehensive collections concerning Buddhism, psychoanalysis, and Jungian psychology, see Molino (1998), Safran (2003), and Spiegelman and Miyuki (1985).

29. As, for instance, exalted by Nicholas Abraham (1994: 98) at the end of his critical review of Pontalis and Laplanche's masterpiece *The Language of Psycho-Analysis*: "[T]he transphenomenal Kernel of this nonscience, which, for more than a few, is already the science of sciences."

30. Here Abe echoes Hui-neng, the Sixth Patriarch of Chinese Zen (Dumoulin 1994; Zimmer 1951: 548). One can also detect in this pronouncement the intimations of that original pre-Oedipal constellation that Kosawa, the pioneer of Japanese psychoanalysis, had formulated as "the Ajase complex" (Okonogi 2005).

31. On the world scale, in this new century, "according to some informed estimates, 3,000 of the existing 6,000 languages will perish and another 2,400 will come near to extinction. This leaves just 600 languages in the 'safe' category, assuming that category to be languages having 100,000 speakers or more. Thus, 90 percent of the world languages are imperiled" (Hale 1998: 192).

32. As one linguist has said, there are no "famous" languages among them. "They are generally known to anthropologists and linguists who specialize in their study" (Ruhlen 1987: 185). The truth is that they were and are primarily studied by missionaries and their more recent non-anointed successors, the Summer Institute of Linguistics (SIL) and the 'new tribes' God-loving Westerners, who are explicitly determined to bring the 'good news' to the native peoples of the world in the medium of their native tongues. Indeed, the program of the SIL is specifically based on a chapter from the Revelations where it is said that there will be no second coming until all the peoples of the world will be able to read the 'good news' in their mother tongue. Of all the news announced to God's creatures, the following is of singular significance, namely, that "the meek shall inherit the world." However, I hasten to emphasize that in Papua New Guinea, especially in the last two decades, it is these missionaries who provide most of the basic help to the peoples in those areas that are bypassed by all development. Because these regions have nothing to offer in the way of economic exploitation, the government has no interest in making any infrastructural investments. As for the reciprocity of missionary work on the global scale, I know a Huli Catholic priest (from the Southern Highlands of Papua New Guinea) who has been working for the last 10 years among drug addicts in the Sydney metropolitan area, principally in King's Cross.

33. I believe that the contributors to this volume reflect such an endeavor, and at this point I wish to thank them all.

34. For comparative discussions of Lacanian and Kohutian frameworks, see the contributions in Gurewich, Tort, and Fairfield (1999).

35. This useful term was coined by W. J. Stein (1970), a phenomenological psychologist. It can also be glossed as "world-empathically." Conceptually, it derives from Heidegger's interpretations of *Stimmung* (mood, attunement) in his *Being and Time*. In psychoanalysis, the best work on the dynamics of the self-world relations is Harold Searles's (1960) *The Non-Human Environment*.

References

Abe, M. 1997. *Zen and Comparative Studies*. Ed. S. Heine. Honolulu: University of Hawaii Press.

Abraham, N. 1994. "The Shell and the Kernel." Pp. 79–98 in N. Abraham and M. Torok, *The Shell and the Kernel: Renewals of Psychoanalysis*, ed. and trans. N. T. Rand. Chicago: University of Chicago Press.

Anzieu, D. 1984. *The Group and the Unconscious*. London: Routledge and Kegan Paul.

Apollon, W., D. Bergeron, and L. Cantin. 2002. *After Lacan: Clinical Practice and the Subject of the Unconscious*. Albany: State University of New York Press.

Atwood, G. E., and R. D. Stolorow. 1984. *Structures of Subjectivity: Explorations in Psychoanalytic Phenomenology*. Hillsdale, NJ: Analytic Press.

Beradt, C. 1968. *Third Reich of Dreams*. Chicago: Quadrangle.

Bidou, P., J. Galinier, and B. Juillerat, eds. 1999. *L'Homme* 149. Special issue, *Anthropologie psychanalytique*.

Boss, M. 1963. *Psychoanalysis and Daseinanalysis*. New York: Basic Books.

_____. 1990. "The Unconscious—What Is It?" *Review of Existential Psychology and Psychiatry* 20: 237–249.

Boyer, L. B. 1979. *Childhood and Folklore: A Psychoanalytic Study of Apache Personality*. New York: Library of Psychological Anthropology.

Brickman, C. 2003. *Aboriginal Population in the Mind: Race and Primitivity in Psychoanalysis*. New York: Columbia University Press.

Brooke, R. 1991. *Jung and Phenomenology*. London: Routledge.

_____, ed. 2000. *Pathways into the Jungian World: Phenomenology and Analytical Psychology*. London: Routledge.

Brown, D., and L. Zinkin, eds. 1994. *The Psyche and the Social World: Developments in Group-Analytic Theory*. London: Routledge.

Castoriadis, C. 1987. *The Imaginary Institution of Society*. London: Polity.

Che Guevara, E. 2000. *The African Dream: The Diaries of the Revolutionary War in the Congo*. Trans. P Camiller, with an introduction by Richard Gott and a foreword by Aleida Guevara. London: Harvill Press.

Cohler, B. J. 1992. "Intent and Meaning in Psychoanalysis and Cultural Study." Pp. 269–293 in Schwartz, White, and Lutz 1992.

Crapanzano, V. 1992. "Some Thoughts on Hermeneutics and Psychoanalytic Anthropology." Pp. 294–307 in Schwartz, White, and Lutz 1992.

Devereux, G. 1967. *From Anxiety to Method in Behavioral Sciences*. The Hague: Mouton.

Doray, B. 1988. *From Taylorism to Fordism: A Rational Madness*. London: Free Association Books.

Dumoulin, H. 1994. *Zen Buddhism: A History*. Vol. 1: *India and China*. Trans. James W. Heisig and Paul Knitter. New York: Simon & Schuster Macmillan.

Eickelkamp, U. 2006. "'Inscribing' Freud: A Critical Review of Celia Brickman's *Aboriginal Population in the Mind*." *Australian Journal of Anthropology* 17, no. 1: 86–104.

Engler, J. H. 1983. "Vicissitudes of the Self According to Psychoanalysis and Buddhism: A Spectrum Model of Object Relations Development." *Psychoanalysis and Contemporary Thought* 6: 29–72.

Ewing, K. P. 1992. "Is Psychoanalysis Relevant for Anthropology?" Pp. 251–269 in Schwartz, White, and Lutz 1992.

Fairbarn, W. R. 1952. *Psychoanalytic Study of the Personality*. London: Routledge and Kegan Paul.

Federn, P. 1953. *Ego Psychology and the Psychoses*. London: Karnac.

Foulkes, S. H. 1990. *Selected Papers: Psychoanalysis and Group Analysis*. London: Karnac.

Freud, S. [1910] 1963. "The Future Prospects of Psychoanalytic Therapy." Pp. 77–87 in *Therapy and Technique*, ed. P. Rieff, trans. Joan Riviere. New York: Macmillan.

_____. [1912] 1963. "The Dynamics of the Transference." Pp. 105–116 in *Therapy and Technique*, ed. P. Rieff, trans. Joan Riviere. New York: Macmillan.

_____. [1915] 1963. "Further Recommendations in the Technique of Psychoanalysis: Observations on Transference Love." Pp. 167–180 in *Therapy and Technique*, ed. P. Rieff, trans. Joan Riviere. New York: Macmillan.

_____. [1915] 1984. "The Unconscious." Pp. 159–222 in *On Metapsychology*. Vol. 11. Pelican Freud Library. Harmondsworth: Penguin Books.

_____. [1917] 1984. "Mourning and Melancholia." Pp. 245–268 in *On Metapsychology*. Vol. 11. Pelican Freud Library. Harmondsworth: Penguin Books.

_____. [1925] 1984. "Negation." Pp. 435–442 in *On Metapsychology*. Vol. 11. Pelican Freud Library. Harmondsworth: Penguin Books.

Fromm, E. 1941. *Fear of Freedom*. New York: Farrar and Rinehart.

_____. 1955. *The Sane Society*. Greenwich, CT: Fawcett.

Gabel, J. 1975. *False Consciousness: An Essay on Reification*. Oxford: Blackwell.

Gillison, G. 1999. "L'anthropologie psychanalytique: Un paradigme marginal." Pp. 43–52 in Bidou, Galinier, and Juillerat 1999.

Giovacchini, P. 1989. *Countertransference Triumphs and Catastrophes*. Northvale, NJ: Jason Aronson.

Glass, J. M. 1974. "The Philosopher and the Shaman." *Political Theory* 2: 181–196.

_____. 1976. "Machiavelli's Prince and Alchemical Transformation: Action and the Archetype of Regeneration." *Polity* 8: 504–528.

_____. 1985. *Delusion: Internal Dimensions of Political Life*. Chicago: University of Chicago Press.

_____. 1989. *Private Terror/Public Life: Psychosis and the Politics of Community*. Ithaca, NY: Cornell University Press.

_____. 1993. *Shattered Selves: Multiple Personality in a Postmodern World*. Ithaca, NY: Cornell University Press.

_____. 1997. *'Life Unworthy of Life': Racial Phobia and Mass Murder in Hitler's Germany*. New York: Basic Books.

_____. 2004. *Jewish Resistance During the Holocaust*. New York: Palgrave.

Green, A. 1999a. "Le psychisme entre anthropologues et psychanalystes: Un différence d'interprétation." Pp. 25–42 in Bidou, Galinier, and Juillerat 1999.

_____. 1999b. *The Work of the Negative*. London: Free Association Books.

_____. 2001. *Life Narcissism Death Narcissism*. Trans. A. Weller. London: Free Association Books.

Grinberg, L. 1990. *The Goals of Psychoanalysis: Identification, Identity and Supervision*. London: Karnac.

Grotstein, J. 1981. *Splitting and Projective Identification*. Northvale, NJ: Jason Aronson.

Gurewich, J. F., M. Tort, and S. Fairfield. 1999. *Lacan and the New Wave in American Psychoanalysis: The Subject and Self*. New York: Other Press.

Hale, K. 1998. "On Endangered Languages and the Importance of Linguistic Diversity." Pp. 192–216 in *Endangered Languages*, ed. Lenore A. Grenoble and Lindsay Whaley. Cambridge: Cambridge University Press.

Heald, S., and A. Deluz, eds. 1994. *Anthropology and Psychoanalysis: An Encounter through Culture*. London: Routledge.

Heimann, P. 1950. "On Counter-Transference." *International Journal of Psychoanalysis* 31: 81–84.

_____. 1956. "The Dynamics of Transference Interpretations." *International Journal of Psychoanalysis* 37: 303–310.

Herdt, G., and R. J. Stoller. 1990. *Intimate Communications: Erotics and the Study of Culture*. New York: Columbia University Press.

Hinshelwood, R. D. 1987. *What Happens in Groups: Psychoanalysis, the Individual and the Community*. London: Free Association Books.

Hopper, E. 2003. *Traumatic Experience in the Unconscious Life of Groups*. London: Jessica Kingsley Publishers.

Husserl, E. 1970. *The Crisis of European Sciences and Transcendental Phenomenology.* Evanston, IL: Northwestern University Press.

Jaspers, K. [1913] 1997. *General Psychopathology.* 2 vols. Trans. J. Hoenig and M. Hamilton. Baltimore, MD: Johns Hopkins University Press.

Jung, C. G. 1969. *The Psychology of the Transference.* Princeton, NJ: Princeton University Press.

_____. 1971. *Psychological Types.* Princeton, NJ: Princeton University Press.

Kakar, S. 1970. *Frederick Taylor: A Study in Personality and Innovation.* Cambridge, MA: MIT Press.

_____. 1981. *The Inner World: A Psychoanalytic Study of Childhood and Society in India.* 2nd ed. Delhi: Oxford University Press.

_____. 1985. "Psychoanalysis and Non-Western Cultures." *International Review of Psycho-Analysis* 12: 441–448.

_____. 1995. "Clinical Work and Cultural Imagination." *Psychoanalytic Quarterly* 64: 265–281. Reprinted in Kakar 2001.

_____. 2001. *The Essential Writings of Sudhir Kakar.* Delhi: Oxford University Press.

Kernberg, O. F. 1998. *Ideology, Conflict, and Leadership in Groups and Organizations.* New Haven, CT: Yale University Press.

Klein, M. [1940] 1988. "Mourning and Its Relations to Manic-Depressive States." Pp. 344–369 in *Love, Guilt and Reparation.* London: Virago.

_____. [1946] 1988. "Notes on some Schizoid Phenomena." Pp. 1–24 in *Envy and Gratitude.* London: Virago.

_____. [1952] 1988. "The Origins of Transference." Pp. 48–56 in *Envy and Gratitude.* London: Virago.

_____. [1955] 1988. "On Identification." Pp. 141–175 in *Envy and Gratitude.* London: Virago.

Koenigsberg, R. A. 1975. *Hitler's Ideology: A Study in Psychoanalytic Sociology.* New York: Library of Social Science.

_____. 1977. *The Psychoanalysis of Racism, Revolution and Nationalism.* New York: Library of Social Science.

Kohut, H. 1971. *The Analysis of the Self.* New York: International Universities Press.

_____. 1977. *The Restoration of the Self.* New York: International Universities Press.

_____. 1996. *The Chicago Institute Lectures.* Ed. P. Toplin and M. Toplin. Hillsdale, NJ: Analytic Press.

Kovel, J. 1981. *The Age of Desire: Case Histories of a Radical Psychoanalyst.* New York: Pantheon.

_____. 1988. *White Racism: A Psychohistory.* London: Free Association Books.

Kracke, W. H. 1979. "Dreaming in Kagwahiv: Dream Beliefs and Their Psychic Uses in an Amazonian Indian Culture." *Psychoanalytic Study of Society* 8: 119–171.

_____. 1981. "Kagwahiv Mourning: Dreams of a Bereaved Father." *Ethos* 9, no. 4: 258–275.

_____. 1999. "A Language of Dreaming: Dreams of an Amazonian Insomniac." *International Journal of Psychoanalysis* 80: 257–271.

_____. 2003a. "Beyond the Mythologies: A Shape of Dreaming." Pp. 211–235 in *Dream Travelers: Sleep Experiences and Culture in the Western Pacific,* ed. I. Lohmann. New York: Palgrave.

_____. 2003b. "Dream: Ghost of a Tiger, a System of Human Words." Pp. 155–164 in *Dreaming and the Self: New Perspectives on Subjectivity, Identity, and Emotion,* ed. J. M. Mageo. Albany: State University of New York Press.

Kracke, W. H., and L. Villela. 2004. "Between Desire and Culture: Conversations between Psychoanalysis and Anthropology." Pp. 175–209 in *Culture, Subject, Psyche: Dialogues in Psychoanalysis and Anthropology,* ed. A. Molino. Middletown, CT: Wesleyan University Press.

Kurtz, S. N. 1992. *All the Mothers Are One: Hindu India and the Cultural Reshaping of Psychoanalysis.* New York: Columbia University Press.

Lacan, J. 1977. *Ecrits: A Selection.* London: Routledge.

_____. 1977a. *Four Fundamental Concepts of Psychoanalysis.* Ed. Jacques-Alain Miller. Trans. Alan Sheridan. New York and London: W.W. Norton.

_____. 1982–1983. "Merleau-Ponty: In Memoriam." *Review of Existential Psychology and Psychiatry* 18: 73–82.

_____. 1985. "Intervention on Transference." Pp. 61–73 in *Feminine Sexuality: Jacques Lacan and the école freudienne,* ed. J. Mitchell and J. Rose. New York and London: W.W. Norton.

_____. 1993. *The Psychoses.* London: Routledge.

Leclaire, S. 1998. *A Child Is Being Killed: On Primary Narcissism and the Death Drive.* Stanford, CA: Stanford University Press.

Lefort, R. 1994. *Birth of the Other.* Urbana: University of Illinois Press.

Lerner, M. 1986. *Surplus Powerlessness: The Psychodynamics of Everyday Life … and the Psychology of Individual and Social Transformation.* Atlantic Highlands, NJ: Humanities Press.

Lincoln, J. S. [1935] 1970. *The Dream in Primitive Cultures.* New York: Johnson Reprint.

Mannoni, M. 1972. *The Child, His 'Illness', and the Others.* Harmondsworth, UK: Penguin Books.

_____. 1973. *The Backward Child and His Mother.* New York: Pantheon.

Meissner, W. W. 1982. *Internalization in Psychoanalysis.* New York: International Universities Press.

Meltzer, D. 1991. "Facts and Fictions." Pp. 49–61 in *The Personal Myth in Psychoanalytic Theory,* ed. P. Hartocollis and I. D. Graham. Madison, CT: International Universities Press.

Merleau-Ponty, M. 1969. "Phenomenology and Psychoanalysis: Preface to Hesnard's *L'Oeuvre de Freud.*" Pp. 81–87 in *The Essential Writings of Merleau-Ponty,* ed. A. L. Fisher. New York: Harcourt, Brace & World.

Merkur, D. 1991. *Powers Which We Do Not Know: The Gods and Spirits of the Inuit.* Moscow: University of Idaho Press.

_____. 1992. *Becoming Half Hidden: Shamanism and Initiation among the Inuit.* 2nd ed. New York: Garland.

_____. 1993. *Gnosis: An Esoteric Tradition of Mystical Visions and Unions.* Albany: State University of New York Press.

_____. 1998. *The Ecstatic Imagination.* Albany: State University of New York Press.

_____. 1999. *Mystical Moments and Unitive Thinking.* Albany: State University of New York Press.

_____. 2001. *Unconscious Wisdom: A Superego Function in Dreams, Conscience, and Inspiration.* Albany: State University of New York Press.

Mimica, J. 1981. "Omalyce: An Ethnography of the Iqwaye View of the Cosmos." PhD diss., Australian National University.

_____. 1988. *Intimations of Infinity: The Counting System and the Concept of Number among the Iqwaye.* Oxford: Berg Publishers.

_____. 1991. "The Incest Passions: An Outline of the Logic of the Iqwaye Social Organisation." *Oceania* 62, no. 1: 34–58; no. 2: 81–113.

_____. 2001. "A Review from the Field (A Critical Review of Gilbert Herdt's *Sambia Sexual Culture: Essays from the Field*)." *Australian Journal of Anthropology* 12, no. 2: 225–237.

_____. 2003. "Out of the Depths of Saurian Waters: On Psycho-Bakhtinianism, Ethnographic Countertransference, and *Naven.*" *Anthropological Notebooks* 9, no. 1: 5–47.

Mitchell, S. A. 1988. *Relational Concepts in Psychoanalysis: An Integration.* Cambridge, MA: Harvard University Press.

Molino, A., ed. 1998. *The Couch and the Tree: Dialogues in Psychoanalysis and Buddhism.* New York: North Point Press.

_____. 2004. *Culture, Subject, Psyche: Dialogues in Psychoanalysis and Anthropology.* Middletown, CT: Wesleyan University Press.

Najeeb, S. 2004. "Sand, Surf, and Sky." Unpublished manuscript.

Neumann, E. 1954. *The Origins and History of Consciousness*. Princeton, NJ: Princeton University Press.

Nishida, K. 1958. *Intelligibility and the Philosophy of Nothingness: Three Philosophical Essays*. Honolulu: East-West Centre Press.

Oden, T. 1967. *Contemporary Theology and Psychotherapy*. Philadelphia: Westminster Press.

Okonogi, K. 2005. "The Ajase Complex and Its Implications." Pp. 57–75 in *Asian Culture and Psychotherapy: Implications for East and West*, ed. W. S. Tseng, S. C. Chang, and M. Nishizono. Honolulu: University of Hawai'i Press.

Otto, R. [1923] 1958. *The Idea of the Holy*. London: Oxford University Press.

Parin, P., F. Morgenthaler, and G. Parin-Matthey. 1980. *Fear Thy Neighbor as Thyself: Psychoanalysis and Society among the Anyi of West Africa*. Chicago: University of Chicago Press.

Petchkovsky, L., C. San Roque, and M. Beskow. 2003. "Jung and the Dreaming: Analytical Psychology's Encounters with Aboriginal Culture." *Transcultural Psychiatry* 40, no. 2: 208–238.

Pontalis, J. B. 1982–1983. "The Problem of the Unconscious in Merleau-Ponty's Thought." *Review of Existential Psychology and Psychiatry* 18: 83–96.

Ricoeur, P. 1970. *Freud and Philosophy: An Essay on Interpretation*. New Haven, CT: Yale University Press.

Roland, A. 1996. *Cultural Pluralism and Psychoanalysis*. London: Routledge.

Ruhlen, M. 1987. *A Guide to the World's Languages*. Vol. 1: *Classification*. Stanford, CT: Stanford University Press.

Safran, J. D., ed. 2003. *Psychoanalysis and Buddhism: An Unfolding Dialogue*. Boston: Wisdom Publications.

Samuels, A. 1985a. "Countertransference, the 'Mundus Imaginalis' and a Research Project." *Journal of Analytical Psychology* 30: 47–71.

_____. 1985b. "Symbolic Dimensions of Eros in Transference-Countertransference: Some Clinical Uses of Jung's Alchemical Metaphor." *International Review of Psycho-Analysis* 12: 199–214.

San Roque, C. 2001. "Coming to Terms with the Country." Pp. 27–52 in *Landmarks: Papers by Jungian Analysts from Australia and New Zealand*, ed. H. Formaini. Manuka, ACT: Australian and New Zealand Society of Jungian Analysts.

Sartre, J-P. 1958. *Being and Nothingness: An Essay on Phenomenological Ontology*. New York: Philosophical Library.

_____. 1960. "The Childhood of a Leader." Pp. 130–220 in *Intimacy*. Trans. L. Alexander. London: Panther Books.

_____. 1963. *Saint Genet, Actor and Martyr*. Trans. B. Frechtman. New York: George Braziller.

_____. 1981–1993. *The Family Idiot, 1821–1857*. 5 vols. Chicago: University of Chicago Press.

Schermer, V. L., and M. Pines, eds. 1994. *Ring of Fire: Primitive Affects and Object Relations in Group Psychotherapy*. London: Routledge.

Schilder, P. 1928. *Introduction to a Psychoanalytic Psychiatry*. New York: Nervous and Mental Disease Publishing Company.

_____. 1942a. *Mind: Perception and Thought in Their Constructive Aspects*. New York: Columbia University Press.

_____. 1942b. *Goals and Desires of Man: A Psychological Survey of Life*. New York: Columbia University Press.

_____. 1950. *The Image and Appearance of the Human Body*. New York: International Universities Press.

_____. 1951. *Psychoanalysis, Man, and Society*. New York: Norton.

_____. 1953. *Medical Psychology*. New York: International Universities Press.

_____. 1976. *On Psychoses*. New York: International Universities Press.

Schneiderman, S., ed. 1980. *Returning to Freud: Clinical Psychoanalysis in the School of Lacan*. New Haven, CT: Yale University Press.

Schwartz, T., G. M. White, and C. A. Lutz, eds. 1992. *New Directions in Psychological Anthropology*. Cambridge: Cambridge University Press.

Schwartz-Salant, N. 1991. "Vision, Interpretation, and the Interactive Field." *Journal of Analytical Psychology* 36: 342–365.

Searles, H. 1960. *The Non-Human Environment*. New York: International Universities Press.

———. 1979. *Countertransference and Related Subjects: Selected Papers*. New York: International Universities Press.

Spero, M. H. 1992. *Religious Objects as Psychological Structures: A Critical Integration of Object Relations Theory, Psychotherapy, and Judaism*. Chicago: University of Chicago Press.

Spiegelman, J. M., and M. Miyuki, eds. 1985. *Buddhism and Jungian Psychology*. Phoenix, AZ: Falcon Press.

Stein, H. F. 1985. *The Psychoanthropology of American Culture*. New York: Psychohistory Press.

———. 2001. *Nothing Personal, Just Business: A Guided Journey into Organizational Darkness*. Westport, CT: Quorum Books.

———. 2004. *Beneath the Crust of Culture: Psychoanalytic Anthropology and the Cultural Unconscious in American Life*. Amsterdam: Editions Rodopi BV.

Stein, W. J. 1970. "Cosmopathy and Interpersonal Relations." Pp. 216–231 in *Phenomenology in Perspective*, ed. F. J. Smith. The Hague: M. Nijhoff.

Stolorow, R. D., B. Brandchaft, and G. E. Atwood. 1987. *Psychoanalytic Treatment: An Intersubjective Approach*. Hillsdale, NJ: Analytic Press.

Sullivan, H. S. 1953. *The Interpersonal Theory of Psychiatry*. New York: Norton.

———. 1974. *Schizophrenia as a Human Process*. New York: Norton.

Tendlarz, S. E. 2003. *Childhood Psychosis: A Lacanian Perspective*. London: Karnac.

Verhaeghe, P. 2004. *On Being Normal and Other Disorders: A Manual for Clinical Psychodiagnostics*. New York: Other Press.

Volkan, V. 1997. *Blood Lines: From Ethnic Pride to Ethnic Terrorism*. Boulder, CO: Westview Press.

Weiner, J. 1999. "Psychoanalysis and Anthropology: On the Temporality of Analysis." Pp. 234–261 in *Anthropological Theory Today*, ed. H. L. Moore. London: Polity Press.

Westen, D. 1992. "Beyond the Binary Opposition in Psychological Anthropology: Integrating Contemporary Psychoanalysis and Cognitive Science." Pp. 21–47 in Schwartz, White, and Lutz 1992.

Zimmer, H. 1951. *Philosophies of India*. Princeton, NJ: Princeton University Press.

Chapter 1

CULTURE AND PSYCHOANALYSIS
A Personal Journey

Sudhir Kakar

My interest in the role of culture in psychoanalysis did not begin as an abstract intellectual exercise but rather as a matter of vital personal import. Without my quite realizing it at the time, it commenced when I started as an analyst more than 30 years ago upon entering a five-day-a-week training session with a German analyst at the Sigmund-Freud-Institut in Frankfurt. At first, I registered the role of culture in my analysis as a series of niggling feelings of discomfort whose source remained incomprehensible for many months. Indeed, many years were to pass before I began to comprehend the cultural landscape of the mind in more than a rudimentary fashion and to make some sense of my experiences, both as an analysand and as an analyst, in cross-cultural therapeutic dyads (Kakar 1978, 1982, 1987, 1989, 1994, 1997).[1]

After undergoing analysis for some months, I realized that my recurrent feelings of estrangement were not due to cultural differences in forms of politeness,

References for this chapter begin on page 43.

manners of speech, attitudes toward time, or even differences in aesthetic sensibilities. (To me, at that time, Beethoven came across as just so much noise, while I doubt if he even knew of the existence of Hindustani classical music, which so moved me.) The estrangement involved much deeper cultural layers of the self, which were an irreducible part of my subjectivity as, I suppose, they were a part of my analyst's. In other words, if during a session we sometimes suddenly became strangers to each other, it was because each of us found himself locked into a specific 'cultural preconscious', consisting of a more or less closed system of cultural representations that were rarely raised to conscious awareness. In my case, what I have termed the 'cultural preconscious' referred to the 'Indian-ness' of an upper-caste Hindu, which I was to spend many years elucidating.

Culturally shared Indian-ness is not an abstract concept, a subject of intellectual debate for academics, but something that informs the activities and concerns of daily life for a vast number of Indians while at the same time guiding them through the journey of life. How to behave toward superiors and subordinates in organizations, the kinds of food conducive to health and vitality, the web of duties and obligations in the family—all are as much influenced by the cultural part of the mind as are ideas concerning the proper relationship between the sexes or one's relationship to the Divine. Of course, for the individual Indian, this civilizational heritage may be modified or overlaid by the specific cultures of one's family, caste, class, or ethnic group. At first glance, the notion of a singular Indian-ness may seem far-fetched: How can one generalize about a billion people—Hindus, Muslims, Sikhs, Christians, and Jains—who speak 14 major languages and are characterized by pronounced regional and linguistic identities? How can one postulate anything in common among a people divided not only by social class but also by India's signature system of caste, and with an ethnic diversity typical more of past empires than of modern nation-states? Yet as attested to by foreign travelers throughout the ages, there is a unity in this diversity that is often ignored or unseen because our modern eyes are more attuned to discern divergence and variance than resemblance. Indian-ness, then, is about similarities rather than differences among the inhabitants of this vast sub-continent, similarities produced by an overarching Indic, pre-eminently Hindu civilization that has contributed a lion's share to what we would call the 'cultural gene pool' of India's peoples.

This civilization has remained in constant ferment through the processes of assimilation, transformation, reassertion and re-creation that came in the wake of its encounters with other civilizations and cultural forces, such as those unleashed by the advent of Islam in medieval times and European colonialism in the more recent past. The contemporary buffeting of Indic civilization by a West-centric globalization is only the latest in a long line of invigorating cultural encounters that can be called 'clashes' only from the narrowest of perspectives. Indic civilization—as separate from, though related to, Hinduism as a religion—is thus the common patrimony of all Indians, irrespective of their faith. Indians, then, share a family resemblance that is seen in sharp relief when it is compared to the profiles of peoples of other major civilizations or cultural clusters. This is why, in spite of persistent academic disapproval, people (including academics in their unguarded moments) continue to speak of "the Indians," as they do of "the Chinese," "the Europeans," or "the Americans," as a necessary and legitimate shortcut to a more complex reality.

What are some of the building blocks of this Indian-ness? Let me begin with the Hindu view of the world, which I have explicated in earlier writings (e.g., Kakar 1978).

The Hindu World-View

Every civilization has a unique way of looking at the world. This world-view, the civilization's center of gravity, is a cluster of ideas that define the goal of human existence, the ways to reach this goal, the errors to be avoided, and the obstacles to be expected on the way. The world-view interprets central human experiences and answers perennial questions on what is good and what is evil, what is real and what is unreal, what is the essential nature of men and women and the world they live in, and what is man's connection to nature, to other human beings, and to the cosmos. For instance, if we look at China (and Chinese societies around the world), we can define the following elements in the dominant Confucian world-view: There is no other world than the one we live in. The ultimate meaning of life is embedded in and not separate from ordinary practical living. The meaning of life is then realized through a personal self-cultivation within the community and through mutual aid in the family, clan, school, and workplace. The glue that binds society is not law but what the Chinese call *li*, a civilized mode of conduct. A predominant feature of the Chinese world-view is a sense of duty rather than a demand for rights.

When we talk of a world-view, we are not speaking of philosophical doctrines that are relevant only for religious and intellectual elites. We are talking about the beliefs and attitudes, many of them not conscious, that are reflected in the lives, songs, and stories of a vast number of Indians. Disseminated through myths and legends or proverbs and metaphors, enacted in religious rituals, conveyed through tales told to children, given a modern veneer in Bollywood films, glimpsed in admonitions of parents as also in the future vistas they hold out to their children, a world-view is absorbed from early on in life—not through the head, but through the heart.

Let me begin with three interlinked elements that compose a major part of the Hindu world-view: moksha, dharma, and karma. My interest in these concepts is not philosophical, textual, or historical; rather, it is psychological. What I want to look at closely here is the contribution of this ancient trinity to the formation of the Indian mind and its reverberations in the thoughts and actions of contemporary Indians.

The Goal of Life

Moksha (which variously means self-realization, transcendence, salvation, a release from this world) has been traditionally viewed as the goal of human life. The idea of moksha is intimately linked with the Indian conviction in the existence of another, 'higher' level of reality beyond the shared, verifiable, empirical reality of our world, our bodies, and our emotions. A fundamental value of most schools of Hinduism (and of the Sufis of Islam), the belief in the existence of an 'ultimate' reality—related to ordinary, everyday reality in the same way that waking consciousness is related to a dream—is an unquestioned verity of Indian culture and the common thread in the teachings of the culture's innumerable gurus. The 'ultimate' reality, whose apprehension is considered to be the highest goal and meaning of human life, is said to be beyond conceptual thought and indeed beyond mind. Intellectual thought, naturalistic science, and other passions of the mind seeking to grasp the empirical nature of our world thus have a relatively lower status in the culture as compared to meditative practices or even art, since aesthetic and spiritual experiences are supposed to be closely related. In the culture's belief system, the aesthetic power of music and verse, of a well-told tale and a well-enacted play, makes them more rather than less real than life.

This emphasis on the spiritual that underlies the practices of the various schools of 'self-realization'—for example, yoga—colors the emotional tone of the way an Indian looks at life. To most Indians, life is a combination of the tragic and the romantic. It is tragic insofar as they see human experience pervaded by ambiguities and uncertainties whereby one has little choice but to bear the burden of unanswerable questions, inescapable conflicts, and incomprehensible afflictions of fate. But superimposed on the tragic, the Indian vision of moksha offers a romantic quest. The new journey is a search, and the seeker, if he or she withstands the perils of the road, will be rewarded by exaltation beyond normal human experience.

The longing to experience 'ultimate reality', this nostalgia of the Indian soul, is a beacon of 'higher feeling' in the lives of most Indians, cutting across class distinctions and caste boundaries, bridging the distance between rural and urban, illiterate and educated, rich and poor. The ironic vision of life, which brings a detached and self-deprecating perspective on the tragic, and in which gods are presumed to have clay feet, is rarely found among Indians. Even for those living in enclaves of Western modernity, an ironic stance toward the spiritual is at most an affectation of a few young people that normally disappears as they age.

If spirituality has been at the center of the Indian world-view, it would be reasonable to expect that it has conditioned the Indian mind, coloring its intellectual, artistic, and emotional responses in certain distinctive ways. In other words, there are various cultural consequences of this belief. One of these is the pervasive presence of hope, even in the most dismal of life circumstances. For centuries, the civilization has conveyed to the growing child the almost somatic conviction that there is a hidden, even if unknown, order to our visible world—that there is a design to life that can be trusted in spite of life's sorrows, cruelties, and injustices. The Indian mind, then, tends to convert even the slightest ray of hope into a blaze of light. Consider this man from a village in Rajasthan who is living in a Delhi slum. He works a back-breaking 14 hours a day on a construction site, lives with six other members of his family in a single-room tenement, and eats, if at all, stale food in a chipped enamel plate. Yet he rejects with surprised astonishment the idea of life having been better in his village. The city with its possibilities—for example, education for his children—has provided him with a sliver of hope. The cynic might see his aspirations for a better life as completely unrealistic, might look on him as someone who clutches at the thinnest of straws, who has never learned that one can hope too much—or in vain. But what keeps this man and so many millions of others cheerful and expectant even under the most adverse economic, social, and political circumstances is precisely this hope, which is a sense of possession of the future, however distant that future may be.

Another consequence of this spiritual orientation (the unshakable belief in a 'higher' reality) is the average Indian's fascination with and respect for the occult and its practitioners. Astrologers, soothsayers, clairvoyants, fakirs, and other shamanic individuals, who abound in Indian society, are profoundly esteemed, for they are thought to be in some kind of contact with the ultimate reality. In India, it is the 'god men', the gurus, rather than the political, social, intellectual, or artistic leaders, who have come to incorporate the childhood yearning for omniscience and perfection in parental figures. The latter, the artists and the scientists, may be respected, but only the former, the gurus, are revered. Their presumed contact with another reality is supposed to confer on them supernatural powers, superhuman status, and a moral excellence that is beyond the ordinary lot.

Right and Wrong

If moksha is the goal of life, then dharma, variously translated as law, moral duty, right action, conformity with the truth of things, is the means through which humans approach the desired goal. Today, there is universal bemoaning of the lack of dharma in social institutions and individual lives. Traditional and modern Indians agree that there is hardly any institution left where those in positions of power have not veered away from dharma. Whereas modern Indians also point to the great social churning that is taking place with the advent of modern egalitarian ideologies, traditionalists see the disappearance of dharma as solely responsible for the social conflict, oppression, and unrest that characterize contemporary Indian society. And as for the dharma of individual lives, at one time, in the long ago utopian past, every person knew that it was not what he did that was important for his spiritual progress but whether he acted in conformity with his dharma. The activity itself—whether that of a shoemaker or a priest, a housewife or a farmer, a social worker serving others and alleviating misery or an ascetic apparently indifferent to the suffering around him—was considered equally good and equally right if it was consistent with dharma

Today, the conservatives contend, the ideologies of Western modernity, including notions of egalitarianism and individual choice, the focus on the importance of material rewards rather than the spirit of human activity, and the tendency to emphasize humankind's aspirations rather than its limits, are accountable for the widespread social envy, unbridled greed, and selfishness plaguing Indian society. Most would achingly agree that of the major elements of the traditional Hindu world-view, dharma is the one that is most endangered and perhaps already crumbling under the impact of modernity. Yet there is one aspect of dharma that continues to be of vital importance in understanding the Indian mind, and not only that of the orthodox Hindu. For even if the many traditional values associated with it are rejected, dharma is still pivotal in the formation of an Indian ethical sensibility. The main feature of this sensibility, in which it diverges from its Judeo-Christian and Islamic counterparts, is a pronounced ethical relativism that has become entrenched in the Hindu way of thinking. For how does any individual know what is right action, that she or he is acting in accordance with moral law and in conformity with the truth of things?

The traditional answer has been that an individual cannot know, since right action depends on the culture of one's country (*desa*), on the historical era in which one lives (*kala*), on the efforts required at a particular stage of life (*srama*), and, lastly, on the innate character (*guna*) that has been inherited from a previous life. An individual can never know the configuration of all these factors in an absolute sense, nor significantly influence them. Nor is there a book with authoritative interpreters such as a church that can help remove doubts as to how an individual should act in each conceivable situation. 'Right' and 'wrong', then, are relative; depending on its particular context, every action can be right—or wrong.

In lessening the burden of individual responsibility for action, the cultural view of right action alleviates the guilt suffered in some societies by those whose actions transgress rigid 'thou-shalt' and 'thou-shalt-not' axioms. Instead, an Indian's actions are governed by a more permissive and gentle, but more ambiguous, 'thou-canst-but-try' ethos. On the one hand, this basic uncertainty makes it possible to take unconventional and risky actions; on the other hand, actions are accompanied by a pervasive doubt concerning the wisdom of individual initiative, making independent voluntary action unthinkable for many who look for psychological security by acting as one's ancestors did in the past and as one's social group—primarily the caste—does at present. The relativism of dharma supports both tradition and modernity, innovation and conformity.

The ethical relativism of dharma has been broadened by the late poet-scholar A. K. Ramanujan to embrace the very way Indians think in most situations. In his stimulating essay, "Is There an Indian Way of Thinking?" Ramanujan (1990) begins his exposition with a survey of Indian intellectuals conducted some 30 years ago in which they were asked to describe the Indian 'character'. As one can imagine, given the Indian talent for self-criticism, the intellectuals wrote quite sharp comments. They all seemed to agree on one thing: the Indian trait of hypocrisy. Indians do not mean what they say, and they say different things at different times. Many Occidental travelers in past centuries have complained about the same thing; in fact, in his 1883 collection of lectures on India, the famed Indologist Max Mueller felt compelled to counter these accusations by including one titled "On the Truthful Character of the Hindus."

The Indian inconsistency is still seen as puzzling: How can a reputed astronomer, working at an institute of fundamental sciences, also be a practicing astrologer? How can the Western-educated executive of a multi-national corporation consult horoscopes and holy men for family decisions? Why does an Oxford-educated cabinet minister postpone an important meeting because the hour of meeting is astrologically inauspicious? These observed traits of inconsistency, however, Ramanujan asserts, are better understood if we recognize that different cultures seem to prefer either context-free or context-sensitive rules in their thought processes and that Indians operate on the basis of context sensitivity rather than context freedom. Let us elaborate.

There is no notion of a universal human nature in Indian culture, and thus we cannot deduce ethical rules such as "Thou shall not kill" or "Thou shall not tell an untruth" or any other unitary law for all humankind. What a person should or should not do depends on the context. Thus, Manu, the ancient Indian law giver, has the following to say: "A Kshatriya (man belonging to the warrior castes), having defamed a Brahmin, shall be fined one hundred [panas]; a Vaishya (someone belonging to the farmer and merchant castes) one hundred and fifty or two hundred; a Shudra (man belonging to the servant castes) shall suffer corporal punishment." Even truth telling is not an unconditional imperative. Here is a quotation from another law book: "An untruth spoken by people under the influence of anger, excessive joy, fear, pain, or grief, by infants, by very old men, by persons laboring under a delusion being under the influence of drink, does not cause the speaker to fall (i.e. it is not a sin)."

The Christian injunction against coveting "thy neighbor's wife" is shared by Hindu law books, which proclaim that "in this world there is nothing as detrimental to long life as criminal conversation with another man's wife." In fact, Hindus are even stricter in defining adultery. Talking to a woman alone in the forest "or at the confluence of rivers," offering her presents, touching her ornaments and dress, sitting with her on a bed are all adulterous acts. The nature of the punishment, of course, depends on the respective castes of the adulterous couple, and there are also exceptions, such as the one that condones adultery with "the wives of actors and singers." In spite of a chapter titled "Other Men's Wives" in the *Kamasutra*, the celebrated text shares the Hindu disapproval of adultery. But it, too, lists exceptions to the rule—for example, if your unrequited passion makes you fall sick—and then proceeds to outline the various ways to seduce other men's wives. Its position seems to be: "You shouldn't do it. But if you must, then these are the ways to proceed. But, of course, you shouldn't have done it in the first place."

Virtues, too, are as dependent on the context as are transgressions. Bravery may be a virtue for the *kshatriya* (warrior), but it is certainly not one for the *baniya* (merchant). Ramanujan remarks that for those adhering to a Western Christian tradition based on the premise of universalization—the Golden Rule of the New Testament—the idea that each class of persons has its own laws and ethics that cannot be universalized must be viewed as baffling and ultimately denigratory.

Context sensitivity is not just a feature of traditional moral law but extends to many areas of contemporary Indian life and thought. The cultural psychologist

Richard Shweder, in comparing descriptive phrases used by Oriyas from eastern India and Midwesterners from the United States, has shown that the two describe persons very differently (Shweder and Bourne 1984). Americans characterize a person with abstract, generic words such as "good" and "nice," while the Oriyas use more concrete, contextual descriptions such as "he helps me" and "he brings sweets." The descriptions provided by the Indians are more situation specific and relational than those of the Americans. They focus on behavior, describing what was done, where it was done, and to whom or with whom it was done, for example, "He has no land to cultivate but likes to cultivate the land of others" or "When a quarrel arises, he cannot resist the temptation of saying a word" or "He behaves properly with guests but feels sorry if money is spent on them." The behavior itself is focal and significant rather than the inner attribute that supposedly underlies it. This tendency to supply the context when providing a description characterizes the descriptions of Indians regardless of social class, education, or level of literacy. It appears, then, that the preferred Indian way of describing people is not due to a lack of skill in abstracting concrete instances to form a general proposition, but rather a consequence of the fact that universal inferences about persons are typically regarded as neither meaningful nor informative.

If truth is relative, something you are never destined to know, then there is no choice but to be tolerant of the truth of others. The roots of the vaunted Indian tolerance, then, may well lie in this context-dependent way of thinking. Yet because of its intimate connection to matters of religious faith, to a person's deepest values, this particular civilizational heritage of ethical action being inseparable from its context does show some variation across religious communities.

While studying violence between Hindus and Muslims in the South Indian city of Hyderabad (Kakar 1996), I also looked at the moral judgments of the two communities regarding their interactions with each other. There are many such interactions in normal times: eating with a member of the opposite community, working with him, punishing a member of the other community who is making fun of your religious symbols or insulting a woman of your community. And then there are the interactions during riots: killings, arson, and rape.

As compared to the Muslims, the Hindus were much more relativistic and contextual in judging a behavior as a transgression and more easygoing in proposing punishment for actions judged as wrong. Irrespective of age and gender, "It all depends" was an almost reflexive response. In responding to cases of interaction with Muslims, the answers were almost always framed in terms of a context, temporal or spatial. The linkage of morality with time would be typically expressed thus: "It [killing] was wrong when times were different but is not wrong now." An individual can thus convincingly state that an action is wrong in right times but right in wrong times. Similarly, space is also involved in moral judgments. Hindus often said that during a riot, actions such as beating up Muslims and looting Muslim shops were wrong if you lived in a Muslim majority area but acceptable if you lived in a Hindu majority neighborhood. As a consequence of this contextual stance, wrong actions by members of the community evoked far less emotion and righteousness than corresponding actions among Muslims.

In this particular instance, Muslims, like followers of other Semitic religions, Christianity and Judaism, were more definite and unambiguous about which actions were right and which were clearly wrong, even during a riot.

Karma, Rebirth, and the Indian Mind

The third essential idea of the Hindu world-view is karma. The popular understanding of karma is expressed by a villager thus: "Even at the time of death man should wish to do good deeds and wish to be reborn in a place where he can do good deeds again. After many lives of good deeds (the living in dharma) a man will attain *mukti* (another word for moksha). If he does evil deeds, his form changes till he falls lower, till he becomes a jar (an inanimate thing)" (Kakar 1978: 44–45). Other Hindus, when pressed for their sense of karma, are likely to express the same twin ideas: first, the cycles of birth and death in which an individual soul progresses (or regresses) through various levels of existence, and, second, the control of this movement by the karma of the individual soul, the balance of 'right' and 'wrong' actions that accompany the individual from one birth to another.

Psychologically, what interests me most in the karma theory is its idea of innate dispositions (samskaras), a heritage of previous life, with which a newborn is believed to come into the world and which imposes certain limits on the socialization of the child. In other words, Indians do not consider infant nature as a tabula rasa that is infinitely malleable and can be molded in any direction desired by the parents. With the cultural belief in the notion of samskaras, there is little social pressure to foster the tenet that if only the caretakers were good enough, and constantly on their toes, the child's potentialities would be boundlessly fulfilled. With the Indian emphasis on a person's inner limitations, there is not that sense of urgency and struggle against the outside world, with prospects of sudden metamorphoses and great achievements just around the corner, which often seems to propel Western lives.

The karmic balance from a previous life and the innate dispositions with which one enters the present one serve to make Hindus more accepting of the inevitable disappointments that afflict even the most fortunate of lives. Yet whereas the notion of inherited dispositions can console and help to heal, it can also serve the purpose of denying individual responsibility. Thus, a 30-year-old patient in psychotherapy, becoming aware of her aggressive impulses toward her husband as revealed in a dream, spontaneously exclaimed, "Ah, these are due to my bad samskaras. However hard I try to be a good wife, my bad samskaras prevent me" (Kakar 1978: 49).

I and Other: Separation and Connection

If each of us begins life as a mystic, awash in a feeling of pervasive unity in which there is no distance between things and ourselves, then the process of sorting out 'me' from 'not-me' is one of the primary tasks of our earliest years.

This task involves the recognition—later taken for granted, at least in most of our waking hours and in a state of relative sanity—that I am separate from all that is not-I, that my 'Self' is not merged with but detached from the 'Other'. The experience of separation has its origins in our beginnings, although its echoes continue to haunt us till the end of life, its reverberations agitating the mind, at times violently, during psychological or spiritual crises.

The Indian gloss on the dilemmas and pain of banishment from the original feeling of oneness, the exile from the universe, has been to emphasize a person's enduring connection to nature, the Divine, and all living beings. This unitary vision of soma and psyche, individual and community, and self and world is present in most forms of popular culture even today. From religious rites to folk festivals, from the pious devotion of communal singing in temples to the orgiastic excess of *holi* (the color of festivals), there is a common negation of separation and a celebration of connection.

The high cultural value placed on connection is, of course, most evident in the individual's relationships with others. The yearning for relationships, for the confirming presence of loved ones and the psychological oxygen they provide, is the dominant modality of social relations in India, especially within the extended family. Individuality and independence are not values that are cherished. It is not uncommon for family members, who often accompany a patient for a first psychotherapeutic interview, to complain about the patient's autonomy as one of the symptoms of his or her disorder. Thus, the father and elder sister of a 28-year-old engineer who had psychotic episodes described their understanding of his chief problem as one of unnatural autonomy: "He is very stubborn in pursuing what he wants without taking our wishes into account. He thinks he knows what is best for him and does not listen to us. He thinks his own life and career are more important than the concerns of the rest of the family" (Kakar 1987: 446).

The high value placed on connection does not mean that Indians are incapable of functioning by themselves or that they do not have a sense of their own agency. What it does imply is a greater need for ongoing mentorship, guidance, and help from others in getting through life and a greater vulnerability to feelings of helplessness when these ties are strained.

The yearning for relationships, for the confirming presence of loved ones, and the distress aroused by their unavailability in times of need are more hidden in Western societies, in which the dominant value system of the middle class prizes autonomy, privacy, and self-actualization, and holds that individual independence and initiative are 'better' than mutual dependence and community. But whether a person's behavior on the scale between fusion and isolation is nearer the pole of merger and fusion with others or the pole of complete isolation depends, of course, on the culture's vision of a 'good society' and 'individual merit'. In other words, the universal polarities of individual versus relational, nearness versus distance in human relationships are prey to culturally molded beliefs and expectations. To borrow from Schopenhauer's imagery, human beings are like hedgehogs on a cold night. They approach each other for warmth, get pricked by the quills of the other, and move away until, feeling cold, they again come closer. This to-and-fro movement keeps being repeated until an optimum position is reached wherein the body temperature is above the freezing point yet the pain inflicted by the quills—the nearness of the other—is still bearable. The balancing point is different in various cultures. In India, for example, as compared to modern European and North American cultures, the optimum position entails the acceptance of more pain in order to get greater warmth.

The emphasis on connection is also reflected in the Indian image of the body, a core element in the development of the mind. In the traditional Indian medical system of Ayurveda, everything in the universe, whether animate or inanimate, is composed of five forms of matter. Living beings are only a certain kind of organization of substances, and their bodies constantly absorb these five elements of environmental matter. For Ayurveda, the human body is intimately connected with nature and the cosmos, and there is nothing in nature without relevance for medicine. The Indian body image, then, stresses an unremitting interchange taking place with the environment, simultaneously accompanied by a ceaseless change within the body. Moreover, in the Indian view, there is no essential difference between body and mind. The body is merely the gross form of matter (*sthulasharira*), just as the mind is a more subtle form of the same matter (*sukshmasharira*); both are different forms of the same body-mind matter—*sharira*.

In contrast, the Western image is of a clearly etched body, sharply differentiated from the rest of the objects in the universe. This vision of the body as a safe stronghold with a limited number of drawbridges that maintain a tenuous contact with the outside world has its own particular cultural consequences. It seems that in Western discourse, both scientific and artistic, there is considerable preoccupation with what is going on within the fortress of the individual body. Pre-eminently, one seeks to explain behavior through psychologies that derive from biology, to the relative exclusion of the natural and meta-natural environment. The contemporary search for a genetic basis to all psychological phenomena, irrespective of its scientific merit, is thus a logical consequence of the Western body image. The natural aspects of the environment—the quality of air, the quantity of sunlight, the presence of birds and animals, the plants and the trees—are a priori viewed, when they are considered at all, as irrelevant to intellectual and emotional development. Given the Western image of the body, it is understandable that the less conventional Indian beliefs concerning the effects on the *sharira* of planetary constellations, cosmic energies, earth's magnetic fields, seasonal and daily rhythms, and precious stones and metals are summarily consigned to the realm of fantasy, being of interest solely to a 'lunatic fringe' of Western society.

It is not only the body but also the emotions that have come to be differently viewed due to the Indian emphasis on connection. As cultural psychologists have pointed out, emotions that have to do with other persons, such as sympathy, feelings of interpersonal communion, and shame, are primary while the more individualistic emotions, such as anger and guilt, are secondary. The Indian psyche has a harder time experiencing and expressing anger and guilt but is more comfortable than the Western individualistic psyche in dealing with feelings of sympathy and shame. If pride is overtly expressed, it is often directed to a collective of which one is a member. Working very hard to win a promotion at work or admission to an elite educational institution is only secondarily connected to the individual need for achievement, which is the primary driving motivation in the West. The first conscious or pre-conscious thought in the Indian mind is "How happy and proud my family will be!" This is why Indians tend to idealize their families and ancestral background, why there is such prevalence of family myths and of family pride, and why role models for the young are almost exclusively members of the family, very frequently a parent, rather than the movie stars, sporting heroes, or other public figures favored by Western youths.

The greater "dividual" (Marriott 1976) or relational orientation is also congruent with the main thematic content of Indian art. In traditional Indian painting, and especially in temple sculptures, for instance, man is represented not as a discrete presence but as absorbed in his surroundings, existing in all his myriad connections. These sculptures, as Richard Lannoy (1971: 78) remarks, are an "all encompassing labyrinth flux of animal, human and divine ... visions of life in the flesh, all jumbled together ... suffering and enjoying in a thousand shapes, teeming, devouring, turning into one another."

I am, of course, not advancing any simplified dichotomy between a Western cultural image of an individual, autonomous self and a relational, transpersonal self of Indian society. These prototypical patterns do not exist in their pure form in any society. Psychotherapy with middle-class Western patients tells us that autonomy of the self is as precarious in reality as is the notion of an Indian self that is merged in the surroundings of its family and community. Both are fictions; their influence on behavior derives not from their actual occurrence but from their enshrinement as cultural ideals. Let us call them visions, and as such the two visions of human experience are present in all the major cultures, though a particular culture may, over a length of time, highlight and emphasize one at the expense of the other. Historically, man's connection to the universe, especially his community, has also been an important value in Western tradition, though it may have been submerged at certain periods of history, especially in the nineteenth and early twentieth centuries. This so-called value of counter-enlightenment is part of the relativist and skeptical tradition that goes back to Western antiquity. It stresses that belonging to a community is a fundamental need of man and asserts that only if a man truly belongs to such a community, naturally and unselfconsciously, can he enter the living stream and lead a full, creative, spontaneous life.

Male and Female

Another fundamental aspect of the Indian mind that differs from its Western counterpart is related to the dawning realization in infancy of the difference between genders. It involves the profound realization of the child that all living beings, especially its beloved caretakers, belong to either one sex or the other. This differentiation is indeed universal, but it is our cultural heritage that further elaborates what it means to be, look, think, and behave like a man or woman.

This becomes clearer if one considers Greek and Roman sculpture, which, we believe, has greatly influenced Western gender representations. Here, male gods are represented by hard-muscled bodies and chests without any fat. In comparison, the sculpted representations of Hindu gods or the Buddha depict bodies that are softer, more supple, and, in their hint of breasts, closer to the female form. Many Buddhist images of Avalokiteswara (the Lord Who Listens to the Cries of the World) are of a slender boyish figure in the traditional feminine posture—weight resting on the left hip, right knee forward; they are the Indian precursor of the sexually ambiguous Chinese goddess Kuan Yin. This minimizing of difference between male and female figures finds its culmination in the *ardhanarishvara* (half-man and half-woman) form of the great god Shiva, who is portrayed with the secondary sexual characteristics of both sexes.

The diminished differentiation between male and female representations in Indian culture is further reinforced by an important, perhaps dominant aspect of religiosity that not only provides a sanction for man's feminine strivings but raises these strivings to the level of a religious-spiritual quest. In devotional Vaishnavism, Lord Krishna alone is male, and all devotees, irrespective of their sex, are female. It is a culture where one of the greatest Sanskrit poets of love, Amaru, is reputed to have been the hundred and first incarnation of a soul that had previously occupied the bodies of a hundred women—where the voice of the Tamil saint-poet Nammalavar, who wrote 370 poems on the theme of love, was always that of a woman. It is a culture where in superior human beings feminine traits are joined to masculine ones. It is a culture where a luminary like Gandhi can publicly proclaim that he had mentally become a woman and that (well before the psychoanalyst Karen Horney) there is as much reason for a man to wish that he was born a woman as for a woman to do otherwise, and take it for granted that he will strike a responsive chord in his audience.

These contrasting cultural interpretations of the universal experience of differentiation are responsible for the insidious British labeling of Indian men (excepting the 'warrior races', such as the Sikhs, Rajputs, and the Jats) as 'effeminate' in the colonial era. Such judgments are a reflexive outcome of deep-seated and rarely examined convictions regarding what is masculine and what is feminine, what is 'manly' and what is 'effeminate'. Between a minimum of sexual differentiation, which is required to function heterosexually with a modicum of pleasure, and a maximum, which cuts off any sense of empathy and emotional contact with the other sex (which is then experienced as a different species altogether), there is a whole range of positions, each occupied by a culture that insists on viewing its stance as the only one that is mature and healthy.

Psychotherapy in Cross-Cultural Dyads

The Hindu world-view, I have repeatedly stressed, is not a system of abstractions to be more or less hazily comprehended during the adult years. It is a fundamental part of an Indian's mind, absorbed by the child in his relationship with his adult caretakers from the very beginning as the underlying truth of the world in which he will spend his life. Rarely summoned for conscious examination, the cultural part of the mind is neither determinedly universal nor utterly idiosyncratic but shares the space with the other two. All three aspects of the mind—the universal, cultural, and individual—are streams that flow into the same river where none of the streams can be 'deeper' than the others. Or, to change metaphors, beginning at birth, the three strands of mind jointly evolve through the life cycle, each constantly enriching, constraining, and shaping the others.

With regard to my own sense of estrangement, what could my analyst have done? Did he need to acquire knowledge of my culture, and, if so, what kind of knowledge? Would an anthropological, historical, or philosophical grounding in Hindu culture have made him understand me better? Or was it a psychoanalytical knowledge of my culture that would have been more helpful? Psychoanalytic knowledge is primarily the knowledge of the culture's imagination, of its fantasy as encoded in its symbolic products—its myths and folktales, its popular art, literature, and cinema.

Besides asking about the kind of knowledge, we also need to ask the question, which culture? Would a psychoanalytic knowledge of Hindu culture have been sufficient in my case? Yes, I am a Hindu but also a Punjabi Khatri by birth; that is, my overarching Hindu culture has been mediated by my strong regional culture as a Punjabi and further by my Khatri caste. This Hindu Punjabi Khatri culture has been further modified by an agnostic father and a more traditional, believing mother, both of whom were also westernized to varying degrees. Is it not too much to expect any analyst to acquire this kind of prior cultural knowledge about his patients? On the other hand, is it acceptable for an analyst not to have any knowledge of his or her patient's cultural background? Or does the truth, as it often does, lie somewhere in the middle?

But now comes the surprise. My analyst was very good—sensitive, insightful, patient. And I discovered that as my analysis progressed, my feelings of estrangement that had given rise to all these questions became fewer and fewer. What was happening? Was the cultural part of my self becoming less salient as the analysis touched ever-deeper layers of the self, as many psychoanalysts have claimed?

Georges Devereux, a psychoanalyst who was also an anthropologist and a pioneer in addressing the issue of culture in psychoanalytic therapy, claimed that in deep psychoanalytic therapy, the analyst needed to know the patient's specific cultural background less fully ahead of time than in more superficial forms of psychotherapy (Devereux 1953). In his conception of psychoanalysis as a universal, a-cultural science, the personality disorders that were the object of psychoanalysis represented a partial regression of (cultural) man to (universal) Homo sapiens. "For this reason," he writes, "children and abnormal members of our society resemble their counterparts in other cultures far more than the normal members of our society resemble the normal members of other ethnic groups" (ibid.: 632). A deep analysis would reveal the same universal fantasies and desires, although, he allowed, the constellation of defense mechanisms could be culturally influenced.

In fact, for Devereux, the most important (and harmful) influence exerted by culture on psychoanalytic therapy was not an analyst's indifference but rather her interest in cultural factors. Devereux rightly pointed to the countertransference danger of an analyst getting too interested in her analytic patient's culture. Sensitive to the analyst's interest, the patient would either gratify this interest by long discourses on his cultural practices or use these as red herrings to divert the analyst from probing deeper into his personal motivations. Freud is reputed to have sent a prospective patient, an Egyptologist, to another analyst because of Freud's own interest in Egyptology.

Most analysts have followed Devereux's lead in maintaining that all those who seek help from a psychoanalyst have in common many fundamental and universal components in their personality structure. Together with the universality of the psychoanalytic method, these common factors sufficiently equip analysts to understand and help their patients, irrespective of the latter's cultural background, a view reiterated by a panel of the American Psychoanalytic Association on the role of culture in psychoanalysis more than 35 years ago (Jackson 1968). There are certainly difficulties, such as those enumerated by Ticho (1971), in treating patients of a different culture: a temporary impairment of the analyst's technical skills, empathy for the patient, diagnostic acumen, the stability of self and object representations, and the stirring up of countertransference manifestations, which may not be easily distinguishable from stereotypical reactions to the foreign culture. Generally, though, given the analyst's empathetic stance and the rules of analytic procedure, these difficulties are temporary and do not require a change in analytic technique. It is useful but not essential for the analyst to understand the patient's cultural heritage.

I believe that these conclusions on the role of culture in psychoanalytic therapy, which would seem to apply to my own experience, are superficially true but deeply mistaken. For what I did, and what I believe most patients do, was to enthusiastically, if unconsciously, acculturate to the analyst's culture—in my case, both to his broader Western, northern European culture and to his particular Freudian psychoanalytic culture. The latter, we know, is informed by a vision of human experience that emphasizes man's individuality and his self-contained psyche. In the psychoanalytic vision, each of us lives in our own subjective world, pursuing pleasures and private fantasies, constructing a life and a fate that will vanish when our time is over. This view emphasizes the desirability of reflective awareness of one's inner states, an insistence that our psyches harbor deeper secrets than we care to confess, the existence of an objective reality that can be known, and an essential complexity and tragedy of life whereby many wishes are fated to remain unfulfilled. I was, then, moving from my own Hindu cultural heritage, which sees life not as tragic but as a romantic quest that can extend over many births, with the goal and possibility of apprehending another, 'higher' level of reality beyond the shared, verifiable, empirical reality of our world, our bodies, and our emotions.

It is acknowledged that every form of therapy is also an enculturation. As Fancher (1993: 89–90) remarks: "By the questions we ask, the things we empathize with, the themes we pick for our comment, the ways we conduct ourselves toward the patient, the language we use—by all these and a host of other ways, we communicate to the patient our notions of what is 'normal' and normative. Our interpretations of the origins of a patient's issues reveal in pure form our assumptions of what causes what, what is problematic about life, where the patient did not get what s/he needed, what should have been otherwise."

As a patient in the throes of 'transference love', I was exquisitely attuned to the cues to my analyst's values, beliefs, and vision of the fulfilled life, which even the most non-intrusive of analysts cannot help but scatter during the therapeutic process. I was quick to pick up the cues that unconsciously shaped my reactions and responses accordingly, with the overriding goal being to please and to be pleasing in the eyes of the beloved. My intense need to be 'understood' by the analyst, a need I shared with every patient, gave birth to an unconscious force that made me underplay those cultural parts of my self that I believed would be too foreign to the analyst's experience. In the transference love, what I sought was closeness to the analyst, including the sharing of his culturally shaped interests, attitudes, and beliefs. This intense need to be close and to be understood—paradoxically, by removing parts of the self from the analytic arena of understanding—was epitomized by the fact that I soon started dreaming in German, the language of my analyst, something I had not done before nor have done since.

The analysis being conducted in German fostered the excision of important parts of my self. One's native tongue, the language of one's childhood, is intimately linked with emotionally colored sensory-motor experiences. When the language used by the analysand is not his or her own, the alien language often lacks what Bion (1963) called "alpha elements." Psychodynamic therapy in a language that is not the patient's own is often in danger of leading to "operational thinking" (Basch-Kahre 1984), that is, verbal expressions lacking associational links with feelings, symbols, and memories. However grammatically correct and rich in its vocabulary, the alien language suffers from emotional poverty, certainly as far as early memories are concerned. To give an example, one of my bilingual patients often uses an impersonal tone characteristic of operational thinking when reporting significant experiences in English and much greater variations in affect when the same experiences are described in Hindi, his native tongue. When in one of his sessions the patient reported, in English, that the previous night he had said to his wife, "Let's have sex," his tone was detached, even slightly depressive. When asked what exactly he had said in Hindi, the answer was, "Teri le loon" (I'll take yours). The much more concrete Hindi expression demanding the use of the wife's vagina, objectifying the person, not only evoked in him greater feelings of an aggressive excitement (and shame while reporting it) but also was associated with fearful memories of childhood play when the same expression was directed at him by an older boy.

How should a Western psychoanalyst, then, approach the issue of cultural difference in his practice? The ideal situation would be that this difference exists only minimally, in the sense that the analyst has obtained a psychoanalytic knowledge of the patient's culture through a long immersion in its daily life and myths, its folklore and literature, its language and music, an absorption not through the bones, as in the case of the patient, but through the mind—and the heart. Anything less than this maximalist position portends the danger of the analyst succumbing to the lure of cultural stereotyping in dealing with the particularities of the patient's experience. In cross-cultural therapeutic dyads, a little knowledge is indeed a dangerous thing, collapsing important differences, assuming sameness when only similarities exist. What the analyst needs is not a detailed knowledge of the patient's culture but a serious questioning and awareness of the assumptions underlying his own, that is, the culture he was born into and the culture in which he has been professionally socialized as a psychoanalyst. In other words, I am suggesting that in the absence of the possibility of obtaining a psychoanalytic knowledge of his patient's culture, the analyst needs to strive for a state of affairs wherein the patient's feelings of estrangement because of his cultural differences from the analyst are minimized and the patient does not cut off the cultural part of the self from the therapeutic situation (or does so only minimally). This is possible only if the analyst can convey a cultural openness that derives from becoming aware of his culture's fundamental propositions about human nature, human experience, and the fulfilled human life and can then acknowledge the relativity of these propositions by seeing them as cultural products, embedded in a particular place and time. The analyst needs to become sensitive to the hidden existence of what Kohut (1979: 12) referred to as the "health and maturity moralities" of his particular analytical school. He needs to root out cultural judgments about what constitutes psychological maturity, gender-appropriate behaviors, and 'positive' or 'negative' resolutions of developmental conflicts and complexes, which often appear in the garb of universally valid truths.

Given that ethnocentrism (the tendency to view alien cultures in terms of one's own) and unresolved cultural chauvinism are the patrimony of all human beings, including psychoanalysts, the acquisition of cultural openness is not an easy task. Cultural biases can lurk in the most unlikely places. For instance, psychoanalysts have traditionally accorded a high place to artistic creativity. However, engaging in visual arts and literary and musical pursuits has not always and everywhere enjoyed the high prestige that it does in modern Western societies. In other historical periods, many civilizations, including mine to this day, placed religious creativity at the top of their scale of desirable human endeavors. Psychoanalysts need to imagine that in such cultural settings, the following conclusion to a case report could be an example of a successful therapeutic outcome: "The patient's visions increased markedly in quantity and quality, and the devotional mood took hold of her for longer and longer periods of time."

I would suggest that for optimal psychotherapy with patients from different cultures, what a psychoanalytical therapist needs is not a knowledge of the patient's culture but a reflective, conscious openness to his own. A therapist can evaluate his progress toward this openness by the increase in his feelings of curiosity and wonder in his counter-transference when the cultural parts of the patient's self find their voice in therapy, when the temptation to pathologize the cultural part of his patient's behavior decreases, when his own values no longer appear as normal and virtuous, and when his wish to instruct the patient in these values diminishes markedly.

It will be evident from my remarks that I have been primarily addressing the issue of psychotherapy in cross-cultural dyads with the assumption that the therapist is Western whereas his or her patient belongs to a non-Western culture. What about the dilemma of a non-Western analyst, such as myself, practicing a Western discipline in an Asian country? Here, the initial feelings of estrangement between the therapist and the patient are not dyadic but have their origin in the therapist. At the beginning of my practice in India, I was acutely aware of the struggle within myself between my inherited Hindu culture and the Freudian psychoanalytic culture that I had recently acquired and in which I had been professionally socialized. My romantic Hindu vision of reality could not be reconciled with the ironic psychoanalytic vision, nor could the Hindu view of the person and the sources of human strength be reconciled with the Freudian views—now also mine—on the nature of the individual and his or her world. With Goethe's Faust, I could only say:

> Your spirit only seeks a single quest
> so never learns to know its brother
> Two souls, alas, dwell in my breast
> And one would gladly sunder from the other.

Some colleagues try to sunder the two souls by unreservedly identifying with their professional socialization, radically rejecting their Indian heritage. Many of them have migrated to Western countries to work as therapists, to all apparent purposes indistinguishable from their Western colleagues. Some who stay struggle to hold onto their professional identity by clinging to each psychoanalytic orthodoxy. Loath to be critical of received wisdom and exiled from Rome, they become more conservative than the pope. Others, like myself, live with the oppositions, taking comfort from the Indian view that every contradiction does not need a resolution, that contradictions can co-exist in the mind like substances in water that are in suspension without necessarily becoming a solution.

I think I resolved this dilemma as do some men in Indian families who, after marrying, are caught up in the conflict between their mothers and wives, each asking the husband/son to choose between them. Unable to make this choice, the men often react by becoming detached from both. I found that the only way I could keep my affection for psychoanalytic and Hindu cultures intact was by loving each less—not by cutting myself off from one or the other but by engaging more critically with each. The loss of a certain measure of innocence and enthusiasm is the price paid for this strategy, a price that may not be too high for preventing a closing of the mind and for keeping intact a curiosity that is not satisfied with easy answers.

Sudhir Kakar is a psychoanalyst and writer who lives in Goa, India. He took degrees in mechanical engineering and economics before training in psychoanalysis at the Sigmund-Freud-Institut in Frankfurt. He has been a Lecturer in General Education at Harvard University, Research Associate at Harvard Business School, Professor of Organizational Behaviour at Indian Institute of Management, Ahmedabad, and Head of the Department of Humanities and Social Sciences at the Indian Institute of Technology, Delhi. He has also been a visiting professor at the universities of Chicago, McGill, Melbourne, Hawaii, and Vienna; 40th Anniversary Senior Fellow at Centre for the Study of World Religions, Harvard University; and a Fellow at the Institutes of Advanced Study, Princeton, and Berlin. Since 1994, he is Adjunct Professor of Leadership at INSEAD in Fontainebleau, France. His recent publications include *The Essential Writings of Sudhir Kakar* (2001), a new translation (with Wendy Doniger) of the *Kamasutra* (2002), the novel *Mira and the Mahatma* (2004), and (with Katharina Kakar) *Die Inder: Portraet einer Gesellschaft* (2006). His 16 books of non-fiction and 4 books of fiction have been translated into 20 languages around the world.

Note

1. This is an expanded and revised version of a paper presented at the "Culture and Psychotherapy in a Creolizing World" seminar at the Department of Psychiatry, McGill University, Montreal, 3–4 June 2004.

References

Basch-Kahre, E. 1984. "On Difficulties Arising in Transference and Countertransference When Analyst and Analysand Have Different Socio-cultural Backgrounds." *International Review of Psychoanalysis* 11: 61–67.

Bion, W. R. 1963. *Elements of Psychoanalysis*. London: Heinemann.

Devereux, G. 1953. "Cultural Factors in Psychoanalytic Therapy." *Journal of American Psychoanalytical Association* 1: 629–655.

Fancher, R. T. 1993. "Psychoanalysis as Culture." *Issues in Psychoanalytic Psychology* 15, no. 2: 81–93.

Jackson, S. 1968. "Panel on Aspects of Culture in Psychoanalytic Theory and Practice." *Journal of American Psychoanalytical Association* 16: 651–670.

Kakar, S. 1978. *The Inner World: Childhood and Society in India*. Delhi and New York: Oxford University Press.

_____. 1982. *Shamans, Mystics and Doctors*. New York: Knopf.

_____. 1987. "Psychoanalysis and Non-Western Cultures." *International Review of Psychoanalysis* 12: 441–448.

_____. 1989. "The Maternal-Feminine in Indian Psychoanalysis." *International Review of Psychoanalysis* 16, no. 3: 355–362.

_____. 1994. "Clinical Work and Cultural Imagination." *Psychoanalytic Quarterly* 64: 265–281.

_____. 1996. *The Colors of Violence: Religious-Cultural Identities and Conflict*. Chicago: University of Chicago Press.

_____. 1997. *Culture and Psyche*. Delhi: Oxford University Press.

Kohut, H. 1979. "The Two Analyses of Mr. Z." *International Journal of Psychoanalysis* 60: 3–27.

Lannoy, R. 1971. *The Speaking Tree*. London: Oxford University Press.

Marriott, M. 1976. "Hindu Transactions: Diversity without Dualism." Pp. 109–142 in *Transaction and Meaning*, ed. B. Kapferer. Philadelphia: Institute for the Study of Human Issues.

Ramanujan, A. K. 1990. "Is There an Indian Way of Thinking?" Pp. 41–58 in *India through Hindu Categories*. ed. M. Marriott. Delhi: Sage Publications.

Shweder, R., and E. J. Bourne. 1984. "Does the Concept of the Person Vary Cross-Culturally?" Pp. 97–137 in *Cultural Conceptions of Mental Health and Therapy*, ed. A. J. Marsella and G. M. White. Dodrecht and Boston: D. Reidel Publishing.

Ticho, G. 1971. "Cultural Aspects of Transference and Countertransference." *Bulletin of Menninger Clinic* 35, no. 5: 313–326.

Chapter 2

ASPECTS OF THE *NAVEN* RITUAL
Conversations with an Iatmul Woman
of Papua New Guinea

Florence Weiss and Milan Stanek

At the end of the 1920s and the beginning of the 1930s, a young British scientist, Gregory Bateson, undertook fieldwork in Papua New Guinea. The most important results were published in 1936 in his acclaimed book, *Naven: A Survey of the Problems Suggested by a Composite Picture of the Culture of a New Guinea Tribe Drawn from Three Points of View.*[1] Following the conceptual leads of Margaret Mead and especially Ruth Benedict, Bateson attempted to establish a general picture of the cultural structure of the Iatmul people, considering in the process various epistemological problems.[2] Much later in the 1970s and 1980s, under the heading of *l'anthropologie structurale* and symbolic anthropology, this orientation became the mainstream of the anthropological interpretation of cultures.

Bateson's work made the Iatmul famous in academic circles, and through numerous private and museum collections that pay testimony to their extraordinary artistic creativity, the Iatmul are well known to the public at large. Out of a dozen categories, Bateson chose to focus on one type of ritual referred to as *naven* in the Iatmul language. In this ritual, a young man, woman, or child is attended to by his or her relatives who perform in three ritualized roles: the mother's brother disguised as a woman, the father's sister disguised as a man, and the mother, who keeps her female attire but is transformed into an ancestral figure. This is made manifest by her behavior and by diverse totemic insignia attached to her body. Commonly, these roles are performed by classificatory relatives in the mother's generation, namely, her brothers, parallel cousins, and sisters-in-law, and by other relatives of different generations who can be identified with the mother, mother's brother, or father's sister.

To be sure, this is not the only Iatmul ritual featuring transvestite behavior, although it is an especially startling one. Mothers come to the fore dancing around their sons or daughters and displaying seductive and incestuous behavior. Having put on women's skirts, mother's brothers pretend that they are their sisters, that they posses a vagina, and that they have delivered these young men or women now facing the ritual performers. To prove this, the maternal uncles fall onto their knees and assume the typical posture of Iatmul women at delivery. Appearing from the opposite side, women in men's attire wielding spears pretend that they have penises and that these young men or women have indeed been engendered through their efforts. Finally, the repertory of bizarre features of the *naven* also includes the mother's brother's act of sliding his buttocks down his uterine nephew's or niece's leg.

During several longer periods of fieldwork among the Iatmul,[3] Milan Stanek and Florence Weiss watched about 20 *naven* performances so that they could add many more details to this instance of women's and men's ritual behavior and relate it to the mythological symbolism. Although ethnographic research is always incomplete, it is nevertheless the case that the successive and cumulative work of many anthropologists has produced an ever more comprehensive and accurate picture of the *naven* ritual and its diverse forms of expression, including the numerous ways in which Iatmul individuals engage in its transvestite performances.

Bateson's (1932, [1936] 1965) and Mead's (1949) original reports on Iatmul culture did not furnish sufficiently comprehensive descriptions.[4] In 1972–1974, a team of post-graduate students from the University of Basel in Switzerland, led by Professor Meinhard Schuster, undertook a wide-ranging ethnographic research in several villages of the central and western Iatmul area. Their study covered many topics, e.g., the economic and kinship systems, the position of women and children, the language and mythology, and the colonial history.[5] Although this work furnished additional information on *naven* (see Stanek 1983a: 276–291, 301–338; 1983b; 1994), neither ritual in general nor the *naven* itself was the subject of a focused research.

Stanek and Weiss did their original research in the village of Palimbei, and subsequently, in 1979–1980, they continued their fieldwork among the Iatmul in co-operation with the psychoanalyst Fritz Morgenthaler.[6] New insights into the significance of the *naven* ritual emerged, particularly through Weiss's ethno-psychoanalytic case study (detailed in Morgenthaler, Weiss, and Morgenthaler [1984] 1987: 144–193). Michael Houseman and Carlo Severi ([1994] 1998), who pooled all the new data on *naven*, attempted a dynamic structural interpretation in relation to a general theory of ritual. Working within a psychoanalytic framework, Bernard Juillerat (1999) formulated a very comprehensive picture of the symbolic structures expressed in the *naven* behavior. Lastly, Eric K. Silverman's (2001) research among the eastern Iatmul brought new descriptions of the *naven* rituals. He also problematized the primary mother-child relationship in connection with the Iatmul men's somewhat fragile masculinity.[7] Thus, the *naven* ritual has once again become a focus of research and analysis. In this article, the authors wish to convey particular insights that were produced through a psychoanalytically oriented series of conversations with Iatmul individuals.

Ethno-psychoanalytic Conversations

The present authors, Milan Stanek and Florence Weiss, were fortunate to meet the Swiss psychoanalysts Paul and Goldy Parin and Fritz Morgenthaler and to join them in their psychoanalytic exploration of different cultures.[8] Together with Morgenthaler, we formulated a research project and during 1979–1980 conducted a series of ethno-psychoanalytic conversations with the Iatmul of Palimbei. We thereby gained a conceptually and empirically richer and more accurate picture of the Iatmul culture. The daily conversations with different Iatmul individuals made it possible to learn more about the emotional background of interpersonal relations in the way they are typically configured in and by the Iatmul culture. This allowed us to attempt a formulation of psychic processes at work in individuals and in groups, thus extending our attention beyond the overt cultural forms of everyday life and ritual.

We published 10 ethno-psychoanalytic case studies, or rather, psychoanalytically oriented conversations with 10 women and men.[9] One of these studies, the conversations between Florence Weiss and the Iatmul woman Magendaua, contains extraordinarily rich and novel information on the psychodynamics of the *naven* ritual. During one of the conversations with Weiss, Magendaua not only performed a sort of micro-version of *naven* directed at her baby but also described seven *naven* performances without being prompted by any leading questions. And toward the end of the conversations, she effected again a sort of *naven* that embroiled Weiss in *naven*-like verbal interactions with her husband.

The group of researchers working in 1979–1980 in Palimbei consisted of four persons: the psychoanalyst and supervisor Fritz Morgenthaler, his son Marco Morgenthaler (at that time a student of anthropology), and Stanek and Weiss, both anthropologists trained in psychoanalysis. The house we lived in stood on a bank of the Sepik River, a 30-minute walk from the Palimbei village situated farther inland. This time we did not intend to engage in anthropological fieldwork; we did not want to speak with our Iatmul acquaintances about their kinship system nor were we eager to participate in ritual gatherings in order to document them. We also did not want to ask our informants to tell us their life histories. Instead, our intention was to speak with our Iatmul partners every day for one hour during three months in order to understand how they experienced their own participation in the social life of their village world.

We decided it would be best to explain at the outset exactly what we were planning to do. Upon arrival and following welcoming greetings, Weiss addressed a gathering of women: "By now I know how you organize your everyday life. I know well your work and your feasts. This time I would like to meet you daily for an hour to take a stroll together with you in your thoughts and feelings in order to get to know what is going on inside you." It is a clearly articulated expression in the Iatmul language and an important Iatmul cultural concept that every individual human being possesses an inner life that is not immediately perceptible to other persons in his or her environment. They found our project acceptable, and the news spread through the village that the whites wanted to speak with individual persons an hour a day. Soon all of us had found partners. But the plan for Morgenthaler to speak with a particular man whom we knew as an expressive *naven* dancer did not materialize. This man was unwilling to participate, and so it happened that we learned about *naven* and its emotional significance mostly from the conversations Weiss had with the Iatmul woman Magendaua.

For the present contribution, Weiss has chosen several passages from these conversations recorded in our book *Gespräche am sterbenden Fluss*, which was published in German in 1984 and in French (as *Conversations au bord du fleuve mourant*) in 1987. When writing our book, we did not try to generalize our results in a comparative perspective, as is common practice in scientific discourse. Rather, we contented ourselves with a few clarificatory remarks. As we saw it, the scientific value of the conversations consisted in rendering authentic information on emotional exchanges between persons representing two different cultures. We were interested in questioning the subjectivity of the researcher, which became so salient in the work of Georges Devereux (1967), and tried to respect the subjectivity of our Iatmul partners. Here we have written a number of additional commentaries to make more transparent the development of the relationship between Weiss and Magendaua and to impart reflections concerning the *naven* since it and its expressive modes became a part of the relational psychodynamic process engendered by the daily encounters.[10] What follows is Weiss's account of her conversations with Magendaua.

My Fellow Counterpart Magendaua

Having already established working relationships with an adolescent woman and a young mother, I sought to engage a third woman, preferably an older one, in daily conversations. I had not met Magendaua during our first stay in Palimbei in

1972–1974 because at the time she was living with her husband in the town of Rabaul in East New Britain. Meeting her for the first time now, she made a strong impression on me. A group of women who were returning in their canoes from a market trip came up to the Sepik bank near our house. As Magendaua, tall and slender, lifted a heavy basket with sago flour from the canoe, our eyes met for a moment. Then she put the burden on her back and went on to the village. From other women I got to know about her and her family.

Although I wanted to ask Magendaua if she would be willing to speak with me on a regular basis, I hesitated for a while because Milan Stanek's conversations with her father-in-law were well under way. But she herself took the lead and approached me instead. Of course, our Iatmul partners did not choose us as interlocutors because of psychic suffering, which is what individuals in Europe do when they make contact with a psychoanalyst. Nevertheless, preexistent experiences and social roles were operative in our situation too. The whites in Papua New Guinea were seen as persons laden with prestige. Except for Magendaua, practically every villager had already had his or her opportunity to strike a deal with us during our first lengthy stay in Palimbei. So apart from the general prestige we were enjoying, Magendaua might have had her own particular motive. She could now seize the opportunity to get to know a white woman and the whole of our group.

Still another motive must have been there from the beginning. Magendaua's father was a clever and commanding man. When in 1927 the Australian colonial administration started to enforce British law in the region, he understood better than anybody else in the village the advantages that co-operation with the colonial power could bring him. He seized the opportunity to become a village headman (*tultul*) in the service of the white government. This social role was hitherto unknown in the egalitarian political structure of Iatmul communities (see Stanek 1991; Weiss 1994c). Supported by the armed police presence, he could exercise a sort of despotic power in the village. His fellow villagers never forgot the forced labor he organized for the colonial administration, along with the fact that he married one young woman after another. During World War II, the Australian administration officers withdrew from the Sepik Province in the wake of the massive invasion by the Japanese armed forces. Knowing full well what was to follow, Magendaua's father also ran away. The villagers discovered him hiding inside a great old tree and shot him down. At that time Magendaua was just a small child. Subsequently, she experienced the severe ostracism that her family endured for some years. As we shall see at the end of our conversations, this sort of contradictory experience with the whites played a role in our relationship. She will identify her father with the mythical image of a wild boar that has lost all connection with its own community and leads a solitary existence in the forest, ready to kill anybody who might approach it.

At the time of our conversations, Magendaua was about 40 years old and had six children, three girls and three boys. She lived in her husband's house together with his father and mother. Her husband's second wife lived in a separate house. Her mother and three sisters, all married and with several children, also lived in the village. Magendaua enjoyed a good social standing because of the family she had married into. Her father-in-law was an old and wise man who possessed great mythological knowledge. He also offered protection and advice to other people. At the time, he was working with Milan Stanek.

Magendaua Makes the First Move

Some days had passed since our first encounter at the bank of the Sepik on market day. I was sitting outside the house with my adolescent partner, engaged in our daily conversation. Magendaua appeared in front of us. She came from the garden carrying a basket of sweet potatoes, her infant child in her arms, followed by three of her other children, a living symbol of good livelihood, plenitude of progeny, and sustenance. She addressed me, and I learned that the sweet potatoes were a gift for the whites. After we exchanged a few words, Magendaua went into our house, delivered the potatoes, and went past us again. I watched her walk away. She turned around and waved at me with her empty bag.

The following day I am off to the village. It is around mid-day. The path leads through a shadeless landscape, with gardens to the left, and to the right Kurupmui creek. I reach the village half an hour later. I walk over the narrow bridge across the creek and arrive at the oldest and largest dwelling house in Palimbei. Magendaua lives here, together with her husband, their six children, and her parents-in-law. Children emerge from underneath the house and call out: "The white woman is coming, the white woman is coming!" I stand still. "Magendaua, are you there?" "Come on up," is the answer from the house. I go up the stairs to the house, and in front of me stands Magendaua. We shake hands and smile at each other.

Now someone in the dark interior of the house calls my name. It is Magendaua's mother-in-law, an old woman. She comes toward me, grasps my chin with a firm grip and pours over me a flood of welcoming words in Iatmul. Then she retreats. Magendaua points to a place next to the door. As we sit down, the children follow suit, watching me with curiosity. I say that we enjoyed the sweet potatoes. Satisfied, Magendaua nods, but then begins to talk about the town of Rabaul, where she lived for seven years. She concludes her description with the statement that she was happy to return to Palimbei. I say: "When I was living in Palimbei seven years ago, you were living in Rabaul. Now both of us are here, and we could have daily conversations together."

Magendaua suggests that we should begin promptly the next day and, like Milan and her father-in-law, meet for our talks in the *haus polis*.[11] We arrange to meet at mid-day. By then, Magendaua would have returned from fishing and would already have made sago pancakes and cooked fish for her family. On the way to the *haus polis* we walk through the village in typical Iatmul manner, with myself at the front, followed by Magendaua, and behind her the children who want to come along. Being curious, the residents of the houses we walk past inquire about our plans. "We are going to the *haus polis*," Magendaua and I reply, taking turns. A much-traveled path runs past this house. Everyone who walks by can see us because the wall that would shield us from the footpath close by is missing. Yet likewise, nobody can pass us unseen. We go up the three steps and sit down in the veranda-like room. It takes a while before the children too have climbed up and found a place close to Magendaua. Then it is quiet.

Magendaua: "This morning I went to the Sepik. Three fish were hanging in my net."

Silence.

"On the way back to the village I walked past your house. It was totally quiet, you were all still asleep."

Silence.

"Back in the village, I gave one fish to my oldest sister. I cut the remaining two into eight pieces, one for each of my six children, my husband, and myself. After I cooked the meal, Milan came to pick up my father-in-law for their conversation. I then asked myself if you too might not come."

Magendaua looks at me in silence.

Florence: "I have come, and you have come too."

Magendaua is silent. The children are becoming restless; they get up and play about. Magendaua admonishes them but to no avail. Now she sends them to the neighbor's house for betel nuts.

Magendaua: "I've had enough of the children disturbing our conversation."

Florence: "Your children are no lame chickens."

As Magendaua is laughing, the three children appear in the door. They come back empty-handed. She winks at me.

Magendaua: "Go to the shop at the end of the village and ask if they have biscuits."

The two older children are enthusiastic; the youngest one does not feel like going and stays. She rambles through Magendaua's bag that is lying next to her on the floor, pulls out a purse, and opens it. Coins fall out.

Magendaua: "Stop it! I will buy sago with these at the market tomorrow."

Florence: "Do you women catch so little fish these days that you cannot barter for sago anymore but need to buy it?"

Magendaua: "When I came back from Rabaul to Palimbei, there were plenty of fish, but now most lakes are overgrown with the salvinia weed and us women catch little fish."

Silence.

"I heard about you and Milan in Rabaul; I was told you are nice people."

Silence.

"One day my brother came to Rabaul and told me that my mother had aged a lot. It was already seven years that I hadn't seen her. When I thought of her, I had to cry. I wanted to return home. My husband too was longing for his father."

A woman passes by. She looks astonished when she sees us, greets us, and walks on. Magendaua waits until she is out of sight.

Magendaua: "She is my husband's second wife. In Rabaul we lived together in one house. She didn't give my husband any food. I threw her out."

Silence.

"She gave birth to only three children, but I have had six. She is a bad woman."

Silence.

"I've run out of sago. Tomorrow I am going to the market. Could you come later, you know how long it takes to go to the forest villages?"

My impression was accurate; Magendaua did wish to engage in daily conversations with me. She proposed to start without any hesitation and delay. In the choice of place she followed her father-in-law. Everybody who was curious could see that she was talking to the white woman. In this first conversation she assumed the role of a mother who provides food for her family. She caught fish, traveled to market in the forest villages, and cooked. Her children were important to her, and four of them assisted her in the first meeting. Later on she would always come carrying her infant child, and sometimes her three-and-a-half-year-old daughter followed her. Magendaua was expressing aggressive feelings toward her husband's second wife and curiosity toward the whites. She watched our house in the morning when we were asleep. She was observing Milan as he was going with her father-in-law to have conversations, and she also demanded to know whether I would come to join her.

In contrast with an ethno-sociological manner of interviewing, this time I did not ask questions in the beginning since I did not wish to determine the themes that Magendaua and I would talk about. I wanted to facilitate an open space for her own interests to unfold. In this manner a discourse developed, the parts of which seemingly remained disconnected: the fish, the house of the whites, the elder sister, and so on. In this sort of discourse Magendaua could follow her ideas and feelings as they emerged in response to the actual and ever changing emotional turns in our relationship. We were at the beginning, and we did not know each other yet.

Difference as Discernment

It takes a certain amount of time for any relationship to develop and for both persons to get to know each other better, especially when there are differences in ideas, behavior, and values. How we deal with these differences will depend on the way we frame our relationship at a particular moment: do we relate in a hierarchic mode or on equal footing or in the flow of mutual attraction? In the ethno-psychoanalytic framework we look for differences in the cultural make-up of the persons in the relationship. In the preface to the French translation of our book (Morgenthaler, Weiss, and Morgenthaler [1984] 1987: 6), Georges

Balandier sums it up: "With ethno-psychoanalysis ... the project becomes more ambitious. To the study 'from the outside' through the observation of cultural behaviors, these disciplines add the study 'from the inside' for which cultural interpretation is done through the knowledge of reactions from individual to individual ... It is a lesson in the apprenticeship in living together, despite the distance between cultures and the internal and external obstacles."[12]

Soon Magendaua discovered that something about my way disturbed her. She was coming late to our meetings, making me wait. In addition, her husband began to interfere. When I go to see her on another day, her husband is standing in the gangway. I learn that Magendaua has gone to the Sepik to set up her net. Her husband tells me that she would be back late and that it makes little sense that I wait. I am astonished and not in the mood to engage in a conversation with him. I take a stroll through the village. At one of the houses, women and children have sat down in the grass. The children are playing, the women are mending their nets and plaiting fish traps. They call me over and I go and sit with them. Milan comes and says: "I'm going home, my interlocutor is ill, there will be no conversation today."

After a while I say goodbye to the women and walk over to the *haus polis*. In the distance I see Magendaua approaching from the river. She waves at me, and once we sit down, I tell her laughingly: "I was beginning to think you would never return from the Sepik. And your father-in-law likewise did not speak with Milan today. When I didn't find you at your house, I thought, Magendaua does not want to speak with me today."

Magendaua listens carefully, turns her head to the side, and hides her face behind her hand.

Magendaua: "You have ideas!"

Silence.

"This morning a tree trunk got entangled in my net. I called my sisters for help. They mocked me: 'Why do you have to hang your net at this very spot where driftwood abounds!' The net was ripped. I took it home and mended it. After I had made pancakes, I went back to the Sepik and hung the net out again. Perhaps a fish can be found in it tomorrow. I was thinking on the way home that surely you would not wait for me. But you did wait."

A girl comes and brings Magendaua's infant, who had been sleeping at home. Magendaua places him in her lap and offers him the breast. Every so often he turns his head and looks at me. Magendaua explains how the women of her village quarter came to have nets. She does not omit a single one. When she is finished with the account, she falls silent for a while.

Magendaua: "My oldest sister catches the most fish. As she does, being older than I."

Silence.

Magendaua winks at me.

"There will be a time when I catch the most fish."

Silence.

"I told my husband that I would bring you sweet potatoes. It is too late today. I'll bring them tomorrow."

Silence.

"Many of my clothes are ripped. I have run out of thread. Could you perhaps give me thread?"

Florence: "I brought only little sewing gear. If you need thread, I can organize some for you."

Magendaua: "I could do with some thread."

Every evening we gather to form our supervision group. Each of us presents his or her conversations of the day. I finished reading the protocol of my last conversation with Magendaua.

F. Morgenthaler: "Magendaua develops anxiety in front of you. She experiences you as uncanny."

F.W.: "Why that? I like her well, I admire her even! She has no reason to be afraid of me."

F.M.: "What I mean has nothing to do with your feelings. Magendaua too, she likes you. This is not the point. Your way is foreign to her. You target so directly and intensely at her. You walk every day half an hour to meet her, and you are taking in her every word. In response to this she comes late to the appointments and lets you wait ever longer in these last days. She is different. She is occupied with the practical problems of her life; she needs fish in her net to feed her family and to exchange a part of it for sago. What she says and hears in the company of other Iatmul women is self-evident to her. You by contrast follow closely every word of hers, you strive to understand what is going on with her. Such an attitude is foreign and incomprehensible for her. When she follows your reasoning, she exclaims: 'What ideas you have!'"

F.W.: "True. A few days ago I experienced strongly how different we are. I had the impression Magendaua is well integrated, cared for, and as for me, I felt being isolated and excluded."

F.M.: "This is on account of the fact that you can only live if you adhere to the internalized image of yourself, whereas Magendaua is a woman who reanimates and renews her image of herself daily through the emotional responses of the group to which she belongs. This is why she continually redistributes everything that she has, and partakes in what others give. We come from a culture where everyone essentially has to rely on him- or herself, demarcating oneself from the other."

F.W.: "But why does Magendaua feel threatened by this?"

F.M.: "She engaged in a relationship with you, and now she feels how different you are. You are like a foreign body, and because you play a role in her group, she feels threatened by you. The differences that you perceive between Magendaua and yourself are differences of personality structure. We first recognized this difference that you now experience to exist between Magendaua and yourself with the Dogon in West Africa. I am not talking about cultural background or total personality—that of the Iatmul differs in almost every aspect from that of the Dogon. I am talking about the ego-organization. The ego-organization of Magendaua shows the characteristic traits of an oral structuration, as we encountered it among the Dogon. In contrast, our ego-organization is saturated with structures that originate in the anal phase of libidinal development. The Dogon, too, experienced us in their relationships with us like foreign bodies and felt threatened by us. We need to consider this aspect of our foreignness, this difference in our personality structure, in your conversations with Magendaua. It must not continue to disrupt your relationship. You tell her that she fears to be devoured when not having anything more to distribute. This alone will not suffice. Her feeling that you are so different will not simply dissipate. Magendaua desires that you and she would be more alike."

I sleep poorly this night. The idea that I might be disturbing the conversations with Magendaua, that our talks might even come to an end soon, is unbearable. I am already at breakfast when Fritz Morgenthaler gets up. He comes toward me and says: "You could succeed with the thread. You must handle the thread in the way Magendaua handles a fish. Not you but I will buy the thread for Magendaua. She asks you and you ask me to procure some thread. In this way you too are an element in a chain and redistribute what you obtain."

I am relieved and know how to speak with Magendaua about the thread. Because since we began our conversations I have been fascinated not only by the way she moves, feels, and thinks, but also her manner of speaking. When Magendaua talks, she loosely lines up diverse episodes; she approaches things via detours. She does not choose the shortest way to the goal. I imagine how I could speak with Magendaua and feel how it suits me. Being playful is not something alien to me.

I find her baking sago pancakes. Next to her is her husband, sitting on a small stool, and some of the children who have lain down on the floor, watching her. He wants to know how the three white men are, but soon leaves for the men's house. Magendaua resolutely takes the last pancake off the hot clay plate, drips water onto it and folds it into a half-moon. She fetches eight little plaited bags from a hook that is hanging from a roof beam. She places a pancake into each bag.

Magendaua: "This one is for Yanamak, this one for Petseri, this one for Pagwiyaman ..."

She says the names of all of her children. She then puts a larger pancake into her husband's bag and finally one into her own. She hangs up all the bags back onto the hook.

Magendaua: "Today I have not caught a single fish. But my sister brought me vegetables which I have cooked."

Florence: "You feed everyone, make pancakes, cook vegetables, catch fish. That's good. If you didn't have anything to distribute they would eat you."

Magendaua: "Oh no, if they did that they would all have to cry because I wouldn't be here anymore."

She points to a mosquito net that is set up in the back of the house.

Magendaua: "Look, there in the corner is a hole, the mosquitoes get in through there. I can't sleep in peace anymore. I would like to mend it and need thread, which I asked you to bring."

Florence: "Fritz is about to go to Wewak in order to fetch his wife Ruth, who is also coming to the Sepik. I told him to get thread for you. Wewak has many shops. He will go to a Chinese shop and find a good thread for you. I explained to him that you want to mend your clothes. I will bring you the thread when Fritz comes back."

As I am talking Magendaua sweeps sago crumbs into the gaps in the floor. We hear the chickens come running down below the house. Happily, I register that Magendaua is enjoying my story. Every so often a quick smile lights up her face, and several times she interrupts her work and looks directly at my face. Next she packs away the broom and lifts the infant onto her hip.

Magendaua: "Come, let's go to our place under the tree."

Two children are following us. While we are talking, they collect little fruit lying under the tree that they share with their mother and me. Magendaua tells me that today a tree trunk got again entangled in her net. Suddenly the baby starts crying.

Florence: "It is the first time that he cries."

Magendaua: "He is sick, that's why."

Silence.

"This morning I saw young women on the Sepik who were returning from a string-band party. They must have been dancing all night. The women were excited. They were beautiful, and they were laughing. Young men were following them in another canoe. One could see from the distance how pleased they were about the women."

Magendaua bends over toward me.

Magendaua: "You know the women of the Sepik. I was like that when I was young."

As we are talking with each other, the baby crawls toward Magendaua and when he reaches her, she lifts him up and places him into her lap. She offers him the breast, briefly pulls it back, and roughly pushes it into the baby's open mouth.

Magendaua: "You are not to eat me. I warn you, don't you dare eat me!"

Florence: "What would happen if your baby ate you?"

Magendaua: "Not thinking he will eat me. But later he would notice that I wasn't there anymore. Then everyone would weep. My children would be very sad, because there would be no woman who could care for them. My husband's second wife can't do it."

Silence.

"I cannot comprehend why we are unable to heed the rules of the Catholics. A man should marry one woman."

Florence: "You had imagined that you could have your husband to yourself. This is why you threw out the second wife."

Magendaua: "Yes, that is so."

Silence.

"I always have to share everything." (She laughs.) "People have said that I used a spell to bind my husband to me. But I don't even know any spells."

Florence: "You don't need spells to bind a man to you."

Magendaua: "I have been pulling your nose for two days. Tonight I will bring you the promised sweet potatoes."

Shortly before dusk I hear a noise coming from the front of our house of someone clearing her throat. I go to the door and see Magendaua. She is standing at the foot of the staircase with four children, the bag with sweet potatoes next to her on the ground. She comes up, and we sit down. Magendaua takes a good look around. The children talk loudly and push each other whenever they discover something special among the many things of the white people. Milan has already said hello to Magendaua. When Fritz and Marco come back from Kanganamun, a neighboring village across the river, I introduce Magendaua to them. It is the first time that she speaks with them. When Magendaua is ready to leave, I accompany her for a bit and then say goodbye. She holds me back: "It is nice at your place: I like the cooking place, the big table and chairs. But the saucepans haven't been cleaned in a long while and are black with char. I will come by tomorrow and clean them."

Witches and *Naven* Dancers

In the days that followed, our relationship changed, and my menacing traits that had disturbed Magendaua faded into the background. We were able to co-operate more in our conversations, as well as in general. We established an exchange of services between the two groups, black and white. For instance, when Magendaua's children became sick, they were transported across the river to the health post of the Catholic mission in our canoe. She in turn cleaned our pans as she had promised, and her husband repaired our floating bridge. After a few days' trip to Wewak, Fritz came back to the village with his wife Ruth. He brought the thread with him, and I forwarded it to Magendaua.

The next day, as I am about to finish the conversation with my adolescent partner in the *haus polis*, Magendaua approaches us in a happy mood.

Magendaua: "Look at these two witches!"

The young woman laughs, and after we say goodbye, I settle with Magendaua in the *haus polis*.

Magendaua: "My children told me that you and Ruth came to the village yesterday. I was on the lake and got home only late."

I tell her every detail of our walk. How we arrived in the village, which path we took, and whom we visited. Magendaua breaks into my account several times, providing the names of those parts of the village through which we had come.

Magendaua: "What a shame! I have nothing that I could give Ruth. I cannot greet her."

Florence: "In such a situation white people simply shake hands."

Magendaua: "We black people know it too. When young people who have been living in a coastal town for a long time come back to the village during holidays, we do a *naven*. Once two sons of my brother returned to Palimbei after they had been away for years. I and my sister put on men's clothes. We played guitar, danced, and sang. An old woman pulled a pig mask over her head. We danced around the two, and after a while they began to weep. They were down because they had left so many relatives behind in the towns and were impressed that we were dancing a *naven* for them."

Florence: "Did you perform as your brother's sister and for this reason dressed in men's clothes?"

Magendaua: "Of course I was a man, I was my brother. If you were to do a *naven* for my children, you too would put on men's clothes. I, being the mother, would dance in women's clothes, and you would perform in men's clothes."

Silence.

"When I saw you speaking with the young woman earlier on, I said you are two witches."

Florence: "What do you mean by that?"

Magendaua: "When the two of us also are sitting together here, people think these are two witches. As witches we discuss which beautiful young man we want to kill. Then we do magic, take his soul, thrash his head, cut it off, and throw it into the Sepik. We could also proceed differently: we don't kill him and take his liver out instead, and whenever we feel like it, bring it out from our hiding place and throw it between us as if it were a ball. When we play with his liver, the young man feels great pain and has no idea why."

Magendaua points to the baby in her lap.

Magendaua: "There are witches who kill and eat such pretty, healthy children."

Florence: "Until now we have only talked about children eating their mothers, but here women eat their children."

Magendaua: "Sure! There are witches who take children out of their grave. They need a piece of human flesh for their magic."

Silence.

"There are no more witches in Palimbei. Only two male witches are left. You know whom I'm talking about."

Silence.

For a brief moment, Magendaua stays silent and, suddenly, shows me her left hand.

Magendaua: "Look, my finger! My husband's second wife bit it off when we were in Rabaul. Relatives had given me wood and metal sheets for the roof, and my husband built a house with it. When I had an argument with his second wife, I wanted her to move out. She wouldn't have a bar of it. A fight ensued. I wanted to punch her in the face. That's when she bit me. She bit off a piece of my finger. I had to stay in hospital for 10 days. When I returned, the argument started all over again, and I bit her in the cheek. I tell you, human flesh does not taste good, it tastes strange. When the children ask me what happened to my finger, I tell them that a rat who was arguing with the first wife bit off a piece of my finger."

For the first time in our conversations Magendaua described a *naven* ritual performed for two young men who had been living for a long time in a colonial town. They returned to spend their holidays in their native village. Magendaua and her sister danced disguised as men (the two young men's *yau*, father's sisters). An old woman (mother's mother, *mbambu*) put on a pig mask representing one of her totemic ancestors. At first, the mood was theatrical and humorous; then the young men broke into tears. In the course of her account, Magendaua imagined me disguised as a man performing a *naven* for her children in the same role of the *yau* as she did in the ritual she was describing to me. After this, both of us could playfully change into witches and kill or enter the bodies of young people in order to take out the best of their inner parts.

The arrival of Morgenthaler's spouse Ruth affected Magendaua in such a way that in the transference, she experienced anew the devouring female phantom, as she had earlier at the onset of our conversations. She avoided seeing Ruth; indeed, she commented on how terribly menacing Ruth was. Under the protection of the splitting, she enjoyed a good relationship with me that was sustained in the conversations and in other activities.[13] Nevertheless, in one of the following conversations she was looking forward to the end of our co-operation; she suggested that we would leave Papua New Guinea soon. In reality, our departure was still a few months away.

We assessed the situation in our supervisory group and concluded that it was not particularly good for the further development of my relationship with Magendaua. If possible, it was preferable to recenter her transference onto me. The next day I will tell Magendaua that we can continue our conversations because there is still plenty of time before my departure. I also decide to attend to her phantasies connected with the splitting without describing their content.[14] In this way I would sustain the personal and emotional value of our conversations and offer myself at her disposition, i.e., give her the opportunity to handle myself in both orientations—'good' as well as 'bad'.

The *Naven* for the Baby

The next meeting with Magendaua was the most exciting moment in the development of our relationship. The emotional dynamics took a new direction when, in my presence, Magendaua displayed toward the small child particular gestures and facial expressions belonging to the *naven* repertory. For her part it was a particularly creative idea, and for the researchers it was a precious gift. After this meeting, the *naven* ritual was to remain one of the most important points of reference in our conversations, and later on she was able and willing to conceive of the *naven* as a sort of intellectual puzzle that can be investigated.

Sequence #1: The Difficulties of Everyday Life

Magendaua: "This morning two women from the neighboring village Malingei asked if they could borrow my canoe, in order to paddle across the river to Kanganamun. I gave it to them, but when I came back to the Sepik in the afternoon, they still hadn't returned. I borrowed the canoe of another woman to check my net. I may have to go again to the Sepik today because I urgently need my canoe for tomorrow."

Florence: "When I was sitting under the tree waiting for you, I thought of our conversations. I was engrossed in my thoughts and pictured how often we have already sat together here and how often we will still speak together. I was thinking of you and how many more times you will paddle out on the Sepik and to the market, and how many tree trunks will still get entangled in your net. We cannot keep count of it."

Magendaua: "As I was cooking a meal for the whole family today, I would have liked to drink some tea, but there was no sugar. My husband probably ate it."

Florence: "You will come to our place. Then Ruth, you, and I will drink tea together."

Satisfied, Magendaua takes her little daughter into her arm.

Magendaua: "I have well-nourished, beautiful children. Only I am skinny. I think of my children and give them food. It is important that their bellies are round and filled."

She lifts up her daughter. "Good, beautiful children I have."

Now she seats the child next to her and looks at me.

Sequence #2: The Sagi, or Mythical Story

Magendaua: "I have to tell you a story. Once upon a time there lived an old couple and two young men together in one house. Everyday the old woman was catching fish, and her rack was packed with fish to the point of collapsing. She did not give any of it to the young men. They then thought: 'Why is she not giving us any fish?' They contrived a plan. They secretly placed a bamboo pipe leading from their mosquito net to the old couple's. During the night when the two old people were asleep, they held one end of the pipe close to their arse-hole and, taking turns, farted into it. The old man woke up first and scolded his wife: 'What are you farting like that for!' With the next fart, the wife scolded her husband. It went on like that for several nights. One day the woman discovered the bamboo pipe and told her husband about it. The two figured something out. The man carved a little slingshot, and when the two young men farted again during the night, he shot little pieces of wood into their arse-holes. Beside themselves with pain, they retracted and helped each other remove the pieces of wood. They thought about how to take revenge. The next morning they went into the grass swamp and hunted a crocodile. They let it lie foul for several days until it began to rot, then they ate as much of it as they could. They went back home and lied down to rest. During the night, they had to shit. They shat and shat until the house was filled and also the staircase and the yard around the house. When the old couple got up at the crack of dawn, they found themselves walking in shit up to their ankles. The fish they caught that day and threw into the canoe were lying in shit. Shortly thereafter the old people died."

Sequence #3: The Naven for a Baby

I say nothing. I think to myself, that really is a mighty story. It all ends in shit and death. What is Magendaua trying to say? I sit there not having a clue. Magendaua calls out to her baby. As he has done a few times before, he has crawled to the edge of the platform from where he could fall down. Suddenly, she rolls her eyes, sticks out her tongue, and wildly moves her torso and legs to and fro.

Florence: "Are you doing a *naven*?"

Magendaua: "Yes, I am doing a *naven*."

Florence: "Because the baby crawled away?"

Magendaua: "Oh no. Because he looked back when I called out to him."

Florence: "You do a *naven* because he looks back?"

Magendaua: "Yes, he did look back."

Florence: "But you do a *naven* when a girl catches her first fish or after completion of the initiation ritual or when somebody from far away returns to the village."

Magendaua: "Yes, that's when we do a *naven*."

Florence: "Does the girl who comes home with a fish or the young men after their initiation also look back?"

Magendaua: "That is so."

Silence.

Sequence #4: The Extended Naven

Magendaua: "This girl from the neighborhood, when she came home with her first big fish, her mothers' brothers, the *wau*, also danced with the women. They had put on skirts and one of them had stashed a big pillow underneath. He kept saying that he was her mother and held his belly in such a way as if he was about to give birth. Another man carried a dog in his arm and gently caressed it as if it were a little child. My oldest sister was dancing along, disguised as a man. She then placed herself in front of one of the *wau* and said: 'You are my wife. Tonight I will make love to you.' He asked back: 'Do you have a penis too?' She simply replied: 'Sure I have a penis. I took it from you and gave you my vagina.' He had nothing to say to that."

Florence: "I have seen the kind of *naven* that you describe. But I had no idea that you mothers do a *naven* already with your babies. And I also didn't know that you do *naven* when your children look back."

Magendaua laughs. Our conversation is over. We get up, she takes her baby into her arm, and when we arrive at the bridge, we say goodbye.

Something remarkable had happened. Magendaua, my fellow interlocutor, with whom I had already been engaged in daily conversations for one and a half months, had produced a sort of *naven* that I had never seen before. I was captivated by the image of Magendaua's infant looking back at his mother. She responded to this seemingly insignificant event with a few body gestures reminiscent of dance choreographies that I had seen in all elaborated *naven* performances. I found especially noteworthy that her facial expressions also came from the *naven* repertory. They represent the mythical mother who, in the imagery of Iatmul mythological culture, is always split into two aspects: the nurturing, good mother and the devouring, powerful, dangerous mother. In the system of totemic names, these two aspects are for the Iatmul differentiated as the ancestral figures Ndanganagwi versus Ndumanagwi.

We are now able to look at diverse forms of *naven* performances from this point of view established by Magendaua with her spontaneously produced baby *naven*. And it is a very fitting perspective, too, since the *naven* for the returning adults is clearly analogous. Today, in these colonial and postcolonial times, when Iatmul men and women return to their native village, often after years of absence, they look with solicitude and anxiety at their folks with whom they grew up. The *naven* for the children who shoot for the first time a duck or catch a big fish can equally be seen from this point of view. We can agree with Bateson's reasoning that they accomplished a sort of great deed that will be taken as an occasion for celebration. But simultaneously the celebrants are also looking back to their childhood. Having brought home the catch to show it to the mother and other relatives, they are beginning to take on the typical role of the Iatmul adults. Through a deed that contributes to the clan's subsistence, the adolescents now come to belong to their society in a new way. They are about to leave behind the children's group, and from the point of view of the mother, they are severing their ties with her. They went out hunting to provide food rather than to receive it. It can be said that the celebrants have returned and look back upon their mothers, upon their relatives, and, as a consequence, upon themselves. Now we can comprehend better what the word *naven* means. It contains the verbal root *ve-* signifying 'looking at': *ve-ga-nde/ve-ga-re* means 'he looks at/she looks at'. The particle *na-* indicates ostentation, as in the French 'Voilà!' (Look at this!).

My work with Magendaua made me aware that since the inception of our ethno-psychoanalytic conversations, I had developed a habit of investigating everything that happened between us in the light of the dynamics of our relationship. I continued asking questions such as "How do I experience my partner? How is this experience changing from one meeting to another? How does she experience me?" Let us look closely at what had happened. At the beginning of our conversations, a particular difficulty emerged. Even if from the outset she was keenly interested in meeting me, Magendaua could not help but experience me as strange. The regularity that I had brought into this relationship, the kind of attention that I directed at her—in short, my overall way of not being an Iatmul woman made her feel anxious and vexed. She would have preferred a different form of relationship: occasionally meeting me, occasionally not, sometimes here, sometimes there, talking as Iatmul women do, about fish and children, about men young and old, the latter being considered responsible for whatever might have gone wrong in the village; sometimes giving, sometimes receiving, changing, and exchanging betel nuts, fish, children. This was, of course, out of the question. I remained who I am, and if she wished, as she did, to continue our conversations, she had to take me as I was.

When I realized—in the supervisory context of our group—what a strain it was for her to deal with me, I took it upon myself to reduce the tension in our relationship. So although being a researcher from Switzerland, I nevertheless was able to temporarily modify certain of my character traits while in Magendaua's company. I began to experience myself as changing: sometimes a woman, sometimes a man, sometimes white, sometimes black; as it were, sometimes I was this, sometimes I was that. The change in me led to a change in Magendaua. She was able to enjoy me better, including my different cultural psychic make-up, and, among other things, I was able to be amused by the role of a witch that she would assume together with me.

On the other hand, Magendaua was at the same time developing an anxiety in connection with Ruth as she had before with me. It looked as if she could not develop and deepen a relationship without experiencing this sort of phantom of a menacing female figure. The early maternal-imago, the pregenital mother in the experience of an infant, represents by no means a special Iatmul phantasy; we know it well in our society, too. Nevertheless, we have different defenses, a different ego-organization to deal with it, more or less consonant with the givens of our own cultural and social structure. By displacing this vile phantom onto the figure of Ruth—whom she had not yet met—she could protect the easier and better relation she was enjoying with me. Concomitantly, our relation became shallower, and I became less important to her. However, by insisting in the first sequence of the last meeting on our mutual work done, that is, by insisting on the value of our relationship and addressing the target of the splitting, I became once more a real and important object.

In the second sequence of the last meeting, Magendaua told me a myth in which we can read the destiny of cathexis, that is, of the emotional investment in a human object, whereby a relationship becomes emotionally deepened. In the myth, the characters deal with cathexis in an aggressively limiting way:

voracious and greedy beings are unsuccessfully warded off and take revenge, with everything ending in excrement and death. Afterwards I realized that with this myth Magendaua had shown both me and herself what would happen to her if she would not be able to fulfill the demands on her, that is, as she experienced me through herself.

In the third sequence it happened that the child looked back, and Magendaua performed her *naven*. I believe the narration of the myth already signified a protection against destructive drives articulated through the phantom of the pregenital mother. They have been symbolized, made accessible to consciousness—for her and for me—and so it became possible again for her to relate to me unimpeded. The *naven* for the baby represented a momentous peak of her psychic transformation: now she was mother and ancestor at the same time. And reciprocally, the small infant who looked back at his mother was also ascendant and descendant, an ancestor and her child all at once.

Furthermore, if the infant was for a moment an ancestor, she herself was a child. For the time being she was freed from her aggressive narrow position. The rigid definitions of social positions becoming blurred, the self-definition and the definition of the other becoming interchangeable, she found an exit out of the narrowing space of destructiveness that continuously bedeviled our relationship and was so aptly contained in the myth. This sort of dependence on the human object, which simultaneously calls forth a destructive turn, is a salient feature of Iatmul social life. And when they wish to maintain their social relations, as Magendaua did with me, they have to go through this movement and find a psychically more flexible or motile mode of sustaining a relationship. I think that the *naven* ritual plays an important role in such transformations.

In the fourth sequence, following my questions concerning the *naven* for the baby, Magendaua described another *naven*, the kind we know well, namely, when several women appear as mothers, others are disguised as men, and a *wau* (mother's brother) is disguised as a woman. The last one incarnates and symbolizes the maternal phantom in a grotesque form, making it consciously accessible to himself and to everybody else present at the scene. The social event of an elaborate *naven* accompanies and steers similar psychic dynamics, probably analogous to the one Magendaua experienced in the last meeting with me.

She Has Something to Tell Me

Two days later Magendaua came to our house to meet Ruth. She didn't feel comfortable sitting with two white women around a table. As Ruth served the tea, Magendaua relaxed and started talking about her last market trip. I translated word for word. For a while Magendaua remained circumspect, but eventually she began to enjoy our company. Her baby, whom she would never leave alone, demanded tea, which she served to him. The following day she came to see me in our house by the Sepik bank, for the first time in order to have our conversations. She mentioned that it would appear that now her infant boy no longer likes her milk but prefers the tea. She asked me, also for the very first time since we began our conversations, for a cigarette. When I offered it to her she said: "Now I am Florence." And after a while she said to her daughter: "I will finish talking to Florence soon. Then you can go with her to her house. She will give you biscuits and you will sleep with her in the mosquito net. If you want, you can go with her to Switzerland. Do you?" The girl looked up at her mother searchingly: she thought for a while then nodded in consent. Magendaua laughed and turned to me: "If you take her away, she will completely forget us. In time she will believe you are her mother. If she would come back one day to our village and you would tell her, she would not believe that I am her mother. So it is."

Magendaua was becoming different. It seemed that she was seduced by the white style, as though she wished to be like I was, not knowing anymore whether she was white or black. Yet from time to time she clung to her own culture, expecting me to speak in Iatmul language instead of Melanesian Tok Pisin, as we had until now. She also tried to involve her sisters and other women in our conversations. I now feared that my relationship with Magendaua had broken down, and I discussed this with our supervision group.

Fritz Morgenthaler made the following interpretation. What I experienced as annoying and incomprehensible in Magendaua's comportment—namely, the caricature of myself, the aggressive demands to speak her language, and her attempts to make me a part of a larger group of Iatmul women—was but an expression of her emotional investment in me. In the next conversations I was to address her desire to 'be a white woman' while simultaneously expressing my deep interest in her cultural life-world. For the sake of the latter topic, I shall go back to the themes pertaining to the baby *naven*. Milan suggested that I consider a possible connection between the *naven* facial expressions and the carved faces typical of the Iatmul works of art.

Just about that time, there began a great initiation ritual performed for a dozen young men. The entire village, especially all the adult men, including Magendaua's husband, was heavily preoccupied with the ritual. Since the abolition of headhunting (in the 1930s for a brief period, then again after World War II), this has remained the most important and elaborate ritual in the central Iatmul villages. At the symbolic level, the young men will lose the maternal blood they received at birth and thus become fully masculine. They will be scarified to make them into adult men. It is their elder brothers, not their fathers, who will cut into their backs numerous short but fairly deep cuts that form an indelible pattern on their skin called the signs of the crocodile. The transformation of the young men is the exclusive domain of adult males. Women are banned from the men's house. Mothers and sisters will see their boys again after the initiation wounds will have healed in the form of conspicuous scars. The initiates will then leave the enclosure while their relatives start performing several elaborate *naven* rituals all at once.

As I walked to the village the next day, I experienced a serene feeling in my soul. Some women I met on the path warned me that Magendaua would not have any time for conversation because she was preoccupied by her current workload. She had to catch fish as well as look after her children and husband.

In my imagination I visualized her tall and slender figure, her smiling countenance, and her tendency to express suddenly and very openly her precise feelings—conflict and aggression no less than other moods of everyday life. I knew
that I had something to tell her; I felt that it would be disappointing for her to
discontinue our conversation.

She is sitting in front of her house, her little daughter next to her. Chickens are
fluttering about, leaping at the crumbs they are throwing them. I take a seat.
Magendaua does not reciprocate my greeting. She only looks at me briefly
and continues to crumble up sago pancakes. I watch her doing it. Yesterday's
discussion crosses my mind, and I grasp that Magendaua is not behaving in a
rejecting manner, but like an Iatmul woman. Her demarcation is not directed
against me. She is sitting with her daughter in front of the house feeding chickens, and I would like to have a conversation with her. She is a black woman,
and I am a white woman. Calmly I say to her:

"Come, let's sit under the tree."

Magendaua: "There are too many mosquitoes there."

Silence.

"It would be much better under the house."

Silence.

"Let's sit under the tree."

As soon as we sit down, the daughter who has followed us begins to fuss. She
wants to go to the Sepik right now and check the fishnet. No amount of per-
suading helps. She continues to fuss.

Florence: "Can you remember our talk when the baby crawled to the edge of
the platform? You called out at him, he looked back, and you did a *naven*."

Magendaua looks at me with astonishment and nods.

Florence: "At that time you told me a secret. If somebody looks back, you do
a *naven*. A lot has happened since that conversation. When you asked for the
cigarette, you nearly became a white woman. Do you remember? You almost
forgot who the Iatmul and who the white woman is."

As I was speaking, Magendaua lifts up her dissatisfied daughter and places her
into her lap. The child calms down and is quiet.

Florence: "You know the carvings on the posts of the ceremonial site."

Magendaua: "You are talking of those that are left of the derelict men's
house?"

Florence: "Yes, I mean those. One of the figures depicted there is sticking his
tongue out like you did when you were doing the *naven*."

Magendaua: "That is so."

Florence: "Many of the figures the men carve resemble it. You told me that
your husband initiated you into the secrets of the men's house. When you
explained the *naven* to me, we came upon a secret the men don't know anything about."

Magendaua lies down stretching out on her back, sticks out her tongue as far as she can, opens her eyes widely and pulls down her lower eye lids with her fingers, shifts her hands behind her ears so that they stand out, lifts her arms and pulls up her legs. She demonstrates faces and gestures of the *naven*.

Magendaua: "The carvings you are talking about are scenes from *naven*."

Florence: "Your men don't know the 'look back' of the child, but you women do."

Silence.

"Do you believe that your husband and father-in-law know what they are depicting in their carvings?"

Magendaua: "They just carve them like that."

Silence.

"Every evening when my husband returns from the men's house, he asks me if we have spoken together."

Florence: "He is busy with the initiation of the young men."

Magendaua: "They are their children now. We women have our own."

She simultaneously embraces the baby and her little daughter. She has just released the two from her embrace when the baby crawls off hurriedly. He stops only at the edge of the platform.

Magendaua: "You are a wild pig."

The tension in our relationship had receded, and both of us were at ease in discussing the *naven*, the initiation—and it would remain so until the end of our conversations, as though the regressive devouring phantasies had been banned by a carver into a piece of wood becoming a work of art.

When Magendaua addressed her infant child as a wild boar, she reminded me about the difficulties of mothering, which, evidently, is neither a pure pleasure nor a mere satisfying woman's prerogative. Magendaua explained to me the mythical image: "The wild boars roam alone. They think only about themselves. When they encounter a human being, they attack. Even a strong man is not able to kill such a boar." Later she will describe her father as a wild boar. By now she had managed to sustain a relationship with a white person without becoming one of these forest spirits. On the following day Magendaua revealed that she had begun to think about the question of the connection between her own facial expressions during *naven* and the carved faces in the men's art.

Magendaua: "I talked to my father-in-law. He said the men carve the scenes from *naven* just like that. They are unaware of the background."

Silence.

"I haven't been able yet to ask my husband."

Florence: "The mother gives the children food. If they have problems, who shall they turn to if not the mother? So it is that your children come to you. I have seen it often. A father cannot do a *naven* for his children."

Magendaua: "Never! A father does not participate in *naven*. He always stands outside. When the mother does a *naven* for her child, it will cry. A child never forgets all the things the mother has done for its welfare."

Silence.

"I believe that the men are jealous of the women. Did you see the young men who just walked across the bridge? None of them carries the sign of the crocodile. They are all as yet uninitiated. These young men lead their own independent lives. They have little to do with their fathers, with adult men generally. This is why they take them into the men's house and cut the sign of the crocodile into their bodies. Only then do they belong to them."

Florence: "The women have the *naven*, and the men have initiations."

Magendaua: "That is so."

Already in the early morning, visitors from neighboring villages arrive in Palimbei. The initiation ritual comes to a close with a big *naven*. For the first time the young men step out from behind the fence around the men's house. They carry on their backs the signs of the crocodile, the signs of their male identity. The men have initiations, and the women have the *naven*. Today the women will dance the *naven* for their sons and nephews, brothers and grandsons. They will transform into sexually seductive and aggressively attacking dancers, whereas the young men will fix their gaze on the ground, seeking to hide their tears behind their hand held up. Magendaua is among the spectators. Excited, she comes toward me and tells me about her sister who, dressed up as a man, took an axe and cut into pieces the staircase to the house of her newly initiated nephew. It was a shame, Magendaua says, that she cannot participate in the dancing. Her time had not yet come.

Extended *Naven*

Magendaua reported on the preparations for the *naven* performances, which were to take place at the end of the initiation when the young men emerge from the enclosure. This was the first time that we had our conversations in her house. As it happened, her husband came up and was surprised to find us there. It was now more than two months since we had started our daily conversations. Throughout this period, he had never intruded upon our conversations, respecting the alliance that had developed between the group of white researchers and his family (his father was working with Milan). Now he took a small stool and joined us. We were seated on the floor as women do. Without hesitation, Magendaua started asking him questions about the carvings. But he had no intention to divulge to us anything of these mythic secrets of men.

Husband: "Scenes from *naven* I just carve like that. I don't know anything exact about it. There are surely mythic stories about them. I do not know them."

He now looks straight at me.

Husband: "Why didn't you bring tobacco for me?"

Florence: "I didn't think of it. I haven't seen you for a long time."

Husband: "You can give Magendaua the tobacco for me. You are a bad woman."

Magendaua's husband is annoyed. The question about the *naven* carvings that Magendaua asked him before was like an invitation to divulge further secrets. He rightly assumes that if Magendaua demands this kind of information when I am around, she would have given away his men's house secrets. And he is furious with me because he holds me accountable for having enticed his wife to do so. He is now enticing me into giving him tobacco. My reaction to his challenge is such as the Iatmul would show. I present myself as ashamed, turn my head away, throw a quick glance at Magendaua and her husband, and then look down on the floor. Now I am changing, half-black, half-white woman, in a manner such as the Iatmul's in their transvestite disguise. Both respond with roaring laughter.

Husband: "I was joking—we are friends."

Silence.

"You and I, we are men, Magendaua is our wife."

Magendaua points to my breasts and says: "A man with breasts?"

Husband (toward me): "Tell her that during initiation, men in the men's house turn into women and develop breasts. I too have breasts."

Magendaua: "I will check this tonight."

Husband: "Tomorrow the initiation will be over, and I will no longer have breasts."

As he is speaking, he gets up, puts the stool away, and goes back into the men's house.

Florence: "How the three of us were just talking, only in *naven* does one talk like this. Your husband, you, and I did a *naven* together. I became a man. I was like a dressed-up *yau*. Your husband turned into a *wau* and claimed he had breasts. All the while you remained the mother."

Magendaua: "That is so."

Magendaua's husband was visibly irritated, as his wife was now asking him about men's secrets. He assumed an aggressively demanding posture: "Give me some tobacco!" This was well justified. Two persons from his closest familial group were conducting daily conversations with the whites, who were rich in material possessions and over whom one could always take advantage. Yet he remained excluded, and, as if this wasn't enough, he was asked to furnish information. The form of his demand was appropriate not just in respect to us whites but also in relation to the social role of Iatmul women who provide daily food and stimulants for their kin. I reacted to his reproach as the Iatmul would do, that is, I acknowledged his right to tobacco, but I concealed my irritation behind a shameful facial expression. I became different, changing my cultural identity. Immediately, he started a *naven*-like verbal altercation with me, and Magendaua took part in it. Now I felt that I had altered myself yet again, this time in respect to my sexual identity—first I was declared to be a husband of Magendaua, then a father's sister in male costume. *Naven* was in the air; several *naven* performances for the newly initiated young men were simultaneously taking place in the village. This contest with her husband further stabilized my relationship with Magendaua.

I Am Not Me, You Are Not You

Relationships between two persons, insofar as they are marked by a deep, mutual, emotional investment, reveal important facts of life. The practice of psychoanalysis consists in a continuously renewed attempt to make transparent the forms and phases of such a relationship—in this instance, between two adults. How did Magendaua experience the relationship with me? How did she deal with it? How did I deal with this relationship? What is the connection of this relationship with the *naven* ritual? We find a comparable intensity in the relationship between lovers or between mother and child. Characteristically, Iatmul life is carried by the ceaseless process of emerging and dissolving groups. All economic, ritual, and leisure activities are group activities. In such groups, the cathexis—the emotional investment in the human object—takes on the particular forms of distribution and fragmentation. Whether a group is in a calm or an aggressive mood, playful or pursuing a task in earnest, it appears that the relationships constituting Iatmul groups sidestep or even prevent the development of a deep cathexis focused on an individual.

As in any culture, every love relationship is continuously under threat from outside or from inside. Conflict and rivalry arise frequently among the Iatmul, individuals struggle with one another, and heavy aggressive feelings are directly expressed. Magendaua reported on such behavior as her co-wife biting off her finger and she, in turn, biting her co-wife's cheek and getting a taste of human flesh. The typical Iatmul solution to this and all other kinds of heavy tension in relationships is to separate. They say that in such a situation one shows one's back to the other. After a while, new encounters will occur between them.

The mother-child relationship is different. As long as the mother does not abandon her child, as long as she provides for her child and enjoys its growth, the mother-child relationship cannot be, to use the Iatmul image, "ended by showing one's back." The infant requires and solicits continuous attention. As Iatmul always say: "Never leave the infant alone." This is a particular form of mutual dependence and cathexis. In Iatmul culture, children quickly become quite autonomous in their social life. Already as babies, carried around by their elder siblings, infants participate in gatherings of the autonomous children's groups that roam without adult supervision. Meanwhile, the mother goes fishing or to the market with her adult female group, unimpeded by the infant. Nevertheless, during the first two years of life, prior to weaning, the mother-child relationship remains a laboratory of cathexes and dependence.

What was the significance of the *naven* Magendaua spontaneously produced for the baby? When I succeeded by my interventions to recenter her transference on my person, she experienced anew a challenge similar to what she is continuously experiencing with the demands of her baby for attention—a baby capable of focusing on her as well as inciting her to focus on it. When she conducts the *naven* ritual, she relates not only to her baby's action but also to mine. She responds to my focusing on her by means of responding to the "looking back" of her infant, that is, by producing a *naven*. Interestingly, the Iatmul integrate the whites into their mythology in a similar way when they equate the whites coming to the Sepik area with their own ancestors coming back from the land of dead. We believe that in the *naven*, everybody who participates acquires a transvestite quality or, more to the point, an altered identity. Magendaua transformed herself into an ancestor. The baby saw (and felt) a transformed mother. For Magendaua also, her baby was transformed into an ancestor. She was no longer just this Magendaua, and he was no longer this baby boy. A third thing had intervened, namely, a mythological dimension of filiation. All Iatmul know that living individuals are incarnations of the ancestors, both recent and from the primeval time. However, this phrasing suggests a simple equivalence of the kind one finds in a dictionary, a sort of logical operation. By contrast, in the lived experience of the ritual action, the transvestitism and additional forms of altering identity allowed Magendaua to ease the emotional pressure in the object dependence and to expand her playground to the network of cultural meanings and behavioral patterns. She thus maintained her psychic motility as well as the level of her ego-functions.

For the Iatmul, a relationship between two people marked by a high level of cathexis seemed to be dangerous. Magendaua employed diverse cultural patterns available to her to manage our relationship as it was developing within the frame of the ethno-psychoanalytic conversations. She played with the idea of leaving me alone and formed projective phantasies about Ruth. She tried to involve several other women in our meetings, and she performed the baby *naven* in front of me. Lastly, helped by her husband, she involved me in a *naven*-like verbal altercation with him. The trajectory of actions in this last-mentioned situation followed the line of elaboration in any typical *naven* performance. His jocular talking style, my shameful gesture, the transvestite mode of experiencing sexual identity in which boundaries and positions are blurred, crystallized, and then dissolved, all seemed to represent well the dynamics of the ritual performance in *naven*. In the course of a *naven*, relationships, identity, and dependency become relativized and fluctuating formations. By going through the ritual action, people are once again able to become active and available in the extended network of social relations.

Magendaua Takes Her Leave

Magendaua received the news that her brother had died in Rabaul, and she joined the mourning community of women. Even in these circumstances, we continued our daily meetings. As my departure approached, I told Magendaua that Milan and I would travel to Rabaul to visit the settlements of Iatmul migrants.

She and her husband gave me a great deal of information about this town in which they had lived for seven years. They told me how to contact people from Palimbei living there.

Magendaua asked me whether I would go with her to the nearby lake the next day. She wanted to show me the damage created by the salvinia weed that infected the waters. Then I would be able to explain to the Iatmul in Rabaul what was happening in the village and why one could now catch fish only in the Sepik River. I soon got the impression that I was going to Rabaul on behalf of Magendaua and her husband.

A day or two later I met Magendaua in a crowded house containing the mourning women. The atmosphere was calm and relaxed. All the women present wanted to know everything about my impending travels. When Magendaua explained that she would like to show me the lake everybody approved. We left the house and the village and walked into the vast grass country. The rising sun was getting hot and the walk seemed to me surprisingly long. Was it because of the sun or that Magendaua was taking an unusual route? She stopped at a small shady grove, and then she looked at the expanse of the lake, slowly making a broad movement with her hand. The surface of the water was completely overgrown with ugly weed as though covered with a thick carpet. No canoe could come through here, and the fish were dying under the salvinia due to a lack of oxygen. After a while we turned back, but before long Magendaua stopped again and pointed to a big old tree.

Magendaua: "My father was hiding in this tree when they shot him."

Florence: "I heard a lot about your father."

Magendaua: "I know. Now you see where he was killed."

Now I understood why she had taken the roundabout way. She wanted to show me the place where her father had been murdered. He took on the shape of a wild boar that tore into pieces all of his murderers. Although all those involved in his murder were long dead, the lone boar stalks forever through the forests and attacks humans. Having resolved now how to deal with my leaving her behind, Magendaua looked back at the cruel destiny of her father. She had begun and maintained a relationship with me, a white woman, without letting herself become seduced by that relationship in the way her father had when he admired and served the colonial power. Magendaua always managed to preserve her autonomy vis-à-vis myself. She was able to hold onto her culture in a creative way as through *naven* performances when she experienced the powerful feelings in our relationship that could tip her off balance, as might have been the case with her father. Magendaua was not in danger of becoming a lonely wild boar incapable of looking back. She knew the expressive pantomimes, and she will continue to roll her eyes, show her tongue, move her body to and fro, wildly rising and lowering her arms and hands. Other people will dance *naven* for her when she will be looking back on those whom she counts as herself.

Florence Weiss holds a position as Senior Lecturer at the Institute of Ethnology at the University of Basel, Switzerland. She is trained in anthropology, political science, and psychoanalysis. She has carried out repeated and extended fieldwork in Papua New Guinea, mainly among the Iatmul people, and has done research in West Africa and, since 1990, in Eastern Europe. She is active internationally as a supervisor in several research projects. Her publications include *Conversations au bord du fleuve mourant: Ethnopsychanalyse chez les Iatmouls de Papouasie/Nouvelle-Guinée* (1987, with F. and M. Morgenthaler), "'Big Man' and 'Big Woman' in the Village—Elite in the Town" (1998, with M. Stanek), *Die dreisten Frauen: Eine Begegnung in Papua-Neuguinea* (2001), and *Vor dem Vulkanausbruch: Meine Freundinnen in Rabaul* (2001).

Milan Stanek is an anthropologist and ethno-psychoanalyst. His appointments include Senior Lecturer at the Institute of Ethnology, University of Zurich (1986–1996); Supervisor at the Verbund für Psychoanalytische Sozialarbeit in Berlin (1997–2003); and, since 2004, Senior Lecturer at the Institute of Slavic Cultures, University of Basel. His publications include "Social Structure of the Iatmul" (1990); "'Big Man' and 'Big Woman' in the Village—Elite in the Town" (1998, with F. Weiss); and "Introduction" in the edited collection, *Chaos und Entwicklung: Theorie und Praxis Psychoanalytisch Orientierter Sozialer Arbeit* (1999).

Notes

1. The book *Naven* was preceded by the article "Social Structure of the Iatmul People," which was published in the Australian journal *Oceania* in 1932. Bateson's first field stay in Papua New Guinea was among the Baining of New Britain in 1927. His first short trip up the Sepik River occurred in 1929. His first longer stay among the Iatmul was in 1930 (6 months in Mindimbit), the second in 1932–1933 (15 months in Kanganamun and Palimbei), and the last in 1938 (8 months in Tambunum). Cf. Bateson (1932: 245; [1936] 1965: 4) and Mead (1964: 349). Cf. also Stanek (1983a: 445n7).
2. See David Lipset's (1982) brilliant biographical as well as theoretical account of Bateson's scientific achievements.
3. Fieldwork was conducted by the authors in 1972–1974, 1979–1980, 1984, and 1989–1990.
4. "*Naven* was a study of the nature of explanation. The book contains of course details about Iatmul life and culture, but it is not primarily an ethnographic study, a retailing of data for later synthesis by other scientists" (Bateson 1965: 280–281; cf. also 257).
5. See Hauser-Schäublin (1977), Schindlbeck (1980), Schmid and Schmid (1992), Schuster (1974), Stanek (1983a), Wassmann (1991), and Weiss (1981). Further publications based on fieldwork among the Iatmul are by Stanek (1982, 1984, 1990, 1991), by Stanek and Weiss (1998), and by Weiss (1987, 1990, [1991] 2001, 1994a, 1994b, 1994c, 1995, [1999] 2001). See the bibliography of M. Schuster in Hauser-Schäublin (1994: 377–388).
6. Fritz Morgenthaler (1919–1984) was a Swiss physician, psychoanalyst, anthropologist, and painter. Salient themes of his work encompass psychoanalytical technique (1978), sexuality (1984), interpretation of dreams (1986), and, with Paul Parin and Goldy Parin-Matthey, ethno-psychoanalysis in West Africa (see Parin, Morgenthaler, and Parin-Matthey [1963] 1966, [1971] 1980). Further publications by Morgenthaler include discussions on the *naven* ritual (1974, 1977).
7. See the critical assessment by Mimica (2003).

8. In the tradition of Sachs ([1937] 1996) and Devereux (1951), the Parins and Morgenthaler had employed the method of regular conversations while doing ethno-psychoanalytic fieldwork in a traditional West African society. They stayed in the communities of the Dogon of Mali, and later among the Agni of Ivory Coast (Parin, Morgenthaler, and Parin-Matthey [1963] 1966, [1971] 1980). See also Boyer and Grolnick (1989).

9. Morgenthaler, Weiss, and Morgenthaler ([1984] 1987) render analytic conversations with six Iatmul persons, Weiss ([1991] 2001) with one woman, and Weiss ([1999] 2001) with three women.

10. Out of over 50 conversations with Magendaua conducted in the field, Weiss recorded 32 conversations in Morgenthaler, Weiss, and Morgenthaler ([1984] 1987: 144–193). In the present essay, Weiss quotes in full 9 of these.

11. Until quite recently, as part of the colonial inheritance, most villages in Papua New Guinea used to have one or several rest houses and a latrine for visiting government patrols. Typically, the patrols were made up of a patrol officer (*kiap*), several policemen (*polis, polisman*), one or several interpreters, and carriers (*kago-boi*). That is why these buildings were called *haus kiap* and *haus polis* (police house). One of the duties of the government-appointed village headmen (*luluai* and *tultul*) was to ensure the maintenance of these houses.

12. "Avec l'ethnopsychanalyse ... le projet devient plus ambitieux. A l'étude 'du dehors' par observation des comportements culturels, ces disciplines associent l'étude 'du dedans' pour laquelle l'interprétation culturelle passe par la connaissance des réactions d'individu à individu ... C'est une leçon d'apprentissage du vivre ensemble, malgré l'écart des cultures et les obstacles intérieures ou extérieurs."

13. Magendaua splits her inner objects into 'good' and 'bad', projecting the bad feelings onto Ruth and conserving the good ones for Florence. This is what we call a 'treacherous collusion' (between Magendaua and Florence) rather than a 'good' relationship, which would inevitably contain ambivalent attitudes properly attached to one and the same person—namely, to Florence.

14. To address the 'content' would mean to tell Magendaua: "Look, your unconscious phantasy of the archaic, menacing mother you have now transferred on the person of Ruth." This sort of 'interpretation' we preferred to avoid. To address the splitting 'in a formal way' would mean here to propose a meeting with Ruth, in order to meet the 'real' Ruth. Then, Magendaua could, hopefully, recenter her phantasm on Florence, i.e., encounter it in Florence and work with it in relationship with Florence.

References

Bateson, G. 1932. "Social Structure of the Iatmul People of the Sepik River." *Oceania* 2, no. 3: 245–291; no. 4: 401–453.

_____. [1936] 1965. *Naven: A Survey of the Problems Suggested by a Composite Picture of the Culture of a New Guinea Tribe Drawn from Three Points of View.* Stanford: Stanford University Press.

Boyer, B., and S. Grolnick, eds. 1989. *The Psychoanalytic Study of Society: Essays in Honor of Paul Parin.* Hillsdale, NJ: Analytic Press.

Devereux, G. 1951. *Reality and Dream: The Psychotherapy of a Plains Indian.* New York: International University Press.

_____. 1967. *From Anxiety to Method in the Behavioral Sciences.* The Hague: Mouton.

Hauser-Schäublin, B. 1977. *Frauen in Kararau: Zur Rolle der Frau bei den Iatmul am Mittelsepik, Papua New Guinea.* Basler Beiträge zur Ethnologie. Basel: Wepf.

_____, ed. 1994. *Geschichte und mündliche Überlieferung in Ozeanien.* Basler Beiträge zur Ethnologie. Basel: Wepf.

Houseman, M., and C. Severi. [1994] 1998. *Naven or the Other Self: A Relational Approach to Ritual Action.* Trans. M. Fineberg. Leiden: Brill. First published in 1994 as *Naven ou le donner à voir: Essai d'interprétation de l'action rituelle.* Paris: CNRS-Éditions.

Juillerat, B. 1999. "Séparation, retour, permanence: Le lien maternel dans le rituel *naven* des Iatmul." *L'Homme* 151: 151–179.

Lipset, D. 1982. *Gregory Bateson: The Legacy of a Scientist.* Boston: Beacon Press.

Lutkehaus, N., C. Kaufmann, W. Mitchell, D. Newton, L. Osmundsen, and M. Schuster. 1990. *Sepik Heritage: Tradition and Change in Papua New Guinea.* Durham, NC: Carolina Academic Press.

Mead, M. 1949. *Male and Female: A Study of the Sexes in a Changing World.* New York: Morrow.

———. 1964. *Continuities in Cultural Evolution.* New Haven, CT, and London: Yale University Press.

Mimica, J. 2003. "Out of the Depths of Saurian Waters: On Psycho-Bakhtinianism, Ethnographic Countertransference, and Naven." *Anthropological Notebooks* 9, no. 1: 5–47.

Morgenthaler, F. 1974. "Die Stellung der Perversion in Metapsychologie und Technik." *Psyche* 12: 1077–1098.

———. 1977. "Verkehrsformen der Perversion und Perversion der Verkehrsformen." *Kursbuch 49.* Pp. 166–182 in Morgenthaler 1984.

———. 1978. *Technik: Zur Dialektik der psychoanalytischen Praxis.* Frankfurt am Main: Syndikat.

———. 1984. *Homosexualität, Heterosexualität, Perversion.* Frankfurt am Main: Qumran.

———. 1986. *Der Traum: Fragmente zur Theorie und Technik der Traumdeutung.* Frankfurt am Main: Edition Qumran im Campus Verlag.

Morgenthaler, F., F. Weiss, and M. Morgenthaler. [1984] 1987. *Conversations au bord du fleuve mourant: Ethnopsychanalyse chez les Iatmouls de Papouasie/Nouvelle-Guinée.* Trans. M. Picard. Genf: Zoé. First published 1984 as *Gespräche am sterbenden Fluss: Ethnopsychoanalyse bei den Iatmul in Papue-Neuguinea.* Frankfurt am Main: Fischer.

Parin, P., F. Morgenthaler, and G. Parin-Matthey. [1963] 1966. *Les blancs pensent trop.* Paris: Payot.

———. [1971] 1980. *Fear Thy Neighbor as Thyself: Psychoanalysis and Society among the Agni of West Africa.* Chicago: University of Chicago Press.

Sachs, W. [1937] 1996. *Black Hamlet: The Mind of an African Negro Revealed by Psychoanalysis.* Baltimore: Johns Hopkins University Press.

Schindlbeck, M. 1980. *Sago bei den Sawos.* Basler Beiträge zur Ethnologie. Basel: Wepf.

Schmid, J., and C. K. Schmid. 1992. *Söhne des Krokodils.* Basler Beiträge zur Ethnologie. Basel: Wepf.

Schuster, M. 1974. "Neuguinea-Expedition des Ethnologischen Seminars der Universität Basel 1972/74." *Information Bulletin der Schweizerischen Ethnologischen Gesellschaft,* Genève 1: 13–17.

Silverman, E. K. 2001. *Masculinity, Motherhood and Mockery: Psychoanalyzing Culture and the Iatmul Naven Rite in New Guinea.* Ann Arbor: University of Michigan Press.

Stanek, M. 1982. *Geschichten der Kopfjäger: Mythos und Kultur der Iatmul auf Papua-Neuguinea.* Cologne: Eugen Diederichs.

———. 1983a. *Sozialordnung und Mythik in Palimbei: Bausteine zur ganzheitlichen Beschreibung einer Dorfgemeinschaft der Iatmul, East Sepik Province, Papua New Guinea.* Basler Beiträge zur Ethnologie. Basel: Wepf.

———. 1983b. "Les travestis rituels des Iatmul." Pp. 163–171 in *Océanie le masque au long cours,* ed. F. Lupu. Rennes: Ouest France.

———. 1984. *Einführung in das Ritualsystem der Iatmul, Mittelsepik, Papua-Neuguinea: Mit Verzeichnis der Ritualobjekte.* Basel: Museum für Völkerkunde, Fiche Sepik-Dokumentation 3–04/05.

———. 1990. "Social Structure of the Iatmul." Pp. 266–273 in Lutkehaus et al. 1990.

———. 1991. "Mythologie und Machtverhältnisse in der primitiven Gesellschaft." Pp. 226–263 in *Ethnologie im Widerstreit: Kontroversen über Macht, Geschäft, Geschlecht in fremden Kulturen,* ed. E. Berg et al. Munich: Trickster.

_____. 1994. "The Naven Ritual of the Iatmul and the Role of Dramatic Techniques in the Ritual Performance." Pp. 27–63 in *Images and Enactments: Possible Worlds in Dramatic Performance*, ed. G. Aijmer and Å. Boholm. Göteborg, Sweden: IASSA.

Stanek, M., and F. Weiss. 1998. "'Big Man' and 'Big Woman' in the Village—Elite in the Town: The Iatmul, Papua New Guinea." Pp. 309–327 in *Common Worlds and Single Lives: Constituting Knowledge in Pacific Societies*, ed. V. Keck. Oxford: Berg.

Wassmann, J. 1991. *The Song of the Flying Fox*. Boroko, Papua New Guinea: Cultural Studies Division, National Research Institute.

Weiss, F. 1981. *Kinder schildern ihren Alltag: Die Stellung des Kindes im ökonomischen System einer Dorfgemeinschaft in Papua New Guinea (Palimbei, Iatmul, Mittelsepik)*. Basler Beiträge zur Ethnologie. Basel: Wepf.

_____. 1987. "Sprache und Geschlecht bei den Iatmul in Papua Neuguinea: Untersuchungen zum Verhältnis von ethnologischer Forschung und Sprachgebrauch." Pp. 151–188 in *Oralité: Beiträge zur Problematik im Umgang mit mündlichen Überlieferungen*, ed. M. Schlechten. Bern: Schweizerische Ethnologische Gesellschaft.

_____. 1990. "The Child's Role in the Economy of Palimbei." Pp. 337–342 in Lutkehaus et al. 1990.

_____. [1991] 2001. *Die dreisten Frauen: Ethnopsychoanalytische Gespräche in Papua-Neuguinea*. Frankfurt am Main: Fischer.

_____. 1994a. "Die Beziehung als Kontext der Datengewinnung: Ethnopsychoanalytische Gesichtspunkte im Forschungsprozess." Pp. 23–47 in *Vielstimmiges Gedächtnis. Beiträge zur Oral History*, ed. G. Spuhler et al. Zurich: Chronos.

_____. 1994b. "Die Unterdrückung der Fraueninitiation: Zum Wandel des Ritualsystems der Iatmul." Pp. 237–259 in B. Hauser-Schäublin 1994.

_____. 1994c. "Rapports sociaux de sexe et structures socio-économiques dans la société Iatmul." *Recherches et travaux en anthropologie* 5: 3–55.

_____. 1995. "Zur Kulturspezifik der Geschlechterdifferenz und des Geschlechterverhältnisses: Die Iatmul in Papua-Neuguinea." Pp. 47–84 in *Das Geschlechterverhältnis als Gegenstand der Sozialwissenschaften*, ed. R. Becker-Schmidt and G.-A. Knapp. Frankfurt am Main: Campus.

_____. [1999] 2001. *Vor dem Vulkanausbruch: Meine Freundinnen in Rabaul*. Frankfurt am Main: Fischer.

Chapter 3

DESCENDED FROM THE CELESTIAL ROPE
From the Father to the Son, and from the
Ego to the Cosmic Self

Jadran Mimica

The people I write about are the four central Yagwoia-Angan territorial groups ('tribes') in the borderlands of the Eastern Highlands, Morobe, and Gulf Provinces of eastern Papua New Guinea (Mimica 1981, 1988, 1991). The empirical domains alluded to in the title are the Yagwoia cultural imaginary (Castoriadis 1987) and the archetypal dynamics that generate their kinship sociality. The specific configuration of relatedness that I will focus on could be glossed as 'patrifiliation'. This, however, is misleading. In terms of the Yagwoia self-constitution, one deals with a living and protracted process of the incorporation of the paternal 'bone'. Although it accounts for the generative dynamics between the father and his male and female children, it is the sonship that gives this osseous incorporation of the father its most acute articulation. The full complexity of this process is the subject of a separate monograph in preparation. Here I provide only one case study exemplifying at once the cosmo-ontological and psychic depths of this vicissitudinous dynamics, which is often marked by overt violence. But with or without such violence, the inner truth of the Yagwoia paternal incorporation is that the father's destiny is to be vanquished and replaced by his son's ascendance to his own procreative masculinity. In this determination of Yagwoia sonship, the incorporation of the father's bone irreducibly carries the signification of his imminent death for the sake of his continuation in the 'bone' implanted in and perpetuated by his son (Mimica 1991).

Given this immanence of life and death in the core of Yagwoia relatedness, I will state that as a realm of human material investments, interests, and activities, the Yagwoia societal field is a libidinal totality. But libido subsumes here its negative modality of mortido. The term 'mortido', which is nowadays rarely used (e.g., McDougall 1995: ix), designates here the destructive mode of psychic energy, which, in view of the Yagwoia facts, is the mirror-inverse of libido (cf. Spielrein [1912] 1994). My conception of libido is rooted in the classical tradition and embraces exactly those salient antinomies that figure in Freud's, Jung's, Abraham's, Klein's, and Fairbairn's formulations. This is so because the Yagwoia mode of existence, which I call 'ouroboric', articulates these antinomies with exuberant transparency and totalizing systematicity. Ouroboros is the archetypal image of the self-eating serpent (Neumann 1954), which among the Yagwoia has a unique mythopoeic manifestation as their self-created, androgynous Imacoqwa (The Great-One-He). This cosmic monad, whose eyes are the sun and moon, embodies, continuously generates, and sustains the world (Mimica 1981, 1988, 1991). Accordingly, he can be characterized as the 'Cosmic Self' and the container of everything that there is. Under the name of Imacoqwa,[1] he can be aptly glossed as the 'Father-of-All', and as such he is the immanent presence in all the denizens of his world-body, specifically in his human progeny. This is why a psychoanalytic exploration of the concrete Yagwoia simultaneously entails the exploration of this archetypal realm of their Cosmic Self.

It will be noted that in this text (and elsewhere, e.g., Mimica 2003b, 2003c, 2006), I consistently write about the Yagwoia un/conscious. I put it so precisely because the relation between consciousness and the unconscious is subject to diverse articulations in different life-worlds. Experientially, their mutual articulation does not conform to a universal dimensional topography, principally in terms of a distinction between psychic interiority and exteriority. Hence my use of the slash in 'un/conscious', which indicates that there is no a priori assumption made as to how and in what mode, if at all, something is unconscious in a given field of experience. This calibration varies between individuals and life-worlds, as well as between different periods within one and the same life-world. In terms of the Yagwoia life-world-specific ontological underpinnings of their experiences and existence, the basic dimensionality of their 'I-ness', such as interiority/exteriority and all its derivatives, is a radically different inner/outer field. Spirits no less than the soul, or any other presences experienced, for instance, in dreams, are not for the Yagwoia 'internal objects' composed of life-memories or archetypal images. They are entities either entirely autonomous (e.g., spirits) and external to a given 'I' (ego) or in a semi-detachable incorporative/excorporative relation with the body and 'I-ness', as, for instance, one's dream-soul-component.

The word 'ego' and its derivations 'egoic' and 'egoity' stress the irreducible boundedness of the primary, bodily sphere of the human experiential field and its constitution with regard to the dialectics of the body ego (Fleiss 1956, 1961; Schilder 1950) and its maternal envelopment (Klein [1932] 1989; Lacan 1977; Mahler, Pine, and Bergman [1975] 1985; Neumann 1954, [1973] 1988; Stern 1985). When I capitalize the word 'Self', I am referring to the realm of the radical, archetypal schemata of experience (Jung 1959, 1968, 1971), which in the Yagwoia life-world is objectified as the ouroboric Cosmic Self. This transpersonal Self is immanent in the egoic selfhood of every living and dead Yagwoia. This, in short, is the sphere of Yagwoia 'agency'. Accordingly, my psychoanalysis is phenomenologically grounded in the Yagwoia life-world. Their psychic being is accounted for with a maximal fidelity to its life-world constitution. So although my use of notions such as un/conscious, egoic self and internal objects is within the framework of psychoanalytic meta-psychological conceptualization, this is done as an interpretive exercise that both maintains and amplifies the ontological originality and existential integrity of the Yagwoia selfhood and life-world.

Among the Yagwoia, all humans are indeed a micro-cosmic manifestation of their macro-cosmos. In this perspective, the psychodynamics of a concrete ego and his or her intersubjective matrix is conterminous with the archetypal dynamics of the ego's life-world and its constitutive imaginary. As an archetypal structure of libidinal dynamics, ouroboros crystallizes the oral-grasping-ocular unity and nucleus of all drives. Here copulation is the mirror-inverse of sucking, biting, eating, looking, grabbing, and evacuation (vomiting, urinating, defecating, ocular emissions). Libido is mortido. The antinomies referred to above *are* intrinsic to the ouroboric libido, i.e., the life-death flow, which, needless to say, in a life-world like the Yagwoia, is the cosmic energy that generates and drives existence in toto.[2]

This intertwining of life and death underscores a specific ouroboric determination of Yagwoia existence (Mimica 1991, 1996, 2003a, 2003b, 2006), whereby there is no life of the human self without the simultaneous co-efficient of self-destruction. Father > son (F > S) incorporative dynamics, for which the indigenous image is 'planting', is taking place correlatively with the mother > child (M > C) incorporative self-circuity, characterized as 'eating'. Its libidinal substance is meat. Accordingly, these two modes of incorporation feed differentially into the kinship matrix, and both are articulated in the total flow of substances and societal exchange.

In the Yagwoia archetypal auto-symbolization of the existential flow, one of the principal images is a variant of the cosmic tree: closed in on itself, the branches and roots completely intertwine, and thus what is up is also down (Mimica 1981,

1988, 2003a, 2006). The F > S 'bone' progeneration figures in this cosmic arbo-real edifice as a process whereby the son, the male offshoot who originates as the hand = branch of his father's trunk = bone (*yekna*), progressively incorporates the father. The son thereby himself becomes the trunk = bone. In this ouroboric dialectic, the *latice* group[3] contains a ceaseless succession of F > S dyads. But the group itself—the container—has to become contained by the bodies it contains because the *latice* always and only subsists as the skeleton of its living members. At the same time, each *latice* group is substantiated in the fleshy envelope of the children external to it. These are the progeny that a *latice*'s women bear for the men of other *latice*s. Being the *latice*'s 'leaves', women detach from the branches and fly off to be the phallic womb-conduits[4] for the differential father > child (F > Ch) self-reproduction and bone self-generation of other *latice*s. The daughter is destined for the generation of the paternal trunk's 'outside' flesh of her children who, for her brother, are his sister's children. The son continues the paternal trunk's 'inside', the bone. In this transformative function, the daughter/woman is the bifurcator of her father's bone-potency. Through her generativity, she always refracts at once her bone-substance as her children's flesh and her husband's own bone (by means of his semen) into her children's bones. Cosmo-ontologically, woman is a phallic self-unity that is immanently self-twining and therefore is the generator of multiplicity. But for her generativity she needs the male inseminator, whose phallic self-unity creates inside her womb the unity of her and his procreative potency (see Mimica 1988, 1991, 2006).

The Case Study: QC and His Son QP

I will now focus on that aspect of the F > S incorporative dynamic which, following his death, will eventually result in the father becoming a benevolent and protective spirit of his children,[5] thus completing the dialectic of the ouroboric dynamics of fatherhood and sonship. The case in point is that of two Iqwaye-Yagwoia men:[6] QC and his son QP.[7] The former was by far the most lethal warrior-killer in the period prior to the abolition of warfare by the Australian government in the early 1950s. In his younger days (from the early 1940s into the 1950s), he was also a shaman and a dream-seer (*wuoca-qale*) who could foretell a person's fate or identify an unknown culprit responsible for, say, a theft or a murder. These were the soul-powers he had originally received from the wild forest spirits. He possessed these powers in addition to his supreme killing capacity, which had been forged as a power of his soul (*umpne*) after his nose-piercing in the context of his all-male inseminatory growth inside the bachelors' house.[8] Importantly, the killing-power component of his soul was co-developed with his shamanistic-visionary powers. However, the latter were virtually extinguished following the death of his mother, whom he used to abuse physically by beating her with a wooden club (*napiye*). Reflecting the common opinion, his son QP told me that it was his father's abuse that had killed her. After her death, his dream-seer vision ceased because, as a spirit of the dead, she depotentiated him by blocking off his soul-powers.[9]

This degree of explicit matricidal self-actualization is rare among the Yag-woia men. Rather, on account of what is, by and large, a volatile (schizoid) structuration of the male contra-sexual (feminine) self-image and the dominance of the primary maternal super-ego (Mimica 2001, 2003b, 2003c, 2006), men's matricidal intentionality is overwhelmingly displaced onto women as wives and onto women in general. It is also transmuted through the pursuit of extra-marital sexual relations in which the aggressive-destructive current is directed at the lovers' husbands. These affairs are a prevalent mode of articulation and sustenance of Yagwoia (male and female) narcissistic equilibrium and 'omni/m/potence'.[10] In QC's case, the articulation of his feminine self-image, mediated by the maternal self-object circuitry, which took on an extremely negative libidinal value, was quite explicitly indicated in the self-evaluation of his fellatio practice.[11] He told his son that because many men had inseminated him, later when he became a warrior and fought, many men wanted to fight only him. Since he was an irresistible attractor, they would come after him, and he in turn would kill them all—that is, engage in destructive 'copulation'.

By contrast, another man, who was QC's co-initiate, gave a self-evaluation that indicates an exact mirror-image of QC's homosexual libidinal determination. Describing himself as a young fellator, he stressed that many inseminators would 'nest' on him because they liked him. He was their pole of attraction.[12] As a consequence of his homosexually primed attraction, later on, when he switched to the heterosexual sector of life, many women yearned for him because he was sexually attractive to them. Indeed, this man was never a fighter of any consequence but had a reputation as an excellent singer (*aapiy-ice*) and fornicator whom women desired. Reciprocally, he desired them, and he acted it out in the appropriate erotic mode. He was not known as a woman abuser and was probably not given to it.

By his own admission, and affirmed as such by other men, QC was a voracious fellator who actively sought numerous men. His son told me that he heard from other men that QC was like an insatiable woman going from one young bachelor to another. They all wondered what kind of man he would become. Then, when he started fighting, they saw the kind of bone-power he had developed. His passive self-positioning is implied in the formulation of the fighting situation in which, as it were, his opponents would attack him rather than him targeting them. However, to the extent that QC's original ingestive-homoerotic desire flourished in warfare, it was lived as such through deadly, efficient, destructive conjunctions.[13] Indeed, I was told that among the Iqwaye-Yagwoia, there was no man who went through more purificatory rites than the old QC. This procedure is obligatory for a killer after he has shattered the skull and brains of his victim. This is the foremost mode of killing a human being—to release the semenal substance from the head-container by shattering it with a war-club. This and this alone is the true deed that makes a man the supreme warrior-killer (*aa'mny malamlace*). All other modes of conjunctive destruction, the most common being shooting with arrows, are overshadowed by the war-club destruction. In this act, the fusion of the killer and the victim is total. The purificatory rite is essential, otherwise the killer will remain impregnated with the blood and marrow (semen = brains) substance of the victim and be exposed to the afflictions of the latter's spirit. One of QC's life-anxieties was from the likely retributions of the spirits of his numerous victims.[14]

In QC, then, the ouroboric libido had primarily the determination of the irrepressible and destructive mortido. It was never sufficiently transformed and expanded into a libidinal generativity of life through erotic bodily conjunction. Although married to four women (three died in the 1960s and 1970s), he had only three children: one by the first, second, and fourth wife, respectively; the third wife was barren. His son was the 'single one', and so were the two daughters, meaning that they had no full cross-sex, same-birth-order brothers.[15]

Starting from mid-adolescence, QC's relationship with his son, QP, became primarily and starkly conflictual and remained so throughout QC's life. The first major conflict ensued when QP went to his mother's help to protect her from one of her husband's numerous beatings. When she died (in the mid-1960s), QP was working as an indentured copra plantation laborer in New Britain, and a few months passed before he learned of her death. In his grief, he burned approximately 25 Australian pounds. Later, when he returned to the village, he burned another 10 pounds and also cut his forehead. All this is symptomatic of the intensity of his symbiotic maternal-feminine attachments, which subsume, of course, his (deceased) mother's brother (MB), and the mother's brother's son (MBS) who succeeded his own father as QP's root 'mother's breast'.[16] Reciprocally, this maternal self-figuration as the mother's son is also symptomatic of his own male-femaleness articulated in his kinship position as a mother's breast (i.e., MB) to his close and classificatory sisters' children.

When QP got married, the relationship between him and his father took on a unilaterally negative and resentful turn. It became evident that QP's father had 'eaten' the shells received for his patrilateral half-sister (i.e., QP's father's first wife's daughter), as well as for his fourth wife's much younger sister. QC took the latter into fosterage with the explicit aim for her to be his son's (QP's) sister for whom he would get a bride-price (shells/money).[17] This is why the girl's upbringing was entrusted to QP's own mother, whose maternal care, and therefore her bodily-substantial self-transmission, had also brought up her son. QP told me that in order to drum into his wife that she should look after this girl as if she were truly her own daughter, QC belabored her—for good measure.[18] QC's view, from which he never deviated, was that in order to make other people obey, you must always be harsh with them or else they will just follow their own will. His most impressive dictum was that when there are too many people around you, you cannot eat in peace. Therefore, you have to kill them off. This was the reason he gave for killing, among others, some of his affinal relations. Overall, QC had a formidable view of human intersubjectivity that he lived by in no uncertain terms. This is why I used to refer to him as Jean-Paul QC, in honor of Sartre, whose dictum "Hell is other people" had unwittingly found an extraordinary resonance in this Yagwoia 'great killer' of human beings.

In the core of every human being dwells an infant. QC had a modicum of infantility, but his most characteristic modality was brought to my attention by children. It concerned his craving for food. Young boys often told me how QC demanded that they give him small rodents and birds that they had caught and fried in the fire. In one respect, they regarded it as appropriate because, as an old man, he was their 'older brother' (*katoqwa*), a coeval. But they also deemed his demands to be fueled by greed, for every Yagwoia will readily acknowledge that small rodents, birds, and lizards are irreducibly the food items for little children and younger women. No man who cares about his manly selfhood and countenance would yield to the cravings of this most embarrassing and compromising mode of alimentary pettiness.[19] QC, quite clearly, had no such qualms.

QC was also renowned for flouting the most widely adhered to Yagwoia dietary taboo against eating python meat. For the Yagwoia, the sheer suggestion of eating snakes is met with unrestrained revulsion. Nevertheless, python meat is reputedly tasty and greasy; it is relished as a delicacy among the Yaqauwye, the Ankave-speaking neighbors of the Yagwoia in the interior of the Gulf Province.[20] Many Yagwoia visit these people especially to attend their mourning termination feasts, which feature opulent quantities of meat, including python meat. But with the exception of QC and another Yagwoia man—his classificatory matrilateral brother, who reportedly gorged on it—no Yagwoia would partake of python meat. On such occasions QC used to mock his fellow Yagwoia by saying to them: "So this something [python meat] is your father!? You all came from this!?" biting into the sumptuous morsel as he did so. In this phrasing he was invoking Imacoqwa (The Great-One-He), the self-created androgynous cosmic monad. One of Imacoqwa's cosmogonic identities is the red python and the species of eel called *ipiye*. QC, then, had no reservations about eating his cosmic Father-of-All (see Mimica 1981).

On one occasion I heard a girl weeping bitterly and throwing tantrums for an hour or so. I eventually went to the homestead to see what was going on. There was a small gathering around the earth oven, and the girl in question was QC's little daughter (by his fourth wife), crying and beating him erratically in spasmodic fits of rage. He was just sitting next to her, impassively enduring her onslaughts. Every so often, when she thrashed him in the face, he would move slightly and angrily growl at her, but without trying to shake her off. It turned out that she had caught a bird that has a characteristic habit of swinging its body while walking on the ground. For this reason it is a prohibited food item for developing female children because later they might develop the same kind of hip-swinging manner of walking and thus unduly advertise their sexuality as if they were only looking for men to grab them. Accordingly, when the girl cooked the bird and was about to eat it, her father told her that, alas, this morsel was taboo for her, so he ate it instead. No amount of explanation as to why it was taboo would placate her, and thus QC put up with his flabbergasted daughter's rage. Other people were rather supportive of QC and thought that he had done the right thing, but one younger man whispered into my ear words to the effect that "we know what kind of man QC is."

As a government-appointed village official (*luluai*), QC did not hesitate to push his interests. He regularly appropriated the fines he would extract from individual villagers who committed various offenses against the government's law. These were heard and settled in the local courts, but instead of taking the fine payments to the government office at the station, QC frequently kept them for himself, especially if they were small amounts.

In respect of shells, QC was as avaricious as he was skilled in acquiring them, and in this he was aided by his relentless desire and will to obliterate. He used to appropriate shells from his vanquished victims. For instance, in the period following the pacification of the northwest Angan regions, he ventured into the Baruya territory accompanied by another great warrior whose specialty was immaculate sharpshooting with bow and arrows. There, in response to a threat, QC killed two men and managed to escape with all their shells. This was in the late 1950s. He also used to go on trading expeditions. But despite all the wealth he gained, by and large, QC did not siphon off any of it to his son. Following his fight over the bride-price shells, in which the son (QP) physically overwhelmed the father, QP made clear to QC that, thereafter, he was not going to look after him for food, meat, or anything else. QP then oriented himself toward a close agnatic and much older brother (QM), who, through another link, was also his classificatory MBS (i.e., male mother). It was to QM that QP bestowed his good filial attitude. Furthermore, having incorporated his father's bone-power, he told his own father QC that for any piece of pork or game he might desire, he should look into QM's feces, because the latter is now like his proper father. QP insisted that the son gets the father's bone in any circumstances, but how he (the son) would relate to his father would depend on whether or not the father looked after his offshoot properly. QC was a "bad man,"[21] and especially a bad father, precisely because, to the extent that he ate the shells that he should have passed on to his son, he was like a man drinking his own semen. Instead, it should be his son's food and the means for his generation (Mimica 1991).

QP's rejection of his father could not be anything more than an expression of a self-conflictual schizoid attitude, for all along, in the ouroboric matrix of kinship self-generation, the predominant determination of relatedness is that of devouring-symbiosis. The father may well be no better than the son's refuse, but he is also the conduit of the primordial phallic bone-potency that has begotten him. The rejection is foremost a negative desire for the total incorporation of that very same potency which the father has in part siphoned, via shells and other means, into himself. In other words, the son who rejects is totally identified with the rejected father.

In QP, as in all Yagwoia initiated after his initiation cohort, all the way to the youngest generations of both men and women, the externally instituted cessation of warfare had not extinguished the reality of the drive to annihilate human life immanent in their life-world, i.e., themselves. Its overt articulation, however, became ever more vicissitudinous and subject to a high degree of self-conscious deliberation and inhibition. This had no parallel in the ouroboric existential milieu prior to its subjection to the 'New Law' first introduced by the Australian colonial state and then continued by the 'independent' national *Gavman* (government) of the 'sovereign' state of PNG.

QP's father embodied to the highest degree the once fundamental egoic value of the destruction of human life, being the irreducible facticity of the life = death flow. In this existential dimension, QP, however, experienced himself with a gradient of ambiguity. During his childhood and initiations (he was nose-pierced in the early to mid-1950s), he had all the diacritical experiences and spirit-showings that eventually would turn a boy under their sway into a deadly warrior. In this respect, the developmental trajectory of QP's soul was akin to that of his father. But because of the external intervention of the colonial government, he had no opportunity to kill a human being in the manner that would make him a true warrior-killer. In the course of his life, QP came to define himself primarily as a man who cares for other men and women and willfully abides by the government law.[22] He thereby posits himself as a "good man," over and against his father, precisely because he would rather preserve than destroy a human being. On the other hand, he often wondered what he would be like if he had grown up in his father's time. Would he have been a great warrior? By saying "I don't know" he would clearly convey a self-satisfied sense of himself, i.e., he knew that he would be both a warrior and a man of knowledge who knows also how to bring warfare to a halt. In this he would follow QNg, his father's patrilateral half-brother, who undoubtedly was the greatest of the Yagwoia "big-great"[23] men in living memory. QP self-consciously identified with him and received from him a great deal of his soul-power, namely, in the form of exquisite esoteric knowledge. QP eagerly imbibed and treasured it.

With regard to his initiatory progression toward his procreative manhood,[24] QP was in the last cohort of the Iqwaye-Yagwoia who endured the full weight of the traditional regime of life bound to the bachelors' house, but minus the most critical feature: the practice of 'sugar-cane eating' (i.e., fellatio). He was in the third cohort of co-initiates nose-pierced and made-by-men (i.e., homo-socialized) after the all-male transmission of the 'bone of bones' (semen) had already been abandoned. But as it happened, QP was also one of those few young men who discovered the practice independently and altogether outside of the traditional context, namely, when they went for the very first time to work as indentured laborers. Since their semen-giver was a white man, back in the village they were said to have received not 'bone' but 'iron', in concord with the view of the white man's (generically) superior power.

In QP's case, his own father and the 'other'[25] father (his father's patrilateral half-brother), QNg, wept upon learning that their son had got the taste of their own *yeki'/t/nye pi'/t/nye* (secret strength), and so of the white man's texture. QNg also told QP that now he would only have to kill a man, and he would be like his own father (F) and father's brother (FB). QNg assured QP that at the time he was nose-pierced, he wanted to show his cohort the basal practice, but other men objected to it.[26] On the whole, QP harbored an ambivalent resentment toward this profound omission. As he saw it, by not being fully shown the inner truth of the men-making practice, the hard work of self-regulation that he endured in his bachelorhood was somewhat void of its inner substance. Moreover, he had not become as fully a man as he otherwise could have, on a par with the older generations of men. There was, then, an ambivalent sense that he was cheated out of the male power that rightfully should have been his possession, just as all the men of yore greedily declare that their 'secret strength' is truly their exclusive possession and as such will vanish with them when they die. There will be no one man left to claim it as embodying it in himself, equally so with the substantiality of all the knowledge-power that belongs to this basal practice, which QP, however, did manage to incorporate to a degree not matched by anyone else. In this, in what I characterize as a 'gnoseophilic'[27] mode, he did amply compensate for missing out on the pure all-male semenal bone-power.

No matter how much QP willfully neglected and disparaged his father, every so often he would make a gesture of reapproach, and QC would do so similarly. As he was getting older, QC continued to voice his rancor with acid brutality fueled by his frustrated omni/m/potence. For instance, in early July 1978, QC had a nasty outburst at the homestead of his agnate, QM, whom his son preferred as a 'father' worthy of his (QP's) care. Early in the morning, QC began to work himself into a rage. He bitterly decried his son's neglect, accusing him of eating pork by himself, never willing to give some to his aging father. Then, when his rage reached the boiling point, he turned on his (fourth, and only surviving) wife, striking her several times with a stick.[28] QM's wife, O, went to her help by trying to stop him. This only enraged QC, and he slammed her a few times. Then QM tried to grab and pull the stick out of his hands, but the old QC in turn managed to hold onto it, exacting in the process a blow or two upon QM. Meanwhile, his wife ran away. Later on QM, who took it light-heartedly, commented: "What kind of a *qwolyana* [old man] is he!? Other men [of his age] would have given up on this kind of hard-headedness [characteristic of younger men]; another man [as old as QC] would work in his children's garden and look after them as if he were their mother. But QC is penis-active, selfish, and tries to be a match for young men!" For his part, QC wrapped up his rage by saying that now that he is old and divested of his strength,[29] they (the entire village collectivity) can look at him and brush him aside as if he were just another man, whereas before they all were his women.

Every so often, QP would give his father some money. For instance, when QP finished building his new house (in 1978), he spent about 30Kina on the payments for the women who cut and brought the *kunai* grass for the roof. Although he had enough of his own cash, he nevertheless accepted 20Kina from QC, who gave it to him as 'help'. Then some time later, QP gambled and won 40Kina. Since QC mentioned those 20K he had given his son earlier, QP gave him the lot (40K) "just to make him happy." When in 1979 QC returned from a very successful shell-finding tour, which took him and several other men all the way to Goroka, he gave QP one or two sets of *nggye-ilyce* (i.e., a set of five cowries) to reciprocate for those extra 20K he had received earlier. Their conflict notwithstanding, the flow of their substance to and fro was also generating their symbiotic rapprochement. In the ouroboric self-circuity, no matter how deeply inflicted the bites and cuts may be, the F > S bone cannot be broken. As the image of the self-eating serpent clearly suggests, the deeper the rupture of the tail, the more of it will be incorporated. There is no other way but from the tail into the mouth, whether from the father to the son or from the self to the mother. Either way, one is always on the way to self-consummation.

The Formation of the Father's Spirit-Presence

QC died in about 1989. To the extent that, while alive, his relationship with his son was fraught with conflict, rancor, and resentment, after his death QC became his son's protective spirit-presence. This was the final actualization of QC's desire, which he expressed while still alive. At that stage he aimed to transmit to QP the vestiges of his shamanistic soul-power for extracting sickness-objects. At times when QC was sick, he—that is, his soul—would have experiences (visions) in which he interacted with the wild forest spirits from whom he had originally received the power to extract sickness-objects. Such experiences have an auto-curative co-efficient and effect, even if the person has not self-consciously intended it as such. In several instances of grave sickness, when he thought that he was going to die, QC (or rather, his soul) would, in his visions, come to a stream with a waterfall and water-pool. Underneath the rock (over which the water falls) he would encounter the spirits of his first two wives, who would immediately ask him about the well-being of their two children, QP and his patri-half-sister Q. They would then pour water on him and send him back to continue looking after their children. After such an encounter, he would revive. It is clear that in his un/conscious, the maternal disposition of the two wives was determined entirely by their concern with their children's well-being. If he were in the throes of the negatively toned feminine imagos[30] (i.e., spirits), the soul encounter would be very different. The spirits would most likely try to pull him onto their side, that is, make him die. Instead, they sent him back to the abode of the living.

In such moments he used to tell his wife to go and fetch his son because he wanted to transfer this (shamanistic) soul-power to him. He often told QP that his soul (*umpne*)[31] had not abandoned him and was residing on his shoulder. As for his soul-power, which facilitated his strong garden work, QC said that he passed it on to QP's sons,[32] specifically those by his senior wife, whom QP came to neglect completely. Since QP was reluctant to acknowledge his first-born son as his own, his father expressly favored the child as his grand-kin replacement. It was his experience of rejection and neglect by QP that conditioned QC's orientation toward QP's neglected wife and her children.[33]

When he died, QC's soul was incorporated through the soul-incorporation rite.[34] This rite is primarily done to ensure that most of the soul-strength of an extraordinarily powerful person—in QC's case, the greatest Iqwaye warrior-killer—is drained away and siphoned into the living young men. Thus, when the rest of the soul becomes transformed into the immortal spirit of the dead (see Mimica 2003a), it will not be very powerful and will not be able to inflict too much harm upon the living. But the soul-incorporation rite notwithstanding, QP locked himself with his father's corpse in his hut and slept by his side for three days, making sure that QC would appear to him in dreams. This is not unusual behavior; some sons do this especially to receive knowledge that the deceased father had not passed on to them while yet alive. QP told me that throughout this period his father's corpse did not smell at all, thereby implying that QC's soul was still with him—otherwise, the body would have begun to bloat and decompose. Following the burial, a large death payment was made to QC's numerous 'mothers'.

Entering QP's '*Innenwelt*': The Dreams

The following dream, which QP had in January 1992, cogently illustrates his '*Innenwelt*'[35] and the reality and the structural significance that his paternal image has in the archetypal dimension of his un/conscious. In terms of QP's ego-consciousness and understanding, his father's spirit (*wopa ilymane*) is permanently present in the exteriority of the world. The spirit's self-manifestation is enabled by the interaction of QP's dream-soul-component, which becomes detached when he is asleep; it is in this condition that the soul can fully see both the spirits of the dead and the wild forest spirits.[36] The dream is quite long, and I will summarize only the first four sequences, while the crucial fifth sequence will receive a detailed examination. The terminal sequence is omitted. Regarding the wider context of this dream, I have to point out the significance of QP's relation to me, which is articulated in many of his dreams. Since my very first fieldwork (1977–1979), QP has cast me as his sister's son (ZS), and that determination significantly configures his relationship with me and my presence in his un/conscious.

The intensity of the psychic (intersubjective) reality of this configuration was brought out in one of his dreams (in approximately 1982), in which he dreamt of his patri-half-sister giving birth to me. QP saw the manifest birth imagery featuring in his dream as representing death, namely, that one of his close sister's children would die. That was certainly the case, and the dream effectively portended the death of QP's FFZS (= ZS), who was very close to him. Again, one can get a sense of the acuteness of the mirror-identity of life = death. This is the diacritical structural determination of the Yagwoia ouroboric libido. The dream imagery was but a specific expression of the Yagwoia cultural-imaginal (archetypal) dimension and, through it, the iconography of their existence.

In 1992 I resumed my field research following a six-year absence. Shortly after my return to the Yagwoia area, I had to fly out to Lae to get supplies. As an event in QP's experience, this resonated with my earlier departure (in 1986) from their world-body, (i.e., the Yagwoia abode). Hence, in the dream, the following occurs:

(1) He first sees an aircraft in which I return from Lae. It lands in a hamlet half-way between his primary residence in the mountains (fringe-forest area) and the government station, where the actual airstrip is located. Our reunion takes place there in the mode of the face-to-face greeting, whereby the full identification is

effected; that is, he is me and I am him. As we are about to start walking up to the village in the ranges, I tell him that an *ilymane* (spirit) is present in our vicinity. He asks where, I point to a stone and tell him to break it (i.e., make a hole). QP proceeds to break it (i.e., make a hole), and then he looks into it.[37] At that point I vanish, while he, startled, is looking for me. As he does so (searching for me), (2) a woman comes his way whom he does not recognize. Her face is blackened with ashes, the sign of mourning. As she heads toward him,[38] (3) his father QC appears. He comes to QP's face[39] and tells him: "It is *ilymane* (spirit)! Run, run away!" and QP duly runs off all the way to Mny (the government station). (4) Here he sees a white man whom he recognizes as Pilip (Philip) and tells him that he would like to learn to speak English. But the latter in turn says that he is not Pilip but Pita IO.[40] In disbelief QP embraces Pita IO's body and thereby establishes that the latter is indeed a black man, despite his white man appearance. QP wants to talk to him, but his father QC comes again and tells him that this is an *ilymane*, and therefore to get away. At this point QP flees so intensely that he flies up into the sky. (5) Having become sky bound, he looks down onto the earth, which has become very remote; he cannot discern trees, grass, or a house. QP is now in the middle between the sky and earth.[41] He worries since he has to descend onto the ground. Just as he is about to descend, a rope quickly drops from the sky all the way to the earth. QP looks up, but there is no tree from which this rope would be suspended. There is only this rope hanging by itself from the sky! QP grabs the celestial rope and comes down to the ground. His father reappears and takes him back to Ylq, his village in the ranges. (6) Here QC shows him his new house, which has all the desirable features associated with white people's dwellings—a tin roof and wooden floorboards.[42] When he sees his father's house, QP becomes overwhelmed with delight. QC tells him: "Later when I leave it, you can take this house. It is truly mine." They talk thus, which makes QP extremely happy.

The protective and profoundly beneficent position of the post-mortal (i.e., spirit of the dead) father-presence in QP's un/conscious could not be made more dramatically manifest. For QP, that was the dream's meaning. He plainly said that his father was now following him all the time, and that no spirit was going to interfere with him, no matter what. Why? "Because," QP said, "my father is staying at my face," and there is no way that a spirit would be able to affect his soul. The father is now in full-face (ocular) relation to him, and, accordingly, QP is repositioned vis-à-vis his father. It is the father who now beholds QP's self-projection and thus mediates his projective (and incorporative) identification with others. We shall see in the discussion of another dream that this facial identification with his father is symptomatic of the overall positive and exclusive articulation of QP's identificatory self-circuitry in and through his father, who is no longer despised and rejected as he was while alive.[43]

In this next dream, too, QP's father protects him from the imminent dangers of a motley collectivity of spirits of the dead, who lurk all over the place and make their living relatives sick, but here there has also occurred a critical event in QP's existential relationship with his own selfhood. I will characterize it as his cosmo-ontological determination, articulated most cogently in the fifth sequence of the dream experience. Every Yagwoia dream is an expression of its dreamer's overall psycho-cosmological equilibrium, that is, the equilibrium between the dreamer's egoity and his or her wider field of selfhood. The latter encompasses simultaneously the ego's living embodiment and its objectification qua and as the concrete world delimited by the sky and earth. In the Yagwoia life-world, the existential image of the world is the objectified image of Imacoqwa, their ouroboric archetypal Cosmic Self (Mimica 1981, 1988, 1991).

In this cosmo-ontological determination, the living dynamism of the 'intra-psychic' landscape, its spatiality and temporality, is simultaneously a manifestation of the fundamental archetypal dynamics of the dreamer's psychic being. Thus, moving through the concrete landscape is also a movement within the universal container—Imacoqwa's world-body. Its internal elemental dimensionality has a unique ouroboric self-mirroring structure whereby the sky mirrors the earth and vice-versa. Note that mirroring entails mirror-reversal, which is articulated in several modalities, all of which are variants of the Moebial-strip or the Kleinian bottle self-circuitry. Among other things, this accounts for the movements of the sun and the moon and their self-alternating effects, such as day and night. These generate the entire spectrum of circadian and seasonal-climatic periodicity and related phenomena, including, of course, the human sleep-wakefulness cycle and most diverse activities that accompany the diurnal > nocturnal self-transformative cyclicity, which creates the cosmic metabolism of the Yagwoia world-body. The Yagwoia cathexis of their 'eco-physical' world is an objective and un/conscious world image lived as their exterior life-world. But exactly as such—that is, as the domain of the 'sensuous' perceptual *Umwelt*—its constitution is the function of the objective schematism of the Yagwoia un/conscious, their '*Innenwelt*'. Through this mediation their 'world exterior' is truly what it is—the absolute reality of their Cosmic Self.[44]

In this perspective, then, the celestial and terrestrial dimensions of QP's oneiric landscape delimit his containment within the world-self. Sky and earth are held in an ouroboric self-alternating conjunction-disjunction by Imacoqwa, and this cosmic container is twined into its immanent male^female self-difference. With his flight into the sky, QP had come into the male[45] pole of the world-body, where Imacoqwa made himself manifest (as the rope) exactly at the critical moment that QP, the dreamer (i.e., his soul-component), had found himself in the mid-point between the sky and earth. The celestial rope is a particular manifestation of the cosmic phallo-umbilicus of which there are several variants (Mimica 1981, 1988). As a celestial post or the ouroboric tree-of-life, this phallo-umbilicus holds sky and earth in a dynamic conjunction. In one case a shaman, when he was sick, was attacked by numerous spirits. However, he was delivered from them into safety because a rock on which he had been placed began to rise into the sky. It did not stop until it reached the altitude at which the attacking spirits could not reach him. In this instance, the archetypal image of the sky^earth conjunction was presenced by a lithic version, the cosmic pillar. In another case, a young man who was under recurrent assaults by the spirits of his dead maternal relatives also saw a celestial rope, but unfortunately he failed to grab it and could not ascend into the sky. In these two instances, the sky^earth conjunction was in the service of an ascent into the sky rather than a descent, as in QP's case. It is vital to be aware of this factual aspect of the Yagwoia archetypal imagination as active in concrete existential situations of Yagwoia individuals.[46] Furthermore, the image of the celestial rope belongs to the scheme of the sun's path as well as the conception of cardinal points and trade relations in the Yagwoia life-world.[47] Still more, in onset experiences of persons who may become shamans, the celestial rope often appears as a multitude of ropes of shells dropping from the sky. Yet another variant of this image is its manifestation as the sun-ray, either one or many. These are also transfigured into the image of the sun's arrow, which causes severe inflammatory skin conditions, including scabies.

In the dream, QP looked for a tree from which the rope might have been hanging, but there was none. In his comments he had no reservation about identifying the rope with Imacoqwa, one of the reasons being that our work was always concerned with him. He also considered the rope's significance in connection with my return after six years of absence. Therefore, the rope (Imacoqwa) had pulled me back, reconnected me to the Yagwoia abode, similarly to the way it enabled QP, in the dream, to come from the sky back onto the ground.[48] When I pointed out that it was QP (not me) who came down that rope, he invoked its solar significance, saying that we all (humans) come from him (Imacoqwa). What he meant by this is that the sun with its rays fertilizes the earth, and everything, humans included, springs out as offshoots from his generative rays. Here the emphasis is on the sun's (Imacoqwa's) paternal inseminatory-protective activity.[49] Implicitly, the fluctuating identity of the sunray as the celestial rope is an ocular phallic-emission since the sun (and moon) is Imacoqwa's celestial eye. This in turn further amplifies its looking-protective significance, which in the dream (although the sun was not manifest) became so through its phallic emission—the rope.[50]

And here is effected the diacritical articulation of QP's overall relation to his paternal imago. What happened in this dream is a double conjunction—not just the facial-ocular positive identification with his human, earthly father's imago (as the protective spirit of the dead), but also the cosmic intercession of his Father-of-All, who is, by means of the sky^earth conjunction, the unity of the world parents, Imacoqwa and Imacipu. Propelled into the sky by his father's urging and his own fear of malignant spirits, QP puts himself momentarily into a situation of, as it were, cosmic disconnection, without a firm tie to either earth or sky. The phallic-umbilicus that binds the ego to its self, the ouroboric matrix of conjoined parents, was momentarily snapped, only to be substituted by the new one that reconnected the sky and earth, thus enabling the dreamer to come down to the maternal earth by his own hand.[51] It is no exaggeration to say that in this regenerative sky^earth conjunction, QP became engendered by the Cosmic Self and self-delivered to his spirit-father, who, most significantly, reappears at the moment when his son touches the earth. In this, his relationship with the paternal imago—indeed, his reconstitution and determination within the all-paternal selfhood—becomes fully actualized. QP has truly accomplished his sonship as a man generated by man, both the particular-human and the universal-cosmic. It can also be said that in this cosmic-axial recalibration of his selfhood, his egoity has become at once more individuated and self-unified under the aegis of the phallo-umbilicus, which is maximally masculine-paternal.[52]

Following his momentous celestial descent, QP returns with his father to their village, where the latter shows him his very own new house, which has the distinctive features of a white man's house. His father tells QP that he will inherit it from him. I will not elaborate on this detail, but suffice it to say that here occurs a further development in the transformation of QP's constellation of egoic identifications, which I have characterized as his 'white man complex'. For the Yagwoia, a house is a paramount image of the bodily-self (i.e., flesh-self), which as such is maternal: the umbilical bellybutton bears the indelible connection to its rootedness in the originary 'house' of the bodily self, the womb-container. In QP's dream, however, this receptacle (house = womb) is provided by his father, and to the extent that QP desires the bodily qualities (power) of the white man, here they come to him in the form of his substituted, fleshy envelope-self, his new paternal house. At this near-terminal point of the dream, the conjunction and identification with me, as his primary and overt white man double, which occurs at the inception of the dream, is transfigured, namely, after the celestial self-disjunction and conjunction. Note that prior to this momentous event, QP's face-to-face identification with me terminates with my disappearance, which leads to the emergence of his father as his primary protector, who also facially (ocularly) identifies with him and then receives him again after QP is delivered to him by the celestial rebirth from Imacoqwa. With this, QP's white man identifications are radically usurped and shaken off, yet reintegrated into a new shape of his self-object identification—the paternal house with the white man features. However, we shall see in the next dream that there was the need for yet another and more radical intervention by his spirit-father to inflict upon QP an ever deeper severance from his white man self-identity.

Disidentification with the White Man Complex

The investigation of the vicissitudes of QP's sonship to his father makes plain that it would be rather trivial to envisage it as a process that has finally produced in his un/conscious the presence of a non-conflictual and an all-good father imago. As it were, all is good that ends well and here—the truly good father is a dead father who has returned as the protective spirit of his living son. Given my quest for a psychoanalytic ethnography that aims to achieve intelligibility of the Yagwoia egoic self in all its depths, it will be far more informative to elucidate the inner nature of this 'good father' imago. What stuff is it made of? In this sphere of the psychic being, what is the meaning of 'goodness'? And what kind of egoic gestalt is this sort of spirit-paternal imago in terms of the agency structuration in the Yagwoia un/conscious?

The next dream, which occurred about one month later (in April 1992), contains ample material for reflection on these questions. For reasons of space, I will present only the second part of the dream as told by QP.

QP is situated at a mourning séance (*aa'ma-ka:ce*),[53] where he and others are singing dirges for a deceased woman whose face he did not see. (1) He is singing thus when his father QC comes and asks him: "Who are you staying with?" QP does not want to tell him that he is staying with Jadran. Keeping quiet, he just looks at his father. (2) Then, as they sing, he sees an airplane landing at Qwaqul-qwe[54] rest-place. I (Jadran) come out of the aircraft and QP shakes my hand. But before he can even start talking to me, his father, QC, comes and hits me in the chest with the hammer-side of his iron axe. I collapse onto the ground while QC proceeds to slice me into pieces with the axe blade. He axes my body into so many pieces as if they are tree-leaves (flying off). My entire body becomes like wood-chip rubbish. Then QP asks his father, "Why did you destroy my sister's son?" QC does not answer, and QP starts weeping bitterly. He turns his face away, so that he no longer sees his father and my axed body, and continues to weep loudly. Then he turns back to the scene because he wants to collect the body pieces, but as he does so he sees that all the body pieces have rejoined, and that I am a bodily whole again, lying sideways. At this point, QP (at last) talks to me (i.e., makes verbal contact): "My Jadran, you've rejoined and arisen again!" He is saying this while I get up and embrace him. He then shouts at the top of his voice that I reassembled, arose, and embraced him, and that "My father didn't kill him!" (i.e., destroyed me irreversibly). As he does so, he also embraces me and continues to announce to the world that I have victoriously regained my bodily life (i.e., reaggregated, become whole again). As he is shouting, he wakes up, wondering whether he truly saw it (i.e., in wakefulness rather than in dreaming).

Given other dreams with similar overt or equivalent substitutive motifs, the foregoing could have been interpreted as either portending good hunting luck (especially since the white man represents the tree kangaroo) or a straight homicide.[55] But in the concrete context of our relationship and (at that time) his engagement with a younger, aspiring local politician, QP saw the axing and reassembling of my body in a different spectrum of existential relevances. In terms of his connection to me, the dream event signified the recovery of the abandoned custom of insemination and other initiatory practices that had all been given up ('destroyed'). That is, through our joined work, these practices were not lost but were being preserved through my 'book', that is, the copious field notes that I have created over the years. Simultaneously, the same motif of bodily destruction and recomposition meant that QP's work with the aspiring local politician might recover and restore the lost connection with the Australian *Gavman*, since this man had an idea of creating an equivalent of the Australian Labour Party that would truly work for the interests of the 'grass-roots' people of PNG.[56] In this perspective, the power of the local custom, through QP's mediation, might re-emerge in the form of a new political group. It was this spectrum of 'destruction' and 'recomposition' that the dream had shown him.

Further probing would have undoubtedly thematized other connections pertaining to hunting, killing, sexuality, and Imacoqwa, with the last figure having a marked connection to the white man theme via the cosmogonic marsupial–tree-kangaroo nexus, which I cannot elaborate here (see Mimica 1981). Nevertheless, I also clearly saw that without any explicit comments on the striking manifest imagery in the dream, QP did assimilate its significance as exactly what his un/conscious, by means of that dream, effected: a disconnection from me and, simultaneously, a certain degree of disinvestment from his 'white man' identifications. As I saw it, this was the result of a very long process that had already been set in motion at the time of my third long-term period of fieldwork, when jealousies between QP and my other collaborators became particularly acute. In 1992, his effective disinvestment was precipitated by my new field site in a different Yagwoia territorial group. Following this dream, I knew that QP accepted this situation in full. In this regard, I could not but be deeply impressed by the blunt reality of the dream and the intelligence of his father's helping spirit figuring therein.

With his first appearance in this second dream, QC makes a direct attack on his son's white man identity by asking him who he is staying with. QP said that in the dream he did not want to disclose the truth, but his father, all the same, took care of it in no uncertain terms. Prior to any verbal contact between me and him, QC had intervened and destroyed me, i.e., his son's preferred 'object' as it was narcissistically charged with his radically bivalent archaic libido-mortido. Both imagos, the spirit-father and the white man (Jadran), are infused with this same non-differentiated libidinal energy in which the destructive force in the dream, clearly manifested by the intensity of the spirit-father's actions, is mirrored by the equipollent force of self-generation (the self-reaggregation of the Jadran imago). The two actions are indeed the actualizations of but one and the same psychic force. This is not just 'the stuff dreams are made of', but the archaic dimension of the psychic being, which is genuinely immortal precisely because its inner ergon is driven by absolute negativity: its mode of self-generation is a ceaseless self-destruction from which alone comes its self-preservation. In the Yagwoia life-world, the foremost manifestation of this primal energic modality of the psychic being is in the immortal wild forest spirits. The spirits of the dead, however, are, so to speak, a manifestation of the second order of immortality. This is because, prior to becoming so, they were mortal human beings, subject to birth, life, and death. Their soul-heat (energy) eventually became transformed into the immortal spirits of the dead. This is not so with the immortal wild forest spirits, who were never born and incarnated in the human realm and thus were never subject to sickness, death, and bodily decomposition. They, in contrast to the spirits of the dead, have always been unborn and undead, that is, *outside* of the flow of life = death to which everything human is subject (see Mimica 2003a).

Seen in the perspective of the tacit Yagwoia cosmo-ontological distinctions and objectifications, the libidinal (psycho-sexual) energy can be constructively subjected to concretizations relative to the originary self-symbolization in its autochthonous, ouroboric life-world. The libidinal 'energetics' manifest in the complementary couplet of QP's spirit-father imago and Jadran is also readily evident in the cosmogonic mythopoeia and in the dreams of individuals who are pestered by the spirits of their dead lovers. For instance, a man is approached by his ex-, now-dead lover, who closes in on him. He pulls a knife and slices her into pieces, but to no effect. She reassembles, becomes a whole body again, and pursues him. He wakes up, overwhelmed with anxiety.[57]

It can be said, then, that QP's imagos articulate a libidinal energetics in which the (homo)erotic mode is conterminous with the irrepressible aggressive-destructive modality.[58] That his cathexis to and incorporation of me was eventually consolidated through his contra-sexual self was already articulated in the dream in which his sister gave birth to me (his sister being the primary mediator of his contra-sexual self). In the dream of the ascendancy of his spirit-father as his self-unifying and positive-protective presence, QP has effectively relaxed his feminine cathexis. He wept over the fact that his father had killed his very own—yet fundamentally alien—white man 'sister's son' (ZS), but he went along with it all the way. The 'good father' did the 'dirty work' (of castration), which is absolutely necessary for QP's self-repossession—not as the male mother of his (alien white) ZS, but as the son who is self-recentered through the now firmly established identification with his own father. QC is the true source of QP's eternal bone and self-value, that is, his authentic and autochthonous ouroboric, narcissistic self-circuitry.

It must be noted that QP's position in the dream is passive; the father does the killing, as unhesitantly and single-mindedly as he did while alive. Next, QP turns away. He no longer wants to see what is going on behind his back, and when he turns around with the intention of picking up the body parts, he finds fulfilled his desire of having his dear object fully restored to life, despite the fact that it had been destroyed just a moment ago. Whatever becomes cathected to the sphere of the ouroboric libido becomes bound to it for eternity—destroyed and pulverized, yes; but renounced or given up, no. There may occur numerous cuts and separations, but every severed part must return to its primal whole and thereby reaffirm it as its inalienable source. And correlatively, its self does not belong to itself but to its matrix-source.[59] Thus, at one level I can say that, thanks to his spirit-father, QP could both have his cake and eat it too. He lost it and got it back with a degree of separation and differentiation from it.

To conclude, the dream makes evident that QP has effected a mode of separation and individuation in relation to his feminine-determined self-object. The intensity of its libidinal value was reduced, while its homo-erotic (i.e. life-affirming-receptive) modality was retained. The active-destructive mode of his narcissistic libidinal circuitry that effected this modification is his father imago, which in the same process has intensified QP's libidinal assimilation of his paternal self-identification. To that extent, by means of his spirit-father, QP's libidinal energetics has become more fully articulated into a self-protective—indeed, self-nourishing—circuitry of what is now a well-tempered mortido bound by and configured into the intelligent agency of the paternal self-object. This, then, is the 'stuff' his 'good father' is made of, and I have no doubt that he will remain so for the rest of QP's life.

For instance, toward the end of the severe drought that affected the region in 1997–1998, QP's first wife, whom he did not favor, died. At first, she did not appear in his dreams. Nevertheless, that she had become a malignant spirit of the dead was clear enough from her children's dreams, in which she appeared. QP readily understood and accordingly told them that he could see from their dreams that she was malignant but that at the same time she was well disposed to them and that they would not get sick. Then, as the health of Y, his favorite and surviving wife, began to deteriorate (she had been sick on and off for many years), QP began to see his dead wife (spirit) in his dreams with the following scenario: she is pulling and dragging a pig into the forest, but QP's spirit-father and his affine (wife's brother) YP come and block her road, whereupon she releases the pig. The pig is QP's sick wife Y, whom the spirit-wife disliked while she was alive. Now that the first wife is dead while Y yet lives, she dislikes her even more. Therefore, the spirit of the dead wife wants to take Y with her so that she too is dead. QP's father's wife's brother (YP) is in fact Y's true father's brother, that is, a close agnatic (classificatory) father. As the paternal spirits of their two respective children, they protect them from this recent arrival, QP's dead wife. In fact, while alive, this wife used to be taken care of by QC (her HF), together with her children. But now, QC is committed only to his son's desire and interests and therefore unreservedly protects his son's ailing wife. In the dreams, apart from blocking the road, the two spirit-fathers also tell the first wife to go back to her own place.

In another, somewhat altered oneiric situation, QP is admonished by his father to take his wife back home. She carries sweet potatoes and has gone astray on a forest path, following the footprints of another man. QP then takes her back home. In another context, the dream could suggest that his wife might actually be attracted to another man. Given her sickness, the dream shows that her soul is in peril. She can be seized by a spirit and dragged away completely, which would mean her death. However, QP's spirit-father was making sure that this did not happen.

When I discussed these recurrent dreams with QP (in 2003), he emphasized that his father's spirit was with him all the time. But he had no illusions about his wife's prospects and was anticipating her death. She had been previously treated unsuccessfully at the local hospital, and she was quite willfully ready to die, as her living became more and more saturated with the insipid pain of being sick yet alive.[60] QP knew that it would not be long before she left him. He felt sorry for himself, then added painfully, yet smiling, that since he is still not completely an old man, he may get a *Hayqwangilyce aapala*, either an A or a C,[61] so that he can bring forth his father's father (QA) or his father (QC). To the extent that he is still virile and procreative, he went on to say, he can get a younger and fertile woman. It would not be good to replace Y with a woman as old as himself; otherwise, the two would just sit inside the *aane acipiye* (food-cook-house) and look at each other.

This image plays on the view of sexual intercourse and child-making as 'food cooking'. An active young couple is, through sexual conjunction, inside the 'house' (i.e., penis in the womb), making a baby. The image of an old, sexually unproductive couple sitting inside a cook-house and just looking at each other suggests an entropic atrophy of the progenitive desire and conjunction. The old couple can only eat the cooked food (i.e., the substitute for the sexual-copulative mode of 'cooking') and look at each other while digesting it. But their looks are not the burning (i.e., cooking) looks of the sexual conjunction and are not fueled by, so to speak, the digestion *à deux* that makes a real baby inside the womb = cook-house. By digesting and looking at each other, the old couple effects no child-generating conjunction. Although themselves contained inside the cook-house ('womb'), they are apart, digesting yet empty of their procreative self-unity in the body of the one who is their third and as such their two-in-one, the fetal being through and in which they will have been replaced. This simple image, then, condenses an entire dialectics of container^contained, being the core of the human ouroboric self-circuity, destiny, and quest for self-creation and self-perpetuation ad infinitum. My ontological amplification of it in terms of the self-generative one^two^oneness is grounded entirely in the immanent mathematicity of the Yagwoia noesis and life-world constitution (see Mimica 1988, 1991).

QP's favorite wife Y died about six months later. With her, he had procreated nine children in all. Two daughters and two sons have grown up; five died in very early infancy or at birth. For a number of years QP had been truly worried that he would not have a son by her. He paid the mortuary payments for the first two dead babies. As for the rest, when his affines, the children's mothers, buttressed their demands for the payments with the pronouncement that these were not just any children but "indeed *our* children," he told them, "You can eat them as they are. They are your marsupials [game-meat] anyway."[62]

Jadran Mimica is a Senior Lecturer in Anthropology at the University of Sydney. He has carried out systematic long-term field research among the Yagwoia-Angan people of Papua New Guinea since 1977. His publications include *Intimations of Infinity: The Mythopoeia of the Iqwaye Counting System and Number* (1988) and "The Incest Passions: An Outline of the Logic of the Iqwaye Social Organisation" (1991). His most recent publication is "Dreams, *Laki*, and Mourning: A Psychoanalytic Ethnography of the Yagwoia (PNG) 'Inner Feminine'" (2006).

Notes

1. Imacoqwa's female mirror-double is Imacipu (The Great-She). The two are identified with the sun and moon as well as with the sky and earth. For the discussion of the primal twinning of Imacoqwa^Imacipu and the symptomatic fluctuation of their luno-solar identity, see Mimica (1981). For the luno-solar quiddity of the human (Yagwoia) soul, see Mimica (2003a: 262–265). For an explanation of the use of the symbol ^ in this essay, see Mimica (2006: 31). It can simply be assumed that any two terms thus connected are totally interdependent.

2. For some, the antinomial modes immanent in psychic energy (libido) and reflected in the formulations of instinctual drives (e.g., the principial Life^Death, Eros^Thanatos, also more recently echoed in the problematics of narcissism, especially in relation to instinctual drives; Grunberger 1979; Kohut 1977) are primarily seen as contradictions that invalidate the formulations themselves. Still worse, those who appeal to 'state-of-the art' developmental neurobiology and neurosciences, or to infant research, think that they, therefore, are really within the truth, and that the notion of libido and its classical formulations (indicated by the great five referred to above, that is, Freud, Jung, Abraham, Klein, and Fairbairn) are an outdated psychoanalytic 'mythology'. In this context, it will suffice for me to say, "They wouldn't know any better," without suggesting that the current knowledge in these fields, including neuro-psychoanalysis (Schore 1994; Solms and Turnbull 2002; Winson 1985), is irrelevant. On the other hand, in characterizing the

Yagwoia libidinal dynamics as ouroboric, which entails a micro-macro-cosmic ego-Self dialectical circuity, I am demarcating its original actualizations in and as their cultural life-world. Accordingly, it cannot be uncritically assimilated into the existing psycho-analytic formulations, including such reworkings as in Lacan's opus. For some recent examinations of the problematics of the death instinct, see Eigen (1995), Green (1999, 2001), Grotstein (1985), and Segal (1993).

3. I use the vernacular term (*latice*) for the Yagwoia groups in order to minimize the avalanche of ideas and associations that would follow if I should characterize them as 'patrilineal'. In this essay, it is not important to provide a detailed exegesis of the inner constitution of the Yagwoia societal field qua group morphology. The latter has neces-sarily to be explicated solely through indigenous images and self-interpretations rooted in the cultural imaginary and its auto-symbolization.

4. An example of women's self-experience as a phallic conduit is detailed in Mimica (2006).

5. This process relates to a separate stream of development of a person's soul-potency, which primarily involves the mediations of the immortal wild forest spirits (*hyaqaye ilymane*) who bestow various powers upon him or her. These are separate, non-human agencies of the generation of a person's soul-powers. When these powers turn out to be the same as one's genitor, for instance, one's father, then one is said to have obtained one's father's soul, although it is not the case that it has been literally transmitted between them. On the other hand, in his more advanced age, a father or some other relative can voluntarily bestow his or her soul-power to his or her child. But equally so, an unrelated person (usually a greedy and jealous shaman) can steal one's soul-power or prevent its development, namely, when it is in the process of acquisition from the wild forest spirits. For an outline of the problematics of mortality and immortality, as well as of the cosmo-ontological determination of the spirits of the dead, in contrast to the immortal wild forest spirits, see Mimica (2003a).

6. Iqwaye is one of the four central Yagwoia-Angan territorial groups or tribes (Mimica 1981).

7. QC's father, QA, is at the inception of his *latice* segment defined by him and his four wives. QC belongs to a patrilateral sibling set totaling 14 brothers and 5 sisters. Issuing from these men is QP's patrisibling set (i.e., his father's brother's children, or FBCh). It in turn includes 32 close agnatic brothers and 12 sisters. In this pool, he has no one full patrilateral sibling. As for their children, for instance, QA's first wife's first-born son's son (who is QP's father's (QC) patrilateral half-brother's son) has in all 21 children. This is a good indication of the field of relatedness generated through polygamous implantation of the bone. All of these numerous agnates are at once the offshoots and the continuation of their *latice* trunk whose nodal bone = trunk = branch = hand is QA, i.e., QP's father's father (FF). Each of his offshoots is himself the part = whole, the hand = branch = trunk = bone who continues to totalize through and in himself the *latice* group oneness. This group-container has the archetypal structuration of the ouroboric tree-of-life, which determines the sense of the *latice*'s self-unity and self-generation with respect to the incorporation (containment) of its living prog-eny (offshoots) (for an illustration, see Mimica 2006). All kin-type notations fol-low the established anthropological convention. Thus, F = father, M = mother, S = son, D = daughter, B = brother, Z = sister, Sb = sibling, H = husband, W = wife. Their com-binations specify various relatedness links, e.g., MBS (mother's brother's son), FZS (father's sister's son), FMBSSD (father's mother's brother's son's son's daughter), HF (husband's father), WM (wife's mother's), and MMBWZH (mother's mother's brother's wife's sister's husband).

8. Although the case of QC can easily invite a comparison with Watson's (1971) classic account of the Tariora's Matoto, this would easily become misleading. The psychoana-lytic-biographical explorations of QC and other Yagwoia warrior-killers require a separate study more fully situated in the generative libidinal matrix of the Yagwoia life-world. Especially the cultural auto-symbolization of the ouroboric flow of life and death has to be given more acute archetypal specifications.

9. This self-experience and self-interpretation are symptomatic of the dynamics of the archaic, maternally determined self-image (ideality) and the super-ego whose erogenous-libidinal structuration is oral-ocular.

10. For this concept of the economy of the archaic narcissistic equilibrium in which, due to its extreme mirror-schizoid bivalency, symbiotic omnipotence and impotence are equipollent and conterminous, I use the term 'omni/m/potence' (see Mimica 2003b: 27).

11. For this practice and social institutional arrangements, see Mimica (1991). For the equivalent practices among the Sambia and the Baruya, see Godelier (1986) and Herdt (1981, 1987). For critical assessments of Herdt, see Mimica (1982, 1983, 2001, 2005).

12. It is of critical significance that in this sort of self-evaluation, the tendency is to place oneself in a passive position. The fellator is the one who is the source of attraction for the men who are drawn to him.

13. For lack of space, I will not discuss the equally formative father-image in QC's un/conscious, which accounts for the overall structuration and the prevalently deadly equilibrium of his libidinal selfhood. His father was killed when he was on a visit to his sister and ZH in the neighboring Yagwoia-speaking tribal group. This eventually escalated into an all-out war that led to the systematic routing of all the enemy settlements. Without the arrival of the Australian colonial government, this tribal group would have undoubtedly been completely destroyed and their lands appropriated by the Iqwaye and, at that time, their Menya-speaking allies, the Pataye.

14. I should mention in this connection that I knew in Goroka a Chimbu man who was in the PNG armed forces. He was a sharpshooter and allegedly had shot a lot of people during the Bougainville campaign. He eventually left the army because, he said, he wanted to make sure that he is way out of the reach of the spirits of all those people he killed.

15. The fourth wife was a late acquisition. In addition to a daughter, she bore him two boys who died in infancy.

16. This is a literal translation of the kin term for MB, who as such is the 'male mother'. After the death of one's basal (*kaule* = tree-base = true) MB, i.e., the one who has the same birth-order as his sister, it is his most senior son who becomes the ego's base or root maternal uncle (i.e., the ego's *kayemu*, or 'his-mother's breast'). All his other brothers are equally upgraded from MBS > MB, i.e., from being referred to as 'my-mother' to 'my-mother's breast', but they are not exactly as 'basal' as the first-born MBS. The new extension of the term *namne* (my-mother's breast) follows primarily the generational equivalence of those who hitherto were classified merely as mothers. The order of seniority of a man's children, however, is determined by the marital order of his wives. Therefore, one's most senior first-born son is not in fact the male born first but rather the first-born son of the very first wife. Therefore, although I may be my father's son born well after his other wives gave birth to his other sons, I am the first in order of filial seniority because my mother is my father's first wife in order of his marital acquisitions. The discussion presented in my monograph in preparation, *Born and Grown from the Bone of the Father: On the Fundamental Theme of the Yagwoia Father-Son Relationship*, gives a good outline of how this seniority scheme is actualized in terms of property transmission and control in a polygamous household and in terms of the libidinal dynamics of the paternal bone incorporation.

17. There was a deeper motivation for this selfishness. QC alleged that his fourth and much younger wife had had sex with his son QP, and this was in all likelihood true. So QC squared with his son by eating the shells. When QC died (in approximately 1989), his wife continued to live with QP, not as his 'mother' but as his woman.

18. Here, a partial motivation was the fact that the fourth wife was much younger than his first three wives. Therefore, the senior wife was likely to feel jealous and unwilling to apply to the fourth co-wife's younger sister the kind of maternal care expected from her.

19. In 1985, a young, married Yagwoia woman with a child had no problems winning the hearts and minds of all those present at the Police Court in Mny when she stated the reason why she wanted to leave her husband and marry another man. She accused

him of petty greediness that he would manifest when shamelessly eating children's and young women's meat that she and her child had procured, while he would rarely, if at all, provide her with pork and game. The man had no argument and stood in painful silence as she detailed these most compromising and embarrassing aspects of his egoity, while some onlookers said that they themselves felt ashamed on his behalf.

20. For these people, see Bonnemere (1996) and Lemonnier (1998).

21. For the ambiguities of the Yagwoia notion of being a 'bad man' yet also a 'great man', see Mimica (2003b).

22. The prototype of this, and for most others, including very much younger Yagwoia, is the Australian governmental conduct for which they have undivided admiration. This, however, is not the same as respect. Respect is a moral attitude that has no reality in the ouroboric mode of self and its un/conscious matrix.

23. For this epithet and usage, see Mimica (2003a).

24. He effectively took in all three women. With the first two he produced 16 children of whom only 8 survived, the other 8 having died in infancy. With the first wife he has 1 daughter and 3 sons, with the second wife, 2 daughters and 2 sons. His third wife was also one of his numerous extra-marital lovers; she was first married to his classificatory matrilateral brother. It is certain that her second son was sired by QP rather than her first and deceased husband IP. Her marriage as a widow to QP was leviratic.

25. This is the exact gloss for the way the Yagwoia specify a classificatory relation: *ung-woqwa* (an/other) in contrast to a *nua* (my-true-x).

26. For this reason, one of QP's co-initiates was reinitiated by his father in another Yagwoia tribal group where the practice persisted until the end of the 1950s. He wanted his son not to miss the experience of the fully fledged practice of men-making (for details, see Mimica 1991).

27. 'Gnoseophilic' (knowledge-loving, in the sense of desire and instinct for knowledge) is equivalent to Melanie Klein's use and conception of "epistemophilic" desire/instinct. Her explication of it ([1932] 1989, [1975] 1988) is presumed.

28. Turning on his wife was an amplified expression of his own omni/m/potence, for he maintained that she had had sex with his son.

29. QC's extreme volatility and lethal aggression was eventually stemmed by a special sorcery performed on him by his own patrilateral half-brother, QNg, who literally depotentiated QC's soul, which made him less volatile and prone to compulsive, violent action. QNg told me that he did this in order to protect QC from the adversity of his fellow villagers. He knew only too well that sooner or later they would put an end to his overbearing behavior by, say, killing him at night in a situation when he would be most vulnerable (e.g., when defecating). QC was fully aware of his brother's action and accepted it as his predicament, no matter how painful it was for him to be depotentiated.

30. Note that his own mother's spirit divested him almost completely of his soul-power.

31. Although spoken in singular and as a whole, the reference is to a particular (or several) autonomous power(s) (here for curing activity) that can be acquired but also lost. The dialectical structure of the soul as being at the same time a simplex and multiplex self-unity of animating 'breathy-heat' is discussed in Mimica (2003a).

32. Although one deals here with profoundly intense projective identifications, from the perspective of the Yagwoia structuration of psychic being, egoity, and intersubjective self-experiences, the contents of the un/conscious are radically externalized regardless of any extra projective activity. Since the basis of self-world relation is incorporative and as such determines Yagwoia intersubjectivity, the experience of being attached to another person as his or her soul-component is indeed an intersubjectively objective psychic fact. In short, it is experiential reality.

33. They often stayed with QC, his wife, and his young daughter in the garden house in the grassland area of the Iqwaye territory, while QP lived permanently with his second, favored wife and her children in the main Iqwaye settlement in the 'upper', forested mountain-range region of the territory. In terms of residence, QC moved to and fro between his

son's and his own garden residence. QP's favored wife was somewhat younger than his neglected wife. He insisted that they had the same marital status because his father had 'marked' (betrothed) and procured them both for him at the same time. QP would refer to this when his older wife would point out that, of the two, she was the first.

34. Likewise with his patri-half-brother, QNg, the grandest of the great Iqwaye-Yagwoia men of yore, who died a year or two before QC.

35. '*Innenwelt*' is a German word meaning 'inner world'. I use it here primarily in the dialectical sense, which presupposes that the inner and outer dimensions are irreducibly co-dependent (Uexkull 1957). The word is in quotes because for the Yagwoia, dreams are not 'inner experience'. Accordingly, QP's 'inner world' is very much an exterior dimension of his existence in the world (see also note 44 below).

36. In terms of Yagwoia self-world experience and understanding of dream reality, the dream is *external* to the sleeping person. Dream events take place in the objective exteriority of the world. Whatever is experienced as being a dream is due to the activity of the dreamer's soul, spirits encountered in the exterior world, and the semblances of living human beings whose ontological determination, however, is indefinite. In discourse, this special status of dream and visionary experiences is often indicated by a verb morpheme, which indicates their separate experiential mode as being different from the certainty of direct wakeful experience. Living humans may be factually encountered 'out-there', or they may be the showings produced by one's soul and/or spirits. Likewise, to the extent that every dream is an event in the world exteriority, the 'physical' factuality of the spatio-temporal dimensionality of that domain is primarily the function of the semblances or the showings of the soul or a spirit. This is why this factuality of the world is determined mainly by its symbolic meaningfulness, which the Yagwoia have developed into a rather stable interpretive framework of symbolic identifications (e.g., in the dream a motif A pictures B, etc.). I deal with a fully developed phenomenology of being as constituted in and for the Yagwoia in their visionary, oneiric, and delusory modes of self-world experiences in another work (Mimica 2006).

37. There are important associational and lexical connections in the sequence spirit > stone > hole. Firstly, stones and cliffs (generically, *hiyekiye* = stone, rock) are passages for spirits. *Ilymane* (spirit) is folk-etymologized as derivative of *ilyce-mane* or *ily-mane* (shit-road, passage), which is similar to *hiyekiye ilymane* = stone-hole, stone-cavity. The latter, however, is prosodically different from the word for spirits, but the connection is nevertheless intimate, as explained above. (For the reasons of the strong anal determination of spirits of the dead in the Yagwoia life-world, see Mimica 2003a.) The stone-opening also indicates the potential movement into the sub-terrestrial (chthonic) dimension, which is to say into the deeper level of the maternal-feminine somatic un/conscious of the dreamer's self. But as will be seen, his movement defines a radically different cosmic-elemental trajectory. In Yagwoia understanding, the fact that in the next moment I vanish and a woman appears is an obvious aspect of dream experience as the work of one's soul and spirits encountered in the oneiric domain. Phenomenologically, the male > female switching of imagos is the manifestation of the immanent bivalency and self-difference of the ouroboric libido and the psychic space within which the ego is at once observer and actor.

38. Note the ocular-identificatory dynamism as it is articulated in the motions of the characters in the dream. He does not know her; he is looking at and scrutinizing her, which generates the field of forces that drive her toward him. In the previous scene, he effected the ocular (face-to-face) conjunction with me, but after I warned him about a spirit, there occurs the disjunction (separation and loss) of the desired object: he opens up the stone, I disappear, and there appears a woman who is heading toward him. She is a source of danger—a spirit. Is she going to hook up (conjoin) with him? She could be any of (the spirits of) his former and now dead lovers, who may, qua conjunction, make him sick.

39. In his account, QP emphasizes the sequence of motion—comes > comes-stands up > in front of his face, articulating thus the erectile (standing-up) barrier that his father's spirit

creates between him (he faces him) and the oncoming woman spirit, whose face is the face of death (mourning ashes).

40. The white man was a European builder married to a PNG woman. His real name was different, but QP misidentified him nominally with another white man of that name. Both were living at the government station at the time. In the dream, the white man carries my identity and the generic aspects of QP's white man identifications. He declares himself to be Pita IO, who is QP's deceased FZS, i.e., his 'son'. The reason he appears as a white man is because he was one of the original three Yagwoia who worked with the first Australian Lutheran missionary, who settled among them in 1954. Pita became like a white man; after his baptism, he denounced the Yagwoia traditional values and became a successful businessman. He was the white missionary's main teacher of the vernacular, and he learned Tok Pisin from the missionary. This was their vital exchange of the speaking substance, although Pita never incorporated the true speech substance of the white man, i.e., English. This is what QP desired for himself—to have that power inside him which is English speech. That is why he tells the white man that he wants to learn to speak it. This would make him more powerful than his rival Pita IO. QP was in an ambivalent conflictual relationship with Pita IO, the resolution of which was undercut by the latter's untimely death. It should be pointed out that these 'white man' personages are all the transfigurations and particularizations of a generic ideal self-object. The 'white man' who inhabits QP's un/conscious (and that of many other Yagwoia) epitomizes the white man's global (generic) power, which QP desires. Originally, the seeds of this self-object became implanted in him when he received a white man's 'iron' (semen), but it became fully developed in the course of his relationship with me, a white ethnographer whom he incorporated completely as his ZS.

41. This is a vitally salient notion of the Yagwoia cosmology. The celestial center, the absolute mid-point of the world-body, marks the *axis mundi* that connects the sky and earth. The terrestrial mid-point is Qwoqwoyaqwa, the center of the universe (Mimica 1981).

42. These have also become the characteristics of the houses of the wild forest spirits, as reported regularly by shamans and those whom these spirits have chosen to empower with their curing powers.

43. What is at work here is the beginning of the transformation of QP's super-ego as it is becoming mediated by the transformed paternal imago.

44. By the same token, this *Innenwelt* > < *Umwelt* dialectics (Uexkull 1957, 1982) constitutes every organismic sphere of being as a concrete life-world of and for a given organismic field, which actively transforms and generates the 'physical' into the livable 'ecological' sphere, for itself and in its own image. All otherness within such a sphere is constituted relative to itself.

45. As I pointed out earlier, the sky^earth are in a mirror-relation to each other. This is because in the Yagwoia life-world, all quiddity is the auto-polar (or bivalent) generative self-unity of maleness^femaleness. Therefore, the sky, although maximally male and paternal, is no less male^female than the feminine and maternal terrestrial realm.

46. This material bears singular import for a constructive reflection on Lévi-Strauss's conception of human mythopoeic noesis, especially as suggested by his famous "canonical formula" and the way it figured in his thought (see Mimica 2003c). For equivalent images of the celestial rope in New Guinea mythopoiea and dreams, see Aufenanger (1960) and Landtman (1917: 447). For a psychoanalytic assessment of Landtman's Kiwai dream, see Roheim (1952: 74–75); for an original commentary on Roheim with regard to Landtman's example, see Hunt (1989: 138–139).

47. In his interpretation of the dream, QP elaborated at length on this significance of the celestial rope.

48. In this one can get a sense of the way the Yagwoia relate themselves through their dreams to their immediate situation, which thereby acquires new relevance and meaningfulness. Reciprocally, dream situations are rendered meaningful relative to the wakeful life circumstances and events therein.

49. From the regional-comparative perspective, a related version of this micro/macro-cosmic generative dynamism is the Baruya procreation belief that every embryo is created through both the man's semen and the sun's fertilization, the latter occurring by the sun-ray penetrating the woman's womb. The sun specifically creates the embryo's eyes, nose, mouth, fingers, and toes (see Godelier 1986: 51). The Yagwoia do not have this particular belief, but it is echoed by the following view. If two unrelated persons resemble each other in facial physiognomy, they are said, in a proverbial sense, that it must have been the sun that inseminated their respective mothers. Solar 'insemination' has the emissive-ocular sense. There are different modalities of the solar 'look'. One can be pierced, touched, and singed by it. The moon's 'look', by contrast, is absorbing, dissolving, and cooling. For the Yagwoia, all humans and everything on earth are generated by the sun and moon, with the sun as the universal father. I explore a full range of luno-solar quiddities in the Yagwoia life-world and their generation of humans as well as of the life-process in general in a separate work on Yagwoia cosmology.

50. It should be pointed out that in QP's self-awareness, the solar-ocular identity of Imacoqwa is quite salient because his *latice* group derives from Imacoqwa's eye—the sun. Other *latice* claim other parts of Imacoqwa's body.

51. As in the first initiation, this primal matrix is ruptured so that the ego's dominant buccal-mammary fusion with maternal self-object is redirected and reconnected to the equivalent but transformed buccal-phallic tie of the primal bone and the phallo-mammary umbilicus that runs through the chain of the junior and senior bachelors who, via fellatio, transmit the all-male semenal flow.

52. We shall see in the next dream that the QP's individuation was specifically effected in relation to the white man complex that had hitherto held sway over him.

53. For a description of Yagwoia group mourning séances, see Mimica (2003a).

54. This place-name, because it figures in the toponymic stock of endearment-names (*ilaye yeuwye*) for QP's *latice*, immediately invokes the identity of his sister's children, to whom alone this class of names applies. Therefore, it prefigures my identity, since it is I who comes out of the airplane at that place. As such, I am literally landing in my macro-cosmic flesh-body locality, which is simultaneously QP's own *latice* bone identity.

55. The same would apply if the conjunction were overtly sexual rather than destructive (for an example, see Mimica 2006).

56. Since this aspiring politician had a university degree, he had a high co-efficient of the 'white man' value attached to him. This too linked him to me. Like some other non-initiated, young, educated men, he also realized that without some knowledge of the local customs—relations between *latice* and territorial groups and land ownership—he could not realistically deal with his people. That is why he sought knowledge and instruction from QP, whose status as a great man of knowledge is genuinely recognized in the entire region.

57. For this sort of ultra-'obsessive' spirit menace, the only effective treatment is a rite that involves first the beating and chasing of the spirit (or spirits), followed by the planting of a cordyline shrub. The efficiency of the rite depends entirely on the power of the spells used in it (see Mimica 2006).

58. This brings to mind the liquid-metal cyborg in the movie *Terminator II*. This perfect killing machine is pure negativity. It has no identity of its own but can assume, by contiguity, a semblance of anything it comes into contact with. It can undergo every mode of destruction, yet it will inevitably reassemble, regain its primary semblance, and carry on with its relentless program of destruction.

59. This is also the fundamental determination of the 'white man' in the Yagwoia self-un/consciousness. Regardless of how they may figure in the sphere of a particular egoity, the Yagwoia see white people generically as descendants of themselves, i.e., of the primal men created by Imacoqwa at the local center of the world-body. This primal ancestor of the white man took off from the center of creation before the separation of the sky and earth, when cosmic darkness still reigned. He took with him (i.e., stole) all the knowledge

that white people now possess, but because this was in truth created by Imacoqwa, the 'white man's' knowledge belongs to the Yagwoia—to the black man, not the white man.

60. For this existential orientation, see Mimica (1996).
61. That is, a woman from the same *latices* as his father's father's mother (A) or father's mother (C). *Hyaqwangilyce aapala* means 'woman from *Hy*', which is the territorial group (tribe) where the two *latices* are predominantly located and from where both mothers of his two ascending lineal forbears came. A usage such as '*X-aapala*', where X is the name of a specific territorial-tribal unit, is the most generic determination of the socio-centric identity of a person. For the logic of this type of marriage, see Mimica (1991).
62. For the logic of Yagwoia self-circuity through social exchange, including the mortuary payments, see Mimica (1991).

References

Aufenanger, H. 1960. "The Ayom Pygmies' Myth of Origin and Their Method of Counting." *Anthropos* 55, no. 1–2: 247–249.

Bonnemere, P. 1996. *Le Pandanus Rouge: Corps, Difference des Sexes et Parente chez les Ankave-Anga.* Paris: CNRS Editions.

Castoriadis, C. 1987. *The Imaginary Institution of Society.* London: Polity Press.

Eigen, M. 1995. "The Destructive Force Within." *Contemporary Psychoanalysis* 31, no. 4: 603–616.

Fleiss, R. 1956. *Erogeneity and Libido.* New York: International Universities Press.

_____. 1961. *Ego and Body Ego: Contributions to Their Psychoanalytic Psychology.* New York: Schulte Publishing Company.

Godelier, M. 1986. *The Making of Great Men.* Cambridge: Cambridge University Press.

Green, A. 1999. *The Work of the Negative.* London: Free Associations Book.

_____. 2001. *Life Narcissism, Death Narcissism.* London: Free Associations Book.

Grotstein, J. S. 1985. "A Proposed Revision of the Psychoanalytic Concept of the Death Instinct." *Yearbook of Psychoanalysis and Psychotherapy* 1: 299–326.

Grunberger, B. 1979. *Narcissism: Psychoanalytic Essays.* New York: International Universities Press.

Herdt, G. 1981. *Guardians of the Flutes: Idioms of Masculinity.* New York: MacGraw-Hill.

_____. 1987. *Sambia: Ritual and Gender in New Guinea.* New York: Holt, Rinehart, and Winston.

Hunt, H. T. 1989. *The Multiplicity of Dreams: Memory, Imagination and Consciousness.* New Haven, CT: Yale University Press.

Jung, C. G. 1959. *The Archetypes and the Collective Unconscious.* Princeton, NJ: Princeton University Press.

_____. 1968. *Aion: Researches into the Phenomenology of the Self.* London: Routledge and Kegan Paul.

_____. 1971. *Psychological Types.* Princeton, NJ: Princeton University Press.

Klein, M. [1932] 1989. *The Psycho-Analysis of Children.* London: Virago Press.

_____. [1975] 1988. *Love, Guilt and Reparation and Other Works 1921–1945.* London: Virago Press.

Kohut, H. 1977. *The Restoration of the Self.* New York: International Universities Press.

Lacan, J. 1977. *Ecrits: A Selection.* New York: Norton.

Landtman, G. 1917. *The Folk Tales of the Kiwai Papuans.* Helsingfors: Finnish Society of Literature.

Lemonnier, P. 1998. "Showing the Invisible: Violence and Politics among the Ankave-Anga." Pp. 287–307 in *Common Worlds and Single Lives: Constituting Knowledge in Pacific Societies,* ed. V. Keck. Oxford: Berg.

Mahler, M. S., F. Pine, and A. Bergman. [1975] 1985. *The Psychological Birth of the Human Infant: Symbiosis and Individuation*. London: Karnac.

McDougall, J. 1995. *The Many Faces of Eros: A Psychoanalytic Exploration of Human Sexuality*. London: Free Association Books.

Mimica, J. 1981. "Omalyce: An Ethnography of the Iqwqaye View of the Cosmos." PhD diss., Australian National University.

_____. 1982. "Review of *Guardians of the Flutes*, by Gilbert Herdt." *Mankind* 13, no. 3: 287–288.

_____. 1983. "Review of *Rituals of Manhood*, ed. by Gilbert Herdt." *Oceania* 54, no. 2: 165–167.

_____. 1988. *Intimations of Infinity: The Counting System and the Concept of Number among the Iqwaye*. Oxford: Berg Publishers.

_____. 1991. "The Incest Passions: An Outline of the Logic of the Iqwaye Social Organisation." *Oceania* 62, no. 1: 34–58; no. 2: 81–113.

_____. 1996. "On Dying and Suffering in Iqwaye Existence." Pp. 213–237 in *Things as They Are: New Directions in Phenomenological Anthropology*, ed. Michael Jackson. Bloomington: Indiana University Press.

_____. 2001. "A Review from the Field (A Critical Review of Gilbert Herdt's *Sambia Sexual Culture: Essays from the Field*)." *Australian Journal of Anthropology* 12, no. 2: 225–237.

_____. 2003a. "The Death of a Strong, Great, Bad Man: An Ethnography of Soul Incorporation." *Oceania* 73, no. 4: 260–286.

_____. 2003b. "Out of the Depths of Saurian Waters: On Psycho-Bakhtinianism, Ethnographic Countertransference, and *Naven*." *Anthropological Notebooks* 9, no. 1: 5–47.

_____. 2003c. "Review of *The Double Twist: From Ethnography to Morphodynamics*, ed. by Pierre Maranda." *Oceania* 74, no. 1–2: 155–157.

_____. 2005. "Review of *Secrecy and Cultural Reality: Utopian Ideologies of the New Guinea Men's House*, by Gilbert Herdt." *Anthropological Forum* 15, no. 1: 94–97.

_____. 2006. "Dreams, *Laki*, and Mourning: A Psychoanalytic Ethnography of the Yagwoia (PNG) 'Inner Feminine.'" Part 1 of 3. *Oceania* 76, no. 1: 27–60.

Neumann, E. 1954. *The Origin and History of Consciousness*. Princeton, NJ: Princeton University Press.

_____. [1973] 1988. *The Child: Structure and Dynamics of the Nascent Personality*. London: Karnac.

Roheim, G. 1952. *The Gates of the Dream*. New York: International Universities Press.

Schilder, P. 1950. *The Image and Appearance of the Human Body*. New York: International Universities Press.

Schore, A. N. 1994. *Affect Regulation and the Origin of the Self: The Neurobiology of Emotional Development*. Hillsdale, NJ: Lawrence Erlbaum.

Segal, H. 1993. "On the Clinical Usefulness of the Concept of the Death Instinct." *International Journal of Psycho-Analysis* 74: 55–61.

Solms, M., and O. Turnbull. 2002. *The Brain and the Inner World*. London: Karnac.

Spielrein, S. [1912] 1994. "Destruction as the Cause of Coming into Being." *Journal of Analytical Psychology* 39: 155–186.

Stern, D. 1985. *The Interpersonal World of the Infant*. New York: Basic Books.

Uexkull, J. von. 1957. "A Stroll through the Worlds of Animals and Men." Pp. 5–80 in *Instinctive Behaviour*, ed. C. Schiller. London: Methuen.

_____. 1982. "The Theory of Meaning." *Semiotica* 42, no. 1: 25–82.

Watson, J. W. 1971. "Tairora: The Politics of Despotism in a Small Society." Pp. 224–275 in *Politics in New Guinea*, ed. R. M. Berndt and P. Lawrence. Nedlands: University of Western Australia Press.

Winson, J. 1985. *Brain and Psyche: The Biology of the Unconscious*. Garden City, NY: Anchor.

Chapter 4

TO DREAM, PERCHANCE TO CURE
Dreaming and Shamanism in a Brazilian Indigenous Society

Waud H. Kracke

The anthropologist Jackson S. Lincoln ([1935] 1970), whose book *The Dream in Primitive Cultures* was the first extensive review of anthropological studies of dreaming in other cultures, argued that dreams in which the dreamer receives a direct message from God, or from one of the deities, are so rigorously defined by cultural belief that they are not amenable to personal interpretation. Dreams of directives or communications from a supernatural figure, which he dubbed "cultural pattern dreams," are held to be so stereotyped in form as not to allow of the expression of any personal meaning that could be interpreted psycho-analytically. Johannes Fabian (1967) goes even further, asserting that because

Notes for this chapter begin on page 118.

the Jamaa cult in the Congo has an elaborated theology of dreams, the dreams of members of that cult cannot ever be understood as the expression of unconscious wishes (cf. Tedlock [1987] 1992a: 21; see also Hunt 1989: 82, 146–149).

I disagree with Lincoln about the uninterpretability of such dreams. Unconscious meaning, as Freud remarked ([1905] 1963: 78), oozes from every pore, and any mental production, no matter how apparently stereotyped, expresses personal meaning. True, the significance of a dream depends very much on what dreaming means for the dreamer in his or her culture, and on the kinds of interpretations that the culture provides for the dreams. In a society where dreams are culturally elaborated, where dreaming may be a space of action as real as waking life, the significance of a dream may be quite different from what it is in a culture in which dreams are 'froth', or the 'random firing of neurons'. Still, dreams are constructed from unconscious thoughts, and the very appearance of a dream of a deity must have unconscious resonances for the person who has the dream.

Can there be dreams that are so rigidly pre-patterned that they can have no unconscious meaning for the dreamer? If this is true, it presents a serious impediment to Freud's theory of dreaming. It seems highly unlikely that there could be two types of dreams, one formed from repressed wishes and conflicts and the other having simply a conscious, manifest form, externally given from cultural belief, with no unconscious basis. Indeed, in Freud's view, the unconscious is expressed not only in dreams but in gestures, in all kinds of daily acts, in thoughts, in any mental production, even if it is most obviously detectable in dreams and in slips of the tongue and similar betrayals that momentarily open a rift to the unconscious (Freud [1900] 1951; [1901] 1956; [1905] 1963: 76–78).

Let us examine this question by looking at dreams in a culture that has a highly developed set of concepts and beliefs about dreams that render them spiritually significant and has traditional modes of interpreting them: the Parintintin Indians of Western Amazonas Brazil.[1] Dreaming has a central place in Parintintin epistemology. For this tropical forest Brazilian people, who ended their migration from the Atlantic coast on the eastern shores of the Madeira River, dreaming is an important way not only of *apprehending* reality, but of acting *in* reality as well. Dreaming is a powerful medium of perception that gives even an ordinary person the capacity to anticipate future events, to pick up the presence of evil spirits, to sense another person's longing for him or her—or, like a shaman in the '*tokáia*'[2] healing ceremony, to communicate with healing spirits such as the Sky People. Anyone who dreams, they say, "has a bit of shaman" (*tem um pouco pajé*) (Kracke 1987).

Dreams merit their own grammatical form in the Kagwahiv language, a Tupí language spoken by groups scattered along the Madeira River and in Rondônia. When dreams are narrated, they are regularly told with a special discourse marker, '*ra'ú*', which is used only in recounting dreams. This particle is a kind of tense marker, suggesting that dreams are felt to have a distinctive place in past time. And it is one of a series of past-tense markers that indicate past events known only through report, not first-hand (Kracke 1979). Like Kwakiutl (Boas 1947: 245), Kagwahiv is quite specific about the epistemological status of statements about the past.

Dreaming is the special province of *pajés*, or shamans. Whereas ordinary people can foresee future states through their dreams, if properly interpreted, shamans can act in their dreams to bring about events. Or rather, they once could act in their dreams, for the last shamans among the Kagwahiv died 20 years ago or more. In their dreams, those who were *'ipají'* (possessed of special powers) could bring about success or failure in warfare or in hunting (*'ohã-mongó'*), or could send their *'rupiguára'* (a shaman's familiar spirit) to bring sickness to someone or to kill him or her. And finally, shamans were literally created in the dreams of older shamans.

The Power of One Who Is *'Ipají'*

A key instrument or agent of a *pajé*'s ability to cause events was his *'rupiguára'*, a kind of spiritual associate or alter ego that had a part in practically all expressions of the shaman's power. When during the *'tokáia'* healing ceremony the *pajé* summoned various spirits to blow on the sick person and sing over him or her, it was the *pajé*'s *'rupiguára'* that would go up to summon the animal spirits, forest demons (*'añang'*), and Sky People. The *pajé*'s *'rupiguára'* that traveled to the abode of the spirits in trance can be seen as a kind of alter ego of the *pajé*, almost translatable as his 'soul'; but the spirits he summoned, insofar as they would obey his summons and come at his bidding, were also his *'rupiguára'* (Kracke 1992: 134–137). When a shaman caused death by singing over a victim's hair, the actual agent by which the death was brought about—the snake or jaguar or disease that killed the person—was the shaman's *'rupiguára'*. And when a shaman dreamed game for someone (*'ohãmongó'*), the animals that allowed themselves to be killed by the hunter for whom they were dreamed are also spoken of sometimes as the *pajé*'s *'rupiguára'*. So if the shaman dreams of someone lying in a hammock, and thus invokes a tiger to kill that person (a hammock in a dream represents a jaguar because of the reticular pattern of the hammock's weave), the jaguar is his *'rupigwára'*: he has literally "caused a tiger" (Borges 1964; see Kracke 2003: 153).

Thus, the various spirits that are influenced or compelled to carry out tasks by a *pajé* are referred to as his *'rupiguára'*. But a shaman also had a spirit that was much more closely identified with him, a kind of alter ego, and this spirit is referred to as his particular *'rupiguára'*. A shaman sometimes had his *'rupiguára'* tattooed on his chest. This kind of *'rupiguára'* is quite closely identified with the individual shaman, for at birth the *pajé* himself was an incarnation of that particular spirit—through the medium of the dream of another *pajé*. A supernatural figure (perhaps the master-spirit of an animal, or the spirit of a disease, or even one of the Sky People) would appear to a *pajé* in his dream and request to be born. This *pajé* would indicate a woman who was ready to conceive to be the spirit's host. The spirit then would enter her womb, to be born as a child destined to become a shaman, with that spirit as his primary *'rupigwára'*. When he was born, the child would be spoken of as the *'jihúva'ga'* (the born one) of the shaman who dreamed his birth (that is, *caused* his birth through his dream). A child may also be spoken of as the *'jihúva'ga'* of its father, so the shaman would 'conceive' a child in a sense analogous to the father's role in conceiving a child. And the spirit that was reborn as the child became the child's particular *'rupiguára'* when the child grew up and was initiated into the shamanic role. It was only through being the *'jihúva'ga'* (literally, the dream-child) of another shaman that one could ever assume shamanic power (Kracke 1992: 139–140).

A shaman's *'rupiguára'* had a particular role in the shaman's dreams as well. According to Paulinho—the oldest Parintintin I knew, a highly intelligent man with a remarkable memory who was my foremost authority on matters of religious belief—the *'rupiguára'* came to a shaman "at night," in his dreams, and told him things. Perhaps that was also when the *'rupiguára'* received its instructions from the shaman.

Dreams and *'Ra'úva'*

The participation of his *'rupiguára'* in a shaman's dreams, if this conception voiced by Paulinho can be taken as representative of general Kagwahiv beliefs, distinguishes them markedly from the dreams of ordinary people. I have never heard the dreams of lay people characterized as something recounted by an external entity of any kind—with the single exception of those dreams that are taken to be communications from the departing *'ra'úva'* of a dying relative. These are dreams in which the dying person appears to the dreamer in a dream close to the time of death. True, the term *'ra'úva'* can refer to an entity something like a soul, and it is used to translate the Christian concept of 'soul' or *alma*. The explanation of the avoidance of eating deer meat when one's child is sick is that (the spirit of) the deer "tramples on the *'ra'úva'*" (*'opyvondý ahe ra'úva-rehe'*). It is alternatively said that the deer's spirit "tramples on the liver" of the sick person, suggesting that the *'ra'úva'*-soul may reside in the liver (Kracke 1991: 227–228, 232). A ghost is sometimes called *'ra'úvaguéra'*, that is, what was once a *'ra'úva'*, a former *'ra'úva'*. But *'ra'úva'* can also simply refer to an image: a picture of a canoe (*'yhára'*) is *'yhára ra'úva'*. The general sense of *'ra'úva'* when it is applied to dream-images refers to the images as illusions, rather than to any notion that the appearances of people and objects in a dream are 'souls' of the things and people that appear in the dreams (Kracke 1979: 127–128).[3]

This term also occurs as a grammatical particle, *'ra'ú'*, which identifies what you are relating as a dream narrative. This dream-telling particle is linked with a past-tense marker, *'ra'é'*, which is used when something that you are telling about as having happened in the past is something that you heard about from someone else or have only indirect knowledge of. (When speaking about an event you witnessed or took part in yourself, you would use a different past tense particle, *'ko'*.) The dream-particle *'ra'ú'*, which occurs in other languages of the Tupí family, seems to have a connotation of unreality or deception. In ancient Guaraní, it was used to indicate something asserted in jest or for deception (*"de burla"*; Montoya 1876: 74).

For the most part, dreams are conceived in mental terms either as the continuation of a train of thought from waking mentation into sleep, as wishful thoughts (Kracke 1979: 135–136; 1999: 260–261), or as predictions—"experiences that reveal emergent possibilities," in Michael Brown's ([1987] 1992: 157) apt phrase (Kracke 1979: 130–132; 1999: 263). Certain specified kinds of dreams, though, are understood in terms of special perception or communication. Nightmares are a sensing of the proximity of an '*añang*', warm dreams of someone indicate that the person is thinking of one and has "spoken one's name," and a dream about a dying person may be a last communication of the departing soul.

The search in dreams for predictions of the future bears closer examination, for it would seem to be a way in which ordinary people approach the power of shamans in their dreaming. Such perceptions of the incipient future are not direct; rather, they are mediated by symbols that must be recognized by the dreamer or by a person (often an older and a more knowledgeable person) to whom the dreamer may recount the dream for clarification. Thus, a dream about a hammock predicts an encounter with a jaguar, due to the similarity between the open-mesh weave of a hammock and the reticular pattern of a spotted jaguar's pelt. Fire predicts fever, and to dream of an old broken-down house foreshadows someone's death—perhaps, but not necessarily, the death of a resident of the house dreamed of. To dream of honey means pregnancy because of an elaborate analogy between the Kagwahiv theory of conception, in which the fetus is nourished by semen of repeated intercourse, and bees' production of honey to feed their larvae. Most of these interpretations are based on some kind of metaphorical analogy, either straightforward (fire = fever) or complex, like the last two. Dreams of wild parties predict success in hunting peccary, a piglike mammal that crashes through the woods in herds. Other interpretations are based on mythic associations. For example, a dream of sexual organs foretells the possible killing of a tapir because of the strong association of that hoofed animal with unbridled masculine sexuality—an association that is codified in a myth in which the tapir is the adulterer. But the point is, first, that this is a form of 'vision beyond current reality' that *anyone* can achieve in dreaming, as is also the perception of '*añang*' in a nightmare, and, second, that it requires a special esoteric knowledge of the symbols in which dream perceptions of the future are coded, a knowledge that is often associated with a feel for the mythic associations of particular animals or objects, which was once the province of the shaman. Indeed, the symbolic equivalences by which one may learn of the future through one's dreams are the same ones that the shaman used to employ to alter the future through *his* dreams. A shaman could ensure successful tapir hunting by dreaming a sexual dream, or could bring peccary to hunters by dreaming of a party—the same metaphorical equivalences used in divining the predictions of everyday dreams.

Nonetheless, although shamanic knowledge may be useful in interpreting a dream, the perception of the future in dreams is always presented as a natural process, unmediated by spiritual entities. Though the foreknowledge of the future is a somewhat shamanlike capacity, and does make any dreamer "a little bit of a shaman," it has never been described to me in terms of spirits communicating knowledge to the dreamer, as the elderly chief Paulinho described the *pajé*'s '*rupiguára*' communicating to him. Conceptually, then, there seems to be a marked distinction between the dreams of ordinary people, which are understood as either thought processes or direct perceptions of spiritual reality, and those of shamans, which involved communication from the '*rupiguára*' and had causal efficacy.

The Experience of Dreaming as a Shaman

When we look at how people report their personal experience of dreaming in private interviews, however, the distinction is not always so sharp. In fact, the idea of dreaming as an expression of shamanic power seems to be implicit in the way that at least some people experience their dreams. For some individuals, dreaming entails a kind of identification with shamanic power.

The way in which this identification with shamanic power is manifested differs considerably from individual to individual. I have seen several instances in which informants experience their dreams as powerful, that is, as having the capacity to realize what they predict. Paulinho, the elderly chief I have mentioned, once dreamed of a fire that consumed the frame of a house in which at the time I was hanging my hammock to sleep. This dream took place when I had just spent some time upriver at a settlement other than the one Paulinho headed, which I think he experienced as an abandonment. As soon as he reported the dream to me, however, he offered the immediate reassurance that on awakening from his dream, he had canceled the fever that otherwise would have ensued for me by performing '*opohãmondók*' (break medicine), the rite of tearing pieces bit by bit off a thatch-palm leaf while reciting lines to void the state of affairs presaged in the dream. He was genuinely concerned lest his angry dream cause me some harm, and felt that he had saved me from it with his nullifying ritual. In another case, Paulinho's wife Catarina complained that she had dreamed game for her son Zeca, but that he had passed up the opportunity by failing to go hunting. Again, she took some credit for the potential for successful hunting that her dream predicted.

At least one person identified himself even more closely, perhaps openly, with a *pajé* in his dreaming. Pedro Neves, a charmingly voluble and cheerfully expressive old man I knew in 1967–1968,[4] whose original name before contact (still sometimes used) was Diré, appropriated the shamanic curing function in his dreams. Pedro Neves (Diré) was a warm, vivacious, and humorous old man who loved to tell myths and ancient tales. He was fascinated with shamanism and loved to recount his visits to his grandfather, the shaman Jahy'ri, at his home '*Čava'egwái*' (Old Man's Tail).[5] So intrigued with shamanism was he, and so nurturing, that once when I had a foot injury and heard him singing by the fire at night, I strongly suspected that he was singing shamanic songs for the healing of my badly infected foot. As I recorded in my field notes: "Last night I woke at 1:30 to see a fire in Diré's fireplace and Diré sitting by it. I had asked him if he knew any songs to heal my foot, and he [had] said no, only an '*ipají*' knows; but I wondered if he was surreptitiously singing."[6] Yet Pedro Neves could not himself take up the calling of an '*ipají*', since (unlike his grandson Carlos, who was dreamed by the '*ipají*' Capitão) his birth had not been dreamed by a shaman.

One evening, when several children were severely sick in the settlement, including his grandson Pedrinho, I passed by Pedro Neves's house and heard him singing a song on his porch. I asked him what it was. "'*Kã'nã*'," he said, and then he told me the following dream, recorded in my field notes:

I dreamed that the '*kã'nã*' [crippled ones] came to Pedrinho's house and blew on him. Now he won't die. [*Ahayhú kã'nã uhu Pedrinho'ga-pýri, ipývo ... ndomanói.*]

Their song that Pedro Neves sang was:

'*ji a'apó nomanomanói*'	I make people not die,
'*nomanói tußei*'.	not die indeed.
'*ji a'apó-kwerá*'	I make them wake up [come to life]

The '*kã'nã*', explained Pedrinho's older brother Carlos, who sat by during my interviews with Pedro Neves, translating when necessary, are humanlike spirits ("They seem like '*añang*', ghosts," [he said]) who live in the forest and blow on people like '*ipají*' to make them better.[7]

Elaborating his dream, Diré said he went up to the sky to bring down the '*kã'nã*'. Thus, he performed in dream just as an '*ipají*' does in the '*tokáia*' curing ceremony (which he had described to me not long before he had this dream): going out (the '*ipají*' in the form of his '*rupiguára*') to bring spirits from their abodes (in the sky, water, or forest, or under the ground) to come and blow on the patient in the healing gesture typical of Tupí *pajés*.

Not a month earlier, when Pedro Neves was sick himself, he told me that he dreamed that the Yvaga'nga, the Sky People, came down and "blew on him, [and] said he would get well."[8] He had said "Sky People," but the specific beings he mentioned—Piarombýra'ga and Mbahíra—are not Sky People. Mbahíra, in fact, is the Tupí creator-hero who in Kagwahiv mythology is bound to earth and lives in rocks. This discrepancy is significant. The Sky People are associated with shamanism: the myth of the founding of the Sky People is also the foundation myth of shamanism, and the curing ceremony is a recapitulation of this myth. The shaman goes to the corners of the cosmos to contact the spirits and call them to the cure, and his spirit-journey recapitulates Pindova'umi'ga's visits to different parts of the universe before going to the sky to make the realm of the Sky People. But the Sky People are also associated with the Harpy Eagle moiety, the moiety represented by high-flying birds, whereas Pedro Neves belonged to the opposite moiety, whose eponymous bird is the ground-dwelling *mutum* or curassow, distinguished for its close family life. Mbahíra, the trickster culture-hero, who created the contours of the rivers and valleys, brought fire to humans from the vultures, and lives in rocks,

is associated with the Curassow moiety. Mbahíra is also endowed with shamanic powers: in the many stories about "The Adventures of Mbahíra" (Nunes
Pereira 1967: 553–582), Mbahíra must resuscitate his hapless companion Itariano, who often comes to grief and perishes in his attempts to copy Mbahíra's
miraculous feats. But Mbahíra is not symbolically associated with shamanism
as are the Sky People. He is never one of the spirits summoned by the *pajé* into
the '*tokáia*' to lend his power for the cure of a patient.

Pedro Neves's inaccurate inclusion of the ground-dwelling Mbahíra among
the Sky People glosses over a dichotomy that is fundamental to Parintintin cosmology and linked with the opposition between the moieties. Since shamanism has a symbolic association with the Harpy Eagle moiety (through the Sky
People), this brings out the very discrepancy in Pedro Neves's own position.
Not only does Pedro Neves belong to the Curassow moiety, but he is performing curative feats in his dreams that he is not entitled to do, since he was not
born a *pajé*. In other words, he is practicing shamanism 'without a license'.

Later, when I was carrying out a series of personal, in-depth interviews with
him, Pedro Neves recounted to me another dream in which he entered even
more directly the world of the '*ipají*'. In a series of dreams in my fifth interview
with him (4 July 1968), he confronted the more menacing and mysterious
aspects of shamanism:

Dream 1: An owl—came, it was eerie ['*ipojý*']. "Here is where you are staying!"
[it said]. I was afraid. An owl's eyes are dark. [He gestures to his eyes.] "Don't
mess with me! Don't be afraid of me," it said. It makes one bleed. [He makes
motions of cutting wrists and sucking blood.]

[I ask in Portuguese, "What did it look like?" or, literally, "How did it appear?"]
It has shamanistic power ['*ipají*']. "You are sick. You will not die," [it says]. It
spoke, and it blew [on him, like a shaman]. That's all. '*Ipají*'—the owl is really
wise ['*okwahaheté*'].

[I repeat the question, "How did it appear?"] Like Yvondéuhu [an '*añang*'],
whose mother is an '*ipají*'. Yvondéuhu shoots a stick of wood, just like a shotgun.
"You go see," said the owl. "Don't fight with us—no more fighting with us."

Dream 2: I had a second dream [about] Kanindéuhu [Blue and Yellow Macaw].
"Ah! Ah! Ah!" it said. "Are you Kanindéuhu?" "I am Kanindéuhu." "You stay
and be my pet ['*renymbáv*']." Kanindéuhu is really beautiful! I say, "You stay
here with me." "I won't stay here. My son will stay with you, named Ararí"
["Little Macaw," in Portuguese, Maracanã].

[I ask, "Who is Kanindé?"] Ararí's father, Kanindé. Ararí is Kanindé's son. [I
ask, "Where does it live?"] In the sky. "You stay, Ararí, don't cry. You'll have
food to eat."

Dream 3: I dreamed of you, too. You were going this way. "What are you cough-
ing now?" Later on, your illness passed ['*opig ndehe*']. The cold said, "I come,
you go far." I said, "Don't give it to me. I'll go far away." The catarrh said,
"We're like that" ['*ore ko natuvẽ*', using the exclusive 'we']. "Don't come," I
said, "I'm going far away."

[I ask, "You saw the catarrh?"] Just like an *'ipajĩ'*. In the old days I didn't see them—catarrh, owls, big snakes—now I see them a lot. [I ask, "What did it look like?"] Bones in front, catarrh was scary ['*ipojý'*]. Just like the smoke of a fire. [I ask, "Who did it look like?"] Just like a *santo* [saint].

Pedro Neves went on to relate two more dreams: one of a deceased son of Boabá, a former playmate of his, who came to see him in his dream "as an '*añang*'" (he said to him "Later Kracke will give you money"); and another about this man's brother, João Boabá, dealing with João's jealous anger at his wife, leading to reflections on the disruptive consequences of jealousy. Whatever the complicated personal feelings these dreams deal with, they express the kind of immersion in the world of shamanic spirits—'*rupiguára'*—that in waking life is normally closed to the uninitiated.[9]

Pedro Neves's relationship with shamanism was different from Paulinho's—much more intense, but also more ambivalent. He was acutely interested in the whole topic of shamanism: it was he who first gave me details of the shaman's dreaming the birth of his successor. As a warm and caring man, he identified with the curing activity of the *'ipajĩ'*. He seemed to aspire at some level to the curative power of the *'ipajĩ'*, as illustrated by the dream in which he brought the *'ikã'nã'* to blow on Pedrinho and cure him. Yet he never claimed shamanic power, nor was it attributed to him. To be sure, he was not dreamed, but more than that, I think he had mixed feelings toward the power of one who is *'ipajĩ'*. In the group of dreams I have just presented, the power is menacing, almost threatening. The owl that represents shamanism in his dream is a stern figure, reprimanding like a parent admonishing a child not to fight—like his grandfather (his mother's father, Iguaharé), whom he had described, in the previous interview two days earlier, scolding his companions for fighting among themselves. In that interview, he described his grandfather, "a great chief," catching his companions in lovemaking and thrashing them. Diré himself escaped a thrashing only because his grandfather did not catch him. Does his fear of the austere figure of the owl in the dream, and the day residue of his grandfather's scoldings, manifest the guilt that he must feel about acting as if he were a shaman in his dreams, confronting illness and giving in to the nocturnal enticements of shamanism? When finally faced with the personified spirit of illness, rather than confronting it confidently with shamanic audacity, he pleads with it to leave him alone, promising to flee far away if it will do so—hardly the attitude of a shaman who is self-confident in his powers. Perhaps this reflects an insecurity he feels about acting in his dreams as a shaman, when he was not born one.

Discussion

The dreams told to me by Pedro Neves have the earmarks of what J. S. Lincoln ([1935] 1970) calls "culture pattern dreams." They are dreams in which a supernatural figure appears to the dreamer, very like the '*rupigwára'* in the dreams of the *'ipajĩ'*, and makes a pronouncement or engages in a dialogue like the dialogues that the shamans of old used to hold with spirits that appeared in the *'tokáia'* (shelter) in the now-defunct curing ceremony. The dream of the *'ikã'nã'* in particular reproduces exactly the way in which the *'ipají'* used to summon spirits to help cure a patient. Thus, the dreams appear to take on a stereotypical cultural form whose significance is to be understood in the context of an important social institution.

Yet at the same time they are very clearly expressions of personal motive and unconscious conflict. The *'kã'nã'* dream expresses a profound wish to be able to intervene with the spirits on behalf of Pedro Neves's sick grandchild, and the third dream of the trilogy of encounters with supernatural beings—his confrontation with the spirit of illness—demonstrates an equal protectiveness toward me. Yet the very menacing quality of the illness in the last-mentioned dream suggests more complicated feelings, perhaps ambivalence toward me and a sense of responsibility for the threat of illness (after all—as Paulinho's dreams more openly confirm—if he has the power to cure illness, he has the power to cause it as well).

An event in Diré's life that may have contributed to focusing his wish to be able to cure was the death of his younger brother, which occurred when Diré was in his early teens. As he told me a few days before relating the dreams, he saved his mother from a war party of the much-feared Mura Pirahã by running into the woods with her, but his younger brother did not escape and was killed. Perhaps his grief over the loss of his brother may have been colored by guilt stemming from sibling rivalry, which the situation of childhood renders highly problematic in Parintintin society (see Kracke 1991: 214). The dream pair he recalls in association to the dreams recounted above juxtaposes two brothers, one of whom, a jealous and violent man, was living in the same settlement where Pedro Neves was staying, while the other was emphatically dead, now an *'añang'*, or ghost.

If the dreams themselves do reflect at one level some measure of stereotyped form, the fact of dreaming them fulfills a wish that helps Pedro Neves resolve his conflicts—the wish to have the curative powers of a *pajé*. For both Paulinho and Pedro Neves, then—and for the latter's wife Maria, as well—it is crucial in understanding the meaning of their dreams to take into account their belief in the power of dreams to have shamanic efficacy in the waking world, for good or ill.

Not surprisingly, it is the elderly Kagwahiv, those who grew up when the shamanic tradition was still strong and who observed or experienced first-hand shamanic cures, whose dreams are most influenced by the shamanic nature of dreaming, and whose very experience of dreaming is shaped by the close association between dreaming and shamanism. Dreams of the next younger generation may be imbued with notions of dreaming as predictions or direct perceptions of others' feelings (as, for example, the belief that one dreams of another person because that person is thinking warmly of one and speaking one's name), or of nightmares as the direct sensing of the presence of *'añang'*. But the sense that dreaming itself constitutes a powerful shamanic activity is something that only the older Kagwahiv exhibit—and not all of them.

Even among those who do, there is considerable personal variation among individuals as to how deeply, and in what way, the identification with shamanism manifests itself in their dreams and in the way in which they experience them. Paulinho was frightened of the potential power of his own dreams—more and more so as I came to know him better—and became increasingly reluctant to talk about his dreams. It was as if this source of power, though universally available, was a dangerous and mysterious domain because it is uncontrollable when one lacks the necessary knowledge possessed by an '*ipají*'. For Pedro Neves, on the other hand, dreaming was his unique opportunity to exercise the healing power of shamanism that he longed to possess yet (as one not born of a shaman's dream) did not have other direct access to, nor the right to practice. His dreams suggest some guilt and fear over his nocturnal exercises in shamanic healing. It was, to be sure, a mysterious and dangerous power, yet for Pedro Neves not unambivalently unwelcome. Pedro Neves and, much later (perhaps only half-jokingly), his wife Maria were the only ones who expressed such open identification with shamanic powers in their dreams.

Culture Pattern Dreams: Some Comparisons

As stated above, many of the dreams discussed in this article have the form of the culturally stereotyped reports of dreams designated by J. S. Lincoln ([1935] 1970) as "culture pattern dreams," in which a supernatural figure brings a message for the dreamer. Contrary to Lincoln's dictum, however, such dreams can be interpreted as expressing personal conflicts. They do have a latent content that is conveyed in disguised form in the dream and can be understood through the dreamers' free associations.

Another example of a culture pattern dream is provided by Erika Bourguignon's (1954) article, "Dreams and Dream Interpretation in Haiti," a classic in the anthropology of dreams. Bourguignon writes of a dream told her by a young Haitian woman who accompanied her on a visit to a family in the country, in which the young woman (the dreamer) was approached by three deities of her household shrine in Port-au-Prince.

> Because I am not in Port-au-Prince, not taking care of the shrine, Mystè Erzili [her name for a print of the Mater Dolorosa] spoke to me thus: that I don't need her, neither her nor Papa Ogun [another deity of her shrine]. She said … "I am happy you came—I need you very much." That is how she said it to me. (Bourguignon 1954: 264)

Here we are apparently faced with a characteristic culture pattern dream, in which a deity addresses herself in dream to the keeper of her shrine with a reprimand concerning lack of vigilance in attending the shrine. Later in the conversation, however, the girl let Bourguignon know that she found it difficult living in the country, away from the city to which she was accustomed. The reproach from her deities in the dream, then, is her own reproach to Bourguignon for taking her away from the city of her home and family.

When the girl recounted the dream in greater detail, it took on a new aspect: it came out that the figure in the dream she interpreted as being "Mystè Erzili" "in fact took the form of a young man the dreamer knew. At this point, she changed her mind and decided that "since it was a man," [the deity] must have been Papa Ogun—although he was dressed in white, not in Ogun's customary yellow." This development provides further possible motives for her wish to return to the city: "I am happy you came—I need you very much" sounds very different coming from a young man of her acquaintance than from the Mater Dolorosa of her shrine! In this case, the theme of supernatural communication lends authority to the expression of a wish in the dream, one which is not supernatural or religious but instead quite personal. The expression of the wish itself is not wholly disguised; rather, it is dissimulated by the interpretation of the dream in religious terms (Kracke 1987: 68–69).

Conclusion

As we can see in both Pedro Neves's dreams and the dream of Bourguignon's field assistant, culture pattern dreams are not as simple as they seem. Certainly, their meaning is colored by the supernatural figures in their content, and by the belief in these two cultures that communication with supernatural figures can take place. But for all that, it is by no means clear that such dreams do not express personal meanings or do not have latent content involving intimate personal wishes.

The culture pattern dreams exemplified in this article express their personal meaning in different ways. In the dream Bourguignon relates, the most personal level of the dream's meaning is directly represented in its images: the image of the young man of her acquaintance who pleads for her return. The disguise is in the overlay of interpretation, the 'secondary elaboration', which makes this young man into an avatar of the *orishá* from her household shrine. For Pedro Neves, on the other hand, it is the very fact of his dreaming of communication with supernatural figures that represents a fulfillment of his deepest wishes: the act of having contact in dreams with spirits makes him (in sleep, at least) an *'ipají'*. His being able to summon the *'ikã'nã'* in his dream gives him the power he longed for, to be able to heal, as he wished he could have healed his brother slain by the Mura Pirahã. His appeal, in one dream, to Mbahíra as one of the Sky People he meets and summons suggests this desire, for Mbahíra's most frequently used shamanic capacity was to bring back to life his ill-fated companion Itariano.

Culture shapes the material from which our lives and our dreams are made. The forms that we think with and to which we are committed, the values we espouse, the language we express them in, are all provided by our culture. But the wishes that move us, that we hide in our dreams, come from more concrete events of our lives: the accidents of our life that leave their mark in the lack that creates our desires—the lack that Bourguignon's assistant felt due to the young man she left behind in Port-au-Prince, as well as her comforting household shrine; the void left in Pedro Neves's life by the death of his brother.

We put together our dreams with all the materials available to us. What we know from our cultural knowledge about the nature of dreaming frames our experience of any dream we have. So it is with culture pattern dreams that represent the dreamer communicating with the gods. Yet the dream itself expresses our own, unique desires, the ones unavailable to our conscious that push us from within.

Acknowledgments

I am indebted to Lucia Villela Kracke for the article's title and for valuable help in editing. Thanks are due, also, to Cliff Wilkerson for suggestions that contributed importantly to the argument of the article. An earlier version was presented at the 35th annual meeting of the American Academy of Psychoanalysis in New Orleans, Louisiana, 12 May 1991.

Waud H. Kracke is Professor of Anthropology at the University of Illinois in Chicago, a research graduate of the Chicago Institute for Psychoanalysis, and a founding and faculty member of the Chicago Circle Association, affiliated with the École freudienne du Québec. He is a member of the American Anthropological Association, of the International Federation for Psychoanalytic Education (IFPE), of the École freudienne du Québec, and of GIFRIC (Groupe interdisciplinaire freudienne de recherche et d'intervention clinique et culturelle). His most recent publications include "A Language of Dreaming: Dreams of an Amazonian Insomniac" (1999); "Dream: Ghost of a Tiger, a System of Human Words" (2003); and, with Lucia Villela, "Between Desire and Culture: Conversations between Psychoanalysis and Anthropology" (2004), the afterword to Anthony Molino's *Culture, Subject, Psyche*.

Notes

1. I lived with the Parintintin for 11 months from February 1967 to September 1968 and in July–August 1973. In 1985, I participated in a FUNAI (Fundação Nacional Do Índio, Brazilian Indian Service) study preparatory to verifying the Parintintin traditional territory as a reservation (an *identificação de terra indígena*). Since then I made annual visits varying from weeks to months until 1992. Fieldwork included a project funded by the Spencer Foundation in 1989–1991 to study the Parintintin adaptation to contact with Brazilian society.
2. I use italics for words in Portuguese or Spanish and single quotation marks around italicized words to indicate Kagwahiv (the Parintintin language). A glossary of Kagwahiv terms is provided below.
3. Theories of dreaming are highly personal. I have written that the concept of '*ra'úva*' does not imply soul travel. For many of my informants, '*ra'úva*' simply refers to the dream-image. João Messias, however, told me in 1985 that in a dream, the dreamer's '*ra'úva*' goes forth and has experiences outside the dreamer's body.

4. He died in Tres Casas in 1973 before I could see him again.
5. Field Notes 1967, vol. 3, p. 57v; Sarilho, 26 November.
6. Field Notes 1967, vol. 2, p. 90v; Sarilho, 21 July.
7. Field Notes 1968, vol. 3, p. 454v; Sarilho, 23 January.
8. Field Notes 1967, vol. 3, p. 59v; Sarilho, 27 November. Neves's nocturnal encounters were syncretic. On another occasion, he had encountered Jesus Christ in a dream (Field Notes 1967, vol. 2).
9. In a somewhat lighter vein, more recently, Pedro Neves's wife Maria also claimed *pajé*-like status for some of her dreams. She claimed to have dreamed (the birth of) one of her grandchildren. His spirit was the spirit of a *tocar disco*—a phonograph!

Glossary of Kagwahiv Terms Related to Shamanism

añang (noun)—ghost of the dead that returns to capture the living; also, forest demons that haunt certain places (such as houses or villages abandoned because of deaths in them). Some of these spirits are named and have personalities.

ipají (descriptive verb)—possessed of supernatural powers. Also used as a noun to denote a shaman, in which use it is a synonym of the Tupí-derived Portuguese term *pajé*.

ipojý (adjective)—uncanny, anxiety provoking, with a sense of supernatural danger.

jihúva'ga (noun)—offspring. A child born as a spirit who entered the mother's womb at the direction of a shaman, who directed that spirit to her in his dream, is spoken of as the *jihuva* or *jihuva'ga* of that shaman.

kã'nã or *ikã'nã* (noun)—the crippled ones. A group of spirits who live by sucking nectar; one of the spirits that can be summoned by a shaman.

ko (grammatical particle)—an evidential past-tense marker used when you are telling about an event you witnessed or took part in yourself. See *ra'é*.

ohãmongó (verb)—to bring success in the hunt or in warfare through dreaming (an activity performed by a shaman, *ipají*).

opohãmondók (verb)—to carry out a ritual by breaking small pieces off a leaf of thatch, one by one, in order to cancel the prediction of a bad dream.

ra'é (grammatical particle)—an evidential past-tense marker used when something that you are telling about as having happened in the past is something that you heard about from someone else, or have only indirect knowledge of. See *ko*.

ra'ú (grammatical particle)—an evidential tense marker indicating that the action or event spoken of occurred in a dream. Occurs in other languages of the Tupí family, either with the same meaning or (as in ancient Guaraní) with a connotation of unreality or deception. See *ko, ra'é*.

ra'úva (noun)—(1) an image, such as a picture; (2) a dream-image; (3) the soul of a dying person, which appears as a dream-image to close relatives, announcing the moment of death; (4) the soul or life principle, which during life resides in the liver (if a deer is killed during the gestation or infancy of a child, the spirit of the deer *opyvondý ahe ra'úva-rehe* [tramples the child's soul with its hooves]; after death, the *ra'úva* turns into a ghost, *ha'úvagwéra* [literally, a former *ra'úva*, or what was previously a *ra'úva*]); (5) used to translate the Christian term 'soul'.

renymbáv (noun)—a pet

rupiguára (noun)—a shaman's familiar spirit, applied both to the spirit within the shaman that carries out his shamanic functions (spirit-journey, knowledge of future, etc.), and to the spirits under his command who carry out the shaman's wishes.

tokáia (noun)—curing ceremony in which the presiding shaman sits inside a small hut (*tokáia*) and the spirits contacted to cure the patient speak through the voice of the shaman.

References

Boas, F. 1947. "Kwakiutl Grammar with a Glossary of the Suffixes." Ed. H. B. Yampolsky and Z. S. Harris. *Transactions of the American Philosophical Society* 37, no. 3: 202(?)–377.

Borges, J. L. 1964. "Dreamtigers." P. 24 in *Dreamtigers*, trans. M. Boyer and H. Morland. Austin: University of Texas Press.

Bourguignon, E. 1954. "Dreams and Dream Interpretation in Haiti." *American Anthropologist* 56: 262–268.

Brown, M. [1987] 1992. "Ropes of Sand: Order and Imagery in Aguaruna Dreams." Pp. 154–170 in Tedlock [1987] 1992b.

Fabian, J. 1967. "Dream and Charisma: 'Theories of Dreams' in the Jamaa Movement." *Anthropos* 61: 544–560.

Freud, S. [1900] 1953. "The Interpretation of Dreams." Pp. 1–625 in *Standard Edition*, vols. 4–5.

———. [1901] 1956. "The Psychopathology of Everyday Life." In *Standard Edition*, vol. 6.

———. [1905] 1963. "Fragment of an Analysis of a Case of Hysteria." Pp. 7–144 in *Dora: An Analysis of a Case of Hysteria*. New York: Collier.

———. 1953–1974. *The Standard Edition of the Complete Psychological Works of Sigmund Freud*. 24 vols. Trans. and ed. J. Strachey, with A. Freud, A. Strachey, and A. Tyson. London: Hogarth Press. (Cited as *Standard Edition*.)

Hunt, H. 1989. *The Multiplicity of Dreams*. New Haven, CT: Yale University Press.

Kracke, W. 1979. "Dreaming in Kagwahiv: Dream Beliefs and Their Psychic Uses in an Amazonian Culture." *Psychoanalytic Study of Society* 8: 119–171.

———. 1987. "Everyone Who Dreams Has a Bit of Shaman: Cultural and Personal Meanings of Dreams—Evidence from the Amazon." *Psychiatric Journal of the University of Ottawa* 12, no. 2: 65–72.

———. 1991. "Don't Let the Piranha Bite Your Liver: A Psychoanalytic and Anthropological Approach to Kagwahiv (Tupi) Food Taboos." *Psychoanalytic Study of Society* 16: 205–246.

———. 1992. "He Who Dreams: The Nocturnal Source of Transforming Power in Kagwahiv Shamanism." Pp. 127–148 in *Portals of Power: Shamanism in South America*, ed. J. Langdon and G. Baer. Albuquerque: University of New Mexico Press.

———. 1999. "A Language of Dreaming: Dreams of an Amazonian Insomniac." *International Journal of Psychoanalysis* 80: 257–271.

———. 2003. "Dream: Ghost of a Tiger, a System of Human Words." Pp. 155–164 in *Dreaming and the Self: New Perspectives on Subjectivity, Identity, and Emotion*, ed. J. Mageo. Albany: State University of New York Press.

Lincoln, J. S. [1935] 1970. *The Dream in Primitive Cultures*. New York: Johnson Reprint Corporation.

Montoya, A. R. de. 1876. *Vocabulario y Tesoro de la Lengua Guarani*. Vol. 2: *Tesoro*. New ed. Vienna: Faesy and Frick; Paris: Maisonneuve y Cⁱᵃ.

Nunes Pereira. 1967. "Experiências e Estórias de Baíra, o grande burlão." Pp. 553–582 in *Moronguetá: Um decameron indígena*. Rio de Janeiro: Editora Civilização Brasileira.

Tedlock, B. [1987] 1992a. "Dreaming and Dream Research." Pp. 1–30 in Tedlock [1987] 1992b.

———, ed. [1987] 1992b. *Dreaming: Anthropological and Psychological Interpretations*. School of American Research Advanced Seminar Series. Santa Fe, NM: School of American Research Press.

Chapter 5

A PSYCHOANALYTIC REVISITING OF FIELDWORK AND INTERCULTURAL BORDERLINKING

René Devisch

My work combines both a phenomenological-anthropological and a psycho-analytic perspective. Through their reciprocal elucidation, I intend to reflect upon my experiences and work. More pointedly, this self-scrutiny of a European anthropologist's immersion in the lives of subaltern subjects in central Africa raises radical questions of an intersubjective, intercultural, and epistemological nature. It calls for a revisiting of the anthropological endeavor, which all too

Notes for this chapter begin on page 145.

often is merely appropriative, objectifying, or even othering. Post-colonial, feminist, and subaltern studies, developing in the context of the West's loss of its central and hegemonic position in today's increasingly multi-centered world scene occupied by heterogeneous civilizations and diverse knowledge systems, have unsettled anthropology. In the course of this decentering, we have witnessed a passage from an architectonic high-low, center-periphery perspective to an understanding of the world as a tapestry made up of a great variety of world-making possibilities, (alter/native) modernities, networks, and transnational and diasporic crossings.

On the one hand, however critical one might be of the ethnocentric (particularly the cognitivist and postmodern) biases and blind spots in today's social sciences,[1] there remains for me, as an anthropologist from the West, a distinct unease with the inescapably alien nature of intrusive anthropological research in local subaltern worlds. The more that I have felt adopted by my African hosts and have come to understand their socio-cultural life-world in its own terms, the more that a certain sensitivity for people's definition of self in the mirror of alterity constructs—conveyed in particular by school education, missionary Christianity, and transregional mass media—leaves me with a gnawing sense of guilt for our colonizing past, its exoticizing and persecutive nature, and hence paranoid imaginaries. Despite this, I continue to feel both a debt and an interpersonal loyalty toward my many Yaka hosts in rural southwestern Congo who integrated me into their lives during my anthropological field research in 1971–1974, or have welcomed me during my annual stays, since 1986, in Kinshasa.[2] On the other hand, my psychoanalytic training,[3] initially only in the Freudian-Lacanian tradition, and my limited clinical practice in Louvain (Leuven) with analysands from Flanders have been broadened by inspiration from Bracha Ettinger's matrixial psychoanalytic perspective on borderlinking, co-implication, and co-poiesis born of "resistance which is also an opening; closing which is also a gift ... insurmountable distance which is encounter" (Ettinger 2000: 93). Borderlinking produces unexpected linkages and co-implications, but it also unties, makes free.

A complementary psychoanalytical and anthropological perspective makes a number of particular assumptions, but principally "it assumes that much thought and activity takes place outside of conscious awareness" (Hunt 1989: 25). Images, fantasies, etiologies, metaphors, and forms of discourse and signification mediate, to some degree unconsciously, people's everyday lives, religious practices, socio-political commitments, and in fact most of their affect, desiring, and bodily involvement within their cultural logics and complex socio-cultural webs of significance. These webs are constitutive of the multi-layered fabric whose patterning reverberates through and between the various fields and levels of body-self, group-life, and world-views. Body, self, group, and world are parts of one another. They inform and recall the experience, not least that of childhood, in each of us, an experience that Obeyesekere (1980) has labeled the "muddy bottom." Such levels of interpenetration are true of any vital network or local group that anthropologists like to study. In other words, this type of psychoanalytic-anthropological perspective assumes the existence of a complex border zone within which the unconscious (transference) dimensions of the anthropological encounter incite a very subtle transformational borderlinking dynamic. These are the affects, emotion, imagination, interlocution, insights, adaptations, empowerment, and exchanges that take place between the anthropologist and the host community. The various phases and contexts of my fieldwork, first in a rural Congolese community and later in suburban post-colonial Kinshasa, have each mobilized a very different dynamic on both an interpersonal and intra-psychic as well as a theoretical and epistemological level. These experiences have further been echoed, during the period of 1980–1986, by my limited anthropological research into bodily symbolism and symptom formation in family medical practices located in Brussels and Antwerp and involving Moroccan, Turkish, and Flemish chronic epigastric patients (Devisch 1990),[4] as well as, since 1990, by my limited psychoanalytical-clinical experience as a member of the Belgian school of psychoanalysis of a Freudian-Lacanian tradition.

To scrutinize from a complementary psychoanalytical-cum-anthropological perspective some of the interpersonal and intra-psychic dynamics in these four fields of research or clinical experience, I have to adopt an unavowedly autobiographical mode. Let me first revisit some of the roots of my anthropological endeavors in earlier years and my studies of philosophy and anthropology in Kinshasa. Indeed, the question comes to mind, what exactly was it in my personal history that drove me to take up a career as an anthropologist and, some twenty years later, to become rather hesitantly involved in the world of Freudian psychoanalysis? I would admit to there being at work something of a spirit of doubt; an effort at mediation, at reconciliation, or, more precisely, at borderlinking between alterities; and, above all else, a concern to acquit myself of a debt toward subaltern people.

Over the years, I have moved from a Lévi-Straussian structuralist perspective to a genuine internal approach to cultural productions and world making in terms of their inner logic and composition (Devisch 1993). My focus is on the intercultural and intersubjective exchange, interaction, and consciousness that yield insight into cultures and site-specific knowledge practices and competences (Devisch 1995, 1996, 2003a). Moreover, it is part of my research endeavor's basic philosophy to promote a multi-vocal anthropology, that is, a polylogue between authoritative cultural voices in diverse sites. Working in the shattered world of suburban Kinshasa has forced me to expose myself to, and to examine from a psychoanalytic-anthropological perspective, the partly defensive and projective intersubjectivity or "self-othering" (Naficy 2000) unfolding in the encounter on the thin line of, on the one hand, the preconception of property, mastery, regulation, choice, rationality, and science and, on the other hand, the elusive *significance* or emergent meaning production that ties in with the proclaimed alien, namely, the non-cognitive, the unsayable, the bodily. This meaning production is developing along the associative chains of forces of desire, anger, and transference, or in line with the perspectivalism of crisis, pain, redemption, normalcy, and their opposites.

Compared to the Congolese subjects with whom I have had the privilege of meeting in their post-colonial settings, my itinerary entails a reverse process. As a descendant, though not by choice, of the Belgian colonizing people, I was initially in search of some form of African adoption as a student of philosophy in Kinshasa and of anthropology at the Congolese University of Lovanium. Then as an anthropologist and later in my capacity as a supervisor of doctoral research,[5] I sought and have continued to seek immersion in, if not integration into, a Congolese community as well as insights about various African societies from within their own rationale, perceptual categories, modes of encounter, and definitions of the subject in the group and the world. My autobiographical-cum-methodological question particularly concerns the interrogation of my own affinity with this predicament of bordercrossing and borderlinking, and the transference and counter-transference operating in that context. I also examine my curiosity about it. I wish to understand the epistemological tracks, the emotional and imaginative states and the ontological presuppositions utilized by the formerly colonized groups (at home and as migrants to the city or in the ex-colony's metropolis) to overcome that estranging othering bestowed on them by the hegemonic (post)colonial models. More concretely, how do the cultural matrices of these African communities filter and calibrate with the masculinist, dualist epistemology effected by the Western bureaucratic nation-state and its colonial endeavor? And how do they respond to the dualist Enlightenment (Cartesian, Hegelian) and phallologic representational patterns of Western academia derived from Western traditions of the book (school and Bible) that objectify scientific observation and present a hierarchical divide between nature and spirit—between matter or world and self, truth, and delusion? And how does the Judeo-Christian conversion and civilizing discourse about heathen pasts and salvific and occidentalized futures of individuals and nations affect black African cultures?

Fieldwork, Academia, and Clinical Practice

First Phase: Initial Encounters with Alterity

My involvement in anthropology has its roots in my own family history, as well as in the various challenges presented by the process of decolonization. My very name, René, which I would later at the age of 14 change to Renaat (at the insistence of my original Flemish culture on authenticity), recycled that of my maternal uncle. On the eve of World War II, some 15 years after having emigrated from Belgian Flanders to French Normandy, he died in 1939 of a brain tumor. My mother, who had cared for her dying brother, abandoned the plan to emigrate and returned to her native Flemish territory to found a family. I can still hear her repeatedly tell me, "I should not have given you your uncle René's name. He died so young." My mother's health had been made permanently fragile due to the deprivations she had experienced as a child of 6 to 16 years in the boarding schools set up for refugee children in the region of Paris during and after World War I. But I retain a distinct memory of the cordial and diligent hospitality she offered to the many farm workers, merchants, and craftsmen who nearly daily crossed the threshold of our large parental farm.

Our home was located along the border formed by the frontier between Belgium and the north of France, within a dozen kilometers of the English Channel. At night we could see the beam of the lighthouse at the port of Dunkirk. Our land formed part of the boundary with that region of France where the adult generation still spoke my Flemish language, whereas my cousins adopted the language of the schools and the French nation. During my childhood (I was born at the end of World War II), a regional trade in contraband based on agricultural produce, tobacco, and spirits took shape in the form of a passionate conspiracy between traffickers struggling to survive and the complicity of the inhabitants of the border area, who often hid the former from zealous customs officers. The family farm, with the active collusion of my father, thus became something of a refuge for small-time smugglers. In my childhood memories and fantasies, this 'frontier' constituted the mainspring of my family history. Powerfully engraved in the local imaginary as a zone of vital borderlinking, this axis was inscribed by the recourse to ruse in confrontations with foreign customs agents.

Fascinated by the diversity of cultures and the encounter with the 'other', I left my home country at the age of 21 for Kinshasa, the capital city of the Democratic Republic of Congo. The manner in which Charles de Foucauld had immersed himself in Touareg life at Tamanrasset in southern Algeria (in 1910–1916) inspired in me the desire for a respectful encounter with the spirit and aptitude of the other, with the purpose of understanding the other on their own terms and without seeking to change them in the slightest. I sought to initiate myself into a Congolese/Zairean culture, to give myself over totally to the world and discourse of my hosts. In such an encounter, I aimed to surpass my own limited cultural horizon and maximally to reduce the interference incurred by my presence as a foreigner. My own philosophical studies undertaken in this period, in the context of a multi-cultural group, were profoundly marked by meetings of and confrontations between cultures. I was fascinated by the militant Négritude movement (supported by the likes of Césaire, Fanon, Sartre, and Senghor), by the beginnings of a 'Bantu philosophy' (Kagame, Tempels), and by the autobiographical interrogation of the double heritage—negro and Occidental—as formulated by writers of the Négritude group. Authors such as Ludwig Binswanger, Martin Buber, Maurice Merleau-Ponty, Claude Lévi-Strauss, and Sigmund Freud, alongside my lively contacts with Koongo society in the region of Kinshasa and Yaka communities farther to the south, drew me in various ways to privilege the study of meaning inasmuch as it is impregnated at the same time with structure and energy, affect, sensuality, and authentic encounter.

My studies in the field of anthropology, carried out successively at the University of Louvain (Leuven) and later at the University of Kinshasa from 1968 to 1971, were a result of my intention to initiate myself in the Bantu genius and to give an attentive ear to the rising spirit of nationalism. Loyally sharing the living conditions of Congolese students in the dormitories of the Lovanium University campus, I was fascinated by the debates launched by the periodical

Présence Universitaire on the issues of Négritude. Students in this milieu questioned the colonial vision that Congolese intellectuals had assimilated, a vision fixed on the civilizing mission of the book (Bible and school), on a reformist modernism, and on the city and state. While the university fully participated in the project of implanting a scientific culture in the Occidental tradition, this student movement adopted the slogan of 'mental decolonization' (the expression is from Mabika Kalanda) and posited itself against the approach of materialist Catholic activism, with colonialist echoes, represented by the numerous Belgians who still dominated the leadership within the university. Indeed, Lovanium University displayed many aspects of a neo-colonial approach aimed at producing instrumental reasoning and a management mentality among the country's future administrative classes. And this dynamic amounted to an even more efficacious colonialism precisely because it was more liberal.

In the 1960s to 1970s, the Occident's colonial imaginary remained dominant among its heirs in the Kinois circles of expatriates and the Belgian Development Cooperation. Paradoxically, in depicting the other in terms of lack while at the same time creating a narrative imaginary field regarding the indulgence, seductiveness, and/or vitalism of the African, the colonizer and later the development experts in fact offered themselves an imaginary space for the self-indulgent consumption of the very thing that was being repudiated by their own colonial or expert development endeavor. The official behavior of the colonizer and development expert amounts to a peculiar fusion in which patriarchal, disciplinary authority is combined with the role of explorer and discoverer of a new, mainly urban ethic-in-the-making. Since the 1950s, Belgian society exported to the tropics its own schizophrenic engagement with reformist or high modernity: it condemned idleness and yet was trapped in its male, desiring fantasy-construct of playful extravagance and innocent and leisurely sexual life in the tropical bush and forest, 'untouched by civilization'. The Flemish novelist Jef Geeraerts (1967) forcefully expresses the self-indulgent ambivalence that the masculine explorer in the tropics feels toward both the technocratic colonial hero and the ascetic petty bourgeois ethic, now in vogue back home, of restraint, redemptive work, and planned social reproduction. Yet both are easily outdone by the narrator's fantasies regarding tropical luxuriousness at the edge of frantic desire and delirious violence associated in particular with allegedly 'wild' voluptuousness or the monstrosity of the pagan witch doctor and sorcerer.

Inspired by my contact with the Négritude movement, I gradually came to doubt the relevance of the Occidental projects of enlightenment and progress, the egocentric and autonomous individual, and the universal mission of (a European-rooted) Christian salvation. We in the student milieus at Lovanium allowed ourselves to be swept away by the appeal of President Mobutu to embrace his program of disalienation proposed under the motto "Recours à l'authenticité" (Resort to Authenticity). His parallel national development plan, Objectif 80 (Goal 1980), promised the nation—which he had newly christened Zaire—palpable socio-economic progress in the ensuing decade. By virtue of their return to authenticity, the Zairean people would ensure their position as heirs of the MPR (Mouvement populaire de la révolution, People's Movement of the Revolution), which would gradually transform itself into a party-state. The "Resort to Authenticity" campaign, in manifold ways, propagated a Zairean identity antonymous to a particular image of whites, portrayed as highly individualistic, susceptible to the power of money, inflexible in matters of technology, and too stringent in regulating time. Mobutist discourse demystified the colonial project and dislodged the Occidentals from their (post)colonial position of paternity and authority in relation to the Zairean people. From this point on, the white man is assigned the role of 'uncle', one that is defined in terms of duties instead of rights with regard to the nationals, who for their part now position themselves as sovereign authors of their own history (Devisch 1994).

In July 1971, I left the university campus. My Zairean co-students had, since 4 June, been conscripted into the armed forces for civic insubordination and lese majesty with regard to the chief of state. I then chose to spend an extended period of time searching experiential insight in a local culture on the basis of listening to the sole voice of the Yaka people living in the margins of the grand stage occupied by the party-state.

Second Phase: The Expatriate Anthropologist and the Host Community's Sense of Borderlinking

From October 1971 until October 1974, I lived among the northern Yaka people of the Bandundu province of southwest Congo, some 450 kilometers to the southeast of Kinshasa. The Northern Yaka inhabit a rural area, with on average some 120 inhabitants per village, located in the thinly populated northern Kwaango region bordering Angola. As my landing point, I chose the chiefdom of Taanda, a relatively autonomous district well anchored in ancestral tradition, the choice having been suggested in these terms by Léon De Beir (1975a, 1975b). A Jesuit missionary, De Beir in 1938–1939 had recorded there in great detail the religious life and ritual practices, and I had brought with me to the field a photocopy of De Beir's manuscript.[6] I lived in the same village, Yitaanda, throughout the period of my field research, leaving it only for brief stays in surrounding villages. My wife Maria interrupted her teaching of physics and mathematics to join me for the last four months of this period in Yakaland.

The onset of this first fieldwork as a novice anthropologist in an alien society evoked my childhood experience at the seashore. Both experiences entailed for me a fear of a loss of identity by being submerged in an indefinable and massive otherness. And yet at the same time, a sense of fascination drove me to let the encounter happen, in an ecstatic amazement, like high tide washing over as I lay on the beach. My arrival in a local community, with neither an invitation nor prior knowledge of my host family, left little room for choice or maneuvering. I had no option but to abandon myself to the most hospitable family in the group, in a complicit and reciprocal exchange of good wishes and seductive promises. I became set apart, sacralized, and thereby disarmed and benign. Indeed, after a few weeks, mourners of the deceased regional chief granted me the status of a native exile.

Ten days after my arrival, the maternal uncle of the ailing Taanda chief, Kapata, begged me to bring some medicines, stating that the request came from the chief himself. His coffin was brought to the village the day I arrived. My appearance at the bedside of the deceased chief, following a thunderstorm in which the hut of his successor was burned down, was perceived by the community as a safe conduct. When its sovereign dies, the community lives in anguish at the prospect that as long as the identity of the chief is in a process of disintegration, his chiefly forces of aggression—believed to take the form of a lightning bolt or a leopard attack—unleash themselves on the chiefdom, whose human and cosmic tissue has been deprived of its principal suture. During a palaver over the succession to the function of chief, a delegate of the superior N-nene dynasty associated me, by way of a mythic narration, to the Taanda chief N-leengi, whom Kapata had succeeded. N-leengi had been exiled by the colonial authorities in 1939 because he had taken part in the millenarian movement *mvungi*. He subsequently died while still in exile at Oshwe, in the Great Lakes region to the northeast of Bandundu. I then found myself received in the Taanda community as an ancestor 'reborn' (*rené*), the death of the one I 'reincarnated' now being dated to 1939.[7] It was by virtue of this identity that Taanda notables several times requested that I intervene at the chiefly tomb "in order that Kapata cease confining the big game with him in his other-tomb." Later, I was solicited to mediate with the N-saka dynasty "in order that the regional dynast N-saka put an end to its wrath against Kapata and his descendants, and restore peace to the Taanda territory."

By closely participating in village life, I was able to gain proficiency in the language and at the same time acquire many basic insights into the Yaka world. With time, the mutual confidence built up with the elders, with whom I often met, eased the way to repeated exchanges and the development of close individual relations with 27 healers; I eventually maintained regular contact with at least 5 of these. These contacts in turn afforded me the opportunity to attend a great number of diagnostic divinatory oracles and to observe closely the healing and/or initiatory seclusion of some 15 patients. Such bonds of generous friendship further serve to engender a sharp and receptive sense of listening, as well as attitudes of enthusiasm and loyalty that enable one to penetrate specialist and initiatic knowledges. I believe that the anthropologist is, in his or her very person and experience, the privileged instrument of research. Already in my second week in Taanda, my adult hosts were amazed at my attitude of "deference and commitment" (*-leembvuka*) in their regard. My supply of medicines and tender of first aid, which often took up to two hours of a day, constituted my gesture of exchange. I continued to do this in the knowledge that the closest dispensary was 60 kilometers distant and in another area where the people of Yitaanda, practically devoid of monetary resources, had no relatives to accommodate and assist them.

Through my performance of a myriad of manual tasks, my assistance in the construction of my hut, my occasional involvement in hunting expeditions or long treks, and my participation in feasts and dances, I defied the stereotypical image of the haughty white man. In view of obtaining the status of an elder or notable, that is, one of sufficient confidence and respect that the group would allow me to be initiated into the heart of its culture, I intentionally adopted in public some of the behaviors characteristic of a Yaka notable. Such behaviors included the ceremonial marks of respect and consideration that notables demonstrated toward each other, their affectation of a certain indifference with regard to the presence and tasks of women and youth, and their forms of greetings. I also closely observed the countless forms of initiatory therapies and everyday practices of health care and medicinal recipes, whereby master and novice, informant and anthropologist invested of themselves intellectually, emotionally, and physically, often in a coalescence of passion and anguish. From all this, a sense of mutual adoption between the anthropologist and the host group was developed.

It appears to me that the presence of a foreign researcher actually incites a group to elaborate on its places and moments of representation of itself to itself, not with the express intention of putting before the anthropologist an idealized mirror of what it is, but in order to fathom, in a new transferential field, its own means of self-definition, invention, and interrogation. This process resembles that of psychoanalysis of non-neurotic individuals. It is not as if the anthropologist provokes the host group to justify, for itself, its own institutions; rather, the researcher incites the community to relive, in a more articulated fashion, the lived experience of this new encounter. This meeting invites the group to re-embrace in a new perspective those elements that give life, consistency, and continuity to the given institution or ritual. The attentive ear and sympathetic gaze of the researcher stimulate notables and cult leaders to explore, more freely and with a certain pleasure, the riches of their language, conventions, and rites.

The core epistemological and anthropological question remains: in which way does the Western anthropologist's endeavor today as a so-called participant in a host society in Africa south of the Sahara, when moved by a post-colonial restorative stance, mark a difference that sets him or her apart from the colonial officer or missionary-ethnographer, the development expert, the post-colonial advocate for human rights, or the culture-sensitive tourist? The bifocality at the core of the anthropological perspective is yet a paradox. It advocates seeing local realities from the perspective of the subjects concerned, all the while self-reflexively observing the activity of others even while engaging in it and subsequently representing those insights in the Western academic traditions of persuasion. To the extent that it is relying on methods of reading and representing the other derived from Western scholarly traditions and on scopic distancing and scrutiny, how much does the ethnographic report still remain an exoticizing, if not othering, mode of representation rather than one of bordercrossing? Does an anthropologist's initial tendency toward border-crossing reflect in fact a more personal search concerned with the estranging stranger within him- or herself? Could the researcher be basically mobilized by an individual (largely unconscious) agenda of borderlinking that is drawn to those dimensions in the host group that reverberate within him- or herself?

A profound respect for diverse ways of life, a capacity for listening and empathy free of prejudices, discreet participation in village life, and a propensity for collective and respectful dialogue together constitute, I believe, the golden road along which the anthropologist can investigate a group and its life-world from the interior. Indeed, erudition, technical know-how, literary skills, or even medical knowledge are being shared or transmitted only in specific interactional settings within such a culture of orality and society governed by strict principles of seniority. The specialist knowledge sharing develops between a talented orator and responsive audience or a healer and patient or a master and apprentice in brief metaphoric wordings or through theatrical evocations with the public as witness. The researcher must then associate him- or herself with the transactional modes of experience and knowledge, as well as with the metaphorical procedures of signification that are at once corporeal, verbal, and scenic. In offering palm wine, cola nuts, and occasionally cloth, it is as if I was providing the Yaka strands by way of an invitation to let me participate in the weaving of a universe of shared knowledges and forces.

At the end of 1974, as we were saying our good-byes to the Taanda chief at the conclusion of our first and longest stay in the field, he asked my wife and me to name our first-born after his lineage. We accepted this gesture of filiation, which henceforth conferred on us the role of transmitters of social identity in the Taanda genealogy. When I first returned to Yitaanda in 1991, to prepare for the making of a film (Dumon and Devisch 1991), I was greeted by the principal reference name that the community had given me: N-ndedyeetu (the white man who became ours). The elders further welcomed me with the epithet, "Mamoosu tukukeembe" (To you we had committed everything).

Because of the distinct gender division of conduct, tasks, and public space in Yaka society, I hesitated to participate in the spheres proper to women. Given my unavowed pact to redress the image of this rural society already considerably disfigured by the (post)colonial gaze, I unconsciously obfuscated in my writing scenes of conjugal violence and of misery, as well as frequent instances of abuse of subordinates at the hands of civil servants and soldiers. On the other hand, I had the opportunity of closely observing the variable sequences of about 15 different *khita* initiatory therapies. I would later elaborate on this in a book (Devisch 1993) dealing with 'gyn-eco-logy' in the broad sense of the term, that is, the capacity for the transmission of life invested in woman, house, and inhabited world (including dwellings, cultivated fields, and zones of gathering and fishing). My research could not of course focus on the subjective experience of women engaged in obstetric care, for example. How would I experientially know about this? But I turned my interest to the work of culture: how does the gyn-eco-logical cult of *khita* inform fertility and its dysfunctions in the life of a woman, the group, and their relations with the world?

Yaka youth, for their part, captivated during their short stay in Kinshasa by a paradoxical affiliation to modernity and by the party-state's ideology, "Recourse to Authenticity," approached me in a manner characterized at once by seduction and resentment. They would confide in me as to how they did indeed view the 'village' and the ancestors as a source of life but above all as a source of oppression. Since my Christian, university, and European background all suggested spontaneously to them an inherent incapacity on my part to comprehend or commend village life, they would question me: "Do you really believe that the old people's fetishes and sorcery bring healing? That they would kill us if we refused to give them the lion's share of our earnings? Do you mean to have us believe that this collection of norms and customs or the counsel of the elders is at all useful in the construction of our great nation?" In response to this frequently posed challenge, I attempted to expose the caricatures that they expected me to play. I was also inspired by the experience my wife Maria was having with fellow women toward the end of our first long stay. Indeed, in my own person I offered to my hosts a space of encounter and a fecund but uncontrollable source of phantasms that step by step associated me with universes that were, after all, unknown to me. To some of them, I represented the figure of the all-knowing white or of a 'doctor' able to remove evil and bring swift healing. Others saw in me a promise of material progress or even a potential source of goods to be acquired by promising me their daughters in marriage, or by manipulating my own avidity for uncovering initiatory or highly protected knowledge.

Third Phase: Anthropology of the Body—Looking from 'There' to 'Here' as If It Were 'There'

I am therefore also much concerned with taking a new look, from the perspective of my African experience, at my own native society and the habitus of North Atlantic scientists. In particular, I wonder whether the Western anthropologist, on returning home and perhaps embracing psychoanalysis or intercultural philosophy, is able to unravel the unthought or deeply suppressed otherness so profoundly present in mainstream North Atlantic consciousness. What transpires, one might ask, beyond the slipstream of ongoing research and the backstage of hegemonic scientific claims? Back in my native Belgian culture in Flanders, I am often upset by the fixedness of a modern, male-biased outlook, propagated in the name of Western science or enlightened rationality and the autonomous subject. For it is this outlook that so relentlessly deploys defensive and projective phantasms with regard to the peoples of Africa south of the Sahara. The latter are ethnocentrically portrayed as the reversal of Euro-American ideals so as to allow us to metabolize a profound anguish with regard to our own instincts and sense of lack, degeneration, and death, or the very real negativity and fear within ourselves.

In my texts on post-colonial Kinshasa (Devisch 1995), the University of Kinshasa (Devisch forthcoming), and particularly the healing communes of the Sacred Spirit (*Mpeve ya nloongu*) (Devisch 2003b), I endeavor to show how much the anthropological encounter unfolds as a complex transferential and counter-transferential embroidery of approval or disapproval, information or exclusion, affection or rejection. Based on the embodied intersubjectivity of anthropologist and host, the meeting between the two forges and reforges their affects, old and new imageries, sensitivities, and intimate memories. It further reshapes the anthropologist insider's understanding of local idioms, conventions, and practices. Inversely, without the capacity of self-critical interpretative insight into his or her native culture, the anthropologist would be unable to develop a critique of his or her interpretation of the host culture. Psychoanalyst and anthropologist share the experience that an inquiry into otherness is simultaneously an exploration into the unknown and alien within ourselves. Paradoxically, this alien element also bears testimony to some universally human condition.

My fieldwork, among the Yaka in particular, and research conducted in Belgium in association with family physicians and psychiatrists (Devisch 1990) opened my eyes to corporeal symbolism and the impact that another culture—ethnic and familial—has on the patient. In the process, I also became more aware of the influence of my own Flemish cultural heritage. In this context, one's attention is directed to the models and mechanisms, above all cultural, capable of determining the form (as in pathoplasty) and conditioning the frequency (incidence) of certain symptoms. My interest was to a great extent captivated by the bodily functions of contact and exchange between the body and the world, namely, the skin, breathing, eating, and sexuality, as well as the senses (touch, smell, hearing, sight, taste) (Devisch 1993: chap. 4). In order to enhance my familiarity as an anthropologist with case studies devoted to certain chronic patients of family doctors in Brussels and Antwerp, I once again was inspired by the manner in which Yaka culture approaches the body and its senses. It was during this period that I formulated the hypothesis of "the three bodies" (Devisch 1993: 132ff.; Devisch and Brodeur 1999: 14ff.). This postulate stresses the extent to which a consonance, a morphogenetic resonance, develops in the subject between corporeal experience, family life, and relations to the world. Indeed, the human body is marked and modeled by a fantastic, mythic, and symbolic anatomy that is mediated by a familial, group, or ethnic culture. Inversely, culture constructs and collectively institutes itself on the basis of corporeal experiences and symbolic functions that are culturally diverse (including significations, identifications, beliefs, cosmological formations, processes of comprehension, and the like).

In the course "Anthropology of the Body," which I taught from 1970 until 2004 as part of the MA program of anthropology at the University of Louvain (Leuven), I attempted to examine how subjects, their community, and their life-world (in their particular locales) each configure one another in culture-specific (symbolic) ways. The course sought to unravel the transvaluation of the symbolic spatial patterning of the social and corporeal registers onto the cosmic, and vice versa. Moreover, the course aimed to develop a 'reciprocal anthropology', looking from 'there' to 'here' as if it were 'there'. This approach was explored by tentatively adopting a three-fields perspective (comprising the correlative physical, social, and cosmic bodies) drawn from research in southwest Congo. This research demonstrated the extent to which the masculine and feminine bodies provide a different repertory of order, namely, a constellation of tangible symbols with the potential of both signifying and shaping the mutual belonging of body-self, meaning, and being in an interweaving between, first, the senses, desire, forces (brought to play in a largely unconscious way), and body-self (the physical body/corporeality of one's identity); second, society (the socio-political body); and, third, the life-world (the cosmic body), shaping among others the space-time dimensions of one's existence. Culture-specific views of and connective processes involving the body, bodily boundaries, and orifices; corporeal functions and growth; and sexuation and reproduction all offer 'natural' symbols for meaningfully figuring and molding the interweaving between the life-world, body-self, society, and culture. These constantly shifting relationships orient, among other things, both the individual's co-shaping of and alignment with the social and political control of autonomy, hierarchy, normality, rivalry, love, virtues and moral sensibility, distinction, courtesy and civility, good fellowship, hygiene, etiquette, disability, and so on.

The course explored the heuristic value of this thesis in two particular transitional phases experienced in Western cultures. In a first part of the course, I examined the transition from the late medieval period to the early modern era, allowing for a particular focus on Flanders.[8] Drawing on such diverse spheres as urban design, surgery, literature, painting, and witch-hunts, I argued that the historical transition in fact entailed a double mutation, first from a basically tactile and oral collective imaginary toward a visual one, and second from a more matri-centered, cyclical, and concentric space-time patterning toward a predominantly viri-centered, lineal, and vertical one. In a second segment, the course focused on the body in the hyper-/postmodern imaginary that has emerged in Western-derived cultural landscapes in the period since the 1970s. We examined, for instance, cyber-feminist praxis in the context of multi-centered networking; artistic, multi-media, and queer movements of exploration taking place at the disintegrating borders of Western hegemony; and multi-/transgendered body cultures shaped by our post-humanistic era's growing awareness of human frailty and multi-form mutability.

Fourth Phase: Toward a Psychoanalytic-Anthropological Approach to Subjectivation in Kinshasa

Since 1986, I have been working for some three weeks annually among the Yaka population in the destitute and poverty-stricken suburban shantytowns of Kinshasa. As fate would have it, these regular visits enabled me to witness first-hand the Luddite uprisings of late September 1991 as well as the violent and widespread military-led plundering by youth gangs in January and February 1993. The violence and ravaging that I witnessed shattered me, I confess, as did my experience of the unrelenting destruction of the suburban infrastructure, the miserable living conditions, and the increasingly desperate life situation and disillusionment of the Yaka population in suburban Kinshasa today. But so did my observation of their paradoxical bricolage of identity creation and obfuscation. While in the shantytowns, where some half-million Yaka live, I felt compelled to incorporate in myself the depressive mood that is prone to breed revolt. This disposition stemmed, in my view, from the unbearable opposition between the misery of the poor and the flagrant arrogance and opulence of the several hundred well-to-do Congolese and expatriate families. The very existence of the latter belied the profound divide between the centers of power and the indigent subaltern.

These experiences forced me beyond the neutral stance of the scientist. I became more and more reluctant to leave out of the picture both the terrible effects of the estrangement, disarray, and entanglement caused by the (post)colonial models and institutions (Devisch 1994, 1995) and the (counter)transferential dimension in my experience of them. Perhaps I have sublimated my deep discomfort with the (post)colonial predicament through my aestheticizing writing on the rural Yaka in the Taanda district, from where a minority of the populace, largely school educated, had emigrated to Kinshasa, and where even fewer people had embraced much of the missionary identity constructs. On the contrary, in suburban Kinshasa, the older Kinois with whom I met—most of the men, at least, being schooled Christians—passed over their ancestral origins in silence, all the while assimilating the antinomic or alienating masks of Zairean modernity in the contexts of the Mobutist state and post-missionary Christianity. They believed themselves to be caught up in the country's march toward a grand party-state, propelled by the drive to enter swiftly into global modernity, more often than not imagined as a world of greater power and a superior way of life and fantasized as a state of abundance, luxury, and ease. I in turn felt strongly estranged by such phantasmic conjectures and the polemics that they spawned, insofar as it appears that my hosts have themselves imbibed the imaginary colonial 'invention' of Africa, a reality unmasked by Valentin Mudimbe (1988). Both the 'traditional' and the 'modern' subjects, as the so-called incarnations of local versus globalizing lifestyles, are fictions of a (post)colonial anthropology and psychiatry. Kinois immigrants' illusory ideals of modern city life and higher education parallel a deep feeling of alienation vis-à-vis the originary space from where they have emigrated. It is an encompassing life-world in which I myself have been adopted, yet a world to which, once in town, I only occasionally bore witness to.

I came to realize, moreover, that during my stay in the rural Yaka world I had concealed from myself the paranoid effects of its saturation with the projections of missionary and colonial representations, as well as the racialized thinking it had absorbed regarding oracy, backwardness, paganism, excess, filth, and sorcery, all seen as the reverse side of the white, civilized world. Until the 1990s, many older Kinois immigrants to Kinshasa's shantytowns felt estranged by their having adopted the paranoid (post)colonial construct of the rural as the inversion of a modern (i.e., whitened, occidentalized) urban modernity. They manifestly perceived the village realm they had left behind, as well as the ancestors inhabiting it, as persecutory obstacles preventing them from fully occupying and domesticating (literally, bringing home) the space of the Occidental other as a source of valid meaning, mastery, and filiation (Devisch 2004). Although half of Kinshasa's population is today under the age of 20 (De Boeck and Plissart 2004), I admit that in the urban context I have maintained my former anthropological disposition of consulting mainly with elders, as if I were unable to listen closely to the younger generation that is apparently less familiar with the fantasies of colonization and its aftermath in the whitened mirror that misrepresents them.

Beginning in 1993, a multi-disciplinary community intervention program aiming to improve health-care services in suburban Kinshasa (Devisch, Dimomfu,

Le Roy, and Crossman 2001) actually led us to reflect on the mind-set of the researchers (Belgian and Congolese social scientists and psychiatrists) involved. A sense of trust and the possibility of dialogue between researchers, healers, and/or health seekers in the suburbs alone are not sufficient conditions for mutual understanding. The modernizing discourse and behavior adopted by the healers, mimicking those learned during (Western) schooling as well as those of the researchers, at least while in their presence, were additional obstacles to achieving a more accurate picture of the dynamics of local health seeking and provision. Only researchers who are familiar with the healer's native tongue, local cultural idioms, and age-old hermeneutics proper to the healing cults are able to circumvent this phenomenon with any credibility.

Moreover, being a product of secularist Western science, the social science researcher such as the psychiatrist is often reluctant to appeal to Christianity, whereas some cult/folk healers are anxious to do. While the healer hopes to establish his or her own connection with modernity through such an association, the researcher is equally anxious to interpose some distance from religion in an attempt to communicate scientific authority and his or her 'university' status. On the other hand, he or she might just as easily—for the sake of research—participate wholeheartedly in a healing service for which, according to the criteria imposed on participants by the faith healers themselves, one must 'have faith' or 'be pure'. Given the omnipresence of Christianity in the capital, it is no surprise that anyone can easily resort to Christian discourse without necessarily being a practicing believer. The problem resides more in the fact that Christianity has been at the forefront of the civilizing mission, particularly where local 'religious' beliefs and practices are concerned, for they are considered a priori 'pagan' or pertaining to magic and fetishism, depending on whether the dominant discourse is religious or scientific. Even the 'modern-educated' Congolese is anxious to avoid too close an association with those local cultural spheres that smack of backwardness and ignorance, for fear that such a relation—or mere contiguity—will make him or her appear equally backward and ignorant.

Quite different perspectives emerge when one looks at the communities of the Holy/Sacred Spirit (Devisch 1996, 2003a). A striking aspect of these groups is that they are centered around mothers as life sustainers and care deliverers. Further, in their religious ceremonies, as in their businesses, members of these groups unabashedly and ingenuously integrate and deploy aspects of both tradition-bound localisms and Western-style modernity. Their pervasive sense of disenchantment with an inaccessible Western-style modernity is expressed through parody and diatribe against missionary Christianity and the hegemonic civilizational pretense of the post-colonial state. Parody in particular has emerged, on the inter- and intra-subjective levels, as an effective means of disalienation by which people seek to 'un-whiten' and free themselves from civilizational paranoia. Members often bear testimony to the deceptiveness of modernity's individualism, technology, consumerism, and hedonism in their frequent rites of public confession. In these sessions it becomes clear that the greed and selfishness associated with such individualism is considered the very work of *sataani*, the local term for the Christian notion of Satan. On the other hand, these communities also provide members with opportunities to put to liberating use some aspects of Western modernity by first submitting them to rites of exorcism before collectively exploiting them in processes of mutual self-help.

Adherents of these prophetic healing communes usually assume my conversion to their faith and ethic, even though they rarely have any idea as to my motivations in attending their celebrations. In terms of their internal logic, these communes presuppose an unending and world-encompassing struggle between good and evil. They demand a strict and binding choice of adherence to the Sacred Spirit and to light and truth, these being seen as the antipole to Satan, darkness, and the delusion of materialism and hedonist consumerism propagated in particular by the transnational media. Through my association with these churches I have often found myself in the position of an adversarial other—an estranged stranger or even persecutor—due to my European origin. This has forced me to examine the paranoid effects of the intrusive white man as representative of modernity.

The life of these faith communities turns very much around the Sacred Spirit, which plays a central role in the healing process of group members, the majority of whom join the group due to one affliction or another. The powers of this healing spirit derive from the surreptitious superimposition of the missionary-taught Christian Holy Spirit and the ancestral spirit, the latter having been overtly diabolized by established Christianity. This concept of spirit is rendered all the more effective by virtue of its capacity to overcome the evil forces afflicting patients and to recapture life-giving energies. The frequent practice of collective trance sets the stage for an effervescent space-time in which the Sacred Spirit re-energizes the entire corporeality, identity, and lived world of the rapt adepts, not just their immaterial 'souls', as whitened Christianity would have it. Through trance the Spirit brings about a re-enchantment of the adepts' world by deploying their own tropes of an awaited messianic world order.

The very physical nature of these moments is enhanced by the role of the leading prophets or prophetesses, who, while themselves in a state of trance, repeatedly strike the body of afflicted members of the congregation with the Bible, suggesting that they are driving out the evil spirits or *sataani*. The rite reflects, however, an act of subtle parody in that here redemption signifies the liberation of those who have come under the attack of deceptive Westernization. Indeed, the Bible is made into a mere mechanism of exorcism. In the performance of the rite, the celebrants are in fact subverting the authority and truth claims of the Bible, mission Christianity, modern science, and the state. The ubiquitous practice of glossolalia in these contexts poignantly illustrates this point: it both parodies and undermines the illiteracy-literacy dichotomy bequeathed by (post)colonial and missionary education. Speaking in tongues represents a travesty of verbal and written meaning while evoking both familiarity and rupture with knowable codes and the authoritarian word. Glossolalia and exorcism, portrayed as an unending metamorphosis of the Sacred Spirit into Satan and vice versa, thus give rise to a terse parody of Westernization and a theatricalization of a clash of civilizations. In this way, the faith-healing communes provide Kinshasa's marginalized slum dwellers with the conceptual and affective energies to resist the subordination of their local worlds and knowledge systems, while giving them a voice with which to 'talk back' to the engulfing globalization. One might ask whether parody is not people's partially successful means to overcome their post-colonial predicament, inasmuch as the post-colony implicitly reproduces the colonizing othering there where it intended to combat it. The versatile Spirit-Satan polarity can be seen as a parodying of the missionary othering.

My intimate knowledge of mediumistic divination and my frequent association with Yaka diviners in suburban Kinshasa shatters Kinois people's self-definition in the mirror of imaginary alterity constructs projected onto them. The practice of divination in town expresses both the cry for the ancestral way of misfortune management and its condemnation in the name of Christian and enlightenment ideals of rationality, self-steering individuality, and the subject-object distinction. Profoundly moved by the disarray of suburban Kinois, my evocation in their midst of divination and its knowledge of the unappropriable otherworldly or invisible order of things urges fundamental questions. Notwithstanding the urban emancipation ideals of modernity and ego-centered selfhood in line with Christian salvation, what valid axiological registers have we to offer in order better to understand misfortune, appease the kin group, domesticate the doom of destiny, and sustain a better life and society? Does there exist a more compelling system of values other than the endogenous socio-cultural view on subject formation, exchange, belonging, kinship, social organization and power, sorcery, and ancestral wrath? In seeking to take the conceptual and behavioral systems of suburban Kinois seriously in their own terms, and to clarify the dynamic of transference between host community and anthropologist, I have been led to the following additional question: how helpful might it be to combine psychoanalytical and anthropological scrutiny in an effort to disentangle the estranging strangeness of the post-colonial subject and the expatriate anthropologist? These questions have in turn suggested a particular research method. Let me sum up a few directions that Claude Brodeur and I have elaborated upon in a joint work.[9]

Cultural activities in their diversity of forms all involve the production of meaning and are thus of great interest to the psychoanalyst and anthropologist alike. Psychoanalysis, particularly that of the Freudian-Lacanian strain, has by and large focused on the domain of phantasmic cultural expressions. Formed during childhood, these psychic constructions are constantly reshaped in one's unconscious throughout one's life. Psychoanalysts, however, could very well bring their attention to bear on cultural performances of very different orders by adapting their strategies and techniques. Approached in its unconscious dimension, any cultural expression could form the object of psychoanalysis, for discourse, whether originating with the individual or the group, is formed and continually refashioned by the subject, group, and life-world.

Given this open definition of the domain and object of psychoanalysis, the question of appropriate methods and investigative techniques arises and, in turn, that of the scientific nature of psychoanalytic discourse. In psychoanalytic consultation, the analyst attempts to listen attentively to an individual while blocking the interference of his or her own discourse in that listening process. Nothing—neither time nor the psychoanalyst's skill or patience—guarantees that the subject's own discourse will in fact emerge. On the other hand, the neutral position required of the analyst cannot indicate total passivity: his or her own discourse serves as an instrument to channel the analysand's discourse back into the consciousness of the latter until the authentic truth of a thought comes to expression. In this sense, psychoanalysis constitutes an art, for it requires from the analyst a particular aptitude to recognize the unarticulated and vulnerable points of a discourse in order to assist the subject in progressively filling in these gaps. And it is only at this point, through the capable intervention of the analyst, that the deep-seated weave of the subject's most personal thoughts can appear.

I suggest that psychoanalysts today have two types of methods at their disposal, the one more purely theoretical and the other largely analytical. In the first instance, one might appeal to the Freudian topical approach, as found in Melanie Klein's theoretical model, or to Jacques Lacan's philosophical approach to text and discourse. However, the challenge to work independently of any speculative model that might be fraught with Western-derived views on person and selfhood has led me to adopt a procedure that I prefer to call an analytical method. Put simply, the aim of such an approach is to identify and bring to light the internal dialectical relations and deep, essential logic of a subject's—whether individual or group—discourse. Here one's attention is drawn in particular to the subject's highly developed sensitivity to context and intersubjective interaction, a sensitivity that is characteristic of Kinois or, for that matter, of a Bantu style of thinking and inhabiting the world. Here, the subject and his or her inner feelings are perceived as contiguous with the encompassing life-world, just as human and spiritual beings are assumed to be co-existent. The skin, the senses, one's fantasy or representations, and one's reputation are held to be the real zones of the self and the other, of the dividual self (cf. Strathern 1988), where discrete subjectivity feeds on intense intersubjectivity and connectedness to the world.

The attentive psychoanalyst then focuses on the fundamental organizing dynamics and principles informing the discourse between two subjects, just as they inform the borderlinking of mother and child, parental and gender relations, or socio-cultural institutions (such as kinship, residence, reproduction, name-giving, seniority, chieftainship, or funerals). The phenomenologically oriented anthropologist is more interested in the historical and context-bound signification of a given institution, the cultural symbolism of the discourse, or the communal emergence of everyday practices or forms of life such as subsistence and extractive strategies. Several different anthropological research strategies are available for the examination of these phenomena. By participating in the thick of the cultural practice they study, anthropologists may seek to enter into the group's very intention or perspective in order to account for its understanding of practice and agency as much as possible in its own terms.

In the encounter with the analysand or host group, the psychoanalyst and the anthropologist find themselves in very different positions, at least in the short term. In the psychoanalytic relation, the honorarium allows for the analysand to recover from a symbolic debt toward the analyst. Conversely, anthropologists, as they enter into an unfamiliar cultural milieu and unknown social networks, require a considerable amount of time before being able to overcome their great uncertainty, a psychological but above all an epistemological one—namely, their situation of being unsettled by modes of knowledge that go against their habitual manner of relating to a topic from the prescribed 'neutral' stance of the researcher. Anthropologists are persistently invited overtly to demonstrate their implication in and define their sympathy toward the group's as yet ungraspable scenario. Interactive and transactional experience in the intercultural meeting, therefore, is not a superficially transparent reality. Expressed in phenomenological terms, the anthropologist seeks to enter the experiential flow of the borderlinking meeting between host group and anthropologist, while respecting the local cultural framing of the encounter.

Inasmuch as it is imagined by each of the other—the host group and anthropologist—the experiential flow is constituted by associative chains, blanks, and suspension points, many of which seem to remain in the realm of the unspeakable and inexpressible. Affects and unconscious motives inform cultural symbols and meanings that are mobilized in the very encounter itself and endow the participants with a kind of energy and with particular associative cultural biases. In the long term, psychoanalytically trained anthropologists, in particular those hailing from formerly colonized nations or marginalized societies, must be capable of listening (with a third ear of empathy and a self-critical attitude) to the often disharmonic medley into which they are drawn. At play here are interactional, representational, transferential, and counter-transferential processes that may reveal, obscure, act out, or even partially overcome the divisions between North and South, between Western-derived social sciences and local-knowledge practices, between descendants of colonizer and of colonized, or between zealous church members and a skeptical anthropologist. In the course of interaction with the anthropologist, the host group enacts elements of its investment in cultural identity. To the extent that in transitional moments and places groups mimic the identity construct they have identified with, their members neutralize in advance their capitulation in the face of a disconcerting political-economic globalization.

Through his or her bifocal sensitivities, the psychoanalytically trained anthropologist is led to interweave a relational self (Nancy 1996) with, on the one hand, his or her hosts and, on the other hand, his or her familial networks at home. Having witnessed so much politico-economic violence in the North-South clash of civilizations during his or her stay with the host group, the anthropologist is perhaps motivated to lay bare the metaphysics, with its essentially Hebrew-Christian and humanist assumptions, feeding the North Atlantic civilizational anxiety with regard to lack and death. This anxiety is silenced in the North by an obsession with advanced, if not almighty, technology and a preoccupation with fine (hedonist) articles of consumption. Yet this same anxiety and mania underpins much of the portrayal by the North of the 'underdeveloped South'. In this light, a bifocal attunement may also help the psychoanalytically trained and self-scrutinizing anthropologist to overcome his or her ambivalence toward some of the Western-derived presuppositions in Freudian psychoanalytic thought, particularly those pertaining to modernity's subject-object division. Finally, such borderlinking between the metaphysical orientations of both the researcher's host and native groups assists the psychoanalytic anthropologist in bringing home his or her multi-layered, intersubjective self, interwoven with others and their life-worlds, both 'here' and 'over there'.

Signifiance and Forces

In my quest to neutralize as much as possible ethnocentric biases, I first attempt to understand subaltern subjects endogenously, that is, in their own terms. My use of the term 'endogeneity' here is certainly not intended to suggest a homogeneity or a substantive autonomous self and clearly distinguished group identity. Rather, I have in mind an inner capacity of subjects and of cultural matrices to exercise self-orientation from an earlier-constituted interiority or a more primary source. Endogeneity pertains to a subject's orientation in opening up to and interacting with a myriad of virtually enriching cultural experiences and borderlinking opportunities offered to him or her, even if these might initially have been perceived as violently intrusive and unsettling.

But how can one express this borderlinking when part of the experience the anthropologist comes to share firmly defies narration or description? What if a cultural institution's singularity resists classical anthropological interpretation? How then should the anthropologist handle institutional secrecy, or deal with a group's acts of violence and deviancy? In other words, in which fields—always plural and intersubjective, heteronomous and partly non-discursive—of drives and desire, memories and longings, power relations and shifting identities, or numinous presences and delusions does the anthropologist's involvement occur? At times, the anthropologist is made a bewildered witness to initiation and divination, healing and trance-possession, sorcerous aggression and perversion; at others, to the ills of the megapolis and the rampant nation-state or the frenzied celebrations in the communes of the Sacred Spirit that parody the salvationist pretense of Christianity and modernity. Yet, above all, does it not remain impossible for the empathic anthropologist to properly convey the essence of a cultural orientation that manifests a certain sovereignty in its creativity or a reluctance to express in words the core of its healing rituals or lethal sorcery (Devisch 2003b)?

In this regard, radical feminist post-structuralist and post-Lacanian approaches assist us in overcoming the anthropologist's all too logo-centered stance. Julia Kristeva (2005; Kristeva and Clément 1998) and, more forcefully, Bracha Ettinger (1999, 2000, 2004) and Gail Weiss (1999) all break with Lévi-Strauss's and Lacan's overemphasis on the symbolic order of language as the realm of society and subjectivity governed by 'the Law of the Father'. Their critique has given me assurance when I have sought to depict the largely non-representational and non-discursive fields of intercorporeity and intersubjective encounter as unruly fields of 'forces'. Bursts of undirected and multi-sensory empathy, along with a shifting consensual and dialogical finesse, make for the experience of encounter, not least in the domain of intercultural fieldwork. I understand the notion of forces in the Freudian sense of pulsion (want, drive, *Trieb*) and in line with Merleau-Ponty's phenomenology of the sensory and affective-relational body. Unlike the Lacanian notion of desire, forces evoke the embeddedness in the flesh of drives, sensations, affects, wants, and imaginaries. Seen from a similar post-structuralist and post-Lacanian perspective, the 'real' is what the subject, such as the participant anthropologist, experiences and imagines as a relevant event, an piece of information, an intent. The real arises out of both a libidinally driven and a discursive transactional setting of fellow subjects. According to Kristeva, the 'real' in an intersubjective encounter, such as the one that produces well-grounded intercultural knowledge, is more akin to what she labels the semiotic than to the empiricist's nude facts, depicted, as they are, by the inductive sociological account of their observable constituents and plots.

Most of the information that I have received from elders and healers, some during rites or a seclusion period, has been gathered while informants were in a very witty or playful mood, for example, while sharing drinks, carving an object, making or repairing some tool, or building a house. Among rural Yaka, the healer's offer of information and self-revelation resembles a trapper-hunter's account of finding the right bait and place to set the trap. These are settings where routine and protocol are overcome by the act of stumbling over the obvious. In his behavior and in the narrative he recounts, the healer resembles a trickster, deploying surprise and giving his clients the opportunity and means to explore a problem. In their very core, divination and healing are founded, so to speak, in dreamwork and in a physicality of knowing. They compose a dynamic of continuous becoming that owes much to the processes of both condensation and displacement, as well as to those of embodiment and metaphoric figuration in the language of the senses. Further, they are disclosed to the anthropologist only in the dense idiom of scenes, moods, and feelings that turn the anthropological encounter into a sensuous intercorporeity.[10]

The French notion of *con-naissance* (colloquially referring to experiential knowing and insight) offers an insightful linguistic rendition of this sensuous intercorporeal and dialogical encounter and mode of comprehension in which the anthropologist is engaged. By virtue of the emotional, hence 'fleshy' (cf. Merleau-Ponty), co-implication of the subjects in a communal action—such as an apprenticeship, a palaver, a marriage, or a therapy—the sharing of knowledge becomes *co-naissance* (literally, co-birth). In its utmost intensity, such knowledge sharing is evocative of a matrixial, trans-subjective border zone emerging in the mother-child life-giving relationships, as depicted perhaps in a somewhat all too paradisiacal manner by Ettinger (1999, 2000, 2004). A similar matrixial borderlinking experience of porosity and sharing-in-difference (for example, at the unstable border zone between the here and there, the living and the deceased, the visible and invisible, the familiar and the alien, the controllable and the uncontrollable, the self and the other) undergirds funerals and mourning, the lucid awakening from a trance-possession or a dream, the bliss of poetry and art, or even humor. Such borderlinking inspires the transworld communication proper to a mediumistic, divinatory oracle, a night-long moon dance aimed at arousing a new season's energies, and various other initiatory or artful states of wonder and becoming. Sorcery, on the other hand, inversely perverts borderlinking into sheer anxiety arousing and destructive bordercrossing.

By Way of Conclusion

My writing on the Yaka problematizes anthropology's classical status defined as a window on the real and the other. Anthropological fieldwork in Africa and its subsequent scholarly report entail major dislocations or shifts from the centrality of the interactional or of the verbal and the observable to the spheres of the event and the transactional, the interior and the invisible. An ethically committed anthropologist, however, cannot continue to exclude from the intercultural encounter what appears to be at odds with the West's secularized world-view, or with its hegemonic modes of sensorialist knowledge acquisition and rational, scholarly knowledge production. My work as an anthropologist and a psychoanalyst, immersed in intercultural encounters marked since the 1960s by the post-colonial predicament, has been beset by certain concerns, of which I will here sketch only three.

A first preoccupation underlying my writing is this: how can the vital world-making practices of particular communities, networks, or institutions (such as religious revival, mediumistic divination or initiatory healing of, say, deeply depressed initiands-patients, or communitarian modes of making decisions or sharing responsibility) grow in rhizome-like ways as webs or matrices across linguistic, cultural, intellectual, and socio-political boundaries? Of particular concern in this regard is the question, can or should the compassionate anthropologist-psychoanalyst espouse, in terms of the host group's canon, the distress or the beauty of the encounter, and hence the dignity and numinous inspiration of the host or the alterity and heteronomy in the cultural milieu of the host group, by way of it becoming part of him- or herself?

A second concern can be formulated in view of what I suggested earlier about the ability of psychoanalysis or intercultural philosophy to unravel the unthought or deeply suppressed levels in mainstream North Atlantic consciousness. Could not the role of anthropology and of psychoanalysis be to privilege *significance*? The latter denotes the generation of interactional and fluid meaning beyond the rigidity of the accepted grounds of truth and of the sensorialist rationalist knowledge production canonized by the Enlightenment. A psychoanalytical-cum-anthropological attention attuned to the intercultural encounter both away from and back home might thus come to grasp and endorse the as-yet-unthought-in-thought here and over there, to comprehend the ever virtual as well as the ceaselessly unfolding and indeterminable, the polymorphous fields of *co-naissance* and intersubjectivity, and the slippery snares of institutional power and the predefined tracks of knowledge. Is it, moreover, the role of the psychoanalytically inspired anthropologist to confront both his or her hosts here and over there with their own estranged self-perception in the mirror of Africanist, Occidentalist, or Orientalist constructs? Does such a 'revelatory' role not exceed the anthropologist's implicit alliance with his or her host community, an alliance that is the very ground for deep intersubjective exchange? Two more questions come to mind. First, if the anthropological encounter is not meant as a therapeutic one, is the psychoanalytically trained anthropologist entitled to envisage such a relationship? Second, to what extent does such zeal reflect a Western-derived anxiety for human perfectibility?

A third concern of the anthropological endeavor I am advocating radically opposes some of the deconstructionist stances taken in postmodern thinking. I compare my position as an anthropologist and psychoanalyst to that of a reluctant joker or trickster figure. In my professional experience I have been deeply and morally touched by the intersubjective encounter with notables in their rural and urban settings with whom I have come to share so much. In my view, the fundamental authority for the anthropologist, as for the psychoanalyst, is precisely the culture-sensitive intellectual and moral interdependence of field and text, fantasies and culture-specific representations, clinical engagement and self-critical reflection, as well as (culturally informed) transference and counter-transference. The type of anthropological and/or psychoanalytical-clinical borderlinking encounter I advocate is nonetheless careful not to impose its own paradigm and avoids restricting the researcher to either of the polar positions of having to look through the window of his or her own world-view or of merely translating the encounter. Both psychoanalysis and anthropology entail the adoption of a healthy skepticism with regard to the accepted claims of reason, truth, and power; to what one is expected to acknowledge at face value; and, for that matter, to any phenomenon or information that appears to be obvious or straightforward. By acknowledging my enrootedness in Flemish culture, I am better able to encounter Yaka society and its cultural framework and horizons in an authentic, situated, yet self-critical and receptive way. Only in this manner can I become a legitimate intermediary or culture broker—or, seen in another perspective, a borderspace—onto whom my hosts can transfer their deeper intuitions and longings about life.

The anthropological encounter inevitably entails an affective dimension. Yet the more that affinity and affectionate fellow feelings grow, the more this encounter is transferential, and such transference is best understood in the literal sense of *diaphorein*, *Übertragung* (i.e., to carry across, beyond; to convey, to open up to one another). *Signifiance* and the forces aroused and arising in the subjectivizing encounter surpass what one can tell or master; they exceed full verbalization or translation, yet at the same time may empower the participants. This encounter is not one of innocence, salvation, or sadness, but it can grow into a genuine human venture for a never-ending polylogue, a mutually enriching co-implication, or an intersubjective and reconciling relation of giving and receiving. In such border zones as genuine hospitality, healing ritual, ecstatic meeting, or humor, one is in a fold of inter-being. Intercultural borderlinks and border spaces unlock unexpected sources of empowerment as well as unsettling modes of meaning and interpretational possibilities, which unfold as loci in worldwide knowledge sharing. Any further development of a psycho-analytically informed anthropology, or of a culture-sensitive psychoanalysis, should draw on this understanding of co-implication and polylogue, so as to emancipate these disciplines and allow them to loosen the ties with their Euro-centric antecedents. Such an approach to the culture-sensitive encounter bears witness to the ever-emerging possibilities for mutually enriching co-implication, artfulness, and dignity, and for coming home as co-constitutive subjects of interweaving 'glocal' (global and local) worlds, which, as Yaka elders used to say, "this is and brings bliss: *kyeesi.*"

Acknowledgments

My research among rural and urban Yaka has been carried out in collaboration with the Africa Research Centre, Department of Anthropology, Catholic University of Louvain (Leuven), Belgium. I acknowledge with gratitude financial support from the Belgian National Foundation for Scientific Research, the Research Foundation—Flanders, the European Commission Directorate-General XII, and the Harry Frank Guggenheim Foundation, New York. The research was also carried out in collaboration with the IMNC (Institut des Musées Nationaux du Congo), as well as CERDAS (Centre for the Co-ordination of Research and Documentation in Social Science for Africa South of the Sahara), based at the University of Kinshasa. I thank Peter Crossman for his editorial help.

René Devisch is Special Emeritus Professor of Anthropology at Catholic University of Louvain (Leuven), Belgium. He was trained in philosophy, anthropology, and psychoanalysis. A member of the Belgian School of Psychoanalysis, he has a very limited private psychoanalytic practice. As co-founder of the Africa Research Centre, he has published widely on the ethnography of the Congo (especially the Yaka and Kinshasa), African religion, witchcraft, and medical anthropology. His publications include *Weaving the Threads of Life* (1993) and *The Law of the Life-Givers* (1999, with C. Brodeur). His most recent work concentrates on the dynamics of local knowledge practices.

Notes

1. Here I take into consideration the works of African thinkers such as Anthony Kwame Appiah, Jean-Marc Ela, Paulin Hountondji, Josephi Ki-Zerbo, Ali Mazrui, Ngugi Wa Thiong'o, and Okot p'Bitek, who call for an adaptation of education and research activities to the polyvalent African contexts. I have elsewhere attempted to examine some dimensions of the as yet poorly understood relationships between Western sciences and endogenous, culture- and site-specific, local knowledge practices in Africa south of the Sahara (Devisch 2005). By 'local knowledge' I mean any professional network's, congregation's, or community's unique genius (and possibly hybridizing creativity) that constitutes and characterizes what its members, in and for the singular and relevant context, meaningfully develop as knowledge, epistemology, metaphysics, and world-view. These studies are part of an effort to overcome ethnocentricity and civilizational ascendancy in the production of scientific discourse and university curricula (Crossman 1999; Crossman and Devisch 2002; Devisch forthcoming; Okere, Njoku, and Devisch 2005).
2. Kinshasa is the capital city of the Democratic Republic of Congo, renamed as Zaire from 1973 until 1996 during most of President Mobutu's reign.
3. There is almost no topic dealt with in this article that has not been scrutinized in a dialogue with Claude Brodeur, philosopher and psychoanalyst in Montreal (and 20 years my senior), pursued since the early 1990s. His most delicate gift of perspicacious empathy has enabled him to stir up and clarify the unthought-in-thought. My colleague-psychoanalysts (Fons van Coillie, Lut De Rijdt, Johan De Groef, Magda Plomteux, Jo Smet, Trees Traversier, Ludi Van Bouwel, Chris Vanstraelen, Jan Van Camp, and Marc Willaert) have, since September 2002, in the very witty ambience of our monthly seminar, shared their inspiring views and radical questions toward bridging the gap between social anthropology and psychoanalysis with a view toward grasping the local and hybrid cultural shaping of our dream-world, self, intersubjectivity, trauma, and memory. We have together sought to address the question, how do the more or less endogenous and exogenous cultural horizons of a subject or a group shape the unconscious, namely, that which escapes the grasp of the individual and group, via their conscious discourse and cultural praxis? This seminar, moreover, continues to help the anthropologist in me to work through my ambivalence toward Western-based, Freudian-Lacanian psychoanalytic theorizing.
4. My research has led me to a number of practical undertakings, which I will not examine in this article. These include research in culture-sensitive psychiatric reform in Tunis (Devisch and Vervaeck 1986), the creation in Brussels of a self-help group for immigrant Turkish women suffering from epileptic-like fits (Devisch and Gailly 1985), and the symbolic-anthropological training of family physicians (at the Department of Family Medicine, University of Antwerp).
5. Some very diverse communities have offered me their hospitality for research (in southwestern Congo and Kinshasa, southern Ethiopia, and Tunis), or for supervision of my PhD students during their fieldwork in Cairo, Kinshasa and western Congo, northern Ghana, northern Israel, southwestern Kenya, northwestern Namibia, southeastern Nigeria, KwaZulu-Natal in South Africa, and northwestern Tanzania.
6. Older people in Yitaanda remembered Father De Beir, one of the few Europeans who stayed there for a few days. Their remembrance, however, added to my guilt regarding the Flemish missionary intrusion, spurring my restorative stance in the post-colonial anthropological encounter. They related De Beir's condemnation of local dignitaries, in particular, those who resisted conversion to Christianity. In 1939, before the eyes of mourners, he had publicly beaten the corpse of a diviner, identifying him as the personification of a heathen institution and hence of Satan. The narrators characterized this act as *mbeembi*, a term for an unwarranted and chaos-causing assault, or an unbearable contravention of domestic intimacy, auguring misfortune to all who witnessed it.
7. That the exile and thus the social death of N-Leengi—whose name I was given at the onset of my fieldwork in early 1974—had occurred in 1939, the year of the death of my

uncle René (literally meaning 'reborn'), whose name I had inherited as my birth name, triggers for me an enigma of some unconscious psychic 'transfusion'.

8. This is in line with the work of, among others, Philippe Ariès, Jean Delumeau, Norbert Elias, and Jacques LeGoff.

9. This and the next three paragraphs elaborate on an earlier attempt, co-authored with Claude Brodeur (Devisch and Brodeur 1999: 249–252), at defining a psychoanalytic-cum-anthropological perspective.

10. In his scholarly writings, Wim van Binsbergen (2003), a Dutch professor of intercultural philosophy at the Erasmus University Rotterdam and director of research at the Africa Study Centre in Leiden, describes his becoming a *sangoma* diviner in Francistown (Botswana). Since his initiation, he has practiced tablet divination in southern Africa and in the Netherlands, where he devised a computer program for *sangoma* consultation that he conducts worldwide via the Internet. Unlike cult initiates or healers such as van Binsbergen, I am as yet unable to trans-subjectively, even less intercorporeally, evoke the necessary links between myself or afflicted patients who sought my help in Kinshasa and the ancestral or healing cult spirits. I can only poetically evoke the spirit realm of my Yaka hosts in southwestern Congo, and have not been able existentially to tie myself in with that most potent invisible realm, namely, *ngoongu*. I depict, all too romantically perhaps, this realm in my writings as their primal maternal life-source, ceaselessly and rhythmically oozing from the womb of the earth (Devisch and Brodeur 1999).

References

Crossman, P. 1999. *Endogenisation and African Universities: Initiatives and Issues in the Quest for Plurality in the Human Sciences*. Brussels: Belgian Administration for Development Co-operation.

Crossman, P., and R. Devisch. 2002. "Endogenous Knowledge: An Anthropological Perspective." Pp. 96–125 in *Towards a Philosophy of Articulation: IKS and the Integration of Knowledge Systems*, ed. C. Odora-Hoppers. Cape Town: New Africa Education Publisher.

De Beir, L. 1975a. *Religion et magie des Bayaka*. St. Augustin-Bonn: Anthropos.

_____. 1975b. *Les Bayaka de M'nene Ntoombo Lenge-Lenge*. St. Augustin-Bonn: Anthropos.

De Boeck, F., and M.-F. Plissart. 2004. *Kinshasa: Tales from the Invisible City*. Ghent: Ludion.

Devisch, R. 1990. "The Symbolic and the Physiological: Epigastric Patients in Family Medicine in Flanders." Pp. 57–74 in *Anthropologies of Medicine: A Reader on North American and European Perspectives in Medical Anthropology*, ed. B. Pfleiderer and G. Bibeau. Bonn: Vieweg.

_____. 1993. *Weaving the Threads of Life: The Khita Gyn-eco-logical Healing Cult among the Yaka*. Chicago: University of Chicago Press

_____. 1994. "Une filiation imaginaire: A propos des images en miroir que Zaïrois et Belges se renvoient." Pp. 72–76 in *Belgique-Zaïre: Une histoire en quête d'avenir*, ed. G. de Villers. Paris: Harmattan; Brussels: Cahiers Africains.

_____. 1995. "Frenzy, Violence, and Ethical Renewal in Kinshasa." *Public Culture* 7: 593–629.

_____. 1996. "'Pillaging Jesus': Healing Churches and the Villagisation of Kinshasa." *Africa* 66: 555–586.

_____. 2003a. "Parody in Matricentred Christian Healing Communes of the Sacred Spirit in Kinshasa." *Contours: A Journal of the African Diaspora* 1: 171–198.

_____. 2003b. "Maleficent Fetishes and the Sensual Order of the Uncanny in South-West Congo." Pp. 175–197 in *Beyond Rationalism: Rethinking Magic, Witchcraft and Sorcery*, ed. B. Kapferer. New York: Berghahn Books.

_____. 2005. "Sciences and Knowledge Practices: Their Culture-Specific Wellsprings." Pp. 104–122 in *Worldviews, Science and Us*, ed. D. Aerts, B. D'Hooghe, and N. Note. Hackensack, NJ: World Scientific Publishing.

_____. Forthcoming. "The University of Kinshasa: From Lovanium to Unikin." In *Higher Education in Postcolonial Africa: Paradigms of Development, Decline and Dilemmas*, ed. M. O. Afolayan. Trenton, NJ: Africa World Press/The Red Sea Press.

Devisch, R., and C. Brodeur. 1999. *The Law of the Lifegivers: The Domestication of Desire.* Amsterdam: Harwood Academic Publishers.

Devisch, R., L. Dimomfu, J. Le Roy, and P. Crossman. 2001. "A Community-Action Intervention to Improve Medical Care Services in Kinshasa, Congo: Mediating the Realms of Healers and Physicians." Pp. 107–140 in *Applying Health Social Science Best Practice in the Developing World*, ed. N. Higginbotham, R. Briceno-Leon, and N. Johnson. London: Zed.

Devisch, R., and A. Gailly. 1985. *"Dertlesmek:* 'The Sharing of Sorrow'; a Therapeutic Self-Help Group among Turkish Women." *Psichiatria e Psicoterapia Analitica* 4, no. 2: 133–152.

Devisch, R., and B. Vervaeck. 1986. "Doors and Thresholds: Jeddi's Approach to Psychiatric Disorders." *Social Science and Medicine* 22: 541–551.

Dumon, D., and R. Devisch. 1991. *The Oracle of Maama Tseembu: Divination and Healing among the Yaka of Southwestern Zaire.* 50 min. film and video in Dutch, English, French, and German Versions. Belgian-Flemish Radio and Television: Science Division.

Ettinger, B. 1999. *Regard et espace-de-bord matrixiels: Essais psychanalytiques sur le féminin et le travail de l'art.* Brussels: Les Editions de La Lettre Volée.

_____. 2000. "Art as the Transport-Station of Trauma." Pp. 91–115 in *Artworking 1985–1999.* Ghent: Ludion.

_____. 2004. "Weaving a Woman Artist with-in the Matrixial Encounter-Event." *Theory, Culture and Society* 21: 61–94.

Geeraerts, J. 1967. *Grangreen 1: Black Venus.* Brussels: Manteau.

Hunt, J. 1989. *Psychoanalytic Aspects of Fieldwork.* London: Sage.

Kristeva, J. 2005. *La haine et le pardon: Pouvoir et limites de la psychanalyse III.* Paris: Fayard.

Kristeva, J., and C. Clément. 1998. *Le féminin et le sacré.* Paris: Stock.

Mudimbe, V. 1988. *The Invention of Africa: Gnosis, Philosophy, and the Order of Knowledge.* Bloomington: Indiana University Press.

Naficy, H. 2000. "Self-Othering: A Postcolonial Discourse on Cinematic First Contacts." Pp. 292–310 in *The Pre-occupation of Postcolonial Studies*, ed. F. Afzal-Khan and K. Seshadri-Crooks. Durham, NC: Duke University Press.

Nancy, J.-L. 1996. *Être singulier pluriel.* Paris: Galilée.

Obeyesekere, G. 1980. *The Work of Culture.* Chicago: University of Chicago Press.

Okere, T., A. Njoku, and R. Devisch. 2005. *All Knowledge Is First of All Local Knowledge.* Special issue of *Africa Development—Afrique et Développement* 30 no. 3: 1–19.

Strathern, M. 1988. *The Gender of the Gift.* Berkeley: University of California Press.

van Binsbergen, W. 2003. *Intercultural Encounters: African and Anthropological Lessons towards a Philosophy of Interculturality.* Münster: LIT Verlag.

Weiss, G. 1999. *Body Images: Embodiment as Intercorporeality.* London: Routledge.

Chapter 6

ON *TJUKURRPA*, PAINTING UP, AND BUILDING THOUGHT

Craig San Roque

Part One: Elegy for Seated Men

> Just like a god he seems to me, that man who sits across from you, so closely attentive to your sweet words.
>
> — after Sappho, fragment 31

'That Man Who Sits Across from You'

Psychoanalysis is mostly about a strange activity that occurs between people, calmly seated, oddly speaking. When two men sat in their conception conversation in Vienna in 1907, the older said to the younger, "And tell me, what do you think

---

Notes for this chapter begin on page 169.

of the transference?" The younger responded, "It is the alpha and the omega of the analytic method." And the older said, "Then you have grasped the main thing" (Jung [1954] 1966: 172).

The capacity of a person to be a psychoanalyst rests upon his or her grasp of theory and aptitude for observational technique in the fieldwork of the psyche, as well as the capability to dwell enough in the "main thing" marked so definitively by Freud as that bittersweet activity generated between persons. The psychoanalyst must be willing to deal with the strange substances that shake one's being when two or three are gathered together in a way that enables matter from that famous 'unconscious' to emerge in bits, groans, and half-formed misunderstandings—to emerge in any shape, from anywhere along the spectrum of love to hate, beauty to terror, self-knowledge to self-delusion.

This matter can be developed further if I slow things down and ask, "Who are these two or three who sit together?" And I am thinking now, remembering occasions sitting in the company of older men—the sort of older men with whom anthropologists often have conversations. Older dark-skinned men who have custodial functions for their specific languages and a cultural obligation. Older men who smell of embedded smoke and kangaroo grease and maybe Log Cabin tobacco.

And the question might be, "What is in our minds as we sit together, you and I?" with the fire simmering, tea stewing, ants busy on the sand, and maybe the heat of coals drifting through the shade of a mulga tree. These settings are fitting for reflective conversations between men of two worlds—indigenous Warlpiri, perhaps, and the traveling Caucasian. Such conversations take place on the edge of campsites, on the edge of settlements, on the edge of and between dreams, between times, between languages, a shimmering, dusty place where nothing much is really what it seems. And nothing spoken is exactly what it might mean and nothing heard is quite what is intended, perhaps. Ambiguous answers and ambiguous tracks of thought are exchanged between persons in exactly the settings where transference phenomena might readily be found, if Freud or Jung had time enough and the chance to sit there long enough—learning, letting go of anticipation, observing the flow of desire and projection. Seated between the eyes of two worlds. This sort of thing.

And thus another question rises about what emerges out of somewhere between a different two men, not an Austrian Jewish doctor speaking German and a Swiss Protestant psychiatrist speaking German words, seeking forms of feeling, edges of image, flurries of body sensation, legs, gut, heart, throat, headache, squinting eyes, nods, moving two minds so differently formed, hunching into conscious enough conversation, seeking to listen. No, not these two but, let us say, a Warlpiri or Pintubi man, speaking Warlpiri, Pintubi languages, and a half-formed English, and maybe a psychiatrist or anthropologist or a lawyer or police prosecutor, the two of them sitting there wondering about a mutual problem: an act of drunken assault, the suicide of a petrol-sniffing boy, the mutilated body of a woman in the creek bed, a traditional man so senseless with sweet white wine that he blurts out age-old secrets in bad company and ought to be speared for it. And if the spear is cast, the men who mete out the sanctioned, traditional punishment will be imprisoned for assault or maybe manslaughter. And they may deserve to be, if they carried out the penalty while drunk or lost their reason while doing it. Irreconcilable parallel laws, cognitive dissonance, daily bread.

Myself, I have sat in many such conversations, the ants busy, the fire dimmed by psychic pain, on a cold concrete floor, dull with ash and grease, supporting so many suchlike conversations, a hundred times, somewhere between two worlds. In the overlap of intercultural conversation, things arrive, if we take the trouble to create between us a "location for cultural experience" (Winnicott 1971: chap. 7) and accept that what might arrive will be perplexity, compassion, humor, irony, whimsical desire, flights of ideas, confusion, resolution—or nothing much except a sense of nowhere to go, other than a slight action here or there, a hunch of the shoulders or shift of the body.

I have thus experienced the realities of the Australian cultural trauma systems, the inter-racial transference milieu where things emerge and merge and re-form at the mercy of that famous 'unconscious', which pushed and pushed the Viennese doctors to discover it and reveal it. And here, in Australia, that 'unconscious' is pushing again, maybe not within us but rather between us, black and white. It is within this 'unconsciousness' of each other that we act, fitfully, hopelessly, being doctors, social care agents, policemen on the edge, lawyers between two laws that barely, rarely meet, barely hear, barely listen, barely see. But still we do the best of a bad enough job. Such things, such reveries are in the background, always there in these conversations between seated men. Two or three gathered together, the ants busy.

I am thinking of these conversations: the one with the boy sniffing petrol behind the garage in Fregon, or the quietly ceremonial old men's conversations at Mission Creek about two laws and the origin of the white man's rights to arrest and sentence a black man, or maybe that muttered laconic exchange in the Toyota Land Cruiser with the man from Finke River (diagnosed as suffering from schizophrenia) as to whether the "snake" curled in his head was going to kill him right now in the car, or maybe later. But the one will I tell you, so as to introduce my theme on the *Tjukurrpa*,[1] is this one about the making of a doctor.

This was a long conversation. It rolled in a vehicle from Alice Springs to Yuendumu and thus to Mt. Wedge and farther west. It rolled, as some conversations do, back east to Sydney and Wollongong and back and forth, again and again. And it roamed also internally, through personal dreams and experiences and clinical encounters. And still it roams, presenting a question about the archetypal basis of the healing profession—the experiential qualification that fits one for practice and the precise nature of the *Tjukurrpa* that supports one's capacity to heal effectively.

The first question put to my psychiatric colleague and myself by the Aboriginal man of whom I am thinking was simply about whether there is any similarity between the way that Aboriginal traditional healers and Western mental health doctors get their skill and recognition. The conversation starter was along the lines of the following: "Psychiatrist, hmmm. Well, you tell me. Do white doctors have to pass through anything? What gives them the right to work? Do they follow *Tjukurrpa* like the *ngangkaris* [witch doctors] do? Or is it only learning from books?"

Good question. It makes one wonder about the grounded, fundamental basis of one's clinical practice, the thing that motivates one to keep on working and be successful, the position on which one stands, the *telos* of one's psychological work. Through such deftly simple questions, I find myself compelled to contemplate the meaning and significance of *Tjukurrpa* as the basis for practice, as well as the substance of another conversation, set against a longer reverie about sugars and alcohol and who or what is responsible for alcohol-related deaths, berserk assaults, family breakdown, sexual derangement. And suicide.[2]

There are thousands of similar conversations going on about "who is responsible" for this and that, like background white noise. Such mutterings are heard today like any other day within the vast, vaguely circumscribed one-third of the continent that makes up the Aboriginal lands, the Aboriginal mind. Here such things as lore and sacred geography keep on mattering, and health and life matters. Yet something life-saving never quite gets to the point, as though some obstacle is there, diverting, repressing, preventing clear thoughts from becoming definitive action.

I wonder what an anthropological investigation might reveal about what goes on in 'the conversation'. Not what this 'black man says', so much, and not what this 'white man says' exactly, but what happens *between* 'black and white' as they are speaking. Because then, I think, we will come to understand more accurately what *Tjukurrpa* is, how it sets us up and prescribes perfect solutions to intractable problems, and how we (black and white) have mutual difficulty in comprehending the theories on which are based our variously proposed perfect solutions. Understanding 'the conversation' in these terms will help us recognize how we break down—how we fail repeatedly.

Yes, I think that is it. I am putting forth the case for the anthropological observation and psychoanalysis of the 'intercultural conversation', a study of the phenomena that emerge between persons—people like those two men seated in Vienna and Zurich in 1907–1910, discovering the significance of what is projected and transferred between them. Here in the fly-blown dusts of the Western Desert, questions will be asked about conversations between people seated halfway between times, between the beginning and the end of local civilizations. What is being projected? What is being transferred between us in exact detail? The material substances, the objects, yes; but the mental substances, the mental objects? How do we grasp the form and feeling of mental substances passing between us in a place like this?

This is the kind of place where it matters what sugar really is and what white sugar transfers to your blood, gut, and brain when you have stopped walking miles every day, hunting lizards and kangaroo meat, eating bush food straight from the ground, a hard-edged kind of roughage, unlike jam from the tin with white-flour bread and fried chicken. And where two liters of port wine end the day, with maybe cannabis in the morning to straighten you out.

Sweet Substance

"Dreaming"—you hear them talk about it, this sweet thing. Sometimes they call it "The Dreaming,"[3] an approximation for English-language speakers. In Arrernte, they call it *Altjerre*, or in the Western Desert language, *Tjukurrpa*, or the Warlpiri, *Jukurrpa*. What does this really mean, this state of things that brings tears to Paddy Sims's eyes, seated cross-legged before a canvas, singing quietly, painting "The Milky Way Story"? This thing that women depict and men define in sand drawings, deft fingers moving upon canvasses stretched on the bare ground or smudged on a backyard cement slab near the Todd River? *Tjukurrpa*, land claims, faraway looks, casually marking this rock and that. Reverence, breaking into song in creek beds, shrugging, walking off. *Tjukurrpa*, lightly held, with a gravity so exquisite, so solid, so omnipresent. *Tjukurrpa*, perhaps the most misunderstood, most ignored, most beautiful, most mysterious, most exploited, most obliterated phenomenon in this country. Strangely provocative, *Tjukurrpa* is seamlessly sewn into the Australian landform, sown as seeds in the mind of a country a long time ago, today. What should I attempt in defining it, this all pervading substance that offers no salvation, no redemption?[4]

Three Definitions of Tjukurrpa

First is a straightforward, heartfelt definition offered by Bob Randall, singer-songwriter (e.g., "Brown Skin Baby"), cultural teacher, and Aboriginal health professional at Mutitjulu/Uluru. In an interview with filmmaker David Roberts, Randall describes *Tjukurrpa* as "[t]he belief of the creation period and the laws that were set down from the beginning. These laws and rules were handed down through ceremonies, it was passed down from one generation to another. So I had to take care of that. It was my responsibility. You separate me from that, and already you've made me weak ... *Tjukurrpa*, in our words, is the belief of creation; like our law, our religion. You look at the past, it is part of the present, and will still be there in the future. It's what non-Aboriginal people refer to as 'the dream time', but it's real. This is *Tjukurrpa* [patting and holding a rock embedded in a hillside]. This is not a rock, only a rock, it is my link to *Tjukurrpa*, and all the stories are in this ... you realize [this rock] it's the *Tjukurrpa*. I have to care for my country, and in caring for my country you have to know its stories and what totemic ancestral beings are associated with that. It's important. And if anything that happened, that was for you to know, to pass on to your kids" (1999; see also Randall 2003).

A second definition of *Tjukurrpa*, conveyed by an informant of Stanner, is quoted by Sutton (1988: 15): "My father said this. 'My boy, look! Your Dreaming is there; it is a big thing; you never let it go [pass it by]. All Dreamings [totemic entities] come from there.' Does the whiteman now understand? The blackfellow, earnest, friendly, makes a last effort. 'Old man, you listen! Something is there; we do not know what; *something*.' There is a struggle to find words, and perhaps a lapse into English. 'Like engine, like power, plenty of power; it does hard work; it *pushes*.'"

A third definition of *Tjukurrpa* was expressed in conversation with Andrew Japaljarri Spencer in April 1990. To set the scene, my colleague Petchkovsky and I are in the back-lane office of the Healthy Aboriginal Life Team (HALT), a petrol-sniffing prevention project based in Alice Springs. We are speaking with Japaljarri Spencer, a Warlpiri member of that innovative social activist team. In the background, going about their work while chatting in several languages, are Christine Spencer, Hinton Lowe, Christine Franks, William Armstrong, and passing family members. We are looking at a painting by Nangala, Andrew's mother. The fine, symmetrical dot painting is about the sugar ant ceremony. The sugar ant belongs in the category of *parma*, or sweet substance. Alcohol also is categorized as *parma*, which in desert life is an essential and sought-after commodity. Desert people need sugar for life-sustaining activities, and in arid lands it is hard to come by. In the liquor shop and the supermarket, however, sugar is cheap and plentiful. And that is a problem.

Andrew says: "This painting is about *parma*, sugar, sugar ant. Different from honey ant. It is like a fly. We have the song for this, for *parma* and for strengthening *parma*. We haven't got the song to send white man's *parma* [sugar] away. We can't get rid of this one. We can only strengthen the good *parma*. The songs for petrol and alcohol must come from the white man; or we must dream new ones. The children [meaning the innocent and uninitiated] can't save the world. You, the white people, have lost your Dreaming. Maybe you don't know the songs for alcohol and petrol. You have to learn [reconnect to] your songs, your whitefellah *Tjukurrpa*. To turn to us, to me [i.e., to Aboriginal people] for the [alcohol and petrol dreaming] songs is too much."

Later Andrew asks straight out: "Do *Kardia* [white people] have the *Tjukurrpa* for *parma*?" I exchange glances with Petchkovsky, my companion in this conversation. We nod to each other. I say, "Yes." Andrew says: "Well, maybe you'd better go and get it. That's your responsibility." I nod, "All right, Japaljarri."

The Ordinary Impact of Dreaming

The idea arose in this conversation that since European culture is responsible for the invention of alcohol, it might therefore hold the 'creation story' (or *Tjukurrpa*) for managing intoxication. Such a creation story might be useful as a conceptual tool to help Australian indigenous people control the problem of alcohol-related destruction wreaked on Aboriginal lives and family structures and thus, perhaps, to help secure a cultural future. This is an intriguing idea, and much subsequent work went into researching and elaborating this concept. The reason for reporting this conversation is not to give an account of that project, which drew logically enough upon the mythologem of Dionysus;[5] rather, the purpose is to note that in this encounter we have a glimpse of the potential of *Tjukurrpa* as a pragmatic force in handling a social problem—alcohol abuse. Bob Randall emphasizes *Tjukurrpa* as creation story, the underpinning of laws of behavior, separation from which makes one weak. Stanner's informant brings out the psychic force, the 'push' in *Tjukurrpa*. And Japaljarri

Spencer suggests that effective control or management of behavior depends upon knowledge of the appropriate *Tjukurrpa*.

The usual reaction of a health-project coordinator might be to counter Japaljarri Spencer's (animistic?) suggestion with a rational, scientifically based response, to produce an 'evidence-based' treatment program adapted to Aboriginal needs, and then to leave it at that. Andrew had suggested that we give serious attention to the 'native solution', and it was this that I set about doing in the development of the Dionysus/Wati *Parrma* or Sugarman project. I am reminded of a phrase in Lévi-Strauss's (1977: 239) *Tristes Tropiques*, wherein he is describing some contention over Eskimo methods of dress and their suitability in handling the environmental conditions within which Eskimo dwell. For some reason, this was questioned by some rational Western visitors. As it turned out, says Lévi-Strauss, "The native solution was perfect; we could only realise this once we had grasped the theory on which it was based." My effort to comprehend *Tjukurrpa* is synonymous with an effort to comprehend the indigenous 'theory' upon which indigenous action in health, law, and cultural maintenance is based.

When one works into such ideas as Japaljarri Spencer's from a practiced, psychoanalytic position, the track is a little different from that of the surprisingly prevalent assumption that I/we (i.e., Westerners or non-Aboriginal persons and institutions in general) already have the perfect solution and that the so-called natives have only to accept the obvious. However, after listening consistently to Japaljarri Spencer in context and in his own terrain, I found that I gradually acknowledged that *Tjukurrpa* might, in itself, contain the theory on which Aboriginal solutions are based. If this were so, I thought, then I was ethically bound to come to know and understand that theory. Moreover, in a personal, empathetic, transferential sense, I allowed myself to appreciate how and why *Tjukurrpa* had such a forceful impact upon human beings and why it was so seriously held to by obviously intelligent and active indigenous men and women. This track is close to Jung's position as outlined in his autobiographical chapter, "Confrontations with the Unconscious," in which he records how he, in his own circumstances, began a reorientation of his working method. Jung (1961: 194) writes: "After the parting of the ways with Freud, a period of inner uncertainty began for me ... Above all I found it necessary to develop a new attitude towards my patients. I resolved for the present not to bring any theoretical premises to bear upon them, but to wait and see what they had to tell me of their own accord. My aim became to leave things to chance. The result was that patients would spontaneously report their dreams and fantasies to me, and I would merely ask ... How do you mean that, where does that come from?" I register this point because the conversation with Japaljarri Spencer marked a shift in myself, not only toward taking *Tjukurrpa* seriously but also in defining a method by which I could come to appreciate it and understand why it is that, as Randall says, the absence of connection to *Tjukurrpa* weakens a person.

Traveling in uncertainty within Aboriginal territories invariably leads to something spontaneously evocative, and much could be written about the value and the disorientation of that experience (San Roque 2000, 2004). One has to allow oneself to cultivate a mode of receptivity to unknown outcomes and a companionship with indigenous associates in an atmosphere of an unpredictable emotional nature. What we find within the Caucasian–Aboriginal Australian relationship is often exceptionally creative yet poignantly destructive, and in an attempt to avoid the latter, my working method developed deliberately along the lines suggested by Jung. This helped, I believe, in the attainment of some relatively successful projects, so long as the partnerships lasted.[6] And it has led to these reflections upon the power of *Tjukurrpa* as a mental influence and a psychological process.

I am using this article to open up the idea that *Tjukurrpa*, like play, is about symbolic realities mingled with actuality (Winnicott 1971), that play is also a basis for thinking and creativity. I have the idea that symbols are painted on bodies and arranged in ceremonies in very specific formations, possibly so that *Tjukurrpa* stories become real in the mind. Understanding how *Tjukurrpa* is laid out may show something about how Aboriginal thought is put together and how things link from country exterior to country interior and even, perhaps, how things pass from one side of the brain to the other. It may be useful to know how Aboriginal thoughts are built; how 'white' or Caucasian thoughts have built up around specific European/Mediterranean/Middle Eastern mythologies and cultural matrices; and how Asian thoughts are constructed around specific Asian mythologies as matrices. To appreciate how culture and cultural history form thinking has a pragmatic and possibly therapeutic purpose for work between black and white Australians. This is based on the idea that our myths and how we employ the myths to which we cling actually reveal how we think and act. Subliminal mythic dream states probably define who we are as a people and affect how we run our nation-state and our international relations. This idea that myth organizes political relations is a concept out of analytical psychology and the emerging theory on how a nation's thought pattern is formed by "cultural complexes" (Kimbles and Singer 2004).

What shapes thinking? The shapers are many, but I am intrigued, for instance, with the way 'country' forms symbolic imagery in the human mind and how established geographic places and accustomed bodily spaces help form a language. In English there are many words and concepts formed, for example, around a common knowledge of boundaries and fences, of walls and roof, foundations and fortress, etc., all patterned upon long association with specific and constructed human boundaries to space. In such ways, certain forms encode our thinking. And further, there is some kind of evolutionary mystery to be unraveled around the continuum of being, which we, as humans, internalize. I speak of the continuum from site to flora to fauna, in multitude forms and activities, and the way in which this continuum of being suffuses, penetrates, fertilizes, and explores the mind of the human being, and especially of those who live in long association with natural worlds and forms, be they in conversation with arid lands and the long horizons of the desert or the expanses of the sea or the surge of rivers, jungles, mountains, volcanoes. Might not desert dwellers have geographically specific images as the geographically specific creators of their specific thought and language patterns?

Understanding how this works might help one appreciate how *Tjukurrpa* works. The phylogenetic spectrum of being in which humans participate is continuously encountered in conversations in Aboriginal country. Indigenous Australians have, as far as I can tell, a subtle notion of the continuity of being between landform, plant, animal, and human, but this notion is not attentive to that progressive evolution of form and consciousness that the Darwinian eye attends upon. Why mention this difference? Because an understanding of geographical spaces, human relationship with the animal world, human phylogenetic history, and especially how we configure this history has significance for how we configure *Tjukurrpa* and also how we might configure a local psychological therapeutic theory and practice. It has to do with the idea of where humans begin and end, from where the human soul appears and to what purpose, how it tells its story, what troubles the soul, and how psychic energies circulate. *Tjukurrpa* addresses and reveals these matters.

Psychoanalysis is concerned with psychic traveling, circulating with therapeutic purpose along the spectrum of being from the earliest forms of becoming to present becoming. It is concerned with following a person from his or her most simple forms of primal thought/feeling to the most complex and abstract forms of thought/feeling/action. As I consider this while in arid country, I think about these specific landforms, bush foods, fruits, lizards, snakes, mammals, and birds that appear in the mind and, simultaneously, in actuality. As I listen to Aboriginal conversations, I find myself in a reverie, wishing I could report such loosely noticed moments and flickering tales of insight to Jung, in archetypal fishing mood, or to Bion, in his "thoughts looking for a thinker" mood, or to Klein, given her intense study of the earliest forms of interior life and of destructiveness as apprehended by her mind when in proximity to children's minds (see Klein 1950; Klein et al. 1973).[7] I am making the point that different things occur in one's mind depending upon *with whom* one is sitting. And *where*. Different ideas form in the mind of psychoanalysts depending upon where they consistently sit—that is to say, in whose proximity they sit and in whose country. Sit attuned in the company of indigenous Australians and note the senses, images, and experiences that arrive in your mind. They might be different from those that materialize when you sit with people in rooms in Melbourne, Zurich, or London. This may seem a truism, perhaps, but in Bion's way, I would say that in Central Australia there are specific "thoughts looking for a thinker." In Japaljarri Spencer's language, *Tjukurrpa* talks to you. *Tjukurrpa* gets "lonely for people."

I sit as others do, sometimes in good company, in trucks, by fires, amid dust and plastic bags and dogs, with old men and women, with petrol sniffers and vigorous painters, and in these sittings certain clusters of thought/feeling forgather. As an agent of agencies employed to solve indigenous health problems, I admit that I have not formed the mental container system that allows localized thoughts to be accurately felt and accurately ordered and consistently followed through into accurate action. This is difficult to do. Learning how *Tjukurrpa* works in situ, in its unique structure, in its specific function and specific symbology may be a very pragmatic step toward taking accurate social therapeutic action.

Summation So Far

I introduce an approach to *Tjukurrpa* as a mental or conceptual system. I suggest that a Bion/Jung nexus offers a potential schema by which psychological thinkers, who value poetic sensibility, might come to appreciate the intricate beauty of the structure of the Aboriginal mental world and the significance of *Tjukurrpa* as a matrix for holding and revealing the continual becoming and rebirth of human life. There is value in passing on to 'the kids' and to uninitiated Westerners the practice of listening to *Tjukurrpa*. Forgetting it, ignoring the psychological significance of 'Dreaming', may be, as Bob Randall suggests, a form of dissociation that mentally weakens us all.

Part Two: Reverie on a Long Road

Kulini

Somewhere between a Stuart Highway roadhouse and the turn-off toward the Anangu Pitjantjatjara Lands, I am thinking about the simplicity of listening. A Pitjantjatjara word cluster, *kulini/kulira/kulilkatinyi* (Goddard 1987) means 'to listen' and also 'to think'. Linguist Ely White has noted that, according to her understanding, "the real business of Aboriginal men is to think; that is to say, to listen—"*Kulini.*"[8] *Kulini* leads us to the business of 'attentive listening' and thus to 'thinking'. It leads me to consider that just as Aboriginal men, whom I know, have sacred objects to which they listen and speak, we, the Caucasians, also have physically numinous mental objects with which we think. I wonder also what objects we carry around in our mental bodies that persistently manifest themselves in Aboriginal country and destroy our capacity for intelligent forethought and action?

The Wreck of the Batavia

There is a novel, *The Accomplice*, by Kathryn Heyman (2003), which is a narrative of a Protestant Dutch woman caught up in the human disasters following the wreck off the West Australian coast in 1692 of the East India Company sailing ship, the *Batavia*. The numinous objects in this story might be 'ship', 'Holy Book', 'money', and 'guns'. But the enterprise founders on the Australian coast, and people resort to murder and cannibalism. Heyman begins her account with a quote from Primo Levi: "The harsher the oppression, the more widespread among the oppressed is the willingness to collaborate with the power." Her story details the effect of collaboration with the prevailing powers (after the wreck). Survival requires that 'good' people lose their voice, their presence of mind. The commander is gone. Acts degenerate. The disaster is the incremental loss of an intelligent and humane mind. My point is that an insidious catastrophe that currently prevails in Central Australia is made possible because significant numbers of people lose the command of intelligent mind and collaborate, paradoxically, with a pervasion of powerlessness. It is not that there is a harsh oppression of native peoples, as such, any more, but perhaps it has something to do with the way certain integrating *Tjukurrpa* of both white and black lose a specific presence in our mind. Heyman, in her account, details in fiction the human wreck of the *Batavia*. The present disaster one might feel around one in Central Australia (and maybe Oceania) should be open not only to fiction (and journalist's fictions) but to precise psycho-anthropological analysis to follow on from the example of Alex Minutjukur and Andrew Japaljarri Spencer and their families, who have consistently attempted a social analysis in their paintings. So too has Tim Leura Japaljarri and the Alice Springs painter, Rod Moss. Their imagery depicts, from inside experience, the wreck of 'culture'.

It might be that a majority of Australians do not know or appreciate just how precisely Rod Moss, Japaljarri Spencer, Minutjukur and company thoughtfully created intimate communications between themselves and those people who also come to dwell in this ancient seabed of desert Australia. Perhaps the name of the ship in which we sail is *Kulini wia*—that is to say, 'No one listens'.

Reverie on a Long Road Again

These things I am thinking, tonight, somewhere in a haze in a yellow truck crossing over the border zone between Pitjantjatjara lands and the South Australian border, leaving behind another futile-feeling conversation with a petrol sniffer and old men who shrug and walk away. Just here, in this brief interstitial 100-kilometer stretch, I think about a place I have pegged in my own mind as the White Noise Café, where we, the white folk, talk in circles, endlessly; and why it is that nothing seems grittily to emerge out of *Tjukurrpa* to save *Anangu* (Aboriginal people) from themselves—and all of us from ourselves. This is a recurrent reverie I know so well. It is like a musical canon, a repeating theme in the 'ethnography of hopelessness and helplessness'. Lévi-Strauss (1977) in his melancholia recognized that prevailing wind of hopelessness among the indigenous Amazonians, just as Theodor Strehlow (1971) did at the end of his *Songs of Central Australia*. These iconic anthropologists were reduced to making half-whispered, existential, diagnostic statements, offered in *tristesse*, offered in response to the mood of a country entering depression. How strangely we fail. Again and again, in country after country.

Part Three: The Undoing of Oneself

Corrupted by Desire

Bion ([1970] 1984: 31–35) advocates that a therapist should come to an analytic engagement with an open mind, uncontaminated with "memory and desire." It could also be advocated that an anthropologist or a therapist ought to be able to come to an intercultural engagement with a mind uncontaminated thus. I doubt very much that this is possible. Or rather, such an openness of mind might be achievable, but how in fact and in detail does one achieve intercultural creativity? The evidence is more likely to show that almost no one has succeeded in cracking the code of a 'successful outcome' in health or law, in social justice or social reconstruction, or even in colonial administration. Most of us (as professionals of ethnic engagement) might confess to failure, and might, in the twilight hours, confess as well to having contributed to the destruction of those cultures and those specific people whom we desired to assist. Or be assisted by. In the process, as perhaps Lévi-Strauss, Strehlow, and Bardon exemplify, one finds oneself finally 'undone'. This phenomenon, in itself, is worth a sensitive, thoughtful ethnography. An analysis.

I came to my meeting with Japaljarri Spencer full of prejudice, expectation, innocence, memory, and desires—and I came with questions (always there are questions). I came with a goal in mind, a desire to get a grip on how the exponents of European and Aboriginal therapeutic traditions and cultures might beneficially find a way of talking to each other about the practice of their craft. This desire both directed and contaminated the way I listened to what Japaljarri Spencer (and his family) conveyed in the fractal fragment of conversation about *parma* and alcohol *Tjukurrpa* that I described above.

When Japaljarri Spencer raised the matter of concern, he naturally enough couched it in terms that made sense to him. Whether or not I understood his issues and communications is open to question, but it would appear that my mind had been prepared in a certain way to make a particular sense of what he was saying. Because my mind had been prepared in a certain way, I took action in a certain way and gathered action about me accordingly. Analyzing the actual detail of these transactions is what I mean about the need for an 'ethnography of failure', that is to say, a description of our intercultural interacting that constructs systems and an analysis of where they fail in precise detail—not with shame or concealment but rather professionally, astutely, in order to diagnose our joint condition. And maybe solve it. So far as I can see, the construct systems turn around this matter of memories and desires and also around the persistent forces coming from our mythic (unconscious) foundations of thought and perception, that is, the *Tjukurrpa*. It might help to appreciate the place that *Tjukurrpa* occupies within the indigenous mind, and how the force or push of the *Tjukurrpa* influences the day-to-day perceptions of every Aboriginal and non-Aboriginal person involved with each other in health, law, economics, social action, and cultural activities. It seems to be a matter of what is felt as real and what is felt simply as passing illusion. I am at a loss about this. I am trying to describe it.

Unquiet Minds

It is a part of the psychoanalytic discipline to conduct an ongoing analysis of one's counter-transference reactions to the other person, the so-called patient. Such a discipline of reflective self-observation seems as useful in the practice of intercultural communication as it is in therapeutic communication. One's training as a psychotherapist prepares one to attend to interpersonal communications in a particularly useful way. The emphasis I place is upon the mode of human attention cultivated within the discipline of psychotherapy and not upon the theoretical constructs of the psychotherapeutic profession. The theories we can take or leave. What we have to work with is the acquired discipline of lucid self-perception, a form of apperception whereby one attempts to observe what is going on between oneself and another, most especially when both are cast into difficult situations and into unquiet states of mind.

Some Implications

Throughout Central Australia and perhaps much of the rest of the country, certainly the northern and western sectors, there is a particular creation power associated with water, water sources, water courses, and water holes. It is tempting to emphasize here the association between waters, serpents, healing activities, and initiation into specific states of being on the edge or overlap of 'dying and creating'. These somewhat esoteric/mystical activities tend to capture (Jungian) attention, but I wish to underline the significance of specific sites for the activity of psychologically significant events. These things do not merely happen 'in the mind' or in some metaphysical archetypal reality absent from actual geographical location. Site is significant. When Japaljarri Spencer spoke of a *Tjukurrpa* for alcohol, I took this to imply that such a story, like all *Tjukurrpa*, would need to be rooted in the actuality of site, in geography with traceable travels of creation beings connecting wine and intoxication to specific sites in the regions of origin. The Dionysus myth does just that. As does the Jesus story, which is exquisitely site-specific with archetypal value.

The implication here is that there are elements and patterns in both the desert Aboriginal and Western mythic repertoire that do have kinship. Strehlow thought so. He tried to demonstrate this in the oral and written cultural forms—the songs of Central Australia and sagas of Old Europe, for instance. Elkin ([1945] 1977) suspected that there might be congruences between the practices of indigenous healers (*ngangkari*) and Western psychiatric practitioners (San Roque 1986: 81–107).[9] I ask myself: Why has it taken so long to be realized and incorporated into psychological practice? What am I missing? What is the secret warfare that goes on between us in Australia that makes such an obvious effort at congruence so difficult to imagine, let alone put into experiential practice?

When I heard a simple outline from Japaljarri Spencer of a specific *Tjukurrpa* as a reference trek for the formation of a *ngangkari* in his own region, with its subject's passage through waterholes, snakes, displacement, rejection, attack, virtual dismemberment, and entry, after perilous journeys, into caves and water, I felt that I was on familiar symbolic territory. Rather than dismissing his iconography for whatever reason, I and my psychiatric colleague committed ourselves to years of gradual engagement with this one story. Much that I have since found in the iconic sequences of the Dionysian matrix, and also in the Oedipal nine-generational saga, presents a repertoire of incidents that are congruent with incidents, symbolic shapes, and patterns in suchlike indigenous Australian traditional stories with which I have become personally and physically involved. The emphasis here is on direct physical and personal engagement with these stories; and if there were ever to be a helpful study of the impact and usefulness of Australian 'Dreaming', then I would suggest that such a study would have to go a lot further than a catalogue and recording of 'Dreaming' stories as objective narratives. It would have to take into account the effects upon persons who have internalized specific *Tjukurrpa* and specific sites (see Petchkovsky and San Roque 1995: 445–450).

Summation

It does appear that basic patterns of both Aboriginal and Caucasian/European/ Middle Eastern foundation/creation stories do reveal a remarkable commonality. Some of the common 'bits' of Caucasian mythic episode and *Tjukurrpa* stories include significant (heroic) beings traveling to specific sites and the effect of those travels and those sites on the visitor. They are marked by the presence of reptilian beings and other numinous proto-human/animal activity; acts of being swallowed and regurgitated by such creatures, or being made small and infantile; beings to whom traumatic events occur; and instances of sexual anarchy, incest, trickery, and deceit by such creatures. There are disappearances into the earth, into landforms, into the sky; appearances out of the sky, out of the earth; travels over ground, underground, in the sky, and among the stars; acts of creation from bodily fluids or functions; losses (and sometimes recovery) of body parts; various tales of male and female supernatural beings in endless gender politics; erotic adventures, comic, tragic, and epic, repeating ad infinitum into endless fights. And always somewhere, there is the presence of good-humored, wily, compassionate beings—sometimes women, sometimes men, sometimes of elder status, sometimes 'innocents'—who advocate cunning, intelligent consciousness, apperception, and the value of wisdom and care gained from experience.

One might note processes within these tales that reflect significant procedures of human inner and outer life. It would take an extensive, locally based study to satisfactorily set out the parallel process between indigenous Australian and indigenous Mediterranean/Caucasian/Northern European mythologies that are central to our contemporary and prevailing cultural matrices. It is probably worth doing if for no other reason than to appreciate each other's idiosyncratic ways of thinking, our cultural anxieties, and our several capacities for self-delusion, in order to provide informed and sophisticated psychological care for indigenous people in distress, especially for those who live in the tensions of parallel or borderline realities/fantasies of the black and the white Australia. Now I want to move on to the intriguing and mysterious matter of how thoughts are made, or what thoughts are made of.

Part Four: Where Thoughts Are Things and Things Are Thoughts

> This rock isn't a rock ... only a rock ... it is *Tjukurrpa*.
>
> — Bob Randall

This Rock ...

Bion, in *Elements of Psycho-analysis* ([1963] 1968: 22–27), describes the terms he will use throughout his project on thinking, thought formation and trans-formation, and the use of mental 'objects' in psychotherapeutic activity. He develops the theme throughout five books. For our purposes here, I deal only with the simplest use of Bion and three of the elements of his system. These are *beta* elements, *alpha* elements, and *alpha* function.

Beta elements refer to "the earliest matrix from which thoughts can be supposed to arise." In this origin state of thought, the proto-elements of the thought domain have the quality of inanimate objects and psychic objects without any distinction being experienced between the two states. In this most primal state of mind, "thoughts are things, things are thoughts and they have personality." "*Beta* elements are not amenable to use in dream thoughts but are suited for use in projective identification. They are influential in producing 'acting out'. They are objects that can be evacuated or used for a kind of think-ing that depends on manipulation of what are felt to be things in themselves as if to substitute such manipulation for words or ideas" (Bion [1962] 1984: 6). I was wondering then, and I still wonder, if we could think of *Tjukurrpa* as the "earliest matrix from which thought can be supposed to arise," using Bion's way of thinking about the matter of mental life. Perhaps one might suggest that in the *Tjukurrpa* state of mind, one might be feeling and seeing inanimate objects and psychic objects as one and the same.

In the *Tjukurrpa* state of mind, it would seem that thoughts are things and things are thoughts. Mountains are snakes, snakes are mountains, rocks are bits of people, bits of people are rocks, and they have personality. These 'things' project themselves into the minds and lives of people, and they act out stories in the topography of the country, rather than in the topography of the interior mind, where mind is considered conventionally as an 'internal' domain. I have been with Aboriginal people whose minds dwell in and roam among snakes as mountains, mountains as snakes—the rocks are people, people are rocks, liv-ing, breathing, doing things in the world, not in the mind, as such. The mind is in the country, or the country is acting in the mind. The question, what is going on in the mind? can be rephrased as, what is going on in the country?

At some point in time, or in human mental evolution, people let their minds play, and *alpha* function, as Bion formulates it, begins to operate on *beta* ele-ments, that is, those concrete, primal, pre-mental things. When this happens, some kind of psychic work is done, and mental transformations take place. This process reflects a fundamental capacity for sustaining human life. The primal *beta* elements become *alpha* elements. That is to say, bits of primal experience acquire a psychic reality, and bits of experience somehow begin to enter into human experience as 'dream thoughts'. As Bion ([1962] 1984: 7) explains it: "*Beta* elements ... differ from *alpha* elements in that they are not so much memories as undigested facts, whereas the *alpha* elements have been digested by *alpha* function and thus made available for thought. It is important to distinguish between memories and undigested facts ... If the patient cannot transform his emotional experience into *alpha* elements, he cannot dream. *Alpha* function transforms sense impressions into *alpha* elements, which resemble, and may be identical with, the visual images with which we are familiar in dreams, namely, the elements that Freud regards as yielding their latent content when the analyst has interpreted them ... Failure of *alpha* function means that the patient cannot dream and therefore cannot sleep."

The Place in the Brain Where Thoughts Assemble

So many times, sitting on bare sand, watching the relaxed yet concentrated seriousness of the way men (or women) painted up their bodies and prepared for a *Tjukurrpa* enactment, I found myself wondering if ceremony might be the communal milieu, the communal container wherein these subtle psychological transformations take place, the place where thoughts are assembled, somehow inside and outside the human mind at the same time. Perhaps ceremony can be understood as a humanly constructed domain where evolutions of consciousness take place and thinking as a mental condition begins, simply by the manipulation of internal/external objects, painted and changed into a kind of numinosity and then carried out in a mental/physical place—a psychosomatic or 'psychoid' event (to use Jung's term), which, by virtue of being shown on 'sacred ground', is somehow also located inside the mental world. There is no Descartian split within such people, as far as I can tell. Inside matters happen outside. Mental events happen in the body moving. The body moving is an idea. I guess that is not so strange really. It is just that I am used to seeing ideas moving as words on a page rather than as bodies on a ceremony ground.

If this is so, and I am coming to the conclusion that it is, then this conception further justifies the decision to present the Sugarman cycle within the format and psychic (trance) space of a ceremony/performance, rather than, for instance, as health-promotion material, video clips, or academic reports. Such complex and abstract mental constructions are too far along the continuum, too far from the *Tjukurrpa* state of mind, where rocks are thoughts and thoughts are rocks.

In the *Tjukurrpa* 'state of mind', if you want to move ideas, you have to paint bodies and move objects as actual things and as psychically charged representations of things/places/beings/rocks. A ceremonial enactment in song and dance is where, collectively, individual and group *beta* elements are worked on and transformed into *alpha* elements, into dream elements and meanings. The ceremonial enactments present simple things as simple moving thoughts. They move, through the container of the ceremony, from a location in the country into a place in someone's mind and thus into everyone's mind. As a result, land forms and mind are fused consciously.[10]

I suggest that as psychic work (*alpha* function) is being done through the singing of a story line, for example, the 'mountains as snakes' become 'snakes as dream', then 'snakes' as dream images assume meanings for men and women, then thoughts, then strings of thoughts and strings of songs, and then fragments of ceremonial action, which are dreams in action. Thus, as psychic work is done, new members (those still out of their mind), the young or uninitiated in the family, are brought into conscious containment by the communal thought systems. Participation in ceremony is participation in the container of shared and developing thinking. Ceremony is, I think, in Bion's terms, *alpha* function in collective action, psychic work in collective operation.

With this possible procedure in mind, perhaps one can understand the significance of what Japaljarri Spencer and others are saying about the need for something to cover or fill the absence of a necessary *Tjukurrpa* in order to hold the space for thinking about something as perplexing in its effect as alcohol is seen to be. When he searched the earliest matrix of Aboriginal experience, Japaljarri could not find psychically significant objects that are imbued with the spirit of intoxication. He could not find, or could not recognize, an element or object that could be used to do psychic work upon, to convert into dream imagery and then thoughts. He needed dream thoughts located in the *Tjukurrpa* before he could authoritatively and passionately form mental conceptions about the behaviors of intoxication. Even if there were to be a container made for a ceremony, Japaljarri and his companions did not know exactly what ceremonial thought-objects had to be brought out from the earliest matrix and then placed into collective view for conscious attention by gathered potential thinkers. The Warlpiri man did not know (I conjecture) the shapes of the animals or plants, the painted designs for the body, the physical or mimetic actions, the words or rhythms of the songs that could be authoritatively sung. Such things have to be sung to give shape to mental concepts and to present conscious prescriptions for action in response to intoxicated behaviors. My friend, literally, concretely, did not know what to think.

Taking it further, if he wanted to send the spirit of alcohol away—that is, become dispossessed of intoxication—he could find no psychic objects in the earliest matrix of thought that he could manipulate physically or mentally in order to use psychic authority over the substance and the behavior. If he wanted to become a healer of alcohol-induced sickness, he could find no dream thoughts and no sustaining psychic or physical objects in the earliest matrix of local *Tjukurrpa* that could form the basis of procedures, ceremonies, songs, or psychic manipulations that would have an effect in the mental domain of his own family. No one listened because there was nothing to sing, except country music, Western rock, or *wama wanti* (give up the grog) songs. There was no deeply structured *Tjukurrpa* music.

Alcohol and intoxication therefore remain as undigested psychic facts for which no one has responsibility, other than to attempt to 'excrete' them. Intoxicated behaviors persist as human objects in chaos in the landscape of the dreaming but are unrelated to or dissociated from the dreaming, with a life of their own, recognized but not internalized, remembered but barely owned as real memories, hardly even dream fragments. Intoxication becomes something that one cannot wake up from and that one cannot go to sleep from—something that exists outside the reach of thought, yet is ever present as psychotic fact. As Bion ([1962] 1984: 7) says: "The patient who cannot dream cannot go to sleep and cannot wake up, hence the peculiar condition when the psychotic patient behaves as if he were precisely in this state." In my understanding, Japaljarri Spencer, as a cultural *ngangkari*, could not (at that time) find or see the psychic objects to extract from the spirit/dreaming body of his community/patients, nor could he find or see the psychic empowerment objects (*maban*) that he could use to insert into the disbanding communal bodies of his kin and bring about the restoration of their sanity. This is why indigenous healers say they have trouble dealing with alcohol 'sickness'.

Restatement: No Tjukurrpa, No Theory

Let me restate this complex, subtle, and probably abstruse theme. When faced with a request to fix a drunk, the indigenous healer, surveying his or her repertoire to handle spiritual, bodily sickness, could find none of the necessary 'thoughts as things, things as thoughts' to manipulate shamanically. There are no empowered story lines to hold or direct the traveling reverie of the healer's mind or hands. No 'snakes as mountains, mountains as snakes' to use to orient a patient's thought lines or recovery lines. No 'rocks as people, people as rocks' to insert into the mind country. No 'objects as power or powers as objects' to inject into the alcohol-dismembered joints. No 'words of power, or powers as words' to whisper into confused ears. No theory. No *Tjukurrpa*.

In short, the potential healer could find no *ngangkari* sequence of psychically effective operations. None of the usual natural objects, geographical locations, or activities at sites could be brought to bear to transform the minds of drunks, who are, literally, out of their indigenous mind and thus in limbo, lost in a country of intoxication. There is no reference point in the topographical dimensions of Aboriginal being or psyche. No place (in mind). No story (in mind). No way of empowering action. The *alpha* function proves impotent. The consequence of this void is that a collective psychosis as a cultural plague occupies the void. In Bion's way of thinking, no one is dreaming these things. No one is waking up, and no one is sleeping the sleep of healthy restoration, so the intoxication events remain as undigested, dissociated *beta* elements. When dreaming, waking, and sleep become disturbed and their realities confused with one another, a person begins to inhabit a psychotic state. In a psychotic state, personal relationships disintegrate. Obligations and the reciprocity of kinship disintegrate. Attention to country disperses and dissociates. Depression results.

Catastrophe, Breakdown, and Story

Meltzer (1978: 62), in his series of lectures on trying to understand Bion, describes Bion's formulations on "Catastrophic Change" as including the search for a "container" to relieve the stress of fragmentation and the hopelessness of ever attaining an integration. The catastrophic nature of the Aboriginal breakdown is almost "unthinkable." It is too emotionally disturbing for most people to comprehend, and that "unthinkability" is the therapeutic problem to be investigated and solved. The instinctive attempt at self-organized healing, which Andrew Japaljarri Spencer and his associates generated through HALT's (1991) work with petrol sniffers and intoxication, also presented itself as a request for an 'object' of therapeutic power. It was not a request for a tranquillizer. The request was for a narrative with substance with which to make sense of a senseless and unimaginably psychotic existential condition.

In Sophocles' *Oedipus*, the issue was the plague and the undisclosed family crime: the killing of an old man, the incest between son and mother, and the consequences of transgenerational traumas. In Australia, the issue is the existential catastrophe, undisclosed family crimes, and an invasion of mind that this particular *ngangkari* has articulated on behalf of his family, culture, and country. Japaljarri Spencer and his kin have articulated their concerns clearly, through succinct, compacted, and complex paintings and through the discourse unfolded from those images in the (now almost forgotten) HALT work. In the course of his many conversations, Japaljarri has plainly said that if the white doctors want to help, there are two necessary steps. First, the white doctors must be cured of their own illnesses (of perception). Second, the white doctors must be incorporated into the family system and have explained to them their family obligations and responsibilities to a specific country/*Tjukurrpa*. That is to say, the solution must involve inclusion.

A mode of operation familiar to analysts is the long, discursive rambling circumambulation of a matter at hand that does not yield to concise, penetrative interpretation. Sometimes for months this circuitous reverie may play like a base theme, just out of consciousness, until one day the matter clarifies into solution. Sometimes deep within the concentration of an analytic session, the therapist realizes that a moment has arrived wherein the patient's most hidden self-recognition has become tangible. This moment of painful self-revelation requires a response from the therapist that calls on all of his or her available experience, understanding, and eloquence. These moments are rare but totally demanding. At such times of intense relational connection, it is as though all of one's life, and the patient's life, passes before one. Such a moment may not last long, but much is packed into it. Something like this has been going on in the long session between myself and Japaljarri Spencer. We are both patient and doctor to each other. The Sugarman events, *Tjukurrpa* ceremonies, and mythic performances are really nothing more than illusions, enactments, hypotheses, experiments in mirroring, attempts at communication. Might this be how you too see these things? Do you understand me? Are we listening properly? Do I understand you? Is it like this?

On Dionysus and Derangement

While Japaljarri Spencer used snake stories and various *Tjukurrpa* idioms to speak with, I began to use Dionysus's character and his activities for intercultural communication. I was happy with the way this character represents a complex, fragmented interlacing of provocatively irrational, amoral, and contradictory adventures, easily matching the snakes and eagles and lizards of Warlpiri and Pintubi country. The god's name changes, his face changes, he carries out acts of apparently mindless violence, disordering the settled world, provoking rage and eroticism. He travels, he appears, he mysteriously disappears. He journeys across countries to the sites of significance. He marries a rejected woman and, paradoxically, holds together a stable marriage. He institutes mysteries of death and renewal, he initiates ceremonial dramas and acts as guardian of theatrical endeavor. He is a spirit of natural fertility and indestructible life, of fluent vegetation, the power of fermentation, and the essence of alcohol. He is attributed with being the quintessence of the human soul, the avatar of intoxication—a creation being who spits grapes and death. He is a narrated container, therefore, wherein it is possible to see *beta* elements and *alpha* elements tangling together. Dionysus presents us with the domain where thoughts are in flux, where bodily emotional processes are fluid, and where the reality of derangement is the fact of life. If 'thoughts are people' and 'people are thoughts', then in Dionysus's ceremony/symbolic drama, most concisely presented in Euripides' the *Bacchae*, we see and feel mad people, and mad thoughts manifest as gods.

In the sleepless dream states of Dionysus/Zagreus actions, mad things travel, dream passions arise ungoverned, mythic acts take precedence over individual wishes, delusions abound, thought disorder reigns—and yet there is a peculiarly liberating logic at work. Despite the chaotic derangement of isolated acts, the whole network of the Dionysus legend hangs together in a loosely knit container of fragmentation and integration that somehow holds sanity, pleasure, ease, and vitality. As far as I can tell, ceremonial theater is not about art; it is all about family obligations and maintaining cultural blood lines. And somehow or other it is about thinking as a communal activity. In my experience, it is within well-organized and well-performed ceremonies that moments of clarity arrive. The rehearsals and preparations are like the long, meandering reverie of analytic work. Japaljarri Spencer insisted that in order to become effective, a *Tjukurrpa* from the European repertoire must also be performed in the manner that Aboriginal *Tjukurrpa* is performed. Hence resulted our several experimental enactments at Intjartnama Outstation in community spectacle, objects swirling through smoke and fire beneath the canopy of wind and stars, with the character of Kronos/Crow cheerfully spearing his father, gleefully swallowing children, resolutely accompanying Captain Cook, dragging a boat up onto the beach, unloading laws. Images from the spectacles, including split brains, broken families, fences, holes in the mind, bottles of rum, bladders of piss, are those of the "greedy *beta* elements" of Western civilization, arriving on the fatal shore "full of a sense of catastrophe, searching wildly for a saturating realisation in the absence of the container (breast)" (Meltzer 1978: 62).

The invasion of the domain of the *Tjukurrpa* by Crow/Kronos (us) and his desperate cohort (us) is "hair raisingly psychotic" (Meltzer 1978: 62). We, the Caucasians, are the bringers of a frenzy, and the substances we bring generate physical and mental breakdown. Searching for a response to this 'unthinkable catastrophe', in which I too participate, Japaljarri Spencer had tentatively, modestly inquired if there might be held somewhere a mental map (a story) that could help him to hold in mind an explanation for the pattern of madness he was witnessing, as he and his family came under the spell of alcoholic intoxication. Probably, there is no story that offers the adequately healing breast. But when Crow steps onto the ceremonial ground, displaying the beginning of white man's madness by swallowing children, when Captain Cook puts on the mask of Dionysus, promising joy but dealing in mayhem, and when socially upright Pentheus paints up his face to quell the manic entourage and ends up dead himself, perhaps then those who sit to watch will find some of the contradictory images they need with which to think about contradictory things. We Europeans have known for a long time that theatrical images can become 'objects' with which to aid clarity of thought. Indigenous people have known the same thing for twice as long.

A Conclusion of Sorts

Talking about the intoxication problem, Bob Randall says, "We see the problem, we really do, but you know, no one knows what to do about it, whose responsibility [it is] … it's a mystery thing." That is the 'mystery thing'—that nothing ever quite works or is sustained long enough to be allowed to work, that health gets worse and many cowboys walk away. There is no grand heroic narrative of Central Australia to write; rather, there is an ethnography of failure. And if such an ethnography of failure were astutely written with a deeply concentrated and applied psychoanalytic eye, perhaps those of us who work in these borderline zones might comprehend where we have all gone wrong or how it is that the destructive and creative elements of human beings turn so precisely and voraciously upon each other in the midst of our own country. I suspect that part of the failure in our black-white relationship is the failure to appreciate the psychological significance of the *Tjukurrpa*.

You will have noted the mood that pervades much of my reflection, and the reflections of others who spend time psychically attentive to the existential realities of life and death in these borderline zones of Australia and southwestern Oceania. It is the mood of a *Tristes Tropiques*, the melancholy of the *Songs of Central Australia*, Strehlow's 'last post'. It is reflected in Geoffrey Bardon's eulogy for the Pintubi painters in his accounts of the Western Desert Art Movement, Tim Leura Japaljarri's bushfire skeleton painting made for Bardon, or Alex Minutjukur and Andrew Japaljarri Spencer's cultural reflection works under HALT's banner. You too may have felt the sense of final, elegiac resignation among the men and women who come and go. This pervasion of feeling is such a significant mood to catch, to psychoanalyze in the truest sense. These works and these moods are a part of Central Australia's 'country' music.

Acknowledgments

This article is dedicated to Andrew Japaljarri Spencer and family, Marlene Nampijimpa Ross and family, Berthe Nakamarra Dixon and family, Larry Jungarai Spencer (deceased), Paddy Japaljarri Sims, Jilly Nakamarra Nelson (deceased), and Wally Jungarai Morris (deceased). Acknowledgment is due to Jude Prichard of Tangentyerre Council Land Care; Barry Cook (deceased); Elva Cook and family from Injartnama, Ntaria; members of the Northern Territory Government Drug and Alcohol Services and NT Correctional Services, 1991–1996; and HALT, Alice Springs, 1988–1992. Thanks are also extended to the Sugarman production members, David Roberts, and the Antipodes Productions film crew, 1996–1999; and to Rod Moss, artist, and his collaborators, Arrenye Johnson and family from Deep Well and White Gate, Alice Springs region. All of whom are more qualified than I to speak on these things.

Craig San Roque is a practicing psychotherapist, qualified from the Society of Analytical Psychology, London; co-founder of the Squiggle Foundation; and a member of the Australian and New Zealand Society of Jungian Analysts. He lectures in a unique Masters Project in Analytical Psychology at the University of Western Sydney, with special interest in the application of psychoanalytic experience to community affairs and cultural anxiety. For many years he has conducted research in cultural psychology, group process, and the interface between therapy and theater. Since 1992, he has been involved with the Aboriginal people of Central Australia, contributing to Aboriginal innovative activities and intercultural dynamics. His most recent publication is "A Long Weekend, Alice Springs, Central Australia" (2004).

Notes

1. The term *Tjukurrpa* and the spelling as used in this article conform to a version of Luritja/ Pintupi usage (Hansen and Hansen 1991). It also appears as *Tjukurpa* in Pitjantjatjara/ Yankunytjatjara style (Goddard 1987), and as *Jukurrpa* or *Jukurpa* in Warlpiri/Amatjerre language group regions. In Arrernte, one will see variations written as *Altjerre, Alchira,* or *Alcheringa.* Fundamentally, the concept is the same, but indigenous language terms vary throughout Australia. [Editor's note: This cosmo-ontological matrix of Aboriginal existence first became known—after Spencer and Gillen's 1904 *The Northern Tribes of Central Australia*—in its Aranda (Arrernte) version of *Alcheringa.* In the course of the long twentieth century, it became generalized for and extended, under both various localized vernacular (*Tjukurrpa, Wangar, mardayin,* etc.) and pan-Australian English glosses ('The Dream-Time', 'The Dreaming', 'The Law'), to virtually all Aboriginal life-worlds that inhabited this continent. Because Carl Strehlow's appraisal of Spencer and Gillen's wording is seldom quoted in literature, I give it here in Obershaidt's translation: "Spencer and Gillen's claim (*Northern Tribes,* p. 745) that 'the word *alcheri* means dream' is incorrect. *Altjirerama* means 'to dream', and it is derived from *altjira* (god) [i.e., ancestral being] and *rama* (to see), in other words, 'to see god'. The same holds true for the Loritja language. *Tukura nangani* = 'to dream', from *tukura* = 'god' and *nangani* = 'to see'. It will be demonstrated later that *altjira* and *tukura* in this context do not refer to the highest God in the sky but merely to a totem god which the native believes to have seen in a

dream. The Aranda language does not render the word 'dream' with *alcheri* but rather with *altjirerinja*, though this word is rarely used. The normal expression of the blacks is, '*ta altjireraka*' = 'I have dreamed'. The word *alcheringa*, which according to Spencer and Gillen is supposed to mean 'dreamtime', is obviously a corruption of *altjirerinja*. The native knows nothing of a 'dreamtime' as a designation of a certain period in their history. What this expression refers to is the time when the *Altjiranga mitjina* [*sic*] traversed this earth" (C. Strehlow [1907] 1991: 1:2).]

2. See HALT's Alice Springs archives, paintings, and publications circa 1987–1992; see also HALT (1991).

3. The invention of this term is often attributed to Stanner. See Stanner (1966, 1979) and Swain (1993: chap. 1).

4. There are varied and rich definitions of Central Australian 'Dreaming'/*Tjukurrpa* by English-speaking writers with a high degree of experience of Aboriginal life and a grasp of how Aboriginal language and metaphysics can be translated into Western concepts. Definitions publicly available through writings and exhibition notes on Western Desert art are most comprehensively treated in, for instance, Sutton (1988), Bardon and Bardon (2004), and Perkins and Fink's (2000) monumental collections. It is not my purpose comprehensively to define and describe *Tjukurrpa*, although some grasp of it is necessary in order to make sense of the arguments and flow of thoughts, especially in the later section of this article. For reliable and available evocations and descriptions extracted through direct immersion, the reader might be referred to Bardon and Bardon (2004), Berndt (1970), Berndt and Berndt (1988), Kimber (2000), Langton (2000), Latz (1995), and Swain (1993); the works of linguists such as the Hansens; and also the fictionalized conversation with Arkady on the theme of the musicality of the *Tjukurrpa* in Bruce Chatwin's (1987) evocative novel, *The Song Lines*. Also included, of course, are the foundation works of formative Australiana anthropologists: Mountford (1976), Stanner (1966, 1979), T. Strehlow (1971), Munn (1970, 1973), Myers (1991), and Morton (1985, 1987, 1989).

5. The Sugarman Project (1993–2000) involved the preparation and production of a series of intercultural community performance events, a rewriting of Greek mythology into a central desert context, an exhibition on the history and origins of alcohol, a doctoral thesis, several multi-media events, and a video documentary by David Roberts. The project, an effort to take *Tjukurrpa* seriously as a basis for therapeutic action, also revealed the kinship between *Tjukurrpa* and European mythological narratives, and thus became an interactive, bicultural story-telling device.

6. Those endeavors included Petrol Link-Up, Intjartnama Rehabilitation Projects, the paintings, Thinking about Young People, Road Story, The Brain Story, Two Laws Story, and the Sugarman Project cultural events.

7. In this article I am approaching only the periphery of the ideas developed by Klein and by Jung. In another setting it might be possible to present the matter in more concise detail. The reader may wish to recall Klein's notions of how human behavior is determined and influenced by "unconscious phantasy," specific symbol formation procedures in the inner world, and the infantile play of desires, conflict, anxieties, defenses, separations, and reconstructions amid the "internal objects" of inner or phantasized life and death (outlined, for instance, in Riviere's introduction in Klein et al. [1973] and subsequent chapters). Jung et al. approach the same zone, I believe, with an archetypal twist that brings infantile phantasy toward connection with adult, culturally specific, and collective expressions of symbol formed around instinctively charged bodily elements. Their perspective also turns around the interplay of destruction, creation, and containment (i.e., Freud's life and death instincts), and all are concerned with the interplay of sexuality, instinctuality, eros, and mourning, and love's destruction by various psychic instruments of schism, hatred, and neglect.

8. HALT, personal communication.

9. At the end of *Aboriginal Men of High Degree* ([1945] 1977), Elkin proposes that a conference be held forthwith to provide a forum within which matters of concern to European and indigenous therapeutic practitioners could be discussed and compared and a working

partnership could be consolidated. Elkin marshaled what evidence he could and presented it formally, requesting that some kind of bicultural exchange occur, which could give an opportunity for practitioners to meet, evaluate, and even validate each other's methodology. In 1986, I attempted to reintroduce the notion of collaborative exchange on matters of practice and training in the field of mental health. I took up Elkin's accounts of the training of a Central Australian traditional healer in the South Australian Ooldea region, comparing it to the stages of a typical psychoanalytical training process. Awareness of the experiential requirements of these two training procedures was a part of my experience when Japaljarri Spencer made his point about the absence of a *Tjukurrpa* to address the abuse of intoxication and later outlined his own story about how traditional healers are 'trained'—or rather, what the *Tjukurrpa* is that underpins the formation of a healer subjected to a traditional procedure within his own group. In November 1986, I presented a paper at the UWS Nepean College conference on Aboriginal studies (San Roque 1986). It was an attempt to foreshadow a way of communicating across the black-white divide by looking for similarities in the respective psychological constructions of reality and by noting the way in which therapeutic training was conducted by indigenous healers and by psychoanalytic therapists. I drew substantially upon Elkin's ethnography. A fuller analysis of initiation experiences (of death and rebirth) whereby a man becomes transformed into a healer is attempted in my unpublished paper "On Babies, Snakes and Water," which was presented at the 1996 Perth ANZSJA Congress.

10. The 'someones' who facilitate this process are the owners of the ceremony, the *Kirda* in Warlpiri, who are bound in reciprocal relationship with the *Kurdungulu*, or 'policemen'. In the non-Aboriginal world, the facilitators of psychic and spiritual transformation are sometimes priests/priestesses as poets of ceremony and sometimes dramatic poets as the creators of theater.

References

Bardon, G., and R. Bardon. 2004. *Papunya Tula: A Place Made after the Story. The Beginnings of the Western Desert Painting Movement*. Melbourne: Miegunyah Press/Melbourne University Publishing.

Berndt, R. M., ed. 1970. *Australian Aboriginal Anthropology*. Nedlands: University of Western Australia Press.

Berndt, R. M., and C. H. Berndt, eds. 1988. *The Speaking Land*. Ringwood, Australia: Penguin Books.

Bion, W. [1962] 1984. *Learning from Experience*. London: Karnac.

_____. [1963] 1968. *Elements of Psycho-analysis*. London: Karnac.

_____. [1970] 1984. *Attention and Interpretation*. London: Karnac.

Chatwin, B. 1987. *The Song Lines*. London: Cape.

Elkin, A. P. [1945] 1977. *Aboriginal Men of High Degree*. 2nd ed. St. Lucia, Australia: University of Queensland Press.

Goddard, C. 1987. *Basic Pitjanjatjara/Yankunytjatara English Dictionary*. Alice Springs, Australia: Institute for Aboriginal Development.

HALT (Healthy Aboriginal Life Team). 1991. *Anangu Way*. Alice Springs, Australia: Nganampa Health Council.

Hansen, K. C., and L. E. Hansen. 1991. *Pintupi/Luritja Dictionary*. 3rd ed. Alice Springs, Australia: Institute for Aboriginal Development.

Heyman, K. 2003. *The Accomplice*. London: Hodder Headline.

Jung, C. G. [1954] 1966. *The Psychology of the Transference. Collected Works*. Vol. 16: *The Practice of Psychotherapy*. 2nd ed. London: Routledge Kegan Paul and Bollingen USA.

_____ (with A. Jaffe). 1961. *Memories, Dreams, Reflections*. New York: Random House.

Kimber, R. G. 2000. "*Tjukurrpa* Trails: A Cultural Topography of the Western Desert." Pp. 269–273 in Perkins and Fink 2000.

Kimbles, S., and T. Singer, eds. 2004. *The Cultural Complex: Contemporary Jungian Perspectives on Psyche and Society*. London and New York: Brunner and Routledge.

Klein, M. 1950. "The Importance of Symbol Formation in the Development of the Ego." Pp. 235–250 in *Contributions to Psycho-analysis: 1921–1945*. London: Hogarth Press.

Klein, M., P. Heimann, S. Isaacs, and J. Riviere, eds. 1973. *Developments in Psycho-analysis*. London: Hogarth Press.

Langton, M. 2000. "Sacred Geography: Western Desert Traditions of Landscape Art." Pp. 259–267 in Perkins and Fink 2000.

Latz, P. 1995. *Bushfires and Bushtucker*. Alice Springs, Australia: IAD Press.

Lévi-Strauss, C. 1977. *Tristes Tropiques*. Trans. J. and D. Weightman. New York: Washington Square Press.

Meltzer, D. 1978. *The Kleinian Development*. Part 3: *The Clinical Significance of the Work of Bion*. Perthshire, Scotland: Clunie Press.

Morton, J. 1985. "Sustaining Desire: A Structuralist Interpretation of Myth and Male Cult in Central Australia." PhD diss., Australian National University

———. 1987. "Singing Subjects and Sacred Objects: More on Munn's 'Transformation of Subjects into Objects' in Central Australian Myth." *Oceania* 58, no. 2: 100–118.

———. 1989. "Mama, Papa, and the Space Between: Children, Sacred Objects, and Transitional Phenomena in Aboriginal Central Australia." *Psychoanalytic Study of Society* 14: 191–225.

Mountford, C. P. 1976. *Nomads of the Australian Desert*. Adelaide: Rigby.

Munn, N. 1970. "The Transformation of Subjects into Objects in Walbiri and Pitjantjara Myth." Pp. 141–163 in Berndt 1970.

———. 1973. *Walbiri Iconography: Graphic Representation and Cultural Symbolism in a Central Australian Society*. Ithaca, NY: Cornell University Press.

Myers F. 1991. *Pintubi Country, Pintubi Self*. Berkeley: University of California Press.

Perkins, H., and H. Fink., eds. 2000. *Papunya Tula: Genesis and Genius*. Sydney: Art Gallery of New South Wales.

Petchkovsky, L., and C. San Roque. 1995. "Wana Tjukurpa." Pp. 445–450 in *Open Questions in Analytical Psychology. Proceedings of the 13th International Congress for Analytical Psychology*. Zurich: Daimon.

Randall, R. 1999. Quoted in *Sugarman* (the documentary film account of the project). Directed by D. Roberts. Sydney: Antipodes Productions (with assistance from Australian Film Finance Corporation).

———. 2003. *Song Man: The Story of an Aboriginal Elder of Uluru*. Sydney: ABC Books for the Australian Broadcasting Corporation.

San Roque, C. 1986. "Psychoanalysis Black and White." Pp. 81–107 in *Proceedings of Nepean College (UWS) Conference on Contemporary Issues in Aboriginal Studies*, ed. B. Wright, L. Petchkovsky et al. Nepean: University of Western Sydney, Fire Bird Press.

———. 2000. "Coming to Terms with the Country." Pp. 27–52 in *Landmarks: Papers by Jungian Analysts from Australia and New Zealand*, compiled by F. H. Formaini. Manuka, ACT: ANZSJA Publication.

———. 2004. "A Long Weekend: Alice Springs, Central Australia." Chap. 3 in Kimbles and Singer 2004.

Stanner, W. 1966 *On Aboriginal Religion*. Oceania Monograph 11. Sydney: University of Sydney Press.

———. 1979. *White Man Got No Dreaming: Essays 1938–1973*. Canberra: ANU Press.

Strehlow, C. [1907] 1991. *The Arand and Loritja Tribes of Central Australia*. Ed. M. F. von Leonhardi. Unpub. trans. by H. D. Oberscheidt. Hermannsburg, Central Australia. (Originally published by Baer & Co., Frankfurt am Main.)

Strehlow, T. G. H. 1971. *Songs of Central Australia*. Sydney: Angus and Robertson.

Sutton, P., ed. 1988. *Dreamings: The Art of Aboriginal Australia*. New York: Viking.

Swain, T. 1993. *A Place for Strangers*. Cambridge: Cambridge University Press.

Winnicott, D. W. 1971. *Playing and Reality*. Harmondsworth, UK: Penguin Books.

Chapter 7

A CARTOGRAPHY OF MENTAL HEALTH

Renata Volich Eisenbruch

Psychoanalysis as a clinical practice entails perspectives on suffering and mental health different from those espoused by psychiatry. Psychoanalysis, though, is on familiar terms with psychiatry, both in hospitals and in consulting rooms. Many who come to the consulting rooms for psychoanalysis are medicated, and many psychiatrists may use the psychodynamic perspective when treating a suffering being. A multitude of disturbances, some quite acute, affect people regardless of their age and ethnicity. Some maladies are characteristic of certain historical periods and their socio-cultural conditions. The epidemic of suicide among adolescents appears to be a hallmark of modern times. Autism, the manifestation of early psychosis and a lifelong disability that impairs social

Notes for this chapter are located on page 185.

interactions and communication, is another malaise. Clearly, social phenomena cannot be dissociated from our approach to mental health, in regard to both the sufferers as well as the services delivered.

Here is an example of how loss of social context may involve loss of meaning. In April 2005, a man was discovered in a suit, dripping wet, on a beach near Sheerness, Kent. He wandered around speechless, looking despondent, his hands gripping music scores. He remained an enigma for the professionals who approached him in order to take care of him. His identity was unknown. If his memory had failed him in relation to his identity, as far as music was concerned, he was a true virtuoso. When admitted to a hospital, he did not speak and the staff supplied him with pen and paper. Determined, he sketched a piano in all its detail. He was led to the hospital's chapel where he started playing Tchaikovsky's *Swan Lake*. He was baptized the 'Piano Man', who, when not having his hands on the ivory keys, was very disturbed and unsettled. The only form of communication for him was music.

Mental health services are replete with such accounts, perhaps not as dramatic but nevertheless dense and complex when examined through psychoanalytic lenses. Chemotherapeutic discoveries have made an undeniable contribution to mental health, and no one could deny the richness of classical psychiatry since the turn of the twentieth century: Kraepelin (1921) distinguished manic-depressive psychosis from dementia praecox, and Clérambault (1927) elaborated his formulation of mental automatism. Psychiatrists, however, conventionally treat manifest clinical conditions as if there was no need to burrow into the psychic meaning. Listening to a number of clinicians, one gains the impression that with the two key afflictions of our time—depression and anxiety—the clinical field is covered.

Psychiatry and Psychoanalysis: Differentiation of Approaches

Psychiatry and psychoanalysis alike are concerned with helping suffering people whose symptoms may prompt a search for help. Psychiatry for the most part considers the symptoms and the manifest phenomenological signs. Psychoanalysis approaches the symptom as a meaning to be deciphered. The significance of each symptom is subtle and unique and is to be integrated into the person's discourse which is impregnated with unconscious elements. The symptom persists; it has a repetitive character. It was after Freud's ([1920] 1940) "Beyond the Pleasure Principle" that the compulsion to repeat moved into the foreground of psychoanalysis. The symptom is no longer seen merely as a form of resistance but traversed by the unconscious and overdetermined by narcissistic investments in which the person finds gratification. Associated with profound suffering, an exacerbated narcissism can often be witnessed today in the psychoanalytical clinic entailing a resistance to the treatment.

The existence of the unconscious that propels the formation of symptoms (as well as of dreams) is addressed through the psychoanalytical process. This process has the ability to restore the importance of the singular experience and history of the suffering person, thereby establishing new configurations in the meaning of life. This is particularly essential in the treatment of adolescents when their previous values lose their meaning and they search for answers to the following question: what do I have to do so that I can be accepted in the adult world? The peer group can be a source of reference to one's existence at this age. The adolescent may feel included in such a group, yet it can also be a source of agony if there is exclusion. Whether there is ostracism or acceptance, adolescence can still be a period of great solitude and turmoil.

It can be argued that the inclusion of psychoanalysis into sociological analysis can enhance certain areas of social research, specifically where traditional approaches have become limited (Paul 1989: 202). My clinical work in a range of countries and culturally diverse settings has led me to develop an ethnographic approach that relates to the human condition understood in an anthropological-existential sense. I shall name it 'ethnography of the subject'—a subject that is born into language and suffers its effects. It is at an early age that language crystallizes a child's symptoms. In this sense, as Jacques Lacan ([1975] 1985: 22) pronounced at a conference in Geneva on 4 October 1975, "The child will effectuate a coalescence between its sexual reality and language." Spoken language leaves its indelible marks. We have been impregnated by the way in which we heard the first words. The parental discourse pre-exists the subject. Arrival into this world as a subject implies a different status from that of a biological being: "The manner of speaking which has been instilled into the subject can certainly carry the mark of the way in which the parents have accepted this child" (ibid.).

Psychoanalysis presented itself from the very beginning as an adventure in the unconscious and the psychic, a remarkable journey through language toward the unknown. These days psychiatry builds itself on biochemical, evidence-based medicine—one would say a new organization of human subjectivity. Although psychiatry specializes in medical care, its status as a science leads to a 'repudiation' of the subject (known in psychoanalysis as 'foreclosure'). The subject is evacuated from the field of psychic causality and what comes to the foreground is the number of manifest phenomena. Depression in modern times has become a biochemical concept. There is a division in the psychiatrist's work. On the one hand we may consider that there is the 'a-subjective' explanation and, on the other, the field of the subject. In the scientific approach, the subject is still there but in a masked way. A psychoanalytic ethnography would seek to overcome this antinomy. If we consider bipolar disorders, there is the paranoid process but also the melancholic one. It is a matter of assessing the position of the subject in life—what is working, what is just working enough, and what is not working at all. It is a question that goes beyond assessment and brings forward the matter of ethics, which concerns not only the relation between the subject and the surrounding civilization but also that of the subject to his or her unconscious desire. It transcends the exaltation of social desires. The experience of culpability, for instance, is closely related to the experience of interdiction. This dialectic leads us to an ethical context.

In "Civilization and Its Discontents" Freud ([1930] 1948: 111) illustrates how peculiarly ethics inhabits human beings: "The element of truth behind all this, which people are so ready to disavow, is that men are not gentle creatures who want to be loved, and who at the most can defend themselves if they are attacked; they are, on the contrary, creatures among whose instinctual endowments is to be reckoned a powerful share of aggressiveness. As a result, their neighbor is for them not only a potential helper or sexual object, but one who may tempt them to satisfy their aggressiveness on him, to exploit his capacity for work without compensation". The subject's relation to his or her outside world is mediated by unconscious phantasy. More important than the modification of the symptom is the modification of the subject's position in the phantasy, that is, the way the subject situates him or herself vis-à-vis his or her unconscious desire.

Karl Jaspers's ([1913] 1997, 1920) phenomenological differentiation between psychiatric and psychoanalytical approaches to mental disorders can be useful as a tool. His distinction is made in terms of "explanation or perception of causal connection" (*erklaren*) and "understanding" (*verstehen*).

PSYCHIATRIC	PSYCHOANALYTIC
Explain	Understand
Symptom	History
Diagnosis	Subjectivity
Disease	Unconscious

Jaspers constructs the opposition between comprehension by the subject (psychoanalysis) and what psychiatrists used to regard as causal explanations that simply clarified what the patient already knew. The latter approach did not help to further the patient's comprehension of what was at stake. By contrast, Lacan has persistently objected to such an opposition between the field of causal explanation and the field of comprehension by the subject. As long as there is an effect of sense in the patient's discourse, the subject is at stake. That is, it is the possibility of articulation in meaning, the implication of the subject in what he or she is saying that justifies the existence of psychoanalysis. How can the subject be an object of investigation?

It was only in 1932 that Freud utilized the term 'subject', referring to it as being liable to split and to suffer cleavages: "If we throw a crystal to the floor, it breaks but not into haphazard pieces. It comes apart along its lines of cleavage into fragments whose boundaries, though they were invisible, were predetermined by the crystal's structure. Mental patients are split and broken structures of the same kind ... They have turned away from external reality, but for that very reason they know more about internal, psychical reality and can reveal a number of things to us that would otherwise be inaccessible to us" ([1932] 1940: 59). Freud states that man, in one respect or another, is divided within himself. It is in a retroactive process, a process of reorganization and 'reinscription' of traumatic and painful events, as well as of fragments of history, that a psychoanalytic knowledge is engendered concerning the splitting of the subject. The reinscription means a new signification of elements that until then could have been immobilizing, a hindrance in the subject's life. This process would lead to a new, hopefully creative dynamic.

Lacan created a new version of the traditional notion of the subject by transforming the subject of consciousness into the subject of the unconscious. He conceptualized the logical and philosophical notion of the subject—of a divided subject—in the context of his theory of signifier. Notably, a signifier is an element in the chain of free association or in the analysand's discourse that represents the subject to another signifier. In order to continue the mapping in terms of this specific conceptualization of the psychoanalytic field, I will take into account three distinct axes. These axes interact with each other and shall be considered in their interplay.

First, there is the environmental axis on which the subject depends for his or her growth. There are cases of migration due to a totalitarian regime, political dictatorship, torture, or political persecution that have led people to depart from their homeland into exile with severe consequences for their mental well-being. In acute cases, such as in autism, we observe how the environment plays a decisive role in promoting or halting the evolution toward this disorder. The exact causes of autism remain unknown, but cases of it and related conditions such as Asperger's syndrome (ASD), known as autism spectrum disorders, have increased in the past two decades. A recent study suggested that the rate can be as high as 116 ASD cases per 10,000 children in some Western countries. The statistics, though, are not significative of the qualitative dynamic process of the psychic and of each individual suffering. There is also the hypothesis that older fathers are more likely to father autistic children. This study advocates that fathers also have a biological clock and that older fathers have almost nine times the risk. Parenting, however, is also influenced by the socio-cultural environment and varies across societies and over time.

Second, there is the symptomatic axis. A psychoanalytic symptom is distinct from a symptom as articulated in medical-psychiatric diagnosis. By diagnosis I mean a questionnaire or mental examination. The diagnosis masks facts that are unknown to the patient and, paradoxically, imposes on the patient the disclosure of symptoms already known to him or her. Psychoanalytic practice distances itself from the diagnosis, if by the latter we understand the operation that consists of ticking on a chart the presence or absence of certain signs before addressing the subject's psycho-social history. Considering the perspective of a psychoanalytic ethnography, the symptom, with correlated complaints and suffering, is to be considered as a formation of the unconscious. Despite the fact that the subject may perceive the symptom as being something foreign to him or her, it results in unconscious gains that lead the afflicted to cling to his or her diseases and correlative forms of suffering. The symptom is therefore another instance whereby the subject finds unconscious satisfaction. It is an intimate aspect of one's being. As Freud ([1917] 1946: 385) points out: "Dealing with a conflict by forming symptoms is after all an automatic process which cannot prove adequate to meeting the demands of life." The symptom is also a fulfillment of an unconscious desire.

Third is the structural axis. The strategies utilized by the subject in the formation of the symptoms, whether knowingly or not, obey a certain structure. It is also through this structure that the subject relates to the organization of the unconscious phantasy. The phantasy mediates the relation between the subject and the world. The Freudian phantasy described in "A Child Is Being Beaten" (Freud [1919] 1947) illustrates the importance of the presence of another child, who not only witnesses the punishment but will also suffer it in its turn. The child places itself in different subjective positions, swinging from passive to active. Following Freud (ibid.: 180): "This phantasy, a child is being beaten, was invariably cathected with a degree of pleasure and had its issue in an act of pleasurable auto-erotic satisfaction. It might therefore be expected that the sight of another child being beaten at school would also be a source of similar enjoyment. But as a matter of fact it was never so... however the experience of real scenes of beating at school produced in the child who witnessed them a peculiarly excited feeling which was probably of a mixed character and in which repugnance had a large share."

This phantasy consists of three phases:

1. *A child is being beaten.*
2. *I am being beaten by my father.* The relation here is dual. The act of being beaten already entails an element marked with erotism.

> This being beaten is now a convergence of the sense of guilt and sexual love. It is not only the punishment for the forbidden genital relation, but also the regressive substitute for that relation, and from this latter source it derives the libidinal excitation which is from this time forward attached to it, and which finds its outlet in masturbatory acts. Here for the first time we have the essence of masochism and the ego is strongly accentuated. We may ask how far the subject participates in the action of the one who aggresses and beats. It is the classical sado-masochistic ambiguity. This second phase, the child being beaten *remains unconscious* as a rule, probably in consequence of the intensity of the repression and can only be *reconstructed* in the course of the analysis. (Freud [1919] 1947: 190)

3. *"My father is beating the child; he loves only me."* In the third phase, the phantasy becomes sadistic. Freud emphasizes that only this form of the phantasy is sadistic because the unconscious satisfaction (in Lacan's terms, *jouissance*) that is derived from it is masochistic. "All of the many unspecified children who are being beaten by the teacher are, after all, nothing more than substitutes for the child itself." In this phase of the phantasy, however, there are three characters: the agent of the punishment, the one who suffers the punishment, and the subject who has the phantasy. The one who suffers is someone whom the subject of the phantasy hates and therefore sees as being rightfully excluded from the parent's preference. The subject who has the phantasy sees him- or herself as being in an exclusive position in relation to the father's affection, as being the father's preferred child, as being the one who has the privilege that the beaten child has forfeited. The subject creates the tension and causality between the other two characters in the phantasy. He or she animates and motivates the action between the other two and also is the instrument of communication between them.

Another illustration of the reconstruction of the phantasy is Freud's clinical case of a five-year-old, 'Little Hans'. While the initial symptom is the fear of being bitten by a horse, Hans's phantasy goes from the transformation of this bite to the unscrewing of the bath. The founder of psychoanalysis writes: "After all, Hans' phobia of horses was an obstacle to his going into the streets and could serve as a means of allowing him to stay at home with his beloved mother. In this way his affection for his mother triumphantly achieves its aim. The content of his phobia was such as to impose a great measure of restriction upon his freedom of movement and that was its purpose. Beyond his hostile and jealous feelings towards his father, his phobia was a powerful reaction against the obscure impulses to movement which were especially directed against his mother—They were sadistic impulses (premonitions, as it were, of sexual relations of some kind) towards his mother" (Freud [1909] 1941: 138).

In his seminar *La relation d'objet*, Lacan ([1956–1957] 1994) analyzes the traversing of the phantasy. Essentially centered on the mother and the mother's desire, this seminar evokes the mother in her capacity as a woman. Lacan refers to female castration—the mother as a subject defined by the lack of an object. In 'Little Hans', the mother was originally an opaque, threatening power, becoming in Hans's phantasy the mother that comes and goes—and with her the whole household (an additional fear of Hans was that the house would collapse). The phantasy then proceeds to the unscrewing of the bath by the plumber. At this stage, in the reconstruction of the phantasy, it is no longer the whole household that is at stake, that is, at risk from the departure of the mother. The metaphoric object in question is a bath that supplies a place for Hans, as Freud ([1909] 1941) comments, "a bath according to his wishes, a bath into which his behind fits perfectly."

Implications for Treatment

As we get referrals from psychiatrists, it is important to situate the differences between the psychoanalytic approach and the psychiatric one. In contrast to the psychiatric treatment, the aim in our psychoanalytic clinical approach is not the removal of the symptom but rather a change concerning the relation that the person has with his or her symptom, which can manifest itself far from its causes. In obsessional neuroses, for instance, the uncertainty of memory is used "to the fullest extent as a help in the formation of symptoms" (Freud [1909] 1941: 233).

Through treatment we aim for the symptom—which at the beginning may have been immobilizing and overwhelming to the point of becoming the person's identity and the fundamental part of his or her life—to be less overwhelming. The symptom becomes just one of the many phenomena that are present in everyday life. The subject ceases *to be* the symptom in order *to have* a symptom (Volich Eisenbruch 2001). Through a psychoanalytic approach, instead of focusing on the symptom, we focus on the unconscious phantasy and on the singularity of each history, with subjectivity taking precedence over diagnostic categories. Finally, instead of speaking of the psychic disease, we speak of the unconscious whose analysis allows meaning to be created by the analysand. This understanding of experiences and suffering—spoken, elaborated, and signified by the patient during the treatment—is of fundamental importance. The dimension of subjectivity, of one's history, is distinct from that of the symptom.

For instance, beyond the question of cyclothymia, the oscillation of extreme affects, there are other essential issues, such as a subject's symbolic place in the family and the place of a child in the unconscious desire of a parent. These are constellations that are constructed during the analytical treatment through the subject's place in the unconscious phantasy. Therefore, the discourse of psychoanalysis accentuates the unconscious phantasy and the subjective implications that it entails. Psychoanalysis has as its primary aim to deal with suffering by accessing the unconscious manifestations that are revealed through transference. The analyst's presence is the repository of the analysand's free associations. The demand is constituted as the word is addressed to the analyst, with the subject demanding an answer for what he or she lacks. Love in transference is what the analysand imaginarily assigns to the analyst as the one who would have what the subject lacks, a supposed knowledge about the analysand. It is fundamental to consider situations on a case-by-case basis, according to each subject's psychic universe, according to the logic of each phantasy that is at stake.

It is noteworthy that the Kleinian and the Lacanian approaches have in common the wish to grasp the phantasy and unconscious life beyond the biological-evolutionary framework of understanding. Construction and traversing of the phantasy is what affords mobility to the subject, giving way to changes in the subject's life. For Lacan, the phantasy is inscribed in a significant structure, such as is illustrated above in the 'child is being beaten' phantasy and the case of 'Little Hans'. Considering the diversity of phantasies of each subject, the traversing of the fundamental phantasy by the patient is also an indicator of the efficiency of the analysis. The modification of the subjective position in relation to the kind of defenses maintained and the unconscious gains and satisfaction found in the symptom are other markers that guide us.[1]

Depression is not necessarily a psychiatric illness. Whereas in medicine the symptom shows up as a dysfunction, when diagnosed according to the classification in DSM-IV or in ICD-10,[2] psychoanalysis approaches the symptom as an enigma—imbued with a particular meaning—and addresses the place of depression in the logic of the unconscious. The two systems therefore utilize different methods of treatment. While selective serotonin reuptake inhibitors (SSRIs), acting on neurotransmitters, is one of the preferred psycho-pharmacological approaches for the treatment of depression, psychoanalysis addresses the question of how the subject is implied, which position he or she occupies in this depression. There is a certain omission of responsibility for one's destiny when one chooses the path of medication, whereby the subject's alienation is reinforced in a chemical effect. Cognitive sciences place cerebral functioning at the origin of knowledge. Psychoanalysis is a process in which the source of knowledge is the symbolic dimension of the unconscious and its implication in one's destiny.

Let us consider another aspect, namely, dissymmetry between paranoia and melancholia. From the very beginning, in his correspondence with Fliess (manuscripts G and K), Freud refers to melancholia as loss and paranoia as mistrust (Masson 1985). He describes melancholia as a bitter regret of something that has been lost, a loss that takes place in the instinctual life. Less focused on the psychiatric approach of the melancholic state, Freud did not identify melancholia with depression; rather, he considered melancholia as a subjective destiny. In his essay "Mourning and Melancholia," Freud (1915) conceived melancholia as a pathological form of mourning. If in the work of mourning the subject succeeds in progressively separating himself from the lost object, in melancholia, on the other hand, he feels guilty about the death, denies it, believes himself to be possessed by the corpse, and identifies with the lost object to the point of losing himself in the infinite despair of an irremediable nothingness. "In melancholia the object perhaps has not actually died, but has been lost as an object of love ... This would suggest that melancholia is in some way related to an object loss which is withdrawn from consciousness, in contradistinction to mourning in which there is nothing about the loss that is unconscious" (ibid.: 245).

The shadow of the object falls on the ego, which becomes, according to the subject, devalued, impoverished and worthless. This form of perpetual lamentation is at the same time the expression of a rebellion at the thought of annihilation of oneself as well as the most extreme manifestation of the unconscious desire for this form of annihilation linked to the loss of an ideal. At the end of his essay "The Ego and the Id," Freud ([1923] 1940) reflects upon death anxiety played out between the ego and the super-ego. It is in melancholia that death anxiety, as a reaction to an internal danger, exposes itself the most. In melancholia we find a ferocious super-ego, a torturer of the ego that is overwhelmed by oppression and can be cornered to the point of committing suicide. The super-ego ceases to be protective and instead becomes a pitiless persecutor to such an extent that the ego feels threatened by it as much as by the most extreme external danger. This dynamic engages the melancholic subject in a genuine feeling of real death.

The subject is the point of emission, as well as the point of reception, of accusations. It is the self-reproach. On the other hand, the paranoid places fault on the side of the 'Other'. Phenomena that assail him or her are assigned to the Other. We can also oppose the melancholic stasis, a certain inertia, to the paranoid sthenia, an excessive mental power of production. Both melancholia and paranoia have an attribute of certitude that does not check for proof. Lacan names this certitude as the 'return in the Real'. Hallucinations, for instance, would be a 'return in the Real' of what could not be resignified by language, of what is not integrated in the system of signifiers. Lacan used the concept of *Verwerfung* (in French *forclusion*, translated in English as 'foreclosure' or 'repudiation') to denote this process. Lacan borrowed this term from Freud, who utilized it in relation to the treatment of a young, wealthy Russian, also known in the psychoanalytic literature as the 'Wolf Man', who came to him for analysis. The process involved in his hallucination of the cut finger was explained by Freud through the concept of *Verwerfung*. It is this term *Verwerfung* that Lacan translates as foreclosure.

In the absence of symbolization, of signifiers that are expelled or not integrated into the subject's unconscious, hallucinations occur in order to represent what is taking place in the subject's life—hallucinations that can represent a default in language. In neurosis, on the other hand, the subject may not have immediate access to certain signifiers. They are however there, behind repression, in a latent way. Forgetting when one is about to enunciate an idea, for instance, may be due to the process of repression that acts on the signifier.

Based on Freudian theory, Lacan makes a diagnosis of the need of a subject. He conceptualizes a logical notion of the subject by elaborating the subject of the unconscious, the subject of desire. This subject is then submitted to the Freudian concept of splitting. The individual and his or her acts are a product of repression, of the splitting between the ego and the subject of the unconscious instance. One may suffer a breakdown, and at this moment, this splitting and articulation between these two aspects of life—the conscious and this other scene that is the unconscious—become even more evident. Freud's metaphor of the crystal mentioned above shows how a structure can be revealed.

The inability of a person to form social bonds in psychosis is a great challenge for the family and the community. Is psychosis out of the therapeutic reach of psychoanalysis? Freud did not believe so. It was through his questioning, derived from his work with psychotic patients, that further psychoanalytical contributions to this field were made. Paranoia, in particular, offers a particularly 'open-cut view' into unconscious processes in a way more accessible to comprehension than other forms of disturbance.

Lacan came across the evidence that psychosis is not a deficit but a psychic organization, another order of the subject. Rather than a deficit, this process is to be considered an enigma. The 'Piano Man' would have been an illustration. In August, four months after his admission to the psychiatric hospital, his identity was revealed. He was a German citizen who, under pressure of unemployment in Paris, traveled to England where he decided to portray himself as a mentally disturbed person. The man used to work with mentally ill patients and is thought to have copied some of their characteristics to convince psychiatric doctors that he had a mental illness (Jacob and Roche 2005). Here is also an illustration of the limits imposed by one's history and constitution. Paradoxically, the means he found to make himself heard was to isolate himself in a deafening silence.

The unconscious is the voice of repressed truth. It is the path through which the truth expresses itself once oneself and others have refused to listen to it. Analysis is instrumental in this process of lifting repression. Painstaking as it might be, it shows a path out of the fatalistic position by encouraging each of us to make an effort to assume responsibility for the unconscious's production.

Responding to External Trauma

Is such a view always true? Can assuming responsibility for the unconscious occur in every circumstance? How can one not be fatalistic in cases of natural disasters? The Indian Ocean tsunami of December 2004 was one of the most devastating natural disasters of our times, claiming hundreds of thousands of lives. In addition, millions of people and entire populations experienced trauma (Ashraf 2005). A remarkable human solidarity could be witnessed after the tsunami had struck. Another disaster brutally exposed US racial divisions. In late August 2005, Hurricane Katrina hit Louisiana, one of America's poorest states, creating in the process squalid conditions, homeless populations, and lethal floods (CDC 2005). Many of the already disadvantaged in the society became refugees; up to half a million people were left homeless. New Orleans gasped for life beneath the water. The scale of devastation and horror was worsened by the armed looting and anarchy. When the water retreated, there was the question of recovery. How does life become viable again for those afflicted by a terrible natural disaster?

It is fair to assign this form of traumatism to a reality that assails from the exterior in the face of which a person is impotent. Terrorist acts many driven by fundamentalism are another element in the list of traumatic events of the present young century. While the field of traumatism is undoubtedly vaster, psychoanalysis can have an impact on efforts to improve the human condition in response to external trauma. The psychoanalytic clinic shows that experience does not acquire its traumatic character merely through intensity as measured on a 10-point scale. Two people can be exposed to the same disaster, leading to traumatization for one but not for the other. The difference depends on how individuals respond with their own phantasy to the catastrophe that affects them. A psychoanalytic ethnography would accentuate the function of the phantasy and the subjective implication in the catastrophe.

The phantasy is a response by the subject to a rupture that has affected the continuity of the subject's history as well as that of his or her community. The phantasy adjusts the convictions, vital expectations, and reactions of individuals. The phantasy is mobilized each time that the subject is affected by anguish. External real danger becomes traumatic when, under the sway of the phantasy, this danger becomes internalized and highly significant for the subject. In other words, traumatism may be one of the possible faces of the phantasy.

Many of those affected by the tsunami interpreted it as a punishment by God. When they comprehended that it was a natural catastrophe in the face of which they could or could not find resources to cope with, they started taking steps to protect themselves and rebuild their lives. This meant that taking on a certain responsibility for their future helped them, if only on a minor scale, to face their anguish and mitigate it. For the affected, the need to reclaim control of their lives and to overcome the feeling of impotence was essential. The tsunami was by no means part of a destiny dictated by the unconscious. No one in the affected areas could have anticipated this natural disaster.

There are instances, however, when one could speak of a destiny in which the unconscious has something to say. We may take as an illustration certain journalists who choose to work in war zones, in countries with a history of kidnapping, or generally in high-risk areas. It is a human tragedy if, like the victims in their reportages, they are themselves kidnapped and subjected to atrocious and squalid conditions, sometimes with fatal consequences. We venture into new fields with an unconscious knowledge that is not always accessible to us. Our unconscious desire will never lose its mystery or its allurement. Its dynamic profoundly affects the direction of our lives. The entire dynamism of the unconscious affects our choices as well as our symptoms. Our capacity (or incapacity) to listen and intervene makes the essential difference.

Conclusion

There is the important and obvious fact that many who could benefit from psychological treatment do not have access to resources. Many forms of intervention are needed to address this problem. Psychoanalysis can make a special contribution in overcoming another form of inaccessibility by addressing the unconscious causes of human suffering. A psychoanalytical ethnography or applied psychoanalysis is especially equipped to open up paths concerning in-depth experiences. It can contribute to human mental well-being across diverse existential conditions through fieldwork in areas affected by natural disasters, war, and poverty and in everyday life. In considering the diversity of contexts as well as the adversities that affect our civilization, it can help bring about a precious understanding. This dynamic process requires the relinquishing of paralyzing doctrinaire positions that are oblivious to the realities of the human unconscious.

Renata Volich Eisenbruch graduated as a clinical psychologist in Sao Paulo, Brazil. She obtained a post-graduate diploma in clinical psychopathology of infants and families from University of Paris XIII, followed by a doctorate in psychopathology and psychoanalysis at the University of Paris VII. She has had extensive experience in child and adolescent psychotherapy at clinics and hospitals, including the Royal Children's Hospital in Melbourne and adolescent units in France. She has worked for over 20 years with migrants, displaced persons, and refugees, originally in Brazil and then in France, in Cambodia, where she trained local allied health professionals in mental health, and in Australia. She teaches at the Faculty of Medicine at the University of Melbourne and is in private practice. Her most recent publication is "Singularities of Adolescence" (2006) in the Brazilian psychoanalytical journal *Percurso*.

Notes

1. As mentioned above, this unconscious satisfaction is also known in the French school of psychoanalysis as *jouissance*.
2. DSM-IV refers to the fourth edition of the *Diagnostic and Statistical Manual of Mental Disorders*, which is published by the American Psychiatric Association. ICD-10 refers to the tenth edition of the *International Statistical Classification of Diseases and Related Health Problems*, which is published by the World Health Organization.

References

Ashraf, H. 2005. "Tsunami Wreaks Mental Health Havoc." *Bulletin of the World Health Organization* 83: 405–406.

CDC (Centers for Disease Control and Prevention). 2005. "Hurricane Katrina Response and Guidance for Health-Care Providers, Relief Workers, and Shelter Operators. *Morbidity and Mortality Weekly Report* 54: 877.

Clérambault, G. G. de. 1927. "Syndrome mécanique et conception mécaniciste des psychoses hallucinatoires." *Annales médico-psychologiques* 85: 398–413.

Freud, S. [1909] 1941. "Notes upon a Case of Obsessional Neurosis." Pp. 153–249 in *Standard Edition*, vol. 10.

———. [1917] 1946. "Mourning and Melancholia." Pp. 239–258 in *Standard Edition*, vol. 14.

———. [1919] 1947. "A Child Is Being Beaten." Pp. 175–204 in *Standard Edition*, vol. 17.

———. [1920] 1940. "Beyond the Pleasure Principle." Pp. 7–64 in *Standard Edition*, vol. 18.

———. [1923] 1940. "The Ego and the Id." Pp. 3–66 in *Standard Edition*, vol. 19.

———. [1930] 1948. "Civilization and Its Discontents." Pp. 59–147 in *Standard Edition*, vol. 21.

———. [1932] 1940. "Introductory Lectures on Psycho-analysis: The Dissection of the Psychical Personality." P. 59 in *Standard Edition*, vol. 22. (Printed title page reads 1933, but actual publication date is 1932.)

———. 1953–1974. *The Standard Edition of the Complete Psychological Works of Sigmund Freud*. 24 vols. Trans. and ed. James Strachey, with Anna Freud, Alix Strachey, and Alan Tyson. London: Hogarth Press. (Cited as *Standard Edition*.)

Jacob, A., and M. Roche. 2005. "Le mystérieux 'homme aux piano' jouait à l'amnésique." *Le Monde*, 12 August.

Jaspers, K. [1913] 1997. *General Psychopathology*. Vols. 1 and 2. Trans. J. Hoenig and M. Hamilton. Baltimore: Johns Hopkins University Press.

———. 1920. *Allgemeine Psychopathologie: Ein Leitfaden für Studierende, Ärzte und Psychologen*. Berlin: Springer.

Kraepelin, E. 1921. *Manic-Depressive Insanity and Paranoia*. Edinburgh: Livingstone.

Lacan, J. [1956–1957] 1994. *Le séminaire, livre IV: La relation d'objet*. Paris: Editions du Seuil.

———. [1975] 1985. "Conférence à Genève sur: 'Le symptôme.'" *Le Bloc-notes de la Psychanalyse* 5: 5–23.

Masson, J. M., ed. and trans. 1985. *The Complete Letters of Sigmund Freud to Wilhelm Fleiss, 1887–1904*. Cambridge, MA: Harvard University Press.

Paul, R. A. 1989. "Psychoanalytic Anthropology." *Annual Review of Anthropology* 18: 177–202.

Volich Eisenbruch, R. V. 2001. *La pathologie organique: Mal énigmatique face à la jouissance et le désir de la mère. Une clinique de la angoisse*. Paris: Les Editions Septentrion.

Chapter 8

PSYCHOTIC GROUP TEXT
A Psychoanalytic Inquiry into the Production
of Moral Conscience

James M. Glass

Political Theory and Human Insecurity

Political theorists have historically argued that disintegration anxiety represents
deep psychological dislocations within the social environment. Unstable political regimes, political violence, disintegrating values, and crumbling borders
suggest radical fissures in the structure of the self, in human nature. Urgency
over decline and disintegration appears, for example, in such famous treatises
as Plato's *Laws*, Hobbes's *Leviathan*, Machiavelli's *Prince*, Rousseau's *Discourse*

References for this chapter are located on page 203.

on the Origins of Inequality, and de Tocqueville's *Democracy in America*. How-ever, the psychological dynamic that establishes disintegration anxiety as a defining political presence is paranoia, and the classic theoretical formulations of political paranoia can be found in the *Laws* and *Leviathan*.

For Plato, anxiety over the resiliency of the polity's borders arose from what he regarded as threats from the passions, from desire subverting the purity of reason. The *Laws* is an administrative nightmare, a set of paranoid institu-tions that see law and administrative practice under the threat of disruption by self-interest. The drones of self-interest subvert reason and political ruler-ship guided by philosophy. Plato constructs a nocturnal council that meets in isolation in the dead of night and serves as guardian for the authority of the laws. The Council protects against intrusion, brackets reason in institutional defenses, and defines legislative purpose. It is acutely aware of the possibil-ity of invasion, disintegration, and attack. What today we would call 'regime maintenance' was Plato's primary concern. But the vigilance of regime mainte-nance depended on a paranoid world-view, on keeping administrators acutely sensitive to the possibility of dangerous intrusions. In some respects, the *Laws* is a more fitting contemporaneous document than Plato's *Republic*, whose visionary, utopian focus seems strangely out of place in the modern world of terror, uncertainty, fear, and displacement. Plato's garrison state, ruled by philosopher kings, protected by a class of militant auxiliaries, sustained by an agrarian mass, is a utopian set piece of fascinating argument and specu-lation. However, real-world anxiety, the omnipresent paranoia over terrorist attacks, and the uncertainty of modern economic life find more resonance in an administrative thicket like the *Laws* than in the pure light of the *Republic*'s philosophic reason.

If the *Laws* might be considered the classical formulation of the paranoid state dedicated to fighting human insecurity, the modern restatement of that position appears 2,000 years later in Hobbes's *Leviathan*, a treatise as fright-ening in its implications for insecurity and paranoia as is Plato's *Laws*. It is almost a genealogical descendant; even though Hobbes never mentions the *Laws*, the psychological factors pushing the construction of sovereignty appear to be quite similar. Both treatises see political authority as a direct response to an essential entropy in the self, and both philosophers take very seriously the corrosive potentiality of desire in producing political claims and demands. Both recommend strong, authoritative institutions as guardians of the political space and as protectors of political speech. Sovereignty, whether it be Plato's noc-turnal Council or Hobbes's mortal god Leviathan, protects against uncertainty and violent assaults on the regime, and, through administrative regulations and laws, reminds subjects that obedience constitutes the highest political good. For Hobbes, sovereign vigilance establishes an inviolable contract between ruler and subject and banishes those "biles and scabs" on the body politic who have the temerity to express political opposition.

Hobbes's sovereign is not human, but rulers are. Flesh-and-blood individuals populate abstract institutions, a recognition that, for example, distinguishes neo-Hobbesians from Hobbes. Even though Hobbes removes the sovereign from the corrosive effects of human desire and vests power in an abstract construction, a psychological understanding of his theory would suggest that sovereignty is subject to the same frailties, insecurities, and vulnerabilities as ordinary human beings. While that was not Hobbes's argument or intent in how he envisioned the form of sovereignty, history demonstrates that sovereigns, including constitutions, possess human properties and biases. Whether the sovereign is a constitution, a terrorist directorate, or a political ideology enacted in regime policy, political action and decision making reflect human, emotive components. No sovereign could leave behind partiality, even though Hobbes believed the messiness of human passion could be banished from political authority.

Further, Hobbes believed the enemy to be, in addition to potential invaders, ideological intruders competing for public attention and challenging in political speech the sovereign definition of good and evil. Hobbes insisted on keeping religious and sectarian claims out of the justifications for sovereignty; its only guidelines should be the maintenance of order. And ideology weakened the sovereign's claim. If ideology were to consume political authority, impartiality and objective judgments would be the first victims. Hobbes had no patience for the divine right of kings or for sectarian political movements such as the Levelers and Diggers or for religious fanatics like the Puritans and Oliver Cromwell. The reasoning of geometry provided the basis for political authority. Geometric proof, once demonstrated, could not be disputed. Subject to common verification, it was an objective explanation for those who understood the proof's logic. It was to be the firm and resolute barrier between madness and rational rulership. Like the geometric construction, the sovereign, untainted by the language of ideology, could not be misunderstood.

But Hobbes's belief that ideology could be banished from rule lay on several mistaken assumptions, the most important being that individuals desiring power could free themselves from political causes and beliefs, the 'Babel' of political claims. And to assume that belief can be banned from the pursuit of political power is not only utopian but ignores the fundamental facts of human nature that Hobbes spends part 1 of *Leviathan* elaborating in such complex detail. Ideology drives the pursuit of power, which in the modern political world often involves phantasies of security and revenge.

A lack of mercy and forgiveness moves the paranoid political construction, and little mercy or empathy appears in the arguments of the *Laws* and *Leviathan*. Nor is there much patience or inclination for long, protracted negotiations to resolve potential conflicts. Hobbes believed that political constituencies, partial interests, would not be selfless enough to muster the necessary resolve and toughness to fight ongoing threats to a stable sovereignty. In this view, what Hobbes calls the "natural condition of mankind," the pre-civil chaos where no "common power" holds individuals in "awe," constitutes the defining fact of modern political life. The "state of war" is everywhere, with no end in sight. Inaction breeds anxiety, and if disintegration anxiety overwhelms the polity, it may sink into madness. Hobbes understood too well the power of madness. We in modern society tend to ignore the power of psychotic constructions and how close to the surface they may be.

Tendencies toward Psychotic Disintegration: Differences in Individuals and Groups

To be psychotic on the individual level is to be in total negation of what Harry Stack Sullivan (1953) called "consensual reality," that is, general and social forms of agreement as to what is right and wrong, normal and abnormal, habitual and extraordinary. It is to see one's actions, which others might regard as bizarre, as normal, sensible, rational, and not out of the ordinary. A young man I interviewed at Sheppard Pratt Mental Hospital in Towson, MD, told me, after a relatively normal discussion, that he could give birth to himself by shoving his head up his anus and then coming out through his belly button. While I expressed some doubt about this, Bill thought I was utterly wrong. It would be fair at that moment to suggest that this young man was psychotic.

What also distinguishes psychosis from consensual reality has to do with epistemology: a theory of knowledge that organizes the world and its facts. Not only did Bill believe he could give birth to himself through his navel, but he also held a series of beliefs and perceptions that involved complex relations between his body parts and various configurations of the interior of his body. Bill believed that (a) he could give birth to himself through his intestines; (b) his head could shrink down, enabling him to travel through his throat, down into his stomach, and then out through a special channel in his eyes; (c) when he felt ill, it had to do with his skin being reversed—the inside had been turned inside out and therefore caused him all sorts of pinprick pains over his entire body. This is just a fraction of Bill's epistemology, but it shows that his method of organizing experience, including moral constructions, had utterly nothing to do with consensual forms of understanding the body and its operation.

In the space between Bill and myself lies a series of violations: he negates my understanding of the world, while I silently refuse to accept his views concerning the interior of the human body. No amount of arguing would dissuade Bill of the belief that his mouth, on occasion, might stretch so wide that he literally could swallow his entire body. That belief is as rigid and fixed in his consciousness as a piling underneath a bridge; it is immovable. That is what epistemology is all about: rigid perceptions and beliefs that anchor the self in the world and situate perceptions in exchanges with the Other. Bill is as firmly fixed in his world as I am in mine. Nothing will change his mind; nothing will change mine. Bill is not 'wrong'; his belief system is 'right' in the sense that it guides his behavior and gives it a moral context. It is wrong for me because I operate from a totally different epistemology. Bill's formal assumptions about the world violate my understanding of consensual reality. I could speak with a colleague about physiology, and we could reach agreement as to the functions of the intestines, the stomach, the anus, the mouth, and so on. But if I told my colleague I could give birth to myself through my navel, he would run like hell from me. Bill operates in a different conceptual and psychological arena. It is not likely that Bill or anyone like Bill would willingly give up his or her epistemology; madness locks in and locks up a self trapped by proofs and demonstrations with origins in logics that are inaccessible to consensual reality.

But it is not realistic to assume that such locked-up theories of knowledge and perception apply only to mad individuals; they also operate with striking power in groups and in group-dependent ideologies. To name an ideology as psychotic means that its appearance has nothing at all to do with normal or consensual patterns of exchange and communication. To argue that group X should be locked up and exterminated in a gas chamber in 2006 in Los Angeles would be crazy, psychotic. To make that argument, however, in January 1942, in a wintry resort just outside of Berlin was not seen as psychotic but rather as normal politics. Psychotic group behavior, which produces enormous anxiety for those named as the 'enemy', becomes a generalizing logic that extends over more than just the internal geography of one's self or mind or being. A psychotic group percept is shared; the ideological formulation brings the group together and creates a shared epistemological system in which everyone believes that what everyone else thinks and does is correct and true. For Auschwitz to have succeeded in Nazi Germany required the mass participation of a number of different groups at all levels in culture and government who agreed that the Jew constituted a terrifying biological threat, "life unworthy of life," and therefore had to be exterminated. It was a belief as powerful on the German consciousness as Bill's belief that he could give birth to himself. Further, in a group-defined psychosis, madness appears in what the group does collectively; it is not to be determined by an examination of the state of mind of individual group members. An individual can be clinically sane but participate in collective, insane actions. What coheres a group action and legitimates its purposes is the group's conscience and how that conscience guides behavior.

Modern Psychological Variants of the Hobbesian Position

Freud, in *Civilization and Its Discontents*, sees the ego as a battleground mediating the demands of the id and the super-ego. Conscience acts as a prohibition on the drives, but it also projects a program of values and action that, while 'civilizing' behavior, may bring with it psychological knots and difficult-to-escape emotional traps. Nonetheless, Freud argues that the super-ego creates for the individual self a set of moral evaluations that guide behavior in the crowded emotional universe of need and desire. This is not a psychotic text but a normalizing one. Conscience confines social action within a range of behaviors broadly considered to be 'consensual' and lawful.

Similarly, on the level of the collective or group, conscience produces belief and induces action in both individuals and groups. Guided by moral imperatives, conscience may attach itself to political argument and ideology, and it possesses enormous power in defining a culture's attitude toward its political agents. Conscience can in fact justify group actions that could be regarded as psychotic. The restraining and civilizing aspects of conscience can, in certain contexts, produce public and political actions that transgress limits and boundaries. What one culture may call 'conscience' may be completely different in another. This development Freud never considered—that the super-ego, rather than being 'civilizing' and representing restraint, could in fact transform into murderous public violence. Vamik Volkan (1997) suggests that conscience infuses ideological programs with a "shared morality," with the corresponding psychological effect of minimizing the dominant group's anxiety. But this conscience that minimizes the dominant group's anxiety may intensify the fear, dread, and anxiety of singled-out groups that are seen to be dangerous and poisonous. The promise of murdering the out-group provides psychological relief for the dominant group.

The young man who shows up at Sheppard Pratt covered from head to toe in axle grease has some very good reason for applying that grease, but he arrives at the hospital because a part of him, a part he has a great deal of trouble communicating with, needs help. His torment drives him to the asylum. But in a group, all believe their beliefs to be true; none feels tormented by their ideology, and all reject anyone or any idea who attacks them. New moralities, attached to ideologies, create visions of possibility and hope. Anything is possible, including the "ability to kill the enemy without remorse" (Volkan 1997: 122). If everyone in the group is saying that X and Y are true, there are no formal procedures for demonstrating disproof. If one argued in Nazi Germany that Jewish blood possessed no imminent threat to German culture, one was regarded not only as scientifically wrong but as a political subversive. Counter-arguments and proofs may exist, but they have no standing or credence in the knowledge factories producing and supporting the ideologies of destruction. For those who choose to look, counter-proofs lie in history, human experience, and the universe of the group's victims.

But the culture refuses to look for proofs negating its dominant assumptions; it refuses to look because those proofs cannot be seen. Counter-arguments possess no validating logics. They have no place or role in the articulating systems of prevailing beliefs. Nazi professors such as Martin Heidegger, Carl Schmitt, Hans Fryer, Karl Haushofer, Hans Namn, and Walter Gross built belief systems, a shared morality, serving as a conscience for German culture, its civil society and political institutions. Conscience as a militant, unforgiving racism entwined culture and mind with politics. No split prevailed between the intellectual and the culture's ideological political agents. Both embraced a value-laden view of the world defined as the need to exterminate the Other. It is a process analogous to the psychotic patient's firm belief that beneath the hospital lie explosive atomic bombs ready to go off at any moment. Nothing in logic, rhetoric, or proof will dissuade the patient of that truth. Similarly with the group, no amount of argument will persuade the German culture that the Jew does not constitute an imminent biological threat to the nation's well-being. Cultural belief systems can be as crazy as individual ones: they have been, and continue to be, responsible for inflicting enormous damage.

A compelling analysis of the power of conscience in the Third Reich, and the contribution of conscience to mass murder and psychotic political behavior, appears in Claudia Koonz's (2003) *The Nazi Conscience*. Koonz argues that the ability to implement mass murder required the translation of good conscience into good action. Cultural and professional leaders understood the moral imperative as a demand for biological cleansing, a shared cultural action receiving the support of major intellectual, political, administrative, and professional sectors of German society. The development of a shared genocidal morality, fed by public consciousness and a group vision, arose from the region of Germany's civil society and fully supported the programmatic aims of the state and the Nazi Party. Conscience played out the phantasies of biological insecurity, and the binding effect of conscience as a politics of exclusion and murder appeared in groups as diverse as rifle and hunt clubs, the Nazi Youth League, local medical associations, reading clubs, and the National Association for the Deaf.

Jews were quartered in ghettos to prevent the spread of "Jewish" diseases; the head of the medical services in occupied Poland was titled chief sanitation inspector; at a symposium outside Krakow in 1942, attended by prominent German scientific researchers and public health specialists, it was suggested by a speaker that the solution to the Jewish "problem" should be annihilation. The audience applauded enthusiastically. The ghettos established in Poland were set up not only to isolate and segregate Jewish populations but also to find suitable environments minimizing physical contact with surrounding areas.

To rid the culture of biological pollutants demanded a cultural super-ego defining human relationships, particularly sexuality, in terms of prohibitions against touching and of phobias regarding 'bad' blood, defective genes, and congenital illness. Sexual contact between Jew and Aryan, the primary focus of the infamous Nuremberg laws, was prohibited and brought with it severe criminal penalties. The insecurity generated by the prospect of an endangered biological future forged radical divisions between clean and unclean, healthy and unhealthy. It is a psychological process akin to the individual psychotic's refusal to touch certain objects or the tendency to see danger in what consensual reality would regard as relatively harmless representations. It is belief—fixed logics—that push the self into fortress-like positions. Yet it is also true that a crazy person is not a group. The relevant audience of the psychotic lies in hidden spaces inside the self. Groups, however, act in public spaces; their behaviors affect other groups and individuals whose epistemologies may hold radically different premises regarding consensual principles. A crazy person holds the delusion inside; it is not generalized. But the culture, in normalizing psychotic beliefs, externalizes radical beliefs as customary behavior. What other societies and cultures would regard as crimes, the normalizing group regards as necessity driven by imminent threat. Jews found themselves increasingly isolated in the society, excluded from all association with Germans. Parks, swimming pools, commerce, medicine, professional practices, administrative law, local zoning regulations, land-use policy, all enforced this radical segregation of 'bad' blood from uncontaminated Aryan bodies.

It was not the SS that became the modern representatives of Plato's nocturnal Council; rather, it was the civil arbiters of conscience, the professions, who defined the epistemology of exclusion, the psychology of boundaries, and the biology of genetics and race—a skin ego built through the aggregations of perceptions. The professors, physicians, scientists, psychiatrists, engineers, mathematicians, accountants, and bankers of the Third Reich formulated the parameters of moral conscience and responded to underlying cultural anxiet-ies over the transgression of racial boundaries. Psychotic beliefs had absorbed not only the institutions but also the range of civil associations responsible for producing the culture's knowledge systems and fixed points of belief. So, for example, if a group says that we have to die so that our spirits can meet the spaceship taking us to the next level of being, you or I out there, in any given audience, at any time of day, can say that the belief is psychotic and transgres-sive, that it violates the norms of consensual reality that you and I understand to be true. While it is crazy for us, it is, of course, not crazy for the group, just as a psychotic's epistemology is not crazy for the individual holding it inside.

If I tell my children that I am leaving the house and will be back in a year because I am going to speak with God, they will consider me crazy. But if a Nazi father tells his children that he is going on special assignment to gas 20,000 Jews in one day, they will consider him a patriot who is saving their country from a terrible poison. What makes the group-based psychosis believ-able is the power of ideology to define individual and group perceptions. Those children believe that their father is doing the right thing because the ideologi-cal system is part of their daily lives. My going to speak with God is not part of my daily routine. It is way out of the ordinary, a textual interruption so transgressive that anyone who knows me will surely say that I have gone com-pletely out of my mind. But this would not be the case with regard to the Nazi father, and in this respect, the criteria for evaluating the psychotic text on the group level are quite different from those for the individual level. A politics is mad or psychotic if it breaks all customary and consensual understandings that I and my audience have with the world. If today I said to you that the purpose of social theory, biology, medicine, mathematics, social science, and physics is to make sure that the world is rid of all poisonous peoples, you would say back to me, "You need psychiatric help—right now!" But in Germany from 1933 to 1945, it was not considered crazy to advocate mass killing and death for those regarded to be biologically and genetically inferior human beings. Indeed, it was just the opposite; it was regarded as a sign of one's devotion, humanity, patriotism, and good sense to advocate the killing of biological impurities. In other words, it was the sign of good and virtuous moral conscience. The psy-chotic text had become normalized.

Koonz (2003: 189) speaks of the "ethnocrats" who forged conscience "appropriate to the tasks ahead" and invented technologies to achieve 'cleans-ing' and 'purification'. Moral conscience motivated the construction of the crematoria, gas chambers, and execution pits and justified their use. In Didier Anzieu's (1989) terms, the culture group's "skin ego," the psychological mem-brane holding the community together, protecting it from disintegration, grew "thicker" because of the society's rigid patterns of exclusion and persecution. Too often we underestimate the power of ideas to define how we treat other human beings. Millions of innocents died in the Germany of the Third Reich because of ideological assumptions generalized throughout the culture in sci-ence, popular literature, cinema, education, technology, and the professions. Those few who regarded Jews as human beings were thought to be crazy or peculiar or "filthy" and corrupt by the vast majority of German citizenry and by the idea-creating mechanisms and centers in the Third Reich. Physicians, biologists, geneticists, public health specialists, infectious disease experts, all promulgated the notion that race purity was threatened by the inherently defective and poisonous Jewish race. If one touched a Jew, it was essential to wash one's hands; if one kissed a Jew, one could be sent to prison; if one had sexual relations with a Jew, one would be prohibited from ever marrying an Aryan person.

According to Koonz (2003: 201), the ethnocrats pondered "racial policies in abstract and theoretical discussions." These policies filtered into the populace, providing guidelines for the arts, sciences, professions, public bureaucracies, and private corporations. Professional schools, universities, research institutes, scientific centers, psychiatric hospitals, the laboratories of Bayer pharmaceuticals, all worked within the moral boundaries of the cultural race agenda and the racial policies of the state. These agendas emerged as a moral consensus, not as a forced imposition on an unwilling populace. The Reich Institute for the Study of the Jewish Question, the Institute for the Study and Eradication of Jewish Influence in German Religious Life, and the Nazi Physicians' League published findings scientifically verifying the inherent danger of Jewish blood. Together, science and popular media promulgated the view that segregation and later the extermination of Jews and Gypsies not only would benefit race hygiene but also would allow Germans to live free of the disintegration anxiety produced by the prospect of biological perversion. The cultural imagery, then, of a biological black hole and the portrayal of Jews and Gypsies as pollutants legitimated a political culture in which murder became normalized as sane, rational public policy.

It is not difficult for ideology to stir up mass insecurity; certainly, events happen in the world that serve to reinforce paranoid fears. Phantasies operating in the political universe possess real-world impact, blurring the distinction between constructed or imagined reality and reality that receives consensual validation. But in addition to concrete dangers 'out there', political policy is subject to being influenced by a psychology of phantasy. It is not unusual historically for political regimes to construct enemies because of intensely held psychological beliefs regarding the danger posed by certain persons, when in fact that danger is non-existent. The defenseless shtetl Jews of Eastern Europe hardly constituted a political and military threat to Nazi Germany.

Phantasy and Political Policy

Koonz (2003: 202) argues that the Germans "converted racial phobias from ideology to credible knowledge" and rationalized the "orderly removal of Jews from mainstream society." Moral conscience as ideology "underwrote the consensus that Jews had no place in Germany." Carl Schmitt, a political philosopher, called for a "healthy exorcism" of the Jews. Not to see the Jew as polluted or diseased was considered wrong thinking and unscientific, the abdication of moral conscience. A Nazi physician assigned to Warsaw argued that typhus in the Warsaw ghetto came not from an innate Jewish tendency to carry typhus but from wretched living conditions, starvation, and lack of adequate medical treatment. He was reassigned to Berlin because his views were considered "unscientific."

Volkan (1997) suggests that intrinsic to the psychology of the self is the need to divide the world into enemies and allies, a process beginning early in psychogenetic development. Further, the process appears in political forms of identification: good self/bad Other transforms into good group/bad group, and the danger of the bad takes on numinous properties through the projection of evil. If the self believes the Other to be the enemy, whatever entity assumes the mantle of enemy becomes in fact the enemy. The political mapping of this psychological dynamic develops similarly. Empirical confirmation of an enemy's threat has little to do with real-world consensual validation but a great deal to do with cultural belief and what ideology projects as sufficient proof and demonstration of danger, for example, German scientists' claim that the Jew is a biologically predisposed carrier of typhus. Phantasy turned to truth, receiving the confirmation of medical science, and in Koonz's view (2003: 259) "deportation and mass murder" became "pre-emptive, psychological self-defense."

Long before the invasion of the Soviet Union, Nazi think tanks produced "volumes of scholarship, lavishly illustrated popular books, press releases, films, conferences, and exhibits that prepared the public for harsh treatment of inferiors" (Koonz 2003: 215). Empirical research motivated by an "ethnic consensus" (ibid.: 225) confirmed the culture's paranoid moral conscience; scientifically objective data brought security to a population worried about its genetic future. Justifying genocide, then, came not from "old-fighter Nazis' coarse hatred for Jews" but from "a deceptively mild and supposedly objective form of racism that ultimately proved to be far more lethal" (ibid.: 125). Interestingly, even after 1945, wives, friends, and associates of major scientific figures setting racial policy insisted that these individuals could not be considered anti-Semitic. After all, Jews were not only biologically different but "dangerous," and their difference justified segregation from the rest of society. Therefore, as outcasts, Jews deserved no empathy. Conscience, in the sense of seeing genocide as morally abhorrent, "did not trouble" (ibid.: 209) German intellectuals "during or after the war " (ibid.: 225).

Moral protest against the brutalization of Jews occurred in rare instances but received no support from the culture or its institutions. Koonz (2003: 272) relates: "What haunts us is not only the ease with which soldiers slaughtered helpless civilians in occupied territories, but the specter of a state so popular that it could mobilize individual conscience of a broad cross-section of citizens in the service of moral catastrophe." Killing Jews signified a consensual moral victory, not "brainwashing" but an enthusiastic embrace of the "public culture" of racism, a "hierarchy of racially based human worth" (ibid.: 273). A society united by "communal celebrations" of race hegemony, visions of "sanctified life in the *volk* ... a religion, a consensual dictatorship ... ethnic fundamental-ism," found murdering to be the highest political achievement (ibid.).

Like individuals, groups can find themselves captured, possessed, or held by paranoid affect whose origins developmentally precede the appearance of language. (It is literally the world of the infant present and alive in the adult. Melanie Klein, Wilfred Bion, D. W. Winnicott, Ronald Fairbairn, and Harry Guntrip were pioneers in demonstrating the behavioral power of the pre-Oedipal universe.) Thomas Ogden (1994: 35) argues that "the paranoid-schizoid posi-tion represents a psychological organization generating a state of being that is ahistorical ... and contributes to the immediacy and intensity of experience." Paranoia may, in its appearance in adult behavior, attack the self's borders, threatening the maintenance of consensual understandings in a world defined by linear or historical causality. In the individual, the more severe the regres-sion to earlier forms of emotional 'being', the more the self may experience breakdown or psychotic developments. Regression brings disorganization and confusion in the self's relation to consensual reality. Paranoid projections may consume consciousness, seriously impairing the self's ability to maintain stable relationships. But in the group, rather than breaking down the collective ego and throwing consciousness into confusion, the appearance of intense para-noid affect, especially as ideology, reinforces resolve, strengthens phantasies of annihilation, and diminishes feelings of insecurity.

Paranoia in the individual may produce a psychotic organization of reality. Psychotic space, in collapsing causality and disrupting linear time, becomes the space of delusion, leading the individual to construct reality through internal psychological projections. Consciousness finds meaning in delusional introjec-tions with scripts and logics that lock the self into a phantasmal world with no exit. In the group, however, the phantasy, rather than remaining internalized, defending against the fear of collapse or a collective state of deadness, attaches itself to instruments of political and social power, mobilizes the culture's under-lying anxieties, and provides a generally accepted explanation for evil. What in the individual would be dysfunctional becomes radically functional in the public space. Delusion as ideology shapes political reality.

For the individual psychotic, the delusional projection remains riveted in a self/self dialogue, immobilizing consciousness in its relations with the outside world but preoccupying the ego in the conduct of its hidden, delusional sce-narios. There may be exceptions; for example, the paranoid schizophrenic may careen out of control and engage in destructive behavior. But schizophrenics generally appear to be mute, sometimes almost catatonic, while the action of the internal world moves at a furious pace. In the group, however, the paranoid/schizoid position assumes organizational and functional purposes missing in the individual. It is almost as if the ideological elaboration of delu-sion, its acceptance by the culture's knowledge centers, and its resonance in a mass audience focuses the group's psychic organization and imparts logic to cognitive operations in the external world. The public representations of moral conscience 'normalize' delusion and enclose reality in new definitions of right and wrong, appropriate and inappropriate.

Ogden (1994: 35) argues that in psychotic individuals, paranoid "qualities of experience" involve a "dialectical process through which the subject is constituted." What makes the subject aware, what gives the subject 'being' are not the memories of historical experience or markers used to designate consensual reality. The subject's psychic constitution emerges from the hermetic logics and moralities implicit in the delusional organization of experience. In the case of the group, that dialectical process appears in normalized ideological constructs, the moral refractory that holds the culture's practical, ethical, and psychological definitions. What in historical retrospect are psychotic forms of identification replace traditional moral designations of experience. For example, in Nazi Germany, mass murder, which in a Judeo-Christian ethic means transgression and violation, becomes in the culture's new moral organization an act of national therapy requiring heroic sacrifice. Yet the action of the group does not derive from historically tested methods of conflict resolution; rather, the new moral view rises from intense psychic pressure generated in synchronic time. And the group turns to action in linear time to enact unconscious phantasies whose aim is to preserve the group from sinking into nothingness (deadness) and unbearable panic over the fear of being contaminated. The belief in the Jew as lethal contaminant drove national policy in the Third Reich, and a shared unconscious fear of contamination played a large role in the techniques and rationalizations for genocide.

The phobia over contamination, driven by paranoid affect, knows no spatial or temporal limitation. In Freud's terms, the feelings subject to mobilization lie deeply buried in a "timeless" unconscious. The right conjunction of political circumstance, cultural development, moral environment, and psychically receptive audience produces a set of public agents ready to rid the culture of its phobic horrors. Ogden (1994: 38) argues: "Psychoanalytic infancy is not restricted to the earliest months of life, instead the notion of the timelessness of the unconscious requires that we view the autistic-contiguous, the paranoid/schizoid, and the depressive positions as together constituting facts of time present in every period of life." Or in the words of William Faulkner, "The past is not dead; it is not even past" (quoted in ibid.: 39). As a collectively shared past, the intensely aversive effects of phobia forged the perceptions driving genocide in Nazi Germany.

As part of infantile psychological development, Ogden examines the "dialectic of splitting and integration," an autonomous operation that through its permutations creates, destroys, and re-creates self and object representations. Not only is the Kleinian subject split (dispersed) among the phantasized internal object relations constituting it, "the splitting process itself represents part of a dialectic of dispersal and unity of the subject, a dialectic of fragmentation and integration, of delinkage and closure, of part-object relations and whole-object relations" (Ogden 1994: 40). It may be useful to look at this process in the context of large group political behavior. "Dispersal and unity ... fragmentation and integration" describe a developmental dynamic central to an ideological explanation of political experience. The phantasy of breaking apart, disintegration anxiety, and phobic aversion incite psychically a set of images, a symbology capable of soothing, containing, holding, and diminishing terror generated by 'bad', dangerous, and threatening objects. Radical action, massive unification, and the demand for blood sacrifice become the instruments of group unity and transcendence over the prospect of paranoid immobility. Phantasies of unification—in the case of Germany, the annihilation of the Jews; in that of Cambodia, the destruction of city dwellers and bourgeoisie—diminish group anxiety and, through the action component of phantasy, create the opportunity for a collective sharing in what the ideology describes as 'healing', 'national therapy', or cleansing. In Anzieu's terms, the group's "skin ego" protects through implementation of the phantasy of unification; action brings new hope to the group consciousness. What Volkan sees as group excitement forges "creative" syntheses, plans, visions, and operations. German land-use and resettlement policies, for example, envisioned the massive movement of thousands of ethnic Germans to newly occupied territories and the forced removal of Jews, "inferior" racial types, and "unlawful" aliens.

Ogden (1994: 40–41) speaks of "intense phantasies of the explosion of the subject ... the intrapsychic pressure for deintegration" and the fear "that disintegration and fragmentation phantasies might lead to death." I am arguing that these phantasies appear in the psychological operations of groups; that phobia generates the fear of collective implosion; that anxiety over contamination and pollution produce countervailing visions (phantasies) whose purpose is annihilation; and that phantasies of political integration have historically been framed in a moral language justifying genocide.

Linking Agent between Group Phantasy and Group Action

Ideology links the group's unconscious phantasy of disintegration and the historical enactment of the project of purification, unity, and rebirth. What Michael Eigen (1996: 54) calls psychic "definition" may be useful in exploring ideology as linking agent: "Definition ... may be used to bind or organize experience." Eigen focuses on the psychological negativity of definition, its exclusionary functions and, in psychosis, its debilitating impact on action and relationship. For political groups, the converse holds true: instead of making life more difficult, definition accomplishes the opposite. As ideology, definition solidifies internally held phantasies about rescue from 'badness'. In the psychotic individual, consciousness finds itself trapped by definitional biases that destroy desire, inhibit communication, and force the self into complex maneuvers to survive the terrifying reality of others. Eigen argues that the "aim of naming [definition] is to stop horrible [psychic] movement" (ibid.). But in political groups, definitional biases intrinsic to ideological explanation, rather than entrapping consciousness, constitute markers liberating consciousness and the group-body from the prospect of contamination. Ideology creates action, but the content of ideology speaks directly to unconscious phantasies motivating its construction. 'Naming', as a function of ideology, refines the meaning of good', provides concrete evidence and argument for exclusion and elimination of 'bad', and develops a new moral language to understand political experience. No room remains for competing moral interpretations; ideology wipes out ambivalence. Eigen quotes Wilfred Bion: "The 'ought' expresses moral violence and omnipotence" (ibid.: 50).

The group 'ought', as ideology, frames the Other's position. No compromise or negotiation exists in this relationship; it is an absolute demand for acquiescence, an omnipotent assertion of power. The group phantasy of redemption and purification reduces the Other's status to that of non-human object filled with pestilence. The group's moral stance justifies physical violence, which neither the state nor its cultural agents question. Moral justification lies in ideological definition, what Eigen (2002: 63) calls a "tyrannical state of mind ... an affective ideology of absolute control"—except that the group experiences ideology not as domination or absolute control but as liberation, an expression of justice, a redress of historical grievance. The group finds its freedom in omnipotent phantasies of delusion, in a glorified destiny free of toxic Others. Most importantly, the ideological umbrella of the group brings security, faith, and the utter certainty that whatever action the agents of the group undertake to protect boundaries is right.

Thus, the German banker who shifts Jewish monies into SS and Reichsbahn accounts enthusiastically participates in a group project, a collective moral undertaking, that brings into its orbit functions as different as managing capital and pushing Jews into gas chambers. The accountant, psychiatrist, physician, banker, railroad engineer, pharmaceutical scientist, university professor, chemicals manufacturer, SS guard, all operate within a moral environment sanctified by ideological definition. Even though the tasks differ, the moral position remains easily identifiable by all actors: killing Jews and Gypsies guards the community from infection, protects Aryan posterity from genetic abnormalities, and restores human security. In Eigen's terms, "extreme states add intensity" (1996: 10), alleviate "annihilation anxiety, and ward off catastrophic formlessness" (ibid.: 60).

What Winnicott (1965: 187) describes as the self's fear of violation may be applicable to ideological formulations justifying mass murder: "Rape and being eaten by cannibals, these are mere bagatelles as compared with the violation of the self's core." What is interesting here is how groups formulate the conditions of violation, the language that is used, and how ideology mobilizes this language of penetration and violation, providing graphic images to reinforce the psychological threat. For example, in Poland, Germans used posters to drive home the point that Jews, as innate carriers of the typhus bug, constituted a threat to public health. Allowing a Jew to touch milk could be poisonous. A Polish professor of mathematics told me that when he was six, his mother took him to a race exhibit set up by the Germans in Warsaw. He remembers hearing a small child scream to his mother, "Mama, look, a Jewish army, a Jewish army!" He turned around expecting to see the exhibit invaded by "hordes" of Jews, but what he saw was this child looking at a closed exhibition case containing thousands of lice and labeled "Jews." Phobic aversion produces reactions like these;

it is akin to the fear of being violated, penetrated. And when phobia becomes a group definition, enforced by graphic public imagery, the group, to protect its core from annihilation, undertakes whatever is required and justifies its actions in language provided by ideological definition.

Paranoia and Organization: Institutional Defenses against Insecurity

Otto Kernberg (1997) addresses the issue of paranoia in organizations and its psychodynamic implications. However, Kernberg sees paranoiagenic behavior as indicative of organizational pathology and regression. It therefore creates dysfunction, breakdown, and confusion; paranoid leaders misuse power, enforce authoritarian procedures, and disrupt organizational morale. What I am arguing is that in certain political environments, paranoid defenses enforce ideological mandates, possess positive and moral outcomes for the culture, and may be consistent with prevailing consensual norms, values, and definitions. Plato's vision reappears in the modern state. Paranoia becomes a psychic engine pushing social policy, bureaucratic initiative, and public policy. The phobia against contaminated blood (Nazi Germany), the dangers to moral purity posed by decadent bourgeois institutions (Cambodia), and the belief in the "international Jewish conspiracy" (neo-anti-Semitism, Wahhabi Islam) suggest, for cultures ideologically dominated by these views, not breakdown or pathology—that is, "paranoiagenic deterioration"—but rather the justification for organizations dedicated to protecting boundary and moral conscience.

Paranoia, elaborated as ideology, produces public technologies for phantasies of world creation and world destruction. James Grotstein (1997) speaks of the symbology of "human sacrifice" that appears in the delusional narratives of paranoid schizophrenics, but which can also be found in ideologies justifying annihilation and in destruction phantasies. In Cambodia, for example, under the Khmer Rouge, ideology demanded the destruction of city dwellers, the decadent professional classes eroding the moral purity of pure communism. These views, in historical retrospect, sound as psychotic as the phantasmic vision of the schizophrenic self. Volkan (1995: 75–76) speaks of "the power of the 'infantile psychotic self'" and how later "self and object images and representations" in the adult derive from "this matrix saturated with affects."

Paranoid imagery in political groups owes its origins as well to shared participation in the imagery of this psychotic core, in the ability and ingeniousness of cultures to elaborate primitive affect in rational argument, public bureaucracies, institutions (Auschwitz), and moralities that view killing as healing. Primitive affect, then, rather than pushing groups into states of psychological dysfunction, becomes on the political level organized into complex moral positions, strenuous research efforts, and coordinated strategies for mass killing. What would immobilize the schizophrenic individual transforms into an energizing dynamic for the group.

Group psychosis differs from individual psychotic projection. Psychotic organization, as the foundation of ideological definition, takes on properties characteristic of schizophrenic delusion, for example, transgression, omnipotent phantasies, the translation of value, and imagery of mass annihilation and domination. But with the group constituted by ideology, psychotic imagery, rather than remaining an internal marker for consciousness (the schizophrenic self/self dialogue), motivates the construction of organizational rationalization and opens up communicative links between political and cultural leadership and the mass audience. Gestapo records from the late 1930s reveal no local protests from Germans to the relocation of Jewish families who for decades had been engaging in commerce and creating friendships in the same villages and towns. The paranoid phantasy regarding contamination had become so powerful, so integrated with national consciousness, that the disappearance of Jews from familiar and long-standing habitats caused hardly a murmur among local populations. It is almost as if the German people, political leadership, and cultural and scientific authority had created a psychological synergy united by the overriding fact of potential contamination and the radical aversion to "diseased" bodies. What today many would regard as psychosis replaced history in defining group relations between Germans and Jews. From the perspective, however, of the culture united by this ideological contamination/purification logic, the phantasy of rebirth and cleansing constituted the highest expression of reason and morality.

Conclusion: Reality Reborn in Phantasies of Annihilation

Psychotic narrative in the self, what Franco de Masi (2001: 80) calls "a psychic strategy directed toward self-annihilation," produces meaning, an unconscious script feeding consciousness and supplying hermetically sealed imagery. This self/self dialogue shuts out the external, consensual world. While it is a "destructive way of dealing with mental" phenomena, delusion does provide reference, orientation, and definition. An "altered, disorganized and destroyed" consensual self gives way to a fabricated, imaginary self, an emotional organization real enough for the schizophrenic. De Masi contends that this "perceptual-altering system includes omnipotent and illusional mental transformations ... a mental catastrophe" (ibid.: 81), that is, psychotic breakdown, with the endgame being Sullivan's (1953) tragically decomposed "hebephrenic," totally cut off from human exchange.

It is striking to compare the function of delusion in the schizophrenic self with its action in overcoming insecurity in the group collective. What de Masi sees as psychotic breakdown appears in the group as an ideological framework, creating vivid oppositions between good and bad. Normalized through the culture's knowledge productions, given authoritative status by the professions, and legitimated through political and social practice, annihilation phantasies dominate the group's habits, actions, and moral arguments. Psychotic positions, elaborated as shared cultural assumptions, devise urgent programs to speed the enactment of an ideological imperative. The Al-Qaeda terrorists engage in a "dialogue" with Western democracies over decadence and immorality by smashing airplanes into the World Trade Center and the Pentagon. In the Third Reich, Jewish pharmacists were required to put a star on medical prescriptions; ghettos were designed to prevent the transmission of contaminated flesh and to segregate Jewish "disease" from surrounding populations. In Auschwitz, the clothes taken from Jews were sterilized in giant boilers before being sent to Germany. National security meant protecting the public from biological contamination, and medical science defined the exclusionary, public health measures necessary to block the transmission of deadly Jewish toxins. It would be difficult to argue today that a belief system requiring the deaths of millions possesses sane, rational components.

The term 'psychotic' is used in an evaluative sense in interpreting political behavior and policy. I am suggesting it may be useful to conceptualize psychotic group states as radical responses to archaic feelings of insecurity, phobic aversion, and paranoia over the fear of being infected by a dreaded, toxic, external agent. In Wilfred Bion's (1961) terms, the unconscious writes the language and behavior of the group; consciousness accepts delusion as truth, and political, cultural, and social institutions grow from shared moral conscience with roots in the delusional rewriting of reality. Concepts of social health, biological therapy, national cleansing, and cultural decadence emerge from a delusional nexus, justifying mass murder and defending the group's psychological boundaries from disintegration and implosion.

James M. Glass is Professor of Government and Politics at the University of Maryland, College Park. He is the recipient of the University of Maryland's Distinguished Scholar-Teacher Award for 2002–2003, and was cited by the Maryland Association for Higher Education as Outstanding Faculty in the state of Maryland for 2004. His most recent books include *"Life Unworthy of Life": Racial Phobia and Mass Murder in Hitler's Germany* (1997), and *Jewish Resistance During the Holocaust: Moral Uses of Violence and Will* (2004). He is currently at work on a project examining group psychoanalytic theories behind mass murder and genocide.

References

Anzieu, D. 1989. *The Skin Ego*. Trans. C. Turner. New Haven, CT: Yale University Press.

Bion, W. 1961. *Experience in Groups and Other Papers*. New York: Basic Books.

De Masi, F. 2001. "The Unconscious and Psychosis: Some Considerations of the Psychoanalytic Theory of Psychosis." In *A Language for Psychosis: Psychoanalysis of Psychotic States*, ed. Paul Williams. New York: Brunner-Routledge.

Eigen, M. 1996. *Psychic Deadness*. Northvale, NJ: Jason Aronson.

_____. 2002. *Rage*. Middlevale, CT: Wesleyan University Press.

Grotstein, J. S. 1997. "Why Oedipus and Not Christ: A Psychoanalytic Inquiry into Innocence, Human Sacrifice, and the Sacred." Parts 1 and 2. *American Journal of Psychoanalysis* 57, no. 3: 193–220; no. 4: 317–335.

Kernberg, O. 1997. "Ideology and Bureaucracy as Social Defenses against Aggression." In *The Inner World in the Outer World: Psychoanalytic Perspectives*, ed. E. R. Shapira. New Haven, CT: Yale University Press.

Koonz, C. 2003. *The Nazi Conscience*. Cambridge, MA: Belknap Press of Harvard University.

Ogden, T. H. 1994. *Subjects of Analysis*. Northvale, NJ: Jason Aronson.

Sullivan, H. S. 1953. *The Interpersonal Theory of Psychiatry*. New York: Norton.

Volkan, V. 1995. *The Infantile Psychotic Self and Its Fates: Understanding and Treating Schizophrenics and Other Difficult Patients*. Northvale, NJ: Jason Aronson.

_____. 1997. *Bloodlines: From Ethnic Pride to Ethnic Tension*. New York: Farrar Straus and Giroux.

Winnicott, D. W. 1965. "Communication and Not Communicating Leading to a Study of Certain Opposites." Pp. 179–192 in *The Maturational Process and the Facilitating Environment*. New York: International Universities Press.

Chapter 9

INTERPRETING NUMINOUS EXPERIENCES

Dan Merkur

Oskar Pfister long ago proposed that religious healing can successfully promote psychotherapeutic change, as gauged by psychoanalytic standards, when the religious practices happen to deploy religious symbolism in fashions that the unconscious super-ego can use to achieve insights. The therapeutic action of religious healing is precisely parallel to the use of symbolism in play therapy (Pfister 1932; see also Devereux 1958; Haartman 2004; Merkur 1995–1996, 2004, 2005). Both procedures rest on an unconscious process that Freud ([1913] 1958: 259) had noted: "Psychoanalysis has shown us that everyone possesses in his unconscious mental activity an apparatus which enables him to interpret other people's reactions, that is, to undo the distortions which other people have imposed on the expression of their feelings." If religious healers can work with religious phenomena to therapeutic effect, there is no reason in principle

---

References for this chapter begin on page 221.

why psychoanalysts should not do the same. It is a question of analyzing religious sublimations by allowing psychoanalytic theories to suggest links among the patient's associations at their level of sublimation.

How may we psychoanalyze religion at its level of sublimation? In this article, I am proposing a new mode of psychoanalytic discourse that is derived from the comparative study of religion. The psychoanalytic appropriation of the discourse implies a sea change. As clinicians, we take interest in our patients' subjective experiences of religion. It is not religions as systems of rites, ethics, tales, doctrines, and social structures but rather individuals' emotion-laden experiences of their religions that clinicians seek to interpret. We ask patients to speak of their feelings about their religious convictions and practices. We are not satisfied with unemotional intellectualizations or claims of conventional emotional attitudes. We ask after fresh emotions that are authentic and heartfelt. Listening is not the same, however, as interpreting. Because classical analysts fantasized that they could be their patients' mirrors, they left themselves out of the picture when they imagined psychoanalysis as a process of bringing to consciousness the contents, meanings, and motivations of patients' subjectivities. Contemporary psychoanalysts instead recognize that we are participant observers, that the psychoanalytic process is a two-person psychology, and that analytic neutrality is not humanly possible. It is inevitable that our values will be present in the interpretations that we offer.

In the present context, I emphasize that psychoanalysts are uncompromisingly committed to a foundationalism that consists, at minimum, of the concepts of mental suffering and its amelioration. Classical analysts medicalized their efforts to help patients 'get better' by thinking in terms of illness and cure. Many contemporary analysts prefer a hermeneutic, humanistic, existential, or other discourse. With the exception of Lacanians, psychoanalysts concur, however, that 'getting better' is not merely 'getting different' in a culturally variable, socially valued way. Therapy is not simply successful social adaptation (Devereux 1970). Clinicians aspire, in some way or ways that we can as yet only vaguely conceptualize, to facilitate a natural and presumably biologically based standard of improvement. Psychoanalysis here parts company with the phenomenological method of comparative religion. We are unhesitatingly committed to an enterprise that aspires toward natural criteria of mental health. Clinicians firmly believe that some religious subjectivities are more wholesome than others. Although we avoid religious dogmatism and apologetics, we are prepared to discover, through clinical and scientific studies, what specifics make a religiosity healthy.

Mysterium Tremendum and *Fascinans*

In *The Idea of the Holy,* a classic contribution to the history of religions that was first published in German in 1917, Rudolf Otto (1950) invented the term 'numinous' to designate the specific quality of religious experiences. He introduced the term in order to denote a quality that is common to the 'holy' and the 'demonic' but is independent of the moral implications of the two traditional concepts. However, the neologism was very rapidly appropriated by theologians as an oblique way of speaking about God. Through van der Leeuw, Wach, Eliade, and many others, Otto's term gained wide employment as a vehicle for smuggling covert theology into the academic study of religion. In the process, the concept that Otto intended lapsed into obscurity.

Otto (1950: 7) was explicitly concerned to discuss "a unique 'numinous' category of value" that is a frequent part of human experience. Considered as a phenomenological category, Otto's concept might be more fittingly expressed in English by inventing the word 'numinosity' to parallel 'beauty' and 'morality'. It is a quality, not an entity. Otto was making a psychological observation, and not a theological claim, when he asserted that "a definitely 'numinous' state of mind … is perfectly *sui generis* and irreducible to any other" (ibid.). Otto remarked that the holy, like the beautiful and the moral, has an aspect or dimension that can be understood only on its own terms. Its experiences can be approached and explained theoretically from sociological, psychological, theological, and other points of view, but the latter do not exhaust its study. Just as it is both possible and meaningful to study beauty as beauty and morality as morality, it is appropriate to study numinosity as numinosity (Merkur 1996).

Otto described numinosity as "non-rational," but Pruyser (1983) drew attention to the cognitive dimension of numinous experiences. He suggested that numinous experiences always involve a "limit situation," a topic that has finality, beyond which it is not possible to think. "Limit situations" become numinous when attempts to exceed their limits precipitate experiences of "*transcendence* and *mystery* … charged with cognitive, ontological, epistemological, and emotional implications" (ibid.: 155–156). "Limit experiences … when man encounters the Holy or Sacred" provoke "the experience of man's contingency on powers beyond his grasp or control" (ibid.: 157). Examples of limit situations include life, death, moral decision, and other decisive moments of unchangeable truth. They may include the sunrise and sunset, starry nights, and other wonders of the environment. The difference between people's reactions to the birth of twins and the births of two singletons again attests to the importance of the cognitive component in experiences of numinosity.

Otto presented a dualistic classification of numinosity that took for granted the traditional metaphysical dualism of German Romanticism. His references to the *fascinans* as "the Dionysiac element" (Otto 1950: 31, 34) alluded unmistakably to the symbolic significance that the Greek god had acquired during late German Romanticism, a generation prior to Otto (Merkur 1993). Bachofen (1967: 63–64) had contrasted Apollonian and Dionysian principles in Greek religion, and Nietzsche (1956) had adopted Bachofen's categories. As a Lutheran clergyman, Otto maintained that God was both holy and one; but Otto's phenomenological writings as a historian of religion should not be confused with his philosophical theology. Whatever may be said of the holiness of God's unknowable essence conceptualizes God as a nuomenological *Ding an sich* (thing in itself). The sense of numinosity that Otto discussed in his phenomenological writings pertained instead to two types of human religious experience: *mysterium tremendum* and *fascinans*.

As an example of the *mysterium tremendum,* with its elements of awe, majesty, urgency, and mystery (Otto 1950: 13–28), consider the following self-report.

> I was lying on my back on a carpet floor one quiet afternoon when I was in my early thirties. I was a graduate student in history of religions at the time. I was deliberately attempting to enter into an experimental religious trance, I think of a spiritualistic nature, but was unprepared for what happened.
>
> My eyes closed, I suddenly perceived inwardly a long cloudbank in an azure sky. A brilliant sun rose above the clouds until it was clear of them; as it rose, it seemed to grow brighter and brighter and I sank deeper and deeper into an intense rapture, a sheer intensity of feeling and concentration excluding all else, even joy. Then, after a timeless moment, the sun gradually began to fade and I gradually became more aware of my surroundings; I began to talk to my wife about what happened. I recall that as the sun faded, more detail appeared. I saw small objects, like planets or planes, circling the sun briefly. Then finally it was lost from view but seared indelibly on my memory. The experience was so powerful that for over an hour afterward I could not do anything, not even read; I just sat in a chair quietly recovering strength and mental orientation.
>
> I have never been quite sure what meaning to give this experience. It was not consciously an experience of oneness, for the sun was simply something I saw, as one might see the sun in the sky, not a cosmic essence I was participating in. It was not even explicitly religious, though I could not help but feel, as soon as I thought about it, that it must have some religious or transcendent meaning. The sun is, of course, a virtually universal symbol of supreme godhead or cosmic essence: Christ is spoken of as the sun, Vairocana is the "Great Sun Buddha" of the East, Surya is the object of daily Hindu devotion, and the Solar Logos is a theme of Hellenistic philosophy. But none of these meanings were emblazoned in my experience. All I knew—and know—was that because of its unique brilliance and intensity, it must encode something very important for me. (Ellwood 1980: 12–13)

The absence of time perception, logical associations, and peripheral attention outside the immediate area of focus suggest that a religious trance, that is, a religiously interpreted dissociative state, was in fact achieved. As to the content of the trance state, the "rapture," the "unique brilliance and intensity," the exclusion of everything including joy except the sun, its quality of having "some religious or transcendent meaning," its lack of associations with a variety of religious meanings that were well known to the subject, all are consistent with Otto's (1950: 29) characterization of "the *positive quality* of the 'wholly other'" that is integral to the *mysterium tremendum.*

An important feature of the *mysterium tremendum* is the intrinsic character of its numinosity. A *mysterium tremendum* is always self-confirming. The sun was manifestly numinous, and it was numinous intrinsically, by virtue of its being. It was numinous because it existed. No further reasoning formed part of the conscious experience of the sun's numinosity. The interior logic of a *mysterium tremendum* is an instance, as it were, of the ontological argument for the existence of God, as the argument might be adapted for cross-cultural purposes (Merkur 1996). The thesis that God is the hierarchically highest being that can be contemplated may be treated as a specific cultural instance of the self-evident numinosity of the 'greater-than-human'. A *mysterium tremendum* is numinous because numinosity is the most awesome, majestic, urgent, and mysterious quality that can be experienced. Otto described numinosity as non-rational, but the term 'irrational' well captures the paradoxical interior logic of the *mysterium tremendum*.

Let us now consider the *fascinans,* the second type of numinosity that Otto recognized. An instructive example may be found in the following self-report.

> When we were travelling to Oregon for my grandmother's funeral I saw a rainbow that was so unbelievably close it was as if it came right through the car. Physically I felt frightened at first and then enormously elated. I felt very much that it was a sign or a symbol of something. I'm still kind of coming to terms with it. (Wuthnow 1978: 62–63)

Although the rainbow was initially frightening, when it became self-evident as "a sign or a symbol of something," the experience turned to elation, in Otto's (1950: 35) phrase, over "the living 'something more' of the *fascinans*." Like the "wholly other," the "something more" is not necessarily conceptualized theistically, and it is misused when it is treated as a covert means to speak theologically. Otto stated that is always "'august' (*augustum*) in so far as it is recognized as possessing in itself *objective* value that claims our homage" (ibid.: 52); but this self-report of "a sign or a symbol of something" well illustrates that "something more" can be experienced quite literally as an intriguing unknown.

The intrinsically metaphoric nature of the *fascinans* is similarly indicated in the following self-report.

> A little group of thatched cottages in the middle of the village had a small orchard attached; and I remember well the peculiar purity of the blue sky seen through the white clusters of apple blossom in spring. I remember being moon-struck looking at it one morning early on my way to school. It meant something for me: what I couldn't say. It gave me an unease of heart, some reaching out towards perfection such as impels men into religion, some sense of the transcendence of things, of the fragility of our hold upon life ... It was always morning, early morning in that day-dream—and here was I, a schoolboy loitering a little, hugging that experience, incapable then of describing it to anyone, even myself, on my way to school. (Rowse 1942: 16; as cited in Paffard 1973: 75)

The full field of sense perception, with the thatched cottages, the orchard, the blue sky, the apple blossoms in spring, constituted a *fascinans* that betokened something more: "It meant something for me: what I couldn't say." A *fascinans* always implies something more than itself. The relation of the *fascinans* to something more is at minimum the relation of a metaphor to its meaning. The signifier signifies a signified that is known but may be unarticulated. The signified may never have been articulated, but there is always at least an awareness that the signifier is metaphoric. The quality of numinosity reflects the limit situation of knowledge. Whenever anything becomes a metaphor of the unknown, the signifier becomes numinous—an instance of the *fascinans*.

In the process, the unknown becomes known with respect to its function as a signified. It is known to be a signified that has significance and meaning.

The verbal unpacking of the metaphor is, however, not part of the unconsciously originating metaphor but instead constitutes commentary on its meaning. The metaphor is a variant of the dream-work (Freud [1900] 1958); its verbal unpacking may proceed either unconsciously, as part of the numinous experience, or consciously, after the metaphor's manifestation. Pre-existing religious ideas—what James ([1902] 1958) called "overbeliefs"—may be integrated with the metaphor in the course of the dream-work, and novel ideas may be formed either unconsciously or consciously as secondary elaborations. Whenever the "something more" of the *fascinans* is discussed in explicitly theistic terms, it is because commentary has contributed either to the numinous experience or to its interpretation.

When the implication of something more develops into a discrete concept of theism, the interior logic of the *fascinans* treats it as a metaphor that often conveys the cosmological argument, as it were, for the existence of a god or God. Consider, for example, the following self-reports.

> In the last five years occasionally I have had overwhelming feelings. Quite frequently I get this feeling on a clear frosty starlight night with or without moon, when I like merely to stand and gaze at the expanse and wonder of the heavens, turning over in my mind thoughts of the maker of these things. (Paffard 1973: 174–175)

> [I asked myself] 'Why, if there is no God, should anything exist in the first place? Indeed, how *could* anything exist? Why not just nothing?
>
> At this moment in my reasoning it was as if suddenly a door had been opened in the mind ... I glimpsed what I can only call the Kingdom of Heaven. For a moment all time seemed to stand still. It was as if I was looking down into a great hall, but unlike an earthly hall it defied description. It was like an intuition of infinity and pure reason. I had caught sight of Truth, which the human faculties in their frailty are unable to grasp. There were the answers to the mysteries of human life and of the existence of the universe. And if I could not understand those mysteries, at least I could know that there is something beyond ...
>
> Then the door was closed quietly and the vision slipped away like a dream. It took me a moment to catch my breath and to remember where I was. I had no doubts about the significance of what I had experienced and felt elated. My interest in the material world, however, was not noticeably diminished, and I continued with my meal and my cabbage, boiled as only the English know how. (Cohen and Phipps 1992: 14–15)

These narratives report instances of the cosmological argument for the existence of God. Because the cosmos exists, and every effect owes to a cause, the existence of the cosmos attests to its creation by a creator.

The interior logic of the *fascinans* may instead involve other logical arguments that require the postulation of something more. Rather than the cosmological argument, a person may ponder the 'argument from design', the argument that the cosmos exhibits a plan or design that attests to an author.

In Jordan, both the apparent proximity of the sky and the enormous magnificence of the scenery would often fill me with a feeling of helpless smallness. This feeling was not unpleasant and was even elevating in a way. Lying in a blanket-roll and watching dawn break over the Dead Sea caused a constriction in my chest and thoughts of man's place in the plans of God. (Paffard 1973: 190)

Another variant might be described as an argument from meaning. It is based on the observation that meaning or significance exists in the cosmos, for which reason it is logically necessary to postulate an intentionality, a source of the meanings.

As I write these pages, other memories of Eton, disconnected and often trivial, surge up. Between obvious growing pains and the stress of constant new adjustments I remember a clear night when, coming back from my tutor's I found myself alone in School Yard. Laying between two buttresses of Chapel, I looked at the stars and felt I could in some way possess even their immensity. The joy of it filled my heart like a revelation, a reassurance that the world of natural beauty means something important to me, and to the world. (Huxley 1970: 54; as cited in Paffard 1976: 43)

When Otto described numinosity as a non-rational experience, he underestimated the *fascinans* as much as he overestimated the *mysterium tremendum*. The *fascinans* is always a rational experience—speculative and inconclusive, to be sure, but nevertheless rational. It is only the *mysterium tremendum* that is irrational.

Numinosity and Anxiety

The relation of the *mysterium tremendum* to the *fascinans* may be illustrated by the following self-report of my own. Some years ago, my wife, two sons, and I took a colleague who was visiting from Europe to see Niagara Falls. After we arrived, we took a ride on the *Maid of the Mist*, a boat that travels on the river below the falls, as close to the falls as it is safely possible to go. We stood at the bow, holding onto the rail. For their safety I braced my sons, who were then perhaps eight years old, between myself and the railing. In a short space of time, the boat made its way under a sunny blue sky through moderately calm water into increasing turbulence and mist. The spray and the mist eventually became so dense that the air was gray and the sky invisible. All that could be seen was the bow making its way forward through the water churning a short distance below. The deafening pounding of the falling water made it impossible to communicate, even by shouting at close quarters.

I was consciously aware that none of us was even remotely at realistic risk, and I momentarily reflected on the fact of my tranquility before my consciousness of the potential danger developed abruptly into a sense of terror at the overwhelming, unthinking, unstoppable force of the immense noise and weight of falling water. I experienced a timeless, quiet quality that in retrospect I recognized as shock. Then the boat, which was no longer making noticeable progress against the current, turned and was rapidly pushed by the current and its motors out of the mist beneath the falls, back onto the open water for its return journey downstream. As my panic subsided, I found myself looking upward, following the falling water to the top of the falls, and scanning the width of the falls. Now I became aware again of the immense volume and force of the water, but I simultaneously recognized the tremendous precision of the power that was displayed. Each droplet occupied its proper place, with not a molecule violating the laws of physics. It was the lawful precision of the water that permitted the boat to go safely into the mist and the splashing spray. I wondered at and was grateful for the power of God.

The first portion of my experience was an instance of the *mysterium tremendum*, with its elements of awe, majesty, urgency, and mystery. The water took on "the *positive quality* of the 'wholly other'" (Otto 1950: 29)—dreadful, shocking, unthinking, and malign. The second portion of my experience, during the return trip, was an instance of "the Dionysiac element in the numen," the *fascinans* (ibid.: 31). The water was now fascinating, an invitation to reflect conceptually, where its fearfulness had previously made thinking impossible. The development of my contemplation of the power and natural lawfulness of the water into thoughts of God illustrates my conceptual unpacking of the immediate metaphor of the water. Experience of the *fascinans* implies but does not disclose "something more," and my theological understanding of the experience preserved the concept of "something more" even as I articulated the signified in theistic terms. As my religious experience continued, I named "something more" as God, but I conceptualized God as radically transcendent of anything I could think. The *fascinans* of the water was a manifest phenomenon whose experience implied the ulteriority of something more and, by so doing, disclosed itself, the *fascinans*, as a mediating agency.

Here is a self-report by the novelist Forrest Reid in which the relation of the *mysterium tremendum* and the *fascinans* again becomes transparent.

It was June, and I was supposed to be working for an intermediate examination, and had a book or two with me even on this blazing afternoon. It was hot and still. The breathless silence seemed unnatural, seemed, as I lay motionless in the tangled grass, like a bridge that reached straight back into the heart of some dim antiquity. I had a feeling of uneasiness, of unrest though I lay so still—of longing and excitement and expectation: I had a feeling that some veil might be drawn away, that there might come to me something, some one ...

My body seemed preternaturally sensitive, my blood moved quickly, I had an extraordinary feeling of struggle, as if some power were struggling to reach me as I was trying to reach it, as if there *was* something there, something waiting, if only I could get through. At that moment I longed for a sign, some definite and direct response, with a longing that was a kind of prayer. And a strange thing happened. For though there was no wind, a little green leafy branch was snapped off from the tree above me, and fell to the ground at my hand. I drew my breath quickly; there was a drumming in my ears; I knew that the green woodland before me was going to split asunder, to swing back on either side like two great painted doors ... And then—then I hesitated, blundered, drew back, failed. The moment passed, was gone, and at first gradually, and then rapidly, I felt the world I had so nearly reached slipping from me, till at last there was all around me only a pleasant summer scene, through which, from the hidden river below, there rose the distant voices and laughter of a passing boating-party. (Reid 1926: 113; as cited in Paffard 1976: 61)

> I have never believed in any formal religion, but I have experienced an emotion that seemed to me religious ... I tried to describe this, but I have been told that I merely described a landscape and a mood, and that the mood had nothing whatever to do with religion. Be this as it may, it was my nearest approach to it, and it was created by some power outside myself. (Reid 1940: 124–125; as cited in Paffard 1976: 61)

Reid knew "a feeling of uneasiness, of unrest" before his religious experience manifested. His feeling of anxiety signaled unconscious resistance to the experience. He presently became conscious of his conflict, as "an extraordinary feeling of struggle, as if some power were struggling to reach me as I was trying to reach it, as if there *was* something there, something waiting, if only I could get through." His sense that something more was just beyond reach ended, however, in a transformation of a *fascinans* into a *mysterium tremendum*. The scenery that had signified something more began itself to be wholly other: "I knew that the green woodland before me was going to split asunder, to swing back on either side like two great painted doors." Reid blamed himself for his failure to sustain the experience that he sought: "I hesitated, blundered, drew back, failed."

My Niagara Falls experience illustrates a psychoanalytic conclusion that I elsewhere explained through close analyses of self-reports of the sense of presence (Merkur 1999). When the boat left the immediate proximity of the falls, my fear dissipated, and my sense of numinosity changed from a *mysterium tremendum* to wonderment at a *fascinans*. In Reid's experience, anxiety prior to the manifestation of the *fascinans* prevented it from manifesting fully, instead converting it into a *mysterium tremendum*. In both cases, anxiety was the factor by which experiences of the *mysterium tremendum* differed from experiences of the *fascinans*. A single limit situation may evoke either or both experiences. When wonderment at the *fascinans* is aroused, the limit situation facilitates thoughts of something more. When anxiety complicates the wonderment, the limit situation is instead experienced as awesome and, in intense cases, as terrifying and dreadful. These negative emotions are inhibiting. They make thinking impossible. The limit situation is experienced in isolation or dissociation. It seems consequently to be alien or, in Otto's terms, wholly other. Coinciding with the isolation of the limit situation in consciousness, the inhibited ideas that constellate something more remain active unconsciously. They manifest consciously but only as they are displaced onto the limit situation, which they transform into a self-validating symbol, the *mysterium tremendum*. Rather than the radically or absolutely transcendent of the *via negativa*, the *mysterium tremendum* involves an idea of relative transcendence or, more precisely, immanence, as is consistent with the *via affirmativa*. Immanence is a symbol in the psychoanalytic sense of the term. It is an irrationally concretized metaphor whose latent content remains something more.

Religion as Delusion, Illusion, and Tenable Speculation

Otto's phenomenology of numinous experiences helps clarify a long-standing confusion in psychoanalytic discussions of religion. In "The Future of an Illusion," Freud ([1927] 1961) argued that religion functions to provide consolation for human limitations. The consolation is necessarily illusory (ibid.: 16–18). In making his case, Freud provided an original understanding and definition of the term 'illusion' (ibid.: 30–31): "An illusion is not the same thing as an error; nor is it necessarily an error ... What is characteristic of illusions is that they are derived from human wishes ... Illusions need not necessarily be false—that is to say, unrealizable or in contradiction to reality ... we call a belief an illusion when a wish-fulfilment is a prominent factor in its motivation, and in doing so we disregard its relation to reality, just as the illusion itself sets no store by verification."

In this formulation, it did not matter whether any given religious doctrine was illusory and valid or illusory and in error. For Freud's purposes, it sufficed that religious doctrines were illusory. "Of the reality value of most of them [religious doctrines] we cannot judge; just as they cannot be proved, so they cannot be refuted ... But scientific work is the only road which can lead us to a knowledge of reality outside ourselves" (Freud [1927] 1961: 31). Whether religious doctrines are right or wrong, they are not susceptible to proof but only to emotional preferences.

In "Civilization and Its Discontents," Freud revised his diagnosis of religion. He termed art an illusion, but religion a mass delusion.

> One can try to re-create the world, to build up in its stead another world in which its most unbearable features are eliminated and replaced by others that are in conformity with one's own wishes. But whoever, in desperate defiance, sets out upon this path to happiness will as a rule attain nothing. Reality is too strong for him. He becomes a madman ... A special importance attaches to the case in which this attempt to procure a certainty of happiness and a protection against suffering through a delusional remolding of reality is made by a considerable number of people in common. The religions of mankind must be classed among the mass-delusions of this kind. No one, needless to say, who shares a delusion ever recognizes it as such. (Freud [1930] 1961: 81)

Freud declined to suggest that religion was more fallacious, now that he called it a delusion, than it had been when he had called it an illusion. He asserted that delusions were a "desperate defiance" of reality that proceeded "in conformity with one's own wishes," but Freud ([1908] 1959) had consistently discussed phenomena as innocent and commonplace as daydreams in similarly alarmist language. For classical psychoanalysis, it was axiomatic that wish-fulfillments compensate for disappointing realities by flying in their face. In such a context, the "mass-delusion" of religion was only slightly worse than the "illusion" of art. The sole substantive difference that Freud adduced was the failure of mass-delusions to be recognized as such. Conversely, illusions are simply mass-delusions that are known to be such.

Freud's indecision as to whether religion is an illusion or a delusion may be clarified, I suggest, by reference to Otto's concepts of the *mysterium tremendum* and *fascinans*. A numinous experience occurs when a sense perception, a fantasy, a concept, or another mental content that concerns a limit situation acquires significance as a metaphor that signifies something more, something intrinsically transcendent of the limit situation. A *fascinans* results unless the experience is complicated by anxiety that collapses the numinous metaphor to become a *mysterium tremendum*, a numinous symbol that is paradoxically self-referring. Because the *mysterium tremendum* is always an ontologically self-validating wholly other, it is always a delusion. It is an unconscious symbol that is subject to the logical error that Whitehead ([1925] 1952) called "the fallacy of misplaced concreteness." Its psychic reality as a meaningful private symbol is wrongly treated as though it were an externally existing reality.

The *fascinans*, by contrast, always has the quality of a religious illusion that is known to be such. Because the *fascinans* is a metaphor that signifies something more than itself, its significance is always subject to interpretation. The possibility of equally plausible multiple interpretations always makes the "reality value" of the *fascinans* uncertain and hypothetical.

Freud's discussion of the illusory nature of religion was advanced by Winnicott (1953) in an article that drew attention to the infant's special attachment to its "first not-me possession," a cloth, teddy bear, or doll that the infant cannot bear to be without. Its importance for the infant is accepted by the family, given social validation through tolerant regard, and surrounded with appropriate ritualized behaviors. In a remarkable intuitive leap, Winnicott (ibid.: 230–231) extrapolated from the "transitional objects" of childhood to a general theory of culture: "I am … studying the substance of *illusion*, that which is allowed to the infant, and which in adult life is inherent in art and religion, and yet becomes the hallmark of madness when an adult puts too powerful a claim on the credulity of others, forcing them to acknowledge a sharing of illusion that is not their own. We can share a respect for illusory experience, and if we wish we may collect together and form a group on the basis of the similarity of our illusory experiences."

With these words, Winnicott endorsed Freud's claim that religion is an illusion. Subject neither to verification nor to falsification, an illusion's treatment as true proceeds out of the wish that it is so, rather than through logical necessity. At the same time, Winnicott reversed the diagnostic significance of illusions. He asserted that illusory experiences range from the transitional objects of infancy through play to creativity and the whole of cultural life. Because illusory experiences are unavoidable, they must be considered normal and healthy. In these contentions, there is little that necessarily differs from Róheim's (1943) view of culture as a system of projections that buffer the individual from natural reality. Winnicott's innovation consisted primarily of a hermeneutic move, a shift in perspective from Freud's rejection of illusion to his own embrace of it.

Winnicott unfortunately failed to offer criteria for deciding when illusion "becomes the hallmark of madness." He stated that illusion is replaced by delusion when a transitional object becomes a sexual fetish (Winnicott 1953: 241), but he did not extrapolate to the context of religion and culture. If some religion is illusory and respectable, some is illusory and mad. How are we to tell the difference? Winnicott (1971: 44) provided only general guidelines in his account of the therapeutic process: "Psychotherapy takes place in the overlap of two areas of playing, that of the patient and that of the therapist. Psycho-therapy has to do with two people playing together. The corollary of this is that where playing is not possible, then the work done by the therapist is directed toward bringing the patient from a state of not being able to play into a state of being able to play."

Pruyser (1974: 112) suggested that "adequate reality-testing is needed to keep the transitional sphere properly bounded, and its content and language consensually validated." Religions have historically permitted illusions to shade over into hallucination or delusion whenever "excessive fantasy formation" has led to "flagrant disregard of the obvious features of outer reality" (ibid.: 115). Pruyser (1983) later added that the integrity of religion as an illusion may also be threatened by an "overdone realism." Through reification, realism "can lead to smothering the imagination and thereby truncating human potentialities" (ibid.: 176). Realists "too fearful of the autistic fantasy going rampant" may additionally fear the illusionistic sphere and seek its abandonment or sup-pression as nonsense. Distortion through realism is also practiced, however, by religionists who apply the canons of knowledge to the concerns of faith. The result is a "slippage of ideas from the illusionistic sphere in which they belong into the realistic sphere where they make a poor fit with the demands of ordinary reality testing" (ibid.: 177). In Pruyser's view, the truth claims of religions may be valid if they are maintained as illusions—that is, as matters of faith—but they are definitely and necessarily false if they are presented as concrete realities.

One may grant Pruyser's point without conceding, however, that "it would be truly civilized if arguments for and against certain beliefs could be handled more playfully, like matters of taste, and without ponderous dissertations about the ultimate nature of reality" (Pruyser 1974: 166). Religion is not a case of *cha-cun à son goût*. People do not argue their religious preferences on subjective, aesthetic criteria. Devotees regularly make universal truth claims on behalf of their religions. Playfulness is warranted, but only to an extent that compares with the circumstance of science. In religion as in science, we deal at best with models, theories, and hypotheses that are open to discussion, but we hold them seriously as the best approximations to truth that we currently know.

Freud presupposed an empirical epistemology when he used the term 'illu-sion'. He assumed that our knowledge of truth is factual, but to his credit he made a career undermining his own epistemology by demonstrating the inevitable subjectivity of knowledge. Working, as I do, with the hermeneutic epistemology that is Freud's legacy, I am persuaded that the whole of abstract conceptualization consists precisely of illusions in Freud's sense of the term. Sense perceptions contain a factual component on which we place illusory spin. Abstract concepts consist of spin exclusively, and science is no exception. Scientific knowledge is intrinsically and inalienably speculative. Scientific findings are heuristic and provisional—never conclusive. They are at best tenable, and alternative conclusions may reasonably be tenable simultaneously.

Speculation is natural, normal, and wholesome in our species. The unwillingness to engage in tenable speculations merits suspicion. Where science addresses perceptible relations between existent quiddities, religion addresses limit situations; but the epistemological statuses of science and religion are otherwise equivalent. There is no avoiding speculation in either enterprise. The illusions of religion are not, as in art, matters of taste and opinion alone. In religion as in science, playfulness is limited to the range of rationally tenable conclusions. Religion is unobjectionable whenever it is speculative but tenable. That which is demonstrably wrong has no claim to serious consideration as knowledge.

Winnicott's conception of therapy as a kind of play may be applied, I suggest, to the phenomenological distinction between the *mysterium tremendum* and the *fascinans*. What is wholly other is always an instance of misplaced concreteness. It is subject to delusional thinking. It is not available for play. By contrast, what is only a sign of something more is available for play. As a sign, it is fascinating. It is subject to interpretation, that is, to hypothetical or illusory thinking. A patient who cannot approach religion playfully, who is fixated on awe at the *mysterium tremendum*, requires a therapy that opens onto wonderment at something more.

Splitting the Sacred and the Profane

Otto's phenomenology of numinous experience differs in several ways from the sociology of the sacred that was initiated by Durkheim. Otto was concerned with subjective human experience, Durkheim with a social status. It was immaterial to Durkheim whether what society designated as sacred was personally experienced as numinous; and it was irrelevant to Otto whether what was personally experienced as numinous was designated by society as sacred. The two categories, numinous experience and sacred status, are partly overlapping, but each includes data that are not addressed by the other.

Durkheim started from the premise that people everywhere impose a dualistic view of the cosmos that categorizes it into the sacred and the profane. Religion pertained to the sacred. It is "a unified system of beliefs and practices relative to sacred things, that is to say, things set apart and forbidden—beliefs and practices which unite into one single moral community called a Church, all those who adhere to them" (Durkheim [1915] 1976: 47). The opposition of the sacred and the profane entails several possibilities of transition. What is profane can sometimes be consecrated, sanctified, or hallowed; conversely, the sacred can be deconsecrated, desecrated, or profaned.

Numinous experience, as Otto conceptualized it, differs significantly. It can be neither made nor unmade. Its circumstance is instead comparable to aesthetic experience. Numinosity is in the eye of the beholder. Anything can be numinous. Nothing is numinous necessarily. When a thing is experienced as numinous, it has been found or discovered to be numinous. A thing that is experienced as numinous on one occasion may not be experienced in the same way on others. One can cultivate an aptitude for experiencing things as numinous, but numinous experience cannot be produced on demand. It is not meaningful to speak of the numinous as having an opposite any more than the aesthetic has one. Just as the category of the aesthetic can be differentiated into a spectrum that ranges from the beautiful to the ugly, so the numinous can be resolved into a spectrum that includes the divine, angelic, miraculous, ghostly, and demonic. The concept of the profane does not belong on the spectrum and is irrelevant to it.

Although what has status as sacred can be experienced as numinous, much that is sacred is not so experienced. In cross-cultural perspective, anything can be sacred, and nothing is necessarily sacred. The emic view within each culture differs, however, from the etic perspective of comparativists. Within any culture, some things are intrinsically sacred and can be defiled or desecrated, others can be consecrated and deconsecrated, and still others cannot be anything but profane. These possibilities are fixed by social conventions, and personal experiences of the numinous do not ordinarily alter them.

Academic efforts to harmonize the two phenomena, numinous experience and sacred status, confound rather than clarify. Numinosity is found; sacrality is made. Numinosity is a naturally occurring category of human values. It consists of awe and wonderment—that is, it consists of wonderment with or without the addition of anxiety. Numinosity can be mystical; everything can be seen as numinous. Sacrality, by contrast, never occurs alone. It is always implicitly conceptualized as one term of an implicit pair. The sacred is always opposed to the profane. The sacred is pure, and there is always a danger of impurity, which is to say, of profanation, desecration, deconsecration, and so forth (Douglas 1966).

Durkheim ([1915] 1976) regarded the sacred as a collective representation, that is, a culturally shared symbol, for the moral authority of society. His formulation compares with Freud's ([1907] 1959, [1913] 1958) original regard for religious ritual as symbolic behavior that displaces "social instincts"—a concept that he later replaced with the super-ego, the moral agency of the psyche. The problem with these views is their inconsistency with the data. Native North American religions, for example, do not include ethics. Prior to Christian influences, Amerindian cultures endorsed ethics on criteria that we may consider secular, pragmatic, and humanistic (Cooper 1931). Religion in these cultures had to do with human relations with the gods and spirits, the accommodation and acquisition of sacred power. Similarly, a "conception of supernatural beings as deeply concerned about the behavior of humans toward one another ... appears to be largely lacking ... in much of Asia and in animism and folk religions generally" (Stark 2004: 470).

Durkheim's account of the sacred fits the orthodox rabbinic tradition in which he was raised much more closely than it does the Aboriginal Australian religions that he contrived to present as moral systems. Polytheistic religions attribute specific taboos to specific gods and spirits, each for individual reasons. The Polynesian concept of *tabu* (set apart) appears in Western scholarship as a generic category, but it pertains to both the avoidance of the polluting of and circumspection toward the sacred (Steiner [1956] 1967: 59–77, 80–86). What is taboo is whatever pertains to a god or spirit whom one wishes to avoid. Also taboo is whatever a revered god or spirit happens to prohibit, as a matter of the entity's personal and often arbitrary preferences.

Not only is the sacred at perpetual risk of defilement, but it is inherently dangerous. It is taboo, off limits, not to be violated. "Everything that is touched by a holy person is consecrated by this very act and can only be used by them … Contact with it is fatal. The divine and the accursed, consecration and defilement, have exactly the same effects upon profane objects. They render them untouchable, withdraw them from circulation, and communicate to them their formidable qualities" (Caillois 1959: 52). The danger of the sacred can be managed, however, through purity. "Purity is acquired by submitting to a set of ritualistic observances. The point above all is to become separated from the profane world in order to make possible the penetration of the sacred world without peril" (ibid.: 38). Free-floating anxiety may be detected in the anxious circumstances that surround the sacred: the perpetual risk of its defilement, its intrinsic danger, and the need for fastidious purity in relation to it. Insofar as what is sacred, in a sociological sense, bears a relation to numinous experience, the element of anxiety indicates that we are dealing in some way with a *mysterium tremendum*, though the relationship is not ordinarily apparent.

I would like to suggest that in psychoanalytic terms, the dualism of the sacred and the profane is symptomatic of the automatization (Hartmann 1958) of numinous experience. Rather than a fresh and immediate manifestation of the unconscious, a *mysterium tremendum* is installed preconsciously within the ego as a more or less stable structure within the personality. Jung (1938: 52–53) described this process as a defense: "What is usually and generally called 'religion' is to such an amazing degree a substitute that … has the obvious purpose of replacing immediate experience by a choice of suitable symbols invested in a solidly organized dogma and ritual … As long as these … work, people are effectively defended and shielded against immediate religious experience. Even if something of the sort should happen to them, they can refer to the church, for it would know whether the experience … was to be accepted or to be rejected." To explain what he meant by "immediate experience," Jung listed "passionate conflicts, panics of madness, desperate confusions and depressions which were grotesque and terrible at the same time" (ibid.: 53). For present purposes, it will suffice to refer to the *mysterium tremendum*.

I understand the phenomenology of the sacred and the profane in terms of two theoretic processes: repression, followed by a partial return of the repressed. When the anxiety that converts an instance of the *fascinans* into a *mysterium tremendum* is sufficiently intense to be paralyzing and traumatic, the ego is unable to resolve the experience into its components and may instead repress the *mysterium tremendum* as a whole. Because Freud regarded the return of the repressed as a failure of defense against quantities of energy that were too great for the stimulus barrier to contain, he regarded the therapeutic value of the latent content of symbols as a fortuitous accident. In my model (Merkur 2001), the return of the repressed is not part of the illness process; rather, it is an initial phase of the healing. Its therapeutic value is no accident. Once unconscious, the repressed *mysterium tremendum* no longer threatens the executive function of the psyche with paralysis and is instead made a topic of unconscious analysis and reflection—in my view, by the creative problem-solving function of the unconscious. The incubation of creative ideas surrounding repressed materials includes symbol formation in order to evade the ego's repressing function and become known, however partially and symbolically, to consciousness.

In Freud's theory of defense, the ego avoids the lability of ever-changing symbolic displacements by installing selected symptoms as routine components of the preconscious ego (Merkur 2005: 37–39). Made part of the preconscious ego, the symptom—in the present instance, the displacement of an unconscious *mysterium tremendum* as a preconscious duality of the sacred and the profane—becomes part of the ego's sense of reality, corrupting it and undergoing reification in the process. The emotionally intense numinous experience is repressed, while an emotionally desensitized substitute is available to consciousness. In the process, the numinosity becomes unavailable for play.

In the case of a repressed *mysterium tremendum*, its unconscious analysis into components is typically symbolized by motifs that are manifestly split into a duality. Splitting is a distinctive type of symbol formation that is much discussed in Kleinian object relations theory (Grotstein 1981). Splitting retreats from realistic perceptions by generating a pair of opposing fantasies: idealization on the one hand and an equally excessive devaluation on the other. In the case of the sacred and the profane, one part of the duality idealizes the positive aspects of the *mysterium tremendum* as sacred, and the other part abhors the negative aspects as profane. The unconscious understanding that the anxiety attached to the numinous is not itself numinous manifests symbolically as an aversion to, and possibly also a conscious anxiety concerning, the profane. At the same time, the split-off, idealized, and emotionally flattened remainder of the *mysterium tremendum* manifests consciously as the sacred.

This return of the repressed is a partial and displaced manifestation of the *mysterium tremendum*. It is not a realistic analysis of the *mysterium tremendum* that would resolve it into its component *fascinans* and anxiety. It is a compromise formation, a substitute, that replaces numinous experience with a duality of the sacred and the profane.

Concluding Reflections

This article is an initial or preliminary discussion of a psychoanalytic approach to religious sublimations at their level of sublimation. Much work remains to be accomplished, both clinically and conceptually, to develop these ideas further. The major points I have made are as follows:

1. For clinical purposes, numinous experiences are the stuff of religion.
2. Numinous experiences are cognitive and emotional responses to limit situations that treat limit situations as metaphors in order to conceptualize the transcendent.
3. Numinous experiences are optimally wondrous. They are instances of the *fascinans* of Otto. They involve awareness that religious metaphors are metaphors and also involve consciousness of something more, which may or may not be elaborated theistically. The experiences are illusory, in the terminology of both Freud and Winnicott; but it is more appropriate to liken them to passionate engagements with scientific ideas. They are speculative but tenable, rational but not necessarily true.
4. Numinous experiences are alternatively greeted with anxiety as well as wonder. The experiences then fall on a spectrum that ranges from awesome to awful. Their symbolic character is not recognized as such. They become subject to the fallacy of misplaced concreteness, and they appear wholly other. Otto termed this category of experiences the *mysterium tremendum*, Freud's term "delusion" applies. It is irrational.
5. Clinical management of a *mysterium tremendum* proceeds by addressing the anxiety that attends the awe. The relief from anxiety facilitates a metaphoric sensibility, transforms the awe into wonderment, and enables a patient who cannot play with religious ideas to become able to play.
6. Religious concerns with the sacred and the profane are symptoms of the repression of numinous experiences. The splitting of the *mysterium tremendum* into the sacred and the profane reduces consciousness of anxiety. The immediate clinical task is to enable the patient to become conscious of the anxiety, to be able to tolerate its full manifestation, and so to be able to experience the *mysterium tremendum* consciously. It would then become appropriate to begin the further task of becoming reflective about the *mysterium tremendum*, in order to transform awe into wonderment.

Why are these shifts in religious experience clinically valuable? An analyst's interpretations of the sacred and the profane in terms of the *mysterium tremendum*, and of the *mysterium tremendum* in terms of the *fascinans*, will provoke resistance in many or most religious devotees. The resistance will stem from the same parts of the personality and will be fixations on the same issues that would be provoked through a conventional psychoanalytic dialogue on the analysand's autobiography—or, in child analysis, through engagement of a child in play. The dynamic resistance is all one and the same. The analyst's point of entry, the point of arousing the resistance and provoking the transference onto the analyst, can as easily and as efficiently be religion as anything else. And the work of therapy can be advanced through a psychoanalytic dialogue on the patient's religiosity and its interpretation as a projection or transference onto something more that repeats aspects of early object relations. It is a question of speaking to the patient about how his or her religious experiences, beliefs, and practices replicate unconscious patterns of fantasy that have prevailed from childhood onward, and how the patient's religiosity fails to pertain to a playful, adult conception of something more.

Whether knowledge of something more is repressed but symbolized in the sacred or a *mysterium tremendum*, or is manifest in a *fascinans*, the concept of something more is implicit in all religiosity and regularly serves as a "transferential figure" (Jacob Arlow, in Grossman 1963: 760). Clinical work may proceed by analyzing the transference projections onto something more, precisely as transferences onto a psychoanalyst may be analyzed. The analyst's interpretations may then be described, in familiar Judeo-Christian terms, as theological analyses of the patient's personal religiosity. The analysis proceeds, however, not merely to identify theological errors, but to determine the sources of the errors in fantasies that arise out of childhood object relations.

Dan Merkur is a psychoanalyst in private practice in Toronto. He holds a doctorate in comparative religion and has taught at McMaster, Queen's, Syracuse, and York Universities, and the University of Toronto. He has published many articles and 11 books, most recently *Unconscious Wisdom: A Superego Function in Dreams, Conscience, and Inspiration* (2001), *Psychoanalytic Approaches to Myth* (2005), and *Crucified with Christ: Meditation on the Passion, Mystical Death, and the Medieval Invention of Psychotherapy* (2006).

References

Bachofen, J. J. 1967. *Myth, Religion, and Mother Right: Selected Writings*. Trans. R. Manheim. Princeton, NJ: Princeton University Press.

Caillois, R. 1959. *Man and the Sacred*. Trans. M. Barash. New York: Free Press. Repr., Urbana and Chicago: University of Illinois Press, 2001.

Cohen, J. M., and J.-F. Phipps. 1992. *The Common Experience: Signposts on the Path to Enlightenment*. Wheaton, IL: Quest Books/Theosophical Publishing House.

Cooper, J. M. 1931. "The Relations between Religion and Morality in Primitive Culture." *Primitive Man* 4, no. 3: 33–48.

Devereux, G. 1958. "Cultural Thought Models in Primitive and Modern Psychiatric Theories." *Psychiatry* 21: 359–374.

_____. 1970. "Normal and Abnormal: The Key Concepts of Ethnopsychiatry." Pp. 113–136 in *Man and His Culture: Psychoanalytic Anthropology after 'Totem and Taboo,'* ed. W. Muensterberger. New York: Taplinger Publishing Company.

Douglas, M. 1966. *Purity and Danger: An Analysis of the Concepts of Pollution and Taboo*. Repr., London: Routledge & Kegan Paul, 1978.

Durkheim, E. [1915] 1976. *The Elementary Forms of the Religious Life*. 2nd ed. Trans. J. W. Swain. London: George Allen & Unwin Ltd.

Ellwood, R. S., Jr. 1980. *Mysticism and Religion*. Englewood Cliffs, NJ: Prentice-Hall, Inc.

Freud, S. [1900] 1958. "The Interpretation of Dreams." Pp. 1–625 in *Standard Edition*, vols. 4–5.

_____. [1907] 1959. "Obsessive Acts and Religious Practices." Pp. 117–127 in *Standard Edition*, vol. 9.

_____. [1908] 1959. "Creative Writers and Day-Dreaming." Pp. 143–153 in *Standard Edition*, vol. 9.

_____. [1913] 1958. "Totem and Taboo: Some Points of Agreement between the Mental Lives of Savages and Neurotics." Pp. xiii–162 in *Standard Edition*, vol. 13.

_____. [1927] 1961. "The Future of an Illusion." Pp. 5–56 in *Standard Edition*, vol. 21.

_____. [1930] 1961. "Civilization and Its Discontents." Pp. 64–145 in *Standard Edition*, vol. 21.

_____. 1953–1974. *The Standard Edition of the Complete Psychological Works of Sigmund Freud*. 24 vols. Trans. and ed. J. Strachey, with A. Freud, A. Strachey, and A. Tyson. London: Hogarth Press. (Cited as *Standard Edition*.)

Grossman, L. 1993. "The Significance of Religious Themes and Fantasies during Psychoanalysis." *Journal of the American Psychoanalytic Association* 41, no. 3: 755–764.

Grotstein, J. S. 1981. *Splitting and Projective Identification*. New York: Jason Aronson.

Haartman, K. 2004. *Watching and Praying: Personality Transformation in Eighteenth Century British Methodism*. Amsterdam and New York: Rodopi.

Hartmann, H. 1958. *Ego Psychology and the Problem of Adaptation*. New York: International Universities Press.

Huxley, J. 1970. *Memories*. London: George Allen & Unwin.

James, W. [1902] 1958. *The Varieties of Religious Experience: A Study in Human Nature*. Reprinted New York: New American Library.

Jung, C. G. 1938. *Psychology and Religion*. New Haven, CT: Yale University Press.

Merkur, D. 1993. "Mythology into Metapsychology: Freud's Misappropriation of Romanticism." Pp. 345–360 in *The Psychoanalytic Study of Society*, vol. 18, ed. L. B. Boyer, R. M. Boyer, and S. M. Sonnenberg. Hillsdale, NJ: Analytic Press.

_____. 1995–1996. "'And He Trusted in Yahweh': The Transformation of Abram in Gen. 12–13 and 15." *Journal of Psychology of Religion* 4–5: 65–88.

_____. 1996. "The Numinous as a Category of Values." Pp. 104–123 in *The Sacred and Its Scholars: Comparative Methodologies for the Study of Primary Religious Data*, ed. T. A. Idinopulos and E. A. Yonan. Leiden: E. J. Brill.

_____. 1999. *Mystical Moments and Unitive Thinking*. Albany, NY: State University of New York Press.

_____. 2001. *Unconscious Wisdom: A Superego Function in Dreams, Conscience, and Inspiration*. Albany: State University of New York Press.

_____. 2004. "Psychotherapeutic Change in the Book of Job." Pp. 119–139 in *Psychology and the Bible: A New Way to Read the Scriptures*. Vol. 2: *From Genesis to Apocalyptic*, ed J. H. Ellens and W. G. Rollins. New York: Greenwood-Praeger Publishers.

_____. 2005. *Psychoanalytic Approaches to Myth: Freud and the Freudians*. New York and London: Routledge.

Nietzsche, F. 1956. *The Birth of Tragedy* [1887] and *The Genealogy of Morals*. Trans. F. Golffing. Garden City, NY: Doubleday.

Otto, R. 1950. *The Idea of the Holy: An Inquiry into the Non-rational Factor in the Idea of the Divine and Its Relation to the Rational*. (1st German ed., 1917.) 2nd ed., trans. J. W. Harvey. London: Oxford University Press.

Paffard, M. 1973. *Inglorious Wordsworths: A Study of Some Transcendental Experiences in Childhood and Adolescence*. London: Hodder and Stoughton.

_____. 1976. *The Unattended Moment: Excerpts from Autobiographies with Hints and Guesses*. London: SCM Press Ltd.

Pfister, O. 1932. "Instinctive Psychoanalysis among the Navahos." *Journal of Nervous and Mental Disease* 76: 234–254.

Pruyser, P. W. 1974. *Belief and Unbelief*. New York: Harper & Row.

_____. 1983. *The Play of Imagination: Toward a Psychoanalysis of Culture*. New York: International Universities Press.

Reid, F. 1926. *Apostate*. London: Constable.

_____. 1940. *Private Road*. London: Faber & Faber.

Róheim, G. 1943. *The Origin and Function of Culture*. New York: Nervous and Mental Disease Monographs.

Rowse, A. L. 1942. *A Cornish Childhood*. London: Jonathan Cape.

Stark, R. 2004. "SSR Presidential Address, 2004: Putting an End to Ancestor Worship." *Journal for the Scientific Study of Religion* 43, no. 4: 465–475.

Steiner, F. [1956] 1967. *Taboo*. Harmondsworth, UK: Penguin Books.

Whitehead, A. N. [1925] 1952. *Science in the Modern World*. 2nd ed. New York: Mentor Books.

Winnicott, D. W. 1953. "Transitional Objects and Transitional Phenomena: A Study of the First Not-Me Possession." *International Journal of Psycho-analysis* 34: 89–97. Repr. pp. 229–242 in *Through Paediatrics to Psycho-Analysis: Collected Papers*. New York: Basic Books, 1958; repr. Brunner/Mazel Publishers, 1992.

_____. 1971. *Playing and Reality*. London: Tavistock Publications. Repr. Harmondsworth, UK: Penguin Books Ltd., 1974.

Wuthnow, R. 1978. "Peak Experiences: Some Empirical Tests." *Journal of Humanistic Psychology* 18, no. 3: 59–75.

Chapter 10

THE RELIGION OF PSYCHOANALYSIS, OR ODE TO A NIGHTINGALE

Shahid Najeeb

Freud would probably have been horrified by the title of this article, for we all know about his intense antagonism toward religion, which he regarded as little more than "the universal obsessional neurosis of humanity" (Freud [1927] 1961: 43). He considered the obsessive magical thoughts and the compulsive rituals that are such central parts of any religion as methods of dealing with anxiety: "[D]evout believers are safeguarded against the risk of certain neurotic illnesses; their acceptance of the universal neurosis spares them the task of constructing a personal one." It is an interpretation that religious people would understandably not concur with, for they think of religion as being something unworldly, something that reaches beyond our human existence. I would not be surprised if religious people judged psychoanalysts, who are mostly atheists, quite severely.

References for this chapter begin on page 237.

However, in the last 20 years or so, there has been a change within psycho-analysis toward religion. Certain psychoanalysts now feel that Freud was per-haps a bit hasty and harsh in his criticisms of religion. These psychoanalysts would probably remain sympathetic to Freud's opinion of orthodox religion, but they would say that within all religions there are streams that can be called spiritual. It is mainly toward these spiritual streams, rather than orthodox religion as such, that there has been a shift in attitude. This shift is basically sympathetic toward the spirituality of religion. Some psychoanalysts, such as Neville Symington (1994: 171), now regard psychoanalysis, at its best, as being a spiritual act. Rachel Blass (2004: 614–634) has recently reviewed and summarized these developments within psychoanalysis. Her basic position is that psychoanalysis has softened Freud's harsh criticism by accepting and rejecting various aspects of religion and by crediting the illusions of religion as being valuable and growth promoting, if they can be understood as transitional objects and phenomena as described by Winnicott (1951: 229–242). In seeking a rapprochement with traditional religion, Blass reasons that both religion and psychoanalysis are searching for truth and that both are based on unconscious memories of early infantile experiences.

I mention these developments in psychoanalysis to emphasize that this presentation is not an attempt to enter these debates, which are mainly about content that can be variously described in Symington's terminology as the dis-tinction between primitive and mature religions or the transformation of bad actions into good. This article, on the other hand, is about the process of reli-gion, that is, the reason why religion exists in the first place. The point of view that will be put forward here is completely indifferent to what kind of religion we are talking about, for what I have to say applies equally to the most primi-tive and the most mature of religions. Likewise, this discussion is indifferent to the aims of religion, whether they are ecstatic, moral, or growth promoting. It is merely the existence of religion that is examined, and it is in this context that psychoanalysis too is examined. For just as we ask, why does religion exist in the first place? we equally ask, why psychoanalysis?

It is the contention of this article that the processes that result in religion are also the processes that result in psychoanalysis and also that these processes are necessary and inevitable. We could not be without them. So there is no attempt here to bring about a rapprochement of psychoanalysis with religion, but much more to illustrate that psychoanalysis is a *form* of religion. This is not because we regard Freud as a modern prophet and his writings as holy writ (though many people might think that is why psychoanalysis is a religion). It is because there is an organic, evolutionary process in mental development that results inevitably in mental creations that go by the name of religion or psychoanalysis. Implicit in this statement is a plea to open one's mind to the phenomenon known as religion and to not be close-minded the moment that the word 'religion' is mentioned.

I will structure this article in the unfashionable Kantian model of thesis, antith-esis, and synthesis. It would appall many literary critics, and certainly all poets, for me to put the burden of this structure on Keats's poem, "Ode to a Nightingale."

Yet I have found it useful to do so, if only to emphasize that poetry is as much a repository of emotional truth as psychoanalysis and religion, and that all three serve very similar human purposes. It is for this reason that Keats's poem shares the title of this presentation. There are many ways in which this marvelous ode can be read, but rather brutishly I will reduce it to the thesis, the painfulness of the human condition; the antithesis, the escape from it; and finally the synthesis, the substance of this article. What follows first is the thesis.

The Pain of Human Existence

The human condition is extremely painful. In his invocation to the nightingale, Keats ([1861] 1906: 255–257) describes the tragedy of our human lives:

> Fade far away, dissolve, and quite forget
>   What thou among the leaves hast never known,
> The weariness, the fever, and the fret
>   Here, where men sit and hear each other groan;
> Where palsy shakes a few, sad, last grey hairs,
>   Where youth grows pale, and specter-thin, and dies;
>   Where but to think is to be full of sorrow
>   And leaden-eyed despairs,
> Where beauty cannot keep her lustrous eyes,
>   Or new Love pine at them beyond tomorrow.

Few descriptions of the realities of human life are as accurate, beautiful, and economical as these few lines. It is not possible to live and be free of old age, sickness, and death. Further, what appears beautiful cannot remain so, and it is also not possible to think without being filled with "sorrow and leaden-eyed despairs." Since this is the painful truth of our lives, there is much motivation to escape it, which forms the antithesis of existence.

The Birth of Soul, God, and Immortality

Now let us move to the antithesis, the escape from the pain of existence. Since time immemorial, humankind has sought comfort in the belief that pain and mortality can be circumvented by some kind of life after death or some kind of immortality. Keats expresses it in this way:

> Thou wast not born for death, immortal Bird!
>   No hungry generations tread thee down;
> The voice I hear this passing night was heard
>   In ancient days by emperor and clown:
> Perhaps the self-same song that found a path
>   Through the sad heart of Ruth, when, sick for home,
>   She stood in tears amid the alien corn;

The same that oft-times hath
Charm'd magic casements, opening on the foam
Of perilous seas, in faery lands forlorn.

However, it is not entirely accurate to state that the concept of immortality came into existence purely as a means to escape the pain of mortality. It is more likely that once the idea of immortality was established, it was used to evade the misery of existence. Of course no one can establish with certainty the origins of such an ancient idea, but it is highly likely that the notion came into existence concomitant with sentience becoming established. I will use the term 'sentience' to mean not merely being aware, but being aware of that awareness. The moment that the mind becomes aware of itself, it has, so to speak, stepped outside of itself and is observing itself. From here it is but a small step to think of the observing function being independent. Since this function does not have physical characteristics, it implies the existence of something that is other than body, something other than mind, something that stands above both, observing both. This is a crucial point in human developmental history, for it is at this juncture that the painfulness of human existence also comes into being. To put it another way, were it not for sentience, the human condition would not be painful. It is not possible to become aware of our existence and not simultaneously become painfully aware of what lies ahead of all of us—namely, old age, sickness, and death. But it is just at this point when sentience comes into being that God, religion, psychology, and soul theory also come into being. I will take each in turn.

Sentience

The special feature of human sentience is that humans are aware of their sense perceptions and their consciousness—and they are aware of that awareness. I see consciousness as a logical evolution of the development of sense perception. Further, I see awareness of that consciousness as an evolution of this same process. It is in this way that stardust, and hence the universe, becomes able first to perceive, then to be conscious, and then to be aware of that consciousness. Nor is this awareness of consciousness confined only to the species experiencing it, for species that are conscious become aware of all else in the universe that exists, consciously or non-consciously. We are seeing an interesting elaboration of this in the conservation movement, where the awareness of one species not only takes into account the existence of other species, but also attempts to serve the interests of these other species by acting on their behalf. Another way of stating this is that humans are functioning as the surrogate mind of both sentient and insentient stardust.

We will have more to say about the centrality of the process of one part of the mind serving to foster the development of other parts of the mind in the development of thought, but for now I want to point out only the evolution of human sentience. In keeping with this developmental scheme, I think it is only the most developed of human minds that are capable of being aware of other minds and serving as surrogate minds for all forms of stardust. It is interesting that psycho-analytic thinking, through a very different paradigm, that of emotional develop-ment, comes to exactly the same conclusion, namely, that care, concern, and compassion for other beings are features of only the healthiest and most devel-oped of human minds. And religious thinking, through yet another paradigm, that of prophet, messiah, or Godly incarnation, preserves in the personalities of these exceptional individuals the same qualities of care, concern, and compassion.

The Development of God and Religion

This brief discussion of the evolution and development of human consciousness, including self-awareness, brings us to another interesting conclusion. If we imag-ine the human mind as functioning as the surrogate mind for the rest of creation, we are but a short step away from the concept of God, who by all accounts func-tions as the mind for the rest of creation. There is nothing that God is not aware of and nothing that God cannot do. This expresses both sentience and the infinite possibilities of the mind. It also suggests a caring and protective function, essen-tially a parental function, which, to wit, is the other leg that God stands on.

I think it would be fair to say that God is an expression of both supra-con-sciousness, that is, consciousness becoming aware of itself, and the projection of our long dependence on our parents. The two are probably interdependent, for it seems that a necessary feature of development is the dimension of time. It takes time for anything to develop, and the more complex the development, the longer it seems to take. Unicellular organisms divide and in that way instantly reproduce fully developed organisms that are developmentally identical to the original organism. More complex organisms require more time to reach the same developmental level as that of the original or parental organism. So it is not sur-prising that the human organism, the most complex organism on Earth, takes the longest period to develop. Within the human organism, the most complex and highly organized organ, that of the mind, requires the most time. We discover that humans spend about a quarter of their lives developing to reach the full mental potential of their parents. In this long period they are dependent on paren-tal minds to a greater or lesser extent. It is to be expected that this long period of incubation should result in the formation of a structural element in the human mind reflecting the necessity of one part of the mind being dependent on another, child upon parents, or human beings upon God. In this way, God is a feature of both supra-consciousness, which takes a long time to fully develop, and the incu-bational parental function necessary for this development. This is not to say that there cannot be ecstatic experiences in which there is a sense of being one with God. The two structures are experienced as one indivisible whole.

The Birth of Psychology

It is well known that the predecessor of astronomy was astrology, which has a factual element. This factual element is based on the movements of the planets and distant stars, and there is no reason to suggest, given that everything in our world is dependent on everything else, that all stardust should not be inter-dependent on other stardust. But mixed in with this factual element are the very human elements of desire, omnipotence, and magic. Chemistry likewise emerged from a mixture: the factual and fantastic elements of alchemy. In the same way, psychology is emerging from ancient soul theory, which also has factual elements woven in with the magical. Nor has psychology emerged com-pletely from this process, for there remain elements in it that are either magical or that deny the existence of the mind altogether.

For those who are offended by the contention that our discipline is the latest offspring of soul theory, we have only to provide evidence of this parentage. The DNA link is unmistakable. The DNA of all thought is the language that carries and communicates it, with an infinite variety of phenotypic manifesta-tions. The root for both 'psychology' and 'psychoanalysis' is the Greek term 'psyche', which the *Concise Oxford Dictionary* describes as "breath, life, soul or spirit." Since we shy away from acknowledging our parentage and from accepting that our science is merely the latest version of soul theory, we are not able to truly benefit from examining our roots and the rich harvest of meaning its investigation might reveal. For instance, we are not then able, as Otto Rank (1930) has done brilliantly, to explore the whole purpose of soul belief, which is to assert human control, such as astrology and alchemy, over the forces of nature. The force of nature that we are particularly concerned with here is mortality. For if psyche is breath, life, soul, or spirit, the whole purpose of soul belief is to control and preserve it, so that it does not willy-nilly slip through our fingers. In other words, soul belief is concerned with ensuring some mea-sure of immortality. I am not suggesting that this is deliberate, planned, or conscious. In fact, the roots of soul belief remain largely unconscious. Before proceeding any further, something needs to be said about mortality.

Mortality and Soul Theory

Mortality has always been problematic for humans, for unlike all other living creatures, only humans are able to imagine and anticipate their own deaths. Of course, other creatures also will do anything to survive, and it could be said that their struggle for survival is based on some kind of unconscious recogni-tion of death. But this recognition is not, as far as I am aware, ever a conscious knowledge of death. Only humans can think of it, be aware of it, plan for it, and communicate about it. The fact that we are able in this way to be conscious of our death and the death of all those around us does not mean that we can eas-ily accept it. This is because life is very dear to us, as it is to all creatures, and because of something much more basic. I think we do not sufficiently appreciate the fact of sentience in the manner I have described. We are constantly aware of the world we live in but are simultaneously also aware of our being aware. This awareness of our being aware is sometimes called 'consciousness of our internal world', because awareness of being aware is a whole inner world of enormous complexity that in many ways mirrors the external world. So deep is this sense of inner watchfulness that it is not possible to imagine it not being there. For instance, when we think of our death, we are nevertheless present in thinking about it. It is almost as if even when we die, our state of consciousness will continue. We cannot imagine ever being without it—alive or dead.

It is in this way that the idea of mortality does not come easily to us. Of course, we do not want to die, but we are also not truly able to imagine dying, for we are always there watching the death. It is never a mere extinction. It is, I believe, this central fact that has had a profound influence on the origins of soul theory. We can see from these considerations that when we die, some part of us continues to watch this dying, a part that could perhaps be called our soul. Thus, we can say that we die but the soul persists. Soul theory exists not only to deny the fact of death, though this is a very important element in all soul belief, but also because of the phenomenal impossibility of imagining such an event. On the other hand, for this very reason it is very easy to imagine the psyche or soul continuing after the extinction of the physical body.

What compounds the problem even further are credible reports of rebirth (Story 1975). These are not all hoaxes, and even one tenable account is sufficient to suggest that something persists after physical death. I am not acquainted with this phenomenon, but reading a number of instances draws one's attention to two features that are fairly constant. The first is that the death of the person who is reborn is usually premature and often traumatic. Apart from reports of the rebirths of Tibetan lamas, I have not come across an account of an old person dying who is then reborn. The second fairly constant feature is that rebirth generally takes place in geographical proximity, usually within the same region or country. It is extremely rare for it to occur in some distant global region, though such instances have been reported. Since I am a psychoanalyst, I tend to reach for familiar psychoanalytical theories, such as projective identification. It might be that rebirth is a special form of this process, but if it is, the whole theory will need to be rewritten. Until that happens, I am content to let phenomena exist that I do not understand without either discrediting them or drawing them forcibly into areas of recognized experience. I mention rebirth here and the associated Tibetan *bardo*, or interval between death and rebirth, merely to highlight the fact that these phenomena contribute to our problem with accepting mortality as being a clearly defined, clean line that limits life. On the other hand, it is this very blurring, this leaking, along with the impossibility of being able to imagine our deaths, that leads to the creation of soul theory.

One particular form of soul theory is of special interest to me—the one that goes by the name of psychoanalysis. I will try to explain why I think psychoanalysis is just one of the latest versions of soul theory.

Psychoanalysis as Soul Theory

Probably the deepest link that psychoanalysis has with soul theory is through the concept of the unconscious, which is central to all psychoanalytic theories. There are of course many different schools of psychoanalysis and many psychoanalytic theories, but to the best of my knowledge, there is none that does not have the unconscious forming an important part of that theory. Of course, what it is that is unconscious, how it affects our everyday lives, and how we might influence it will vary with the theory. But it would be hard to imagine something that goes by the name of psychoanalysis that did not have some formulation about the unconscious. What is so important about the unconscious? I will offer some suggestions.

First, when we talked about other creatures not being aware of their death, I mentioned that their behavior might suggest an unconscious awareness of death, that is, maybe things go on in the organism that the organism is not aware of. We also talked about unicellular organisms having, if you like, an unconscious awareness of propagation, otherwise, why propagate? This sense of things happening in the organism that the organism is not aware of, but which are nevertheless essential and central to that organism, goes back a long way. Freud always talked about his own version of the unconscious, and we in turn talk about Freud's version, as if it is the only version of unconscious that exists. Perhaps we do not sufficiently understand how deep and how central this concept is to all forms of life, for it is an essential feature, albeit unconscious, of all life to desire to continue living and to propagate that state. So if psychoanalysis is about life and if an unconscious desire to live and propagate is central to life, then it is not mere coincidence that the unconscious is central to psychoanalysis.

Secondly, Freud's understanding and description of the unconscious came from his interpretation of dreams. Since antiquity our ancestor's soul theories were heavily reliant on dreams, for it was dreams more than anything else that demonstrated the incontrovertible existence of the soul. When one sleeps, one is dead to the external world, but the internal world (or soul) is very much alive in dreams. Dreams have long been seen as evidence of the soul's independence from the body and hence of its immortality. To this day, people view their dreams as not being of this world but rather as having predictive value, as being a glimpse into the world of the future. Soothsayers and prophets have since time immemorial relied heavily on dreams, citing them as evidence of their ideas. Is there anything new in psychoanalysis that uses dreams in much the same way? Of course, we do not use dreams to predict the future, but we do claim, like our ancestors, to know the meaning of dreams. More importantly, we use dreams to substantiate our theories, especially the theory that is central to psychoanalysis—the unconscious. It could be said that for our ancestors, everything one needed to know about the soul was to be found in dreams. We psychoanalysts say that everything one needs to know about the unconscious can be found in dreams. We have merely replaced the term 'soul' with 'unconscious', and because we deny our connection with our ancestor's soul theories, we do not see the similarities.

Thirdly, there is something about the unconscious that suggests that it belongs to another realm, providing a link to immortality. No psychoanalyst talks about the unconscious being immortal, but there is something called the group unconscious that seems to have a life of its own, independent of the individuals constituting it. But perhaps more central to our everyday work, there is an unconscious dialogue that takes place between the psychoanalytic dyad that seems to have a life of its own. Only periodically and occasionally do we become aware of the rhythms and features of this other dialogue, this other life, which exists parallel to the current one. This parallel existence has much in common with soul theory, for instance, when we say things such as: "The formal procedure of psychoanalysis is time limited and finite, but the process of psychoanalysis persists throughout one's life." We might even go so far as to say that this process, which was a parallel process during psychoanalysis, might govern the conduct of one's life till the very end.

Synthesis

To recapitulate the structure of this presentation, we first talked about the pain of mortality, then about the origins of sentience, God, soul theory, and mortality. Now we will attempt to bring them together in a synthesis. I will preface this synthesis with another verse from Keats's "Ode to a Nightingale." For me it is the most moving verse of this poem, and it carries within it the essence of this presentation.

> Darkling I listen; and, for many a time
>> I have been half in love with easeful Death,
> Call'd him soft names in many a musèd rhyme,
>> To take into the air my quiet breath;
> Now more than ever seems it rich to die,
>> To cease upon the midnight with no pain.
>>> While thou art pouring forth thy soul abroad
>>>> In such an ecstasy!
> Still wouldst thou sing, and I have ears in vain –
>> To thy high requiem become a sod.

On the first reading of this verse, one is inclined to think that what is being sought is just death, or an escape from pain through death. Thus, the intent of this verse—escape from pain—seems to be similar to the previous one. But I think there is a crucial difference, for in this verse, it is not just death that is being sought—it is death "while thou art pouring forth thy soul abroad in such an ecstasy!" It is the "while" that makes an enormous difference, for though death is taking place, it is in the presence of the singing of the nightingale. The singing of the nightingale at this point is surely also Keats singing and singing in such an ecstasy! The song that is being sung carries the essence of the bird and the essence of the poet so beautifully melded together. It might be at this point that there is a transformation of death into painfully beautiful singing. The song is a feature of the singer's pain yet is separate from the singer, and that is why the song is able to carry pain and the terror of death.

So it can be said that in this verse, the pain of existence (the thesis) is overcome neither by death nor by immortality (the antithesis), but by something else that brings about a transformation of the pain within the mind of the person experiencing it. It is important to emphasize that the pain is still there; it has not ceased nor has it been denied. The singing of the nightingale that has entered the mind brings about the crucial transformation, the synthesis of pain and the capacity to bear it. The pain of existence is cradled in what we have referred to as the soul of existence. The pain of existence without a soul is meaningless. Soul theory devoid of the pain of existence, like many contemporary psychological theories, is equally meaningless. When they come together, there is a sense of coherence, meaning, and comfort. We need to explore this process by which it becomes possible both to experience pain and also to bear it.

Beginnings

I believe it is an illusion to think that the mind can develop on its own, for I believe that the human mind is essentially an inter-relational structure. In maintaining that the mind is a relational structure, I am merely summarizing and paraphrasing an enormous body of psychoanalytic literature, which can be condensed into a couple of sentences. The first is by Winnicott (1960: 39), who states that there is no such thing as an infant independent of the maternal care provided by its mother. The second is by Bion ([1962] 1977: 36), who asserts that the mind needs maternal reverie in order to survive and develop, without which the mind deteriorates and dies. Both are essentially saying the same thing in slightly different ways.

Having traversed the origins of sentience, God, and soul theory, we are now in a position to draw them together into a causally interdependent relationship. We saw that sentience, in the sense of awareness of consciousness, is a logical and necessary evolution of consciousness, and that God and soul theory are logical and necessary products of this same process. We could say from this perspective that a complex chicken has evolved from the origins of life—the egg, if you like. But we are now asking, perhaps very controversially, how could there be an egg without a chicken? What we are positing is a development of our earlier idea that all organisms have an unconscious desire to live and propagate, though there is nothing in their consciousness that would suggest such awareness. We are saying in the same way that it might be this very unconscious process that produces consciousness in the first place. The rather crude model we have is that of the chicken laying the egg, or maternal care or reverie being necessary for the development of mind. This of course is no doubt true, for there can be no egg without a chicken, infant without maternal care, or mind without reverie. But we are now saying that an egg necessarily posits a chicken, an infant a mother, and a mind reverie. They do not exist independent of each other, so it is nonsense to ask which came first, chicken or egg. It is likewise naive to interpret Winnicott or Bion crudely as saying that it is maternal care that produces the infant or that reverie produces mind. It would be truer to the spirit of Winnicott's writings to say that when he beheld the infant, he simultaneously beheld maternal care and that he could not separate one from the other. Likewise it would be truer to say that when Bion beheld a functioning mind, he became aware of an interdependence of mind and reverie or 'container-contained'. He came to this opinion from his observation that when there appeared to be a container without the contained or something contained without the container, what he saw was a severely dysfunctional mind or a mind functioning in the dimension of psychosis.

Disjunction of Container-Contained or Lies and Truth

Those familiar with the work of Bion might accept what I have just stated, but there is a piece of his work that does not sit comfortably with this interpretation. It concerns his theory about lies and the thinker. I will quote a few sentences that summarize his view and then try to understand these statements from an interdependent perspective. The quotation comes from his book *Attention and Interpretation* (Bion [1970] 1977: 100–103):

> Provisionally, we may consider that the difference between a true thought and a lie consists in the fact that a thinker is logically necessary for the lie but not for the true thought. Nobody need think the true thought: it awaits the advent of the thinker who achieves significance through the true thought. The lie and its thinker are inseparable. The thinker is of no consequence to the truth, but the truth is logically necessary to the thinker. His significance depends on whether or not he will entertain the true thought, but the thought remains unaltered.
>
> In contrast, the lie gains existence by virtue of the epistemologically prior existence of the liar. The only thoughts to which a thinker is absolutely essential are lies. Descartes's tacit assumption that thoughts presuppose a thinker is valid only for the lie.

These words are a powerful and persuasive description of what Bion means by lies. Part of the power of this argument comes from his contrast of the lie with what he calls the truth. This contrast can be misleading. Bion maintains that the pre-existence, pre-eminence, and necessity of the liar are the foundation of a lie. The lie is a lie because it is a feature of the personality of the liar, and yet the liar makes out that it is not so. That is the basic lie. The truth, on the other hand, is not a feature of the personality of the person espousing it and as such is indeed independent of human agency. Bion thus overstates his case by asserting that true thought awaits the arrival of the thinker. This may of course be true, but there is no way that we can possibly know this. It is the same as saying that before the advent of an organism, there exists a desire to live. While this may be so, we can never know about this until the arrival of the organism. In the same way, we can never know about the truth until the arrival of the thinker.

What distinguishes truth from lies is the fact that truth cannot be owned by anyone; for instance, the wish to live and propagate cannot be owned by anyone, nor are they the features of some particular person. The truth is something that is necessary and inclusive, not voluntary and exclusive. Or we can say that truth and thinker are different aspects of the same reality, but lies and the liar are not. The liar can choose a particular lie to propagate, and the lie dies with him or her. However, there is no choice when it comes to the truth, for truth will always endure ("Satyam eva jayate"—Upanishads) and is imperishable. Truth never changes, though over time we come to appreciate more and more of it, and this greater awareness is commensurate with the growth and development of the person who discovers and uses it. Lies do not endure for long. They keep changing rather than enduring, and they are eventually detrimental to the person who harbors them.

Singer and the Song

Returning to Keats and the nightingale's song, I think we are now in a better position to understand the relationship of the singer to the song. Keats is in pain, enormous pain. But in his pain he recognizes the pain of all humanity, so already in this recognition he has moved beyond his personal pain. He understands that his pain is an integral part of the pain of existence, of being alive. It is not possible for his pain to exist independently of the pain of humanity. Likewise, there can be no such thing as the pain of humanity without the pain that we all have some experience of. They are both different aspects and dimensions of the same thing, particular and universal, container and contained. But this is not the only dimension of Keats's existence. A central feature of his experience is his poetry, which wells up in him like the song of the nightingale. This poetry is probably the most important aspect of his existence, for it gives meaning to the rest of his existence. His pain does not disappear, but having various significations assigned to it makes it bearable. This difference is an important one, for it is the difference between what Bion calls the experience of the pain that one rids oneself of and the pain that is suffered. I believe it is possible to suffer pain only if the pain can be put into some kind of context that gives it coherence and meaning that thereby contains it. Thus, the song of the nightingale, and Keats's own song, gives meaning to the pain that Keats suffers and hence makes it endurable. This song is a particular instance of song that is universal, the song of the nightingale, your song, my song. These lines of Keats have meaning for us, for even though we did not write them, they resonate within us. They are part of our song, or we are part of that greater song. And we have seen that the song carries within it pain, for it is pain that produces the song, and it is song that carries the pain, universally and individually, container and contained.

What I have said about Keats and the nightingale is true also of the thinker and the true thought, of experience and its formulation. But this needs some elaboration. It is not easy to understand that the process of thinking is inherently painful. We think a thought and it does not hurt, so we conclude that thinking must also be painless. But any kind of sustained or productive thinking *is* painful, as is evidenced by the many ways we avoid thinking in this manner. We have numerous means of numbing our minds so that they do not think, from using drugs such as alcohol to watching television constantly and indiscriminately. We shy away from thinking because it requires effort and because it is painful. We have seen that in order to develop, thinking requires maternal care or reverie. As the capacity to think develops, it facilitates greater capacity to think, or, to state it another way, maternal reverie gradually becomes part of one's own reverie, thus facilitating the development of thought. This development of thought by giving context to one's existence makes the pain of existence that much more bearable or sufferable. If the capacity for thinking is not developed, less thinking can be borne, less pain can be endured. Instead of being suffered, pain gets either numbed or ejected, often forcefully in external intemperance or physical violence. Or alternatively, pain fragments the mind.

Concluding Thoughts

There are many kinds of thinking, but we are here concerned only with those kinds of thinking that give meaning to our existence and, in doing so, make the pain of it a little more endurable. Soul theory is the most basic and most persistent way of giving meaning to our existence and thus making it bearable. I understand religion as a process that collects concordant clusters of soul theory, preserving them in scriptures and various rituals and practices. This is how I have come to understand psychoanalysis— as being merely the latest repository of clusters of soul theory preserved in rituals and practices. But there is nothing disparaging about such a description, for in our discussion about maternal care and reverie, we have come to recognize that such organization is necessary to provide containers of human experience.

It is in this way that I regard soul theory, religion, and psychoanalysis as evolving naturally and necessarily from human existence and experience, acting as containers of that existence and experience. But we have also seen that consciousness of human existence cannot exist without some way of being able to think about it, and while this thinking about it stands outside the experience, it is yet an inherent part of that experience. In other words, maternal reverie that is necessary for thought to develop is an inherent part of thinking. It is not that soul theory or religion evolves from man as some scientists say. Or that man emerges from religious beliefs as religious people would have us believe. It is truer to say that that they are both organically and mutually necessary dimensions of all human existence; you cannot have one without the other. Every thought is reciprocally related to the thinker that thinks it, as indeed is every chicken to every egg.

There is only one way in which I think psychoanalysis differs from other soul theories. While all soul theories take as a given the existence of the soul, psychoanalysis examines the creation, structure, and function of that soul. Psychoanalysis exists as a product of experience, yet it is always examining how it is such a product. It is consciousness examining consciousness and hence necessarily what is unconscious. The process extends to experience, for psychoanalysis examines all experience, including the experience of psychoanalysis, and it is the experiences of psychoanalysis that provide the structures that allow the examination of these experiences. Psychoanalysis is the process of the soul examining itself, of thought examining thinking, and of life examining its meaning.

Yet even as I put matters this way, I cannot help but feel that the essence of what I am trying to say might well be lost in all the words and ideas that I am using to convey that essence. I do not have the economy of the poet. If I did I would probably say something like:

> Now more than ever seems it rich to die,
> To cease upon the midnight with no pain.
> While thou art pouring forth thy soul abroad
> In such an ecstasy!

I would like to convey the feeling of how the pain of existence is transformed so richly by wordless birdsong, for it is birdsong that gives meaning to existence. And when birdsong gives meaning to existence, then one becomes part of that experience seamlessly. All that can be heard is Keats and the nightingale pouring forth their songs in such an ecstasy of joy, a joy that carries within it the rich scarlet thread of pain that is such an inherent part of being human. We cannot be human without that pain, and we cannot carry that pain without our songs. But please do not ask whether what you hear is Keats or the nightingale singing, or whether it is the ecstasy of the singer or the song. Please only listen and in listening quietly fade away. So that eventually there is only the singing and nothing outside it.

Shahid Najeeb is a psychiatrist (Fellow of the Royal Australian and New Zealand College of Psychiatrists) and a member and training psychoanalyst of the Australian Psychoanalytical Society. He works full-time in private clinical practice in Sydney as a psychoanalyst and psychotherapist. Apart from his interest in clinical psychoanalysis, he is interested in the interface of psychoanalysis with literature, religion, and culture. His publications include "The Body of Psychoanalysis and Its Narcissism" (2003), "The Benefits of Psychoanalysis to Spirituality" (2002), and "The Significant Other: Clinical and Ethical Issues Involved in Treating a Patient in Isolation" (1996).

References

Bion W. R. [1962] 1977. *Learning from Experience*. Pp. 36–37 in Bion 1977.
_____. [1970] 1977. *Attention and Interpretation*. Pp. 100–103 in Bion 1977.
_____. 1977. *Seven Servants*. New York: Jason Aronson.
Blass, R. B. 2004. "Beyond Illusion: Psychoanalysis and the Question of Religious Truth." *International Journal of Psychoanalysis* 85: 615–634.
Freud, S. [1927] 1961. "The Future of an Illusion." Pp. 5–56 in *The Standard Edition of the Complete Psychological Works of Sigmund Freud*, vol. 21, trans. and ed. J. Strachey, with A. Freud, A. Strachey, and A. Tyson. London: Hogarth Press.
Keats, J. [1861] 1906. "Ode to a Nightingale." Pp. 255–257 in *The Golden Treasury of English Songs and Lyrics*, ed. F. T. Palgrave. London: Everyman.

Rank, O. 1930. *Psychology and the Soul: A Study of the Origin, Conceptual Evolution, and Nature of the Soul*. Baltimore and London: John Hopkins University Press.

Story, F. 1975 *Rebirth as Doctrine and Experience: Essays and Case Studies*. Kandy, Sri Lanka: Buddhist Publication Society.

Symington, N. 1994. *Emotion and Spirit*. London: Cassell.

Winnicott, D. W. 1951. "Transitional Objects and Transitional Phenomena." Pp. 229–242 in *Through Paediatrics to Psycho-Analysis*. London: Hogarth Press.

———. 1960. "The Theory of the Parent-Infant Relationship." Pp. 35–65 in *The Maturational Process and the Facilitating Environment*. London: Hogarth Press.

SUBJECT INDEX

Ajase complex, 18n30
alpha and *beta* elements (Bion), 40, 162, 163, 164, 165
Apollonian and Dionysian, 206, 211
argument from design, 209
Asperger's syndrome, 177
Auschwitz, 190
autism, 177
automatization (Hartmann), 218
Avalokiteswara (the Lord Who Listens to the Cries of the World), 37

bardo (states, Tibetan), 230
Baruya procreation belief, 103n49
bipolar disorders, 175
borderlinking, 122, 123, 125, 128, 129, 139
Buddhism, 10
    emptiness (*sunyata*), 11
    no-self, 11
    and psychoanalysis, 10–12

Captain Cook (mythologem), 167, 168
celestial rope, 89
    as cosmic phallo-umbilicus, 90–91
    as solar emissions, 91, 103n49
Central Australian Aboriginal life-worlds, 8, 17n23, 148–171
"Child Is Being Beaten, A" (Freud), 178
Christianity, 135
cognitive sciences, 180
colonial imaginary, 126
compulsion to repeat, 174
co-naissance, 141, 142

Congo, 7
    as the background of Rene Devisch's Yaka ethnography, 8
    Jamaa cult, 107
    and twentieth-century geopolitics, 7, 16–17n20, 21, 22
conscience, 190, 191
container-contained (Bion), 234, 235
contamination, 197, 200, 201
'Cosmic Self' (among the Yagwoia), 78, 79, 90, 91
cosmic tree/tree-of-life, 79, 90, 98n7
cosmological argument, 209
cross-cultural dyads and psychoanalytic context, Kakar on, 37–42
    Devereux's view, Kakar on, 38–39
culture, role in psychoanalysis, 25–26

depression, 175, 180
diagnosis, 177
Dionysus (mythologem), 153, 154, 160, 166, 167, 168
disintegration anxiety, 186
Dogon (Mali, West Africa), 55
dreaming (*Tjukurrpa*), 5, 150, 151, 152, 154, 155, 156, 157, 159, 160, 161, 162, 163, 164, 166
    as internal geo-psychic object, 5
dreams
    experience of, grammatically marked, 101n36, 107, 109
    given birth through, 108
    in Haiti, 116–117
    nightmares, 110

NAMES INDEX